Britten on Music

Britten

on Music

Edited by

PAUL KILDEA

UNIVERSITY PRESS

OXFORD
UNIVERSITY PRESS

Great Clarendon Street, Oxford OX2 6DP

Oxford University Press is a department of the University of Oxford.
It furthers the University's objective of excellence in research, scholarship,
and education by publishing worldwide in

Oxford New York

Auckland Bangkok Buenos Aires Cape Town Chennai
Dar es Salaam Delhi Hong Kong Istanbul Karachi Kolkata
Kuala Lumpur Madrid Melbourne Mexico City Mumbai Nairobi
São Paulo Shanghai Taipei Tokyo Toronto

Oxford is a registered trade mark of Oxford University Press
in the UK and in certain other countries

Published in the United States
by Oxford University Press Inc., New York

First published 2003

British Library Cataloguing in Publication Data
Data available

Library of Congress Cataloging in Publication Data
Data available

ISBN 0-19-816714-8

1 3 5 7 9 10 8 6 4 2

Typeset by Cambrian Typesetters,
Frimley, Surrey
Printed in Great Britain
on acid-free paper by
Biddles Ltd.,
Guildford & King's Lynn

For Paul and Verlie

ACKNOWLEDGEMENTS

For permission to reproduce Britten's essays and interviews I acknowledge the Britten Estate Limited, its current chairman Colin Matthews, and its former chairman, Donald Mitchell, with whom I have often discussed this volume.

I am grateful to the support of the Britten–Pears Library, Aldeburgh, for allowing me access to manuscript and some printed articles. I would thank in particular Pam Wheeler, Anne Surfling, Judith Tydeman, Nicholas Clark, and Judith LeGrove for their careful checking of source material. I am also grateful to Judith for her index. I thank Keiron Cooke for his help in selecting the photographic plates, and Jenny Doctor, former Director of the Library, for her stimulating ideas throughout this project, and for her expertise on the BBC and recorded sound. As ever, Rosamund Strode's detailed knowledge of Britten, his music, and his colleagues was of great help and stimulation; for this I thank her. I am grateful to Tim Day for his help in uncovering various recordings held in the National Sound Archive.

Introductory notes from Faber Music scores are © copyright Faber Music Ltd., and are here reproduced by kind permission. Essays 62, 65, 72, 75, 91, 98 are © copyright Faber & Faber Ltd., and are reproduced by kind permission. Essay 69 reproduced by kind permission of *The London Magazine*. Essay 73 reproduced by kind permission of John Warrack and by courtesy of *Musical America* archives. Essay 85 reproduced by kind permission of Opera Canada Publications. Essay 88 reproduced by kind permission of Mrs L. P. Rosenthal. Essay 91 reproduced by kind permission of Donald Mitchell. Britten's 1966 interview with Edmund Tracey reproduced by kind permission of Sadler's Wells. Essay 100 reproduced by permission of Victor Gollancz. Essay 101 reproduced by kind permission of Weidenfeld and Nicolson. Essays 50, 74, 94 reproduced by kind permission of John Amis. The note on *Noye's Fludde* reproduced by kind permission of Colin Graham. I would like to thank Jonathan Ward for permission to reproduce his translation of the Credo from Verdi's *Otello*. Britten's various radio interviews with Eric Crozier reproduced by kind permission of the Eric Crozier Estate. I am grateful to The Society of Authors as agent for the Provost and Scholars of King's College Cambridge for permission to reproduce his interview with E. M. Forster. The interview with John Piper reproduced by kind permission of Clarissa Lewis. All contributions to Aldeburgh Festival programme books reproduced by kind permission of Aldeburgh Productions.

While every reasonable attempt has been made to identify and contact copyright holders of material printed here, the author shall be pleased to hear from organizations or individuals he has been unable to trace.

I would also like to express my gratitude to the various people who interviewed Britten during his lifetime, both for their permission (or that of their estates or employers) to reproduce articles and transcripts here, and for the often perceptive and probing questions they put to him.

I am grateful to Mrs Osman for permission to reproduce Kurt Hutton's fine photographs. I am also grateful to Nigel Luckhurst for permission to reproduce his portrait of Britten on the cover. The photographic plate of Britten's and John Pounder's childhood play 'The Precious Documents' is reproduced by kind permission of Madeleine Pounder.

I am grateful to Bruce Phillips for his initial interest in and support of the book. I am similarly indebted to Cyril Ehrlich. I would also like to thank Mary Worthington, Sophie Goldsworthy, Michael Wood, Jacqueline Smith, and the OUP production and design departments for the care they took in the publication of this book.

CONTENTS

PART III. 1956–1965

'All a poet can do today is warn'

PART IV. 1966–1976

'My mind beats on'

PART V.
Introductory Notes

ON BRITTEN'S MUSIC

ON THE MUSIC OF OTHER COMPOSERS

LIST OF PLATES

ABBREVIATIONS

ACGB	Arts Council of Great Britain
AFPB	Aldeburgh Festival Programme Book
ASCAP	American Society of Composers, Authors and Publishers
BBCWAC	British Broadcasting Corporation Written Archives Centre
BPL	Britten–Pears Library, Aldeburgh
EOG	English Opera Group
GB-ALb	Britten–Pears Library, Aldeburgh
ISCM	International Society for Contemporary Music
Mitchell and Reed	Donald Mitchell and Philip Reed (eds.), *Letters from a Life*, vol. i: *1923–39*; vol. ii: *1939–45* (London: Faber & Faber, 1991)
NSA	National Sound Archive

INTRODUCTION

In August 2001, as this book was nearing completion, the novelist, newspaper columnist, and opera librettist Philip Hensher dared to suggest in the *Independent* that Britten's music really isn't much chop. August is a lazy news month in England and, on cue, BBC Radio 4's *Today* programme picked up the gauntlet. Hensher was invited onto the programme to explicate his thesis; Colin Matthews, composer and chairman of the Britten Estate Limited, was pitted against him. The saintly Sue MacGregor participated in an illuminating exchange:

HENSHER: The thing to remember about the *War Requiem* is that it was an official commission for the opening of Coventry Cathedral. It's full of very highly sound, almost politically correct one might say, views on war, on the importance of reconciliation, etcetera, etcetera, etcetera. The trouble is that no one ever listens to the music.

MACGREGOR: Don't they?

HENSHER: I mean that metaphorically. I mean Stravinsky said that he couldn't hear the music for all the Battle-of-Britten sentiment. What people are really listening to is the sentiment and not actually the quality of the music, I think, which is actually not that high.

MACGREGOR: And you think Benjamin Britten's reputation really doesn't extend very greatly beyond our shores?

HENSHER: I think that's true. I mean it's noticeable that most of Britten's pieces that are still popular are not the kind of abstract pieces, not the concert pieces, but the pieces with some sort of meaning to them—you know, *Peter Grimes*, or the *War Requiem* . . .

MACGREGOR: Or *Let's Make an Opera*.

HENSHER: Yes, exactly that. Once you take away the meaning, and if you don't speak English you won't understand what the *War Requiem* is going on about, then all you've got is the music.[1]

Colin Matthews, perhaps wondering if such a bald critique had ever been levelled at, say, *Tristan und Isolde*, replied sanguinely: 'I don't think Britten needs me to defend him . . .', before picking apart Hensher's litany of gripes and factual errors.

The interview was fascinating on a number of levels—not least because Hensher is an intelligent commentator with a passion for contemporary art music: what does it tell us, for instance, about Britten's reputation today? What

[1] BBC Radio 4, *Today*, 4 Aug. 2001.

does it suggest about the currency or legacy of Britten's 'conviction pieces'? How universal are the stories, the complicated emotional liaisons Britten created on stage, and the musical language used to create them? And, finally, what does the exchange imply about the *public* role of artists and their work, then and now—something of which Britten felt strongly.

The compilation of the writings and interviews in this book came about through aims considerably more modest than a need to answer such questions. Its origins were in a desire to see if a composer whose *métier* was word-setting could possibly be as tongue-tied, as inarticulate, as he protested throughout his life. Such protests were frequent and often public: 'I am a very bad speaker. I always think of what I wanted to say afterwards.'[2] Or: 'Artists of course are the last people who should talk or write about art, especially their own.'[3] Or: 'I admit that I hate speaking in public. It is not really a matter of shyness, but because I do not easily think in words, because words are not my medium. This may surprise some people, but I suppose it is the way one's brain is made.'[4] And when not public, there were the many scrappy drafts of talks or articles, surrendered to Peter Pears, his partner for almost forty years, and covered with corrections in his hand, that suggest an easy abdication of confidence or conviction in the face of Pears's more overt literary skills. Yet how was it possible that someone so sensitive to poetry could be insensitive to the rhetorical nuances of prose? How conceivable was it that someone whose real literary education was at W. H. Auden's side could remain unconfident in his proclamations on matters cultural or political? (Both had left Gresham's School armed with the advice 'That everyone shall be able to argue, to debate, to read aloud, and to lecture', which Auden made one of the guiding principles of 1930s literary England.[5]) Such incongruities suggested that a compilation of Britten's words would be interesting in the very least; at most, incongruousness might be exposed as disingenuousness—perhaps Britten affected a verbal shyness as a form of rhetoric or defence? Either way (or most likely somewhere in between), collecting these words on music was sure to shed some light on Britten's creative process. Anything more ambitious—including countering criticisms such as Philip Hensher's (as yet unarticulated) or a determination to reassess Britten's contribution to British culture—was not the original motivation for this volume.

Yet the cyclical nature of both criticism and an artist's posthumous reputation has brought these very questions, twenty-five years after Britten's death, well within this book's skeletal remit. It is clear, for instance, from Charles Osborne's perceptive interview with Britten (Essay 69) that Philip Hensher's

[2] Essay 29. [3] Essay 67. [4] Essay 60.

[5] Written in Britten's English notebook for Lent term, 1929 (*GB-ALb* 2–1000784).

criticisms *were* articulated long ago—although by someone else. Osborne brought to Britten's attention the criticisms of quite another young writer of the *War Requiem*:

OSBORNE: Incidentally, one of our younger poets—a great admirer of your music—recently said to me that he was somewhat disturbed by a 'sweetness' in the *War Requiem*. I *think* I see what he means, though I don't in fact share his feeling. He said that, for this reason, he preferred—rather irrelevantly, I thought—your *Midsummer Night's Dream*.

BRITTEN: I don't, of course, understand what your friend is referring to, though I can't see any great defect in sweetness as long as it's not weakness. I can't imagine, though, how the *War Requiem* could be considered sweeter than *A Midsummer Night's Dream*.

Britten further admitted to Osborne that some of his right-wing friends loathed the *War Requiem*. ' "Though the music is superb, of course," they'd say. But that's neither here nor there to me. The message is what counts'—to which Osborne replied, thoughtfully, in his conclusion: 'But the music *is* the message, as its composer knows full well, and those who begin by loving the sound are in dire peril of having to admit the sense.'

Thus two literary/dramatic appraisals of the one work present themselves—one contemporary, one retrospective. Each argues from a similar platform before coming to a conclusion diametrically opposed to the other. Today, Osborne would no doubt disapprove of Hensher's tree surgery, his efforts to dissect music from motive in this particular composer, and would question the inference that Britten thought up his sermons and serpents before shoe-horning them into a well-rehearsed musical formula. (The second part of Osborne's sentence is less accurate, painting as it does Britten as a mythological Siren, luring in unsuspecting passers-by who either navigate the tides or crash on the rocks.) Yet Hensher would no doubt counter Osborne with his assessment that the music just isn't very good.

Where does a volume of Britten's writings and interviews slip into this virtual argument? What it can't do is make the musical construction of a Britten work any different; the *War Requiem* will remain the same, its 'sweetness' or its 'sentiment' intact. But it does provide a rationale for Britten's compositional motives, since in this volume Britten articulates many of the messages he so often couched in his works in highly ambiguous terms—which was for him both a dramatic device and a disguise. Yet whether masked in music or revealed in words, on this—Britten's genuine belief in the power of art to change society, and the responsibility of the artist to use this power—we all agree. For this reason alone, Britten himself would not argue with Hensher on at least one of his criticisms. As Britten said in 1964: 'The text of my *War Requiem* was perfectly in place in Coventry Cathedral—the Owen poems in the vernacular, and the words of the Requiem Mass familiar to everyone—but it would have been pointless in Cairo or Peking.'[6] Communication, as these essays demonstrate, was an issue of paramount importance to Britten.

* * * *

Quite apart from the personal motives it suggests, this volume can also be read anthropologically—*Peter Grimes*, after all, was contemporary with the formation in Britain of the Arts Council, a permanent opera company at Covent Garden, and the BBC Third Programme, three organizations with which Britten maintained close links from their inceptions; their creative endeavours and Britten's intertwined and overlapped from then on. Yet a few codicils must be sketched for those hoping to read this volume as a history of post-war English cultural achievement. Although the sound and shape of Britten's prose remained pretty consistent throughout his life—a sturdy, knockabout style befitting an intelligent public-school boy—its function changed dramatically over the forty years of writings, interviews, and speeches represented in this collection. Unlike his letters, which were never conceived as public proclamations (no matter how his voice changed in them, depending upon who was the recipient), the tone of his published articles in particular is precisely illustrative of his own evolving reputation on one hand, and shifting cultural boundaries in England on the other. The first of these is easier to demarcate than the second: levels of discretion and disclosure varied in the different periods of Britten's life. The street-fighting nerve of his earliest essays, when he had little reputation and much ambition, would have been out of character for the composer of *Gloriana*. From *Peter Grimes* onwards, his rapid reconstruction as a major artistic figure meant he became more careful in what he said. Not being a politician, journalists didn't bother checking his earlier thoughts on any given subject, eager to pounce on the slightest indiscretion or prise open the smallest gap between the position articulated then and his current thinking. And not being a politician, there were occasional, revealing slips, which earned him the disapproval of funding bodies, fellow musicians, music institutes, and critics (this was pre-1960, when unwise utterances by political figures were considered way too important or revelatory to be published automatically).

The shifting cultural (and social) boundaries in England after the war are harder to detect in Britten's writings. He never wrote about homosexuality, for example, despite the Wolfenden Report and the slow dance towards legalization in 1967, and despite his visible relationship with Pears. His disdain for various musical trends from the mid-1950s onwards was only occasionally articulated explicitly. But this is the trick of Britten's essays. Such disdain is

[6] Essay 72.

present in every comment he ever made about the responsibility of artists to communicate and be of use to society; you were either relevant as an artist or were resident in an 'ivory tower'—Britten's common expression of incomprehension and dismissal. Relevance demanded a language easily understood by those willing to listen to high art in an age of the Vietnam war and the Beatles, in an era of Stockhausen and Darmstadt. Similarly, although ideas about sexuality are not openly expressed in his writings, his fundamental concern about 'man's inhumanity to man', on whatever basis or due to whatever prejudice, threads through his words as it does his music.

Certainly his approach to writing was not that of Michael Tippett, another successful British opera composer of Britten's generation, who could not help but speak candidly about music, philosophy, and sexuality, and who perhaps found greater fluency in his compositions by arguing his creative ideas in prose. But as Tippett said of Britten in his obituary: 'It seems to me that certain obsessions belonged naturally to the works of art which he produced. I don't think it matters at all that they may not in any way have belonged to his personality. I refer to a deep sense of cruelty upon people, cruelty as a suffering. A sense, I think, also of the fragility of all existence, leading him to a sense of death.'[7] And although overt arguments about this cruelty or this fragility do not flow over from Britten's music to his writings, as they do with Tippett, knowing that they drove his creativity suggests that we must treat the layers and ambiguities of his written words with the care with which we attempt to identify and respond to these factors in his music. As Britten himself said in 1951: 'It is a proud privilege to be a creative artist, but it can also be painful. Great artists have been destroyed by their consciences.'[8] As Western society so quickly seemed to squander the hard-won trophy of peace, as Britain attempted first to manufacture a high-art cultural industry in the period immediately following the war and then import a popular one from America, Britten felt strongly the proud privilege and responsibility of being a creative artist. Yet his words and music tread the finest of lines between expressing and repressing the core values of his conscience.

* * * *

This volume is a 'complete edition' of Britten's writings (at least as complete as current scholarship allows)—those published in his lifetime and those that remained as unfinished drafts or were given as speeches. He was not as prolific as Percy Grainger, for instance, thus the agony of selection and exclusion has been a welcome absence from the editorial process. Certain radio and newspaper interviews included here help to complete a historical narrative signposted

[7] *The Listener* (16 Dec. 1976). [8] Essay 33.

by his forty years of prose writings and speeches. The selection criterion was that the interview illustrate something of Britten that his writings do not. Thus a number of existing BBC recordings and transcripts do not appear in this book—a long, rambling interview with Britten and Pears upon their return from South America in 1967, for example. Yet the equally long, but far more revealing interview with Britten, Eric Crozier, and E. M. Forster when they were effecting the revisions to *Billy Budd* does find a place here (Essay 57). For similar reasons, one radio script on *Peter Grimes* and a transcribed interview on *Children's Crusade* are included in Section V—contradicting this section's remit as a collection of Britten's programme notes, but nonetheless positioning the two pieces in the most appropriate part of the book.

The history of talk programmes on BBC radio is slightly complicated: in the first few decades of radio, discussions were mostly pre-recorded, transcribed, and then rerecorded by the original participants with transcriptions in front of them. The existing NSA recording of Britten, Eric Crozier, and John Piper, formally and rather stiffly discussing the creation of *Albert Herring* (here transcribed and reproduced as Essay 22), is a perfect example. Many of these scripts survive on microfilm in the BBC Written Archive Centre, as do later transcriptions of live or pre-recorded programmes when such formalities were no longer observed, but when the importance of such talks as a BBC (and, perhaps, a historical) resource was recognized. When such transcripts have been used as the source for essays in this book, I have silently corrected grammar, phonentical misspellings, and certain facts, since these were clearly misheard or misunderstood by the BBC transcriber, or simply reflect the transcriber's interpretation of the recorded interview. As historical documents such details should perhaps be preserved; yet in doing so, Britten's thoughts and words would actually be misrepresented. And pages of verbal hesitations and collisions today make poor reading—at least in this format. In a number of instances it is possible to compare BBC transcript with BBC recording, which convinced me that such editing is necessary for this volume, while at the same time being true to Britten. It also makes these 'historical' transcriptions consistent in style with those I have made from recordings. Source material is anyhow cited and may be accessed and compared. And as with each transcript, the full interview—as opposed to the edited version that was often broadcast—is included in this volume.

Having tried and failed to come up with a generically encompassing word for the various pieces in this volume, I have settled on 'Essay', which although inaccurate is nonetheless used to refer to articles, interviews, transcripts, and speeches alike. The items have been ordered chronologically according to publication or transmission date, although significant discrepancies between when a piece was written or an interview given and when it received its public airing have been noted.

Two bookends have suggested the utilitarian division of essays and interviews into four sections. His first article was written in 1936, his last in 1976; grouping the essays in ten-year periods (eleven in the final instance) seemed a sensible way of presenting the material. Yet something more than healthy pragmatism emerges from these groupings. However coincidental, the periods identified (1936–45, 1946–55, 1956–65, 1966–76) reflect significant stages in Britten's life and music. His life and public role would not be the same after the premiere of *Grimes* in 1945; his trip to the Far East from late 1955 to early 1956 influenced his compositional aesthetic and restocked his dramaturgical armoury; and the final ten years or so of his life were marked by a concentration of energy on his expanding Aldeburgh Festival, and a misplaced conviction that he was losing touch with contemporary musical ideas.

The themes that I consider important for each of these divisions, along with a chronology detailing important works and events in each period, are intended to place Britten's thoughts and words into a social and musical context, but are not meant to force extraneous meaning onto the essays where none was intended. They serve as a reminder that readers should look below the surface of the printed word, should consider the pieces in terms of a linear narrative; but in each case nuanced interpretation is left up to the individual. For this reason, footnotes have been kept to a minimum.[9] The sources for published articles, talks, and broadcasts are given in each instance. Britten recycled a number of his writings; each version has been included if significant alterations in context, his thinking, or scholarship are evident (his various notes on the *Sinfonia da Requiem*, or on Purcell's *Dido and Aeneas*, for example), excluded if more or less a direct copy or translation. One piece had to be constructed from poor or ambiguous sources (Essay 67), but this has been undertaken with care and as much circumstantial evidence as exists.

Where drafts of published articles are significantly different from the published version or are illustrative of specific points, I have included the pertinent passage as a footnote. On one or two occasions, when Britten was responding in print to a specific article or newspaper story, I have included the provocative article—or an extract of it—as a footnote. I have also included cross-references to help those who will dip into the volume rather than read it from cover to cover. For this reason, some details in the footnotes are repeated.

[9] More detailed biographical information on Britten can be found in Humphrey Carpenter, *Benjamin Britten: A Biography* (London: Faber & Faber, 1992), or Donald Mitchell and Philip Reed (eds.), *Letters from a Life*, vol. i: *1923–39*; vol. ii: *1939–45* (London: Faber & Faber, 1991).

The spellings of the original publications have been retained, since they are often a useful reminder of the country (or journal) in which a piece first appeared. Such details have not been inserted into transcriptions of foreign radio interviews; although this would be philologically correct, it would also be desperately pedantic (these transcriptions conform to OUP house style). Britten's drafts reflect the format of the manuscript as far as possible, and certainly retain his misspellings. Titles of the original pieces have been retained where they exist; others of my invention are distinguished in the source information. Titles of specific compositions in Part V are standardized according to *Benjamin Britten: A Catalogue of the Published Works* (Aldeburgh: The Britten–Pears Library, 1999) or *The New Grove Dictionary of Music and Musicians* (London: Macmillan, 2000). In the Contents list the date of each note is specified; in the text the date of composition is included in each heading. Programme notes of dubious authorship have not been included in this volume, although notes and articles of joint authorship have been.

What emerges from this volume, to me, are some of the jigsaw pieces long missing from the public representation of a complex, deep-thinking, paradoxical artist. Collections of writings of other composers may be more dazzling in prose style (Grainger), or less measured in their value judgements (Tippett); but this volume allows those interested in Britten's music to trace its philosophical origins. For all the diversity in his compositional style, some of his philosophical notions were well formed from his early years as a published prose writer, and remained consistent throughout his life. Compare, for example, Essay 9 (1942): 'those who sell music as if it were a kind of breakfast-food' with Essay 72 (1964): 'It is one of the unhappiest results of the march of science and commerce that this unique work, at the turn of a switch, is at the mercy of any loud roomful of cocktail drinkers—to be listened to or switched off at will, without ceremony or occasion.'

In an essay that touches on what *he* sees as the link between words and music, Britten sees very little comfort in continuity (Essay 67):

> I hate talking about my own music, or my own musical inclination, & avoid it whenever I can. But having broken the rule here, I reserve the right to change any of my opinions whenever I want to. These opinions included liking or disliking any of the great figures of the past (a purely personal matter, derived from temporary needs, which must seem irritating & bewildering to other people). They include a reluctance to treat contemporary subjects in opera—preferring the parable technique. They include a dislike of listening to songs, operas & so on in a language I can't understand, & a dislike of singers who don't sing their words clearly or perhaps more important, don't <u>use</u> their words, but equally of singers who forget that music has line and tune as well as words. They include . . but one could continue indefinitely.

Yet this is a theoretical world he describes, a declaration of rights rarely engaged. Britten did soften his early opinion of Sibelius (Essay 78), as indeed he hardened it concerning Beethoven, but tales of him playing through works of Brahms to test whether his earliest assessment (bad) had altered (it hadn't) are more representative of Britten's artistic character and certainty than the occasional public reassessment.

The huge biographical interest in Britten over the last ten years or so has on the one hand sometimes overshadowed the music itself (something Britten would have hated), and on the other has suggested that Britten held greater claims for its or his significance (something he would have mocked). Both hands join in the arguments articulated at the beginning of this introduction; it is only appropriate, then, that in a volume of his words on music, Britten is allowed to rebut them:

> All of us—the public, critics, and composers themselves—spend far too much time worrying about whether a work is a shattering masterpiece. Let us not be so self-conscious. Maybe in thirty years' time very few works that are well known today will still be played, but does that matter so much? Surely out of the works that are written some good will come, even if it is not now; and these will lead on to people who are better than ourselves.[10]

Good *did* come, whether it was advances in post-war British culture, or in wider public awareness of ideals Britten held close to his heart. Criticizing these now appears churlish, for Britten was addressing the audiences of his day, in the language he thought would best deliver his message. And although he was determined to be a *relevant* composer, the above extract suggests that he was quite aware that the nature of his relationship with his audiences would change over time.

Quite another extract—this from a mock 'Collected Poems of Benjamin Britten' ('Limited Edition of One Copy. This is No. One.') written some time between 1939 and 1941—implies that Britten might even have foretold Philip Hensher's critical assault, for the preface to this edition of two modest poems ('ô my pussy cat' and 'ghosts%'), 'is 'reprinted from the Dictionary of National Biography.2001':

> From the very scanty available evidence, it would appear that the subject of this memoir came into the world on the 22nd day of November, 1914 or more likely 1915. It seems that from his earliest years he was given to composing long and serious poems of an obscure and apparently religious nature, indeed legend has it that when his infant fingers could not yet hold a pen, he was found one morning seated at a typewriter in the middle of the seventieth canto of an Anacreontic Ode on the Joys of Mysticism, a work which alas! was for ever lost, when during the Great Paper Famine of 1953, the

[10] Essay 82.

whole of the valuable first edition was used (one can only conclude) for other, less exalted purposes. . . . But enough of speculation. After all, a man is judged by his works, not by his idiosyncrasies.[11]

Self-mocking proof, surely, of a sense that 2001 would be his *annus horribilis*, his critical nadir. Yet the opposite is true: twenty-five years after his death (fifty after the Great Paper Famine of 1953), Britten remains much performed throughout the (non-English) world, deadly serious proof, surely, that the themes that preoccupied him in his music are all too relevant today. And so it is that this volume of essays helps to remind those who listen to Britten's music of the simple truths, and the tortured paths towards expression of these truths, at the centre of the many great works of this reluctant public speaker.

[11] *GB-ALb* 1–02053788. Typed unsigned document, although the language, syntax, ideas, and prep-school humour and imagery suggest that Britten was the author.

PART I

*

1936–1945

'Oh but the unloved have had power'

INTRODUCTION AND CHRONOLOGY

Britten's writings in this period are unlike anything he later penned. Unbridled by lasting fame and public expectations, and buoyed by his well-developed sense of ambition and destiny, his essays attack any number of shibboleths and errant knights. In this, of course, if Auden was not always standing at Britten's shoulder, he was at least sharpening his pencil. Even when American domicile and war had intervened, when Britten's absence from England provoked censure and outrage in bodies ranging from the Royal Philharmonic to the *Musical Times*, when his artistic colleagues Auden and Isherwood were under fire in the *Spectator* and the House of Commons, he kept up his attack on the musical and political complacency of the country he had left behind. His defence of Mahler (Essay 10) is on one level a remarkably prescient piece about a composer whose true worth would really only be discovered once the LP record had eclipsed its short-breathed predecessor in the early 1950s, but on quite another level it is an attack on English concert programming, on the narrow-minded subscription to a symphonic canon defined to a large extent by Brahms's death in 1897. To Britten, those who sought a broader definition, such as the BBC's Edward Clark (Essay 2, the second of four essays written by the jobbing composer to supplement his meagre income), were fighting the same battle that he and his fellow artists (more commonly writers than musicians) were fighting. His piece on 'England and the Folk-Art Problem' (Essay 8) draws battle lines—admittedly not of his own authorship (English pastoralists had long been slogging it out with Teutonic infiltrators)—which he fervently believed would define the future of British music. Moreover, the Auden poem quoted at the end of the article represents Britten's artistic creed in this period:

> Compelling all to the admission
> Aloneness is man's real condition,
> That each must travel forth alone
> In search of the Essential Stone,
> 'The Nowhere-without-No' that is
> The justice of Societies.

In this, Britten was not arguing for isolation; rather he was referring to the lucidity that comes from journeying beyond the status quo. As a conscientious objector back in England, such attacks were impossible. Yet in 'Vienna' (Essay 16), written in the closing months of the war, he argued for a united humankind, one that recognized the value of culture and heritage as a civilizing and uniting force, one that defied the corruption and destruction of war. It is a subtle piece about wresting back power from those who had assumed it since 1939. As Auden phrased it in *On This Island* (set by Britten in 1937), 'O but the unloved have had power, | The weeping and striking, | Always; time will bring their hour'. Britten's own music for the rest of his life was a continuation of this journey, an attempt to grant power to the unloved and disenfranchised, to bring them their hour; yet in no other period was his prose writing so outspokenly connected with the ideals of his musical compositions.

1936 Completes score for *Night Mail*, a collaboration with W. H. Auden and others, for the General Post Office Film Unit, for whom he began working the previous year; composes incidental music for Montagu Slater's play *Stay Down Miner* (Left Theatre), and Louis MacNeice's translation of *The Agamemnon* (Group Theatre); composes *Our Hunting Fathers*, Op. 8, concurrent with the Spanish Civil War, *Russian Funeral*, *Soirées musicales*, Op. 9, and the score for his only feature film, *Love from a Stranger*.

1937 Mother dies; commences friendship with Peter Pears; completes *Pacifist March*, with a text by the future librettist of *The Rape of Lucretia*, Ronald Duncan; composes a number of theatre, film, and radio scores, including *The Ascent of F6* (Group Theatre); composes *Variations on a Theme of Frank Bridge*, Op. 10, for Boyd Neel and the Salzburg Festival, *On This Island*, Op. 11, *Mont Juic*, Op. 12 (with Lennox Berkeley), and a number of short Auden lyrics.

1938 Moves into the Old Mill at Snape in Suffolk; continues to write theatre and radio scores, including *On the Frontier*; composes his Piano Concerto, Op. 13, for himself and the BBC Proms; meets Aaron Copland; sets Randall Swingler's *Advance Democracy*; applauds Chamberlain's efforts in Munich.

1939 Composes *Ballad of Heroes*, Op. 14; follows (with Pears) Auden and Isherwood to North America; consummates relationship with Pears; composes *Young Apollo*, Op. 16 (which he withdraws after the first performance), Violin Concerto, Op. 15, *Les Illuminations*, Op. 18, *Canadian Carnival*, Op. 19; accepts Japanese government commission for *Sinfonia da Requiem*, Op. 20, and commences work with Auden on choral operetta *Paul Bunyan*, Op. 17.

1940 Seriously ill for much of February and March; gives numerous recitals throughout the year with Pears, for which he realizes Purcell songs and arranges the first of his many folksongs; composes *Diversions*, Op. 21, *Seven Sonnets of Michelangelo*, Op. 22 (his first work written especially for and dedicated to Pears), *Introduction and Rondo alla Burlesca*, Op. 23, No. 1.

1941 *Sinfonia da Requiem* premiered in Carnegie Hall, with the New York Philharmonic conducted by John Barbirolli; discovers *Listener* article on George Crabbe, which prompts a desire to return to England; *Paul Bunyan* is given its premiere at Columbia University; composes *Matinées musicales*, Op. 24, *Mazurka Elegiaca*, Op. 23, No. 2, String Quartet No. 1, Op. 25 (a commission of Elizabeth Sprague Coolidge), *Scottish Ballad*, Op. 26, and his

'Occasional Overture', published posthumously as *An American Overture* to avoid confusion with his later *Occasional Overture* (1946); resentment of Britten's absence from England spills over into the press.

1942 Awaits passage back to England; is commissioned by the conductor Serge Koussevitzky for an opera based on Crabbe's poem *The Borough*; sails to England, during which time he composes *Hymn to St Cecilia*, Op. 27, and *A Ceremony of Carols*, Op. 28; registers as conscientious objector; continues to give concerts with Pears under the auspice of the Council for Encouragement of Music and the Arts; asks Montagu Slater to write the libretto for *Peter Grimes*, the scenario of which Britten and Pears had already completed; works on a number of propaganda programmes for radio; meets E. M. Forster at performance of the *Seven Sonnets of Michelangelo*; cycle is subsequently recorded by HMV.

1943 Composes *Serenade*, Op. 31, for tenor, horn and strings, which is first performed in October; composes Prelude and Fugue, Op. 29, for Boyd Neel, *Rejoice in the Lamb*, Op. 30, for Walter Hussey, and *The Ballad of Little Musgrave and Lady Barnard* for the prisoners of Oflag VIIb in Germany; publishes his first volume of folksongs; meets Michael Tippett.

1944 Works mainly on *Peter Grimes*, although manages to realize a number of Purcell songs for his recitals with Pears; records the *Serenade* for Decca, the beginning of a lifelong, almost exclusive, relationship with the company; composes *Festival Te Deum*, Op. 32, and a number of Auden lyrics from *Christmas Oratorio* (later published by Auden as *For the Time Being*), which Britten intended to set in full, but didn't—partly because of its dense poetry, partly because of the breakdown of his friendship with its author.

1945 Completes *Peter Grimes*, Op. 33, which is given its premiere at Sadler's Wells in June; composes *The Holy Sonnets of John Donne*, Op. 35, following his concert tour with Yehudi Menuhin of German concentration camps; composes String Quartet No. 2, Op. 36, and his most elaborate film score ever, published as *The Young Person's Guide to the Orchestra*, Op. 34.

1 Soviet Opera at B.B.C.: Shostakowitch's 'Lady Macbeth' (1936)

'Oedipus Rex' broadcast on February 12th, and 'Lady Macbeth' broadcast on March 18th with Albert Coates conducting, are the most important events of this season's B.B.C. concert programmes.[1]

Shostakowitch belongs to the school of young Soviet composers. His latest opera *Katrina Ismailowa* is a love story which is treated very naturalistically. The opera had a tremendous success in Prague and other Western European countries.

'Oedipus Rex' demonstrated Stravinsky's remarkable sense of style in drawing inspiration from every age of music and in leaving the whole a perfect shape, satisfying every aesthetic and emotional demand. But since the established idea of 'originality' dies hard, it is easy to see why Stravinsky's later works are regarded with disfavour. Another difficulty is his later method of dramatic composition. The set, stylised musical numbers, the Latin words, and the masks worn by most of the actors combine to give the impression of an impersonal comment on Sophocles' drama rather than a re-enactment of it.

A deep contrast to this method appears in 'Lady Macbeth.' Here the music is the terrible sadistic drama itself, and it is only in the remarkable entr'actes that Shostakowitch makes detached comments on the previous gruesome events on the stage.[2]

Let us hope that the critics have given this work a better welcome than they handed to 'Oedipus Rex.' One London critic expressed amusement at Jocasta's lovely aria in Act II. But maybe it is a compliment to the music to have stirred up any emotion in him at all.[3]

Source: *World Film News* 1/1 (Apr. 1936).

[1] Both works were recent and unknown in England—*Oedipus Rex* (1926–7), *Lady Macbeth of the Mtsensk District* (1930–2). Shostakovich himself later revised *Lady Macbeth* as *Katerina Izmaylova* (1956), the title given to the second production of the work, in Moscow in 1934, which curiously opened only two days after the first (in Leningrad). This revised version was first produced in 1963. See also Essay 83.

[2] This was a technique Britten later employed in his 'Sea Interludes' and Passacaglia in *Peter Grimes* (1945).

[3] It has not been possible to identify the critic. The autograph draft of this article (*GB-ALb* 1–9400196) is in many ways more interesting than the version published:

> Two of the most important events for the musician this season are B.B.C. concert performances of works intended for the theatre. Both by contemporary Russian-born composers, they form an interesting contrast. One being the work of a universally-acclaimed figure, who seems to have disappointed the public with his later work; the other by a young man of steadily growing reputation, but who is yet more of an intellectual cult than a composer of importance to the general public. One a product of pre-revolution

days—now living in France; the other a member of the Soviet regime, living and apparently revelling in the present conditions.

Stravinsky's 'Oedipus Rex',—opera-oratorio after Sophocles, text by Cocteau (put into latin by Daniélou)—was performed under Ansermet at Queen's Hall on Feb. 12th. The enthusiasm of the conductor did not seem to have spread to the performers. The chorus sang accurately enough, but with dull tone and not much vitality. The attitude of the orchestra seemed the same; while the soloists, with the exception of Oda Slobodskaya who sang beautifully, though the part of Jocasta lies too low for her, seemed quite at sea. Oedipus was entirely mis-cast; the bel canto of a latin tenor is needed rather than teutonic 'Tristan' style.

One of the peaks of Stravinsky's output, this work shows his wonderful sense of style & power of drawing inspiration from every age of music, and leaving the whole a perfect shape, satisfying every aesthetic demand. And of course, as the established idea of originality dies so hard, it is easy to see why the later works of Stravinsky are regarded with such disfavour. Another hard nut to crack is the typical later-Stravinsky method of the drama. The combination of set stylised sections in the music, the latin words, the masks worn by most of the actors, give the impression of an impersonal comment on Sophocles, rather than a re-enaction of the Drama.

It is this attitude which shows the greatest contrast to Shostakovitch's Lady Macbeth (Queen's Hall, March 18th, under Albert Coates), which is a realistic production of the terrible sadistic story. Here the music is the drama itself, and it is only in the remarkable entr'acts that Shostakovitch makes impersonal comments, on the gruesome events on the stage.

Let us hope that the critics will give this work a better welcome than they gave to 'Oedipus Rex'. One London gentleman expressed amusement at Jocasta's great and beautiful aria in Act II. But perhaps it is a compliment in itself to have stirred him to any emotion at all.

2 Wireless Concerts lose Edward Clarke (1936)

News comes that Edward Clarke [*sic*] has left the B.B.C.[1] The bold scope and high standard of the Contemporary Concerts have been largely due to his perseverance. Both listeners and the B.B.C. music department will regret his going.

The most important music broadcasts announced for May are Alban Berg's violin concerto, completed shortly before his death last year, and Vladimir Vogel's *Wagadu*, a work for chorus and small orchestra. The Berg is scheduled for May 1st, and the Vogel for May 16th. The month's music will also include relays from Covent Garden opera house. The season opens on April 27th with *Die Meistersinger*. This will be broadcast in its entirety, a procedure almost unprecedented for the B.B.C.

The Berg concerto will be played by Krasner[2] and conducted by Anton von Webern, himself a composer and close friend of Berg during his lifetime.[3] Von Webern's series of Workers' Concerts in Vienna drew crowded houses, and won him wide fame as a conductor.

Vladimir Vogel, Russian composer living in Switzerland, is best known for his fine *Storm March* for brass, and for two rhythmic studies for orchestra.[4] The choral writing of *Wagadu* is said to be difficult to a degree of virtuosity.[5]

It is a pity that no room has been found for novelties in this season's opera. Practical difficulties may bar the production of Berg's *Wozzeck*, but means surely exist for the staging of Shostakovitch's *Lady Macbeth*. The broadcast of this work in March stirred up interest and discussion in many musical quarters. Why should Weinberger's delightful *Schwanda* be dropped when, with a little nursing, it might deservedly become a popular favourite?[6]

Source: *World Film News* 1/2 (May 1936), 10.

[1] Edward Clark (1888–1962), visionary English music administrator and conductor, whose work as a BBC music programmer, particularly in London from 1927, brought a wide array of contemporary music before the listening public. He left the BBC because of accusations about financial irregularities on a BBC business trip and changes to his programming of a Symphony Orchestra tour. He married Elisabeth Lutyens in 1942.

[2] Louis Krasner (1903–95), American violinist, who commissioned and gave the first performance of Berg's Violin Concerto.

[3] Anton Webern (1883–1945), Austrian composer and conductor, pupil of Schoenberg. Britten's opinion of him fluctuated throughout his life. See below e.g. Essay 69.

[4] Wladimir Vogel (1896–1984), Swiss composer of Russian and German descent. Vogel wrote four rhythmic studies: *Ritmica funebre*, *Ritmica scherzosa*, *Ostinato perpetuo*, *Ritmica ostinata* (1930–2).

[5] *Wagadus Untergang durch die Eitelkeit* (1930), for soprano, alto, bass-baritone, chorus, speaking chorus, and five saxophones.

[6] Jaromír Weinberger (1896–1967), American composer of Czech birth. His opera *Švanda dudák* (Schwanda, the Bagpiper) of 1926 was his most successful piece, receiving over 2,000 performances by 1931.

3 BBC Programming: Holst, Vaughan Williams and Poulenc (1936)

For June–July the musical programme of the B.B.C. are not its brightest. There is the usual sprinkling of light orchestral and classical chamber music programmes, suitably interspersed with part-songs by the various teams of B.B.C. singers octets and choruses. But for the more adventurous listener there is not much excitement.

The Canterbury Festival on when Dr. Boult is taking down section of the B.B.C. orchestra, contains Holst's St. Pauls Suite as the sole representation of 20th Century music.[1] [This charming work for strings alone will not be found particularly exhilarating for the admirers of Berg or Bartok.][2] Let the interested listener note the final passage, exacting both for the technique and nerves of the leading first violin—a tactless, and may we suggest, not particularly successful experiment on the part of the composer.

Vaughan Williams' piano concerto will be played by Harriet Cohen on .[3] Not one of the most popular works of this [illegible] laureate of English musicians, though its admirers rejoice in the Lisztian flavour of the piano writing, and in the Central European atmosphere of the harmony—Bartok being put in his place, no doubt.

Poulenc will play some of his piano music on ----- His recent output is singly devoted to that instrument, he himself being a pianist of the first rank. The academicians [*sic*] attitude to Poulenc is gradually changing from that of pained surprise to that of patronising approval—which must be trying for this young Frenchman, once member of Les Six, and still on the ambitious side of forty. He is known principally in England for the trio for Oboe, Bassoon & piano—the classic for that combination, and for his entertaining ballet the 'Homeparty' (Les Biches)—produced [by Diagilev] in London about ten years ago with choroeography by Nijinska.[4]

Source: Autograph draft (*GB-ALb*). This was most likely intended for *World Film News* 1/3 (June 1936).

[1] Adrian Boult (1889–1983), English conductor, here given his academic title by Britten most likely as a gesture of disdain.

[2] Crossed out by Britten.

[3] Harriet Cohen (1895–1967), English pianist and champion of contemporary British music. Vaughan Williams dedicated his Concerto to her.

[4] Serge Diaghilev (1872–1929), Russian impresario, misspelt and crossed out by Britten. Vaclav Nijinsky (1889–1950), for a period Diaghilev's lover, was principal dancer in a number of infamous ballet productions by Diaghilev, including *Les Biches* (1923) by Poulenc (1899–1963). See Essay 71 for more on Britten's later friendship with Poulenc.

4 'As You Like It' Walton's Music (1936)

That the directors of 20th Century Fox Film Corporation should have invited one of the 20th century stars of British music to write for one of its biggest productions is very creditable indeed.[1] But the invitation seems to have exhausted their enterprise. His name, perhaps symbolically, is absent from the programme, and the opportunities he has had for writing serious film music seem negligible.

There is, of course, the Grand Introduction over the credit titles—pompous and heraldic in the traditional manner. There is a Grand Oratorio Finale with full orchestra, based on Elizabethan songs, in which a bunch of Albert Hall contralti is very prominent. Both these are written with great competence, and indeed Walton is incapable of any sort of inefficiency.

But apart from suitable *Waldweben*[2] noises at the beginning of each sequence, which tactfully fade out as the action starts, that is the whole of Walton's contribution to *As You Like It*.

Once [*sic*] cannot feel that the microphone has entered very deeply into Walton's scoring soul.[3] A large orchestra in which strings are very prominent has been used, and in the accompanying pastoral music one is conscious of the energetic ranks of the London Philharmonic sweating away behind the three-ply trees.

As far as he is allowed, Walton makes one or two musically apt suggestions. The introduction is very neatly dovetailed into the chicken-yard, and Leon Goossens on the oboe mixes very creditably with the Wyandottes.[4] Also a neat and poetic use of the leitmotiv *Rosalind* is to be noted.

But the music for *As You Like It* is not the advance on *Escape Me Never* which we all expected.[5]

Source: *World Film News* 1/7 (Oct. 1936), 46.

[1] *As You like It*, based on Shakespeare's play, directed by Paul Czinner, with a cast that included Elisabeth Bergner, Laurence Olivier, and Sophie Stewart.

[2] *Waldweben* ('forest murmurs'), orchestral interlude in Wagner's *Siegfried*.

[3] As the ensuing articles and interviews show, Britten remained fond of Walton. The relationship was not always without tension (yet Walton was a witness at his Appellate Tribunal hearing in June 1942; see Essay 11), although Britten's comment here is no doubt more to do with his recent employment by the GPO Film Unit and his interest in exploiting sound technology for effect, on a scale and budget considerably smaller than that available to Walton.

[4] Leon Goossens (1897–1988), English oboist. He was professor of oboe at the Royal College (1924–39) when Britten was a student there, and was well known to him by the time of this review. Britten dedicated his *Phantasy* (1932) to Goossens, who gave the first performance of it in a BBC broadcast in August 1933. The wyandotte is an eponymous heavy-weight fowl, a breed originating in late 19th-century New York. It is not clear if Britten here is commenting on the historical incongruity of introducing these fowls into an Elizabethen setting.

[5] Walton had also written music for Czinner's 1935 film *Escape Me Never*, also starring Elisabeth Bergner.

5 American Impressions (?1940)

First of all the size. Coming from England where, I believe, there is no place more than 80 miles from the sea, the immense distances one can travel here and is expected to travel here are unbelievable. The other side of the Atlantic the journey of two hundred odd miles between London and Paris is, for the majority of Englishmen an event only to be undertaken after much thought and preparation and one which will clearly distinguish one year from another. Here the number of miles has no such significance. Americans commute distances which Englishmen travel for their summer vacations.

* * * *

And not only size in distances, in opportunities. For a musician this is especially obvious. If, as a composer, he has a success with an orchestral work, there are over 60 first-class orchestras to play this work[1]—in England there are perhaps six. If a singer, a tour of only the women's clubs of this country will keep him busy for several months. I am told that music is the third largest industry in this country, and having spent some time in the Middle West listening to a Band Clinic, in which a University Band of some 300 strong took part, and talking to numberless directors of similar bands, I can well believe this. The demand for music of all types is enormous, and serious composing should be a most profitable business.

* * * *

Serious composing should be a most profitable business, and for a few it is. But for many serious and capable composers the reverse is sadly true. I think I know some of the reasons, as the position in England, before the last year or so of 'emergency', was analogous. Too many composers have grandiose ideas. They worry too much about posterity. They have mapped out for themselves a little path-way of 'original development' and must not deviate to the left or to the right. They will not condescend to write simple or direct music, or to please this or that director or producer. There is a way of pleasing most people and still not hurting one's aesthetic standards, and that, I feel, should be the aim of a composer. It is this idea of the divine right of a creative artist that has terrified so many officials and business men who hold the purse-strings. I was horrified by the badness and dullness of most of the serious music played in the Band Clinic I mentioned above. Why is the young serious composer not

Source: Typescript, n.d. (*GB-ALb* 1–9900027). This draft later formed the basis of 'An English Composer sees America', Essay 6.

[1] Originally '30', with note in margin: 'Is 30 correct? BB'.

writing for these bands? He should study the demands and then persuade the publishing houses, easily the most unenterprising section of the American musical world, to understand that a musical education is an asset and not a liability.

* * * *

The publishers in this country are sadly unenterprising. Compared with the number of performances that contemporary American compositions receive and the enterprise of the recording companies, the publishers lag far behind. It is little use having large hire libraries filled with works written in not always legible manuscript. Well printed scores and parts make all the difference in the world to the performers and many times must influence conductors making up their programmes. It is partly the fault of the composer, who is not business-like enough to realise that publishers must balance their books. If in addition to his Sinfonia Tragica (in B flat minor) he showed the hesitant publisher six school songs, some violin studies, or a sonatina for Bass Clarinet and Piano, the results might be more favourable.

* * * *

But in spite of feeling mostly in the mood of Sinfonia Tragica these days, the American musician should feel fortunate to be living this side of the Atlantic Ocean. Here matters artistic and cultural have not been put away to make room for gas-mask and the ration card. The radio is used as propaganda for tooth paste and not for forms of government. Here at least the musician can look forward to a future, and a future that is bright with opportunity.[2]

[2] America joined the war the following year, following the Japanese bombing of Pearl Harbor in Dec. 1941.

6 An English Composer Sees America (1940)

In April of last year, I left England on a vacation trip across the Atlantic, a vacation rather from the general European atmosphere than from overwork.[1]

I spent two months in Canada, and since last August have been chiefly in and around New York with occasional visits to the Middle West. I have found this country enormously stimulating, and, as I have met many of the chief figures in American music today, I have had perhaps as good an opportunity as most foreigners of comparing conditions in this country with those in their own.

* * * *

There has been recently a lot of correspondence about American music and the treatment of American composers. It has been the chief topic of conversation in many musical circles to which I have been introduced, and it has been the subject of many articles and essays.

Let me say straightaway that, in my opinion, the American composer has little to grumble at; compared with English composers, nothing. Whatever struggle American music may have had in the past for its fair share of public recognition, today the composer here, compared with his English brother even in normal times, has a very rosy prospect.

In the first place, as far as I can see, there does not exist in the minds of most audiences here the deadening distinction, so common in England, between 'music' and 'contemporary music.' This in part may have been caused by the British Broadcasting Corporation's mistaken policy of giving a full-sized concert once a month by music of [*sic*] contemporary composers (generally of the most formidable and unattractive kind); and with this gesture, having done its duty to 'contemporary music,' it returns with a sigh of relief to the normal programs of 'music.'[2]

* * * *

This distinction has been aggravated by the modern music enthusiasts themselves, who have not always been very discriminating in their praise, and

Source: *Tempo* (American edn.) 1/2 (Apr. 1940), 1–3.

[1] Article was completed on 19 Mar. 1940 and first appeared in the *New York Times*, 24 Mar. 1940. In Britten's autograph draft (*GB-ALb* 1–02053789), this opening sentence was followed by: 'The six years since I left the Royal College of Music had indeed been strenuous ones, filled as they were with "occasional composing", the occupation which forms such a large part of the contemporary composer's life. But my real object was for a time at any rate to escape the spiritual fogs which have settled so closely upon "the most famous island in the world".'

[2] See Jennifer Doctor, *The BBC and Ultra-Modern Music, 1922–1936* (Cambridge: CUP, 1999) for an explanation of BBC programming policies in the period concerned.

have made the same mistake of giving entire concerts of modern music. This, separating as it does the two audiences, is obviously fatal. Contemporary music should take its place in concert programs side by side with the well-tried masterpieces; it should be judged solely on its merits as music.

American audiences appear to be less prejudiced in this respect than English ones. Most of the symphonic programs include a twentieth-century work, and the halls do not seem to be any the less full. American composers should be very definitely helped by this attitude, in their efforts to be heard, and, to judge from the concert and radio columns of the Sunday papers, it is undoubtedly the case. Since the beginning of the season, modern music generally has been continually broadcast, and American music in particular has received outstanding encouragement from such festivals as the one organized by ASCAP and, more recently by WNYC, as well as the fine concerts of American music given by Dr. Koussevitzky.[3] The programs of the Boston and New York Symphony Orchestras contain American works, as do the programs of the symphonic bodies all over the country.

In England, too, there is no such organization as the WPA,[4] which according to the press, has performed 7,332 American compositions by 2,258 native or resident composers! I wish that the American musician could see the programs of the B B C Symphony, the London Philharmonic Orchestra and the London Symphony Orchestras. He would not think himself so hardly used.[5]

* * * *

Generally speaking, unless one has become a national institution (a process which requires many white hairs and forty years of being snubbed and rejected), one is limited for performance of new works to the London branch of the I.S.C.M.,[6] with its few concerts a year and exclusively highbrow audience; to occasional semi-amateur performances organized by well-meaning but often inefficient enthusiasts, or to very infrequent and strangely

[3] ASCAP: American Society of Composers, Authors and Publishers. WNYC: New York radio network, with its own radio orchestra. Serge Koussevitzky (1874–1951), Russian-born conductor and arts patron, conductor of Boston Symphony Orchestra (1924–49) where his commissions included Bartók's *Concerto for Orchestra* (1942–3, rev. 1945), Messiaen's *Turangalîla-symphonie* (1946–8), and *Peter Grimes* (1945).

[4] WPA: Works Progress Administration, an independent agency formed by the Roosevelt administration in 1936 and funded by Congress to provide jobs for the unemployed and to facilitate the creation of public works of art. Under its banner were the Federal Arts Project, the Federal Music Project, and the Federal Theatre Project.

[5] Again, as Doctor establishes, this is part of the mythology of 1930s concert programming, already in the making.

[6] ISCM: International Society for Contemporary Music.

timed radio performances, few of which reach the general concertgoing public.[7]

Here the composer has a chance of obtaining commissions from radio and phonograph companies. In England these are even rarer than chromatic timps. Here there are private fellowships; I know of nothing of the kind in England. In America perhaps the printing of modern music has lagged behind performances, and in this respect the publishers seem scarcely to have realized that a printed work stands a much better chance of establishing itself in the regular repertory than a sometimes illegible score, and parts that may not have been too well copied and have been thumbed and blue-penciled from Boston to Los Angeles. Phonograph companies on this side have been much more enterprising, and many works by the not so old have been 'disked' and many are to come.[8] On the other side of the Atlantic, the great publishing houses automatically issue a few contemporary scores each year, but to be recorded is for most composers a rare privilege.

All this is not to say that the struggle of the young and unknown composer is not often heartbreakingly difficult here as everywhere. But I am sure that his opportunities are greater in this country than in any other country in the world.

* * * *

To the outsider, however, the struggle which American music has had for recognition, and which has resulted in the present comparatively happy situation, has left behind it at least one potential source of danger. This is the very real danger of excessive nationalism.

In the first place, in their efforts to do justice to the American cause, conductors and performers may not always exercise an objective criticism in their choice of works to offer the public. They may be prejudiced by the fact that these works are written by Americans. No one would deny that this country has been magnificently hospitable to European composers and artists. But what always has mattered and always will matter is that the works in question should be good. No accident of nationality has ever excused a composer for writing bad music.

In the second place, the composer must be alive to the danger of consciously trying to create what he imagines to be a national style. I realize that many young American composers wish to produce something different from the rather tame imitations of the European masters, from Grieg to Hindemith, that

[7] This was the experience of many of Britten's contemporaries, although not his own.

[8] See Chapter 6 of Paul Kildea, *Selling Britten* (Oxford: OUP, 2002), for an examination of Britten's recording history.

have been turned out in this country for some time. But I am sure that a complete rejection of the great European tradition is equally fatal, for, after all, that tradition is nothing but centuries of experience of what people like to hear and what players like to play.

* * * *

In England the position has been very similar. At the turn of the century, young English composers were sick to death of the preponderating German influence which had been stifling English music for 150 years. There were two reactions to this: one on the part of practicing musicians like Elgar and Frank Bridge, who realized the value of the classical tradition yet whose utterances were characteristically English; the other, and temporarily more influential, reaction was that of the folksong group. This group adopted English folksong as the chief influence in their work, and disregarded most of the lessons Europe had to give. It held up the progress of music for twenty-five years, but it has now entirely subsided, since audiences found it monotonous melodically and harmonically, and clumsy in form and orchestration. It was founded on a style which was too personal to its instigator and in its imitators forced and unnatural.

* * * *

Let American composers take warning from this. There is no more malignant disease than nationalism. Why not make the best of both worlds? With lessons learned from Europe, let an American style develop naturally and without forcing, which it surely will do, if the composer takes notice of what is going on around him and writes the best music he can for every occasion that offers itself. Besides having the largest concert organizations in the world and the obvious advantages of Hollywood, this country has an educational system unparalleled in size and scope, and the demand for good, simple music in this direction is enormous. There are school operas to be written, pieces for the numberless school children learning to play instruments, and, above all, there are the bands which are such a feature of this country and have been so neglected by the serious composers.[9]

[9] Percy Grainger excepted, whom Britten greatly admired. Britten's draft concluded with: 'It is by supplying the best possible music for these different demands that a real American tradition will be formed; and judging by the splendid start it has made, and by its good fortune in possessing in Aaron Copland, as important and vital a composer as any living, an example to the young composer, this tradition has every chance of becoming a great one.'

7 On Film Music (c. 1940–1)

LEYDA: In answering the following questions, illustrate, wherever this is advantageous and possible, by a reference to a film for which you have written the music, and quote from the score.

1. Do you assist in the choice of sequences for which music is to be written?

BRITTEN: If possible—in my experience in documentaries, yes, in Commercials, no.

LEYDA: 2. To consider first the single film sequence—do you work on the music from the script or from the finished film sequence?

BRITTEN: All depends on the kind of film. In some documentaries I have done, the picture was cut to the music after the latter was recorded—a luxurious procedure.

LEYDA: 3. (*a*) Does your musical imagination have to fit itself to particular details dramatic or visual of film sequences; or is it free to produce its own musical terms for the essence or quality of the sequence as you see it?

BRITTEN: It depends on the character of the film. Usually if the picture is serious one finds a musical equivalent to the emotions being shown on the screen. If the picture is lighter, or a cartoon, a lot of synchronization with details on the screen can be used.

LEYDA: 3. (*b*) What—in one case or the other—is the effect of your procedure on 1) the music, 2) the film?

BRITTEN: (1) If the music is free of the fetters of synchronization, it can be more interesting qua music—but that is not so important, as I don't take film music seriously qua music anyhow—(2) See 3 (*a*) above.

LEYDA: 4. Do you take anything into account outside the dramatic and visual elements of the film sequence—for example, the level of musical understanding of the film audience?

BRITTEN: It is usually impossible to underestimate the musical intelligence of the film audiences—certainly commercial ones. Documentary audiences incline to be more high-brow, but not necessarily more intelligent.

LEYDA: 5. What difference are you aware of that is produced in the music by the fact that you are composing it for a film sequence and not for a sequence in any other dramatic medium?

Editor's title.

Source: The questions were devised by the film historian Jay Leyda and circulated to Marc Blitzstein, Paul Bowles, Britten, Aaron Copland, Henry Cowell, Ernest Krenek, and Karol Rathaus, and were answered by Britten some time in the period 1940–1, while the composer was living at 7 Middagh Street, Brooklyn. Questionnaire is kept in The New York Public Library, and is reproduced in Mitchell and Reed, ii. 896.

BRITTEN: The technical side of the recording. The possibility of gradual fades in and out. And most obvious of all, that only 1/10th of the audience's attention is on the music.

LEYDA: 6. Is the possibility of the length of the particular film sequence being reduced or increased after the entire film is completed a difficulty for you in composing the music for the sequence?

BRITTEN: One usually allows for that kind of thing when writing the score—marking possible 'cuts' or 'repeat bars'.

LEYDA: 7. Do you find that the special facilities of sound recording for films—for example, the number and placing of microphones, the combining of sound track in re-recording—provide additional resources for your music?

BRITTEN: Certainly. The possibilities of re-recording are endless. Interesting sound perspectives can be achieved by the use of several microphones.

LEYDA: 8. Do you orchestrate the music, and if not do you feel this as a limitation?

BRITTEN: Always.

LEYDA: 9. Bearing in mind the degree to which you as a composer of an opera would control the dramatic shaping of the libretto, are you as the composer for a film, consulted about the dramatic or visual elements?

BRITTEN: In documentaries nearly always—in commercials never.[1]

LEYDA: 10. Is there anything in composing music for the film sequence that necessitates a change in your usual method of composition?

BRITTEN: Usually greater speed, so that one is not so free to reject as when composing in one's own time. In moments of greatest emergency, one has to write straight into the orchestra parts, which is not my usual method! Personally, even in times of ease, I always write film music straight into score—which is not such a feat as it sounds since I use as small an orchestra as possible.

LEYDA: 11. To proceed now from the problem of the single film sequence to the problem of the entire film:

(*a*) Do you feel the need of unifying the passages of music within a film as you would unify them in any other musical work?

(*b*) Have you found that the film permits this or that it makes it more difficult or even impossible?

(*c*) Have you been able to satisfy this need?

BRITTEN: (*a*) Certainly. I believe that the audience (usually unconsciously) gets a feeling of satisfaction from that.

(*b*) It is usually possible.

[1] Britten only ever composed the score for one commercial film, *Love from a Stranger*, for Trafalgar Films (Nov. 1936).

(*c*) By using the same kind of scoring throughout; same kind of musical material.

LEYDA: 12. Are the conditions under which you compose music for film satisfactory or would you like them to be changed, and if so how changed?

BRITTEN: No I should always like to be consulted during the writing of the script; have what time & materials (kind of orchestra) I want; have as much money and publicity as the star actors get. Faint hope![2]

[2] There are resonances here of Schoenberg's comments reproduced in the *New York Times*, 28 Jan. 1940, on the composition of film scores: 'I would be willing to write music for a film. . . . I would want $100,000 for the score. They must give me a year to write it and let me compose what I want. And, of course, I would have to say something about the story.'

8 England and the Folk-Art Problem (1941)

There have been so few outstanding composers in England since the turn of the century, it is hardly surprising that America knows little of that country's musical fashions; for it is the minor composers who most clearly indicate the trend of the age. Roughly speaking there have been two major schools, and the conflict between the two has influenced everybody. The outstanding figures whose personalities may be said to have given each school its particular character were Elgar and Parry.

Elgar represents the professional point of view, which emphasizes the importance of technical efficiency and welcomes any foreign influences that can be profitably assimilated. Parry and his followers, with the Royal College of Music as their center, have stressed the amateur idea and they have encouraged folk-art, its collecting and teaching. They are inclined to suspect technical brilliance of being superficial and insincere. This difference may not be unconnected with the fact that Elgar was compelled to earn his living by music, whereas Parry was not. Parry's national ideal was, in fact, the English Gentleman (who generally thinks it rather vulgar to take too much trouble). From Parry and his associates there arose a school of composers directly influenced by folksong, to which belonged virtually every composer known here until recently, except of course, Elgar and Frank Bridge. This may seem surprising to many Americans who have come to regard Elgar as synonymous with England. But he is, in fact, a most eclectic composer, his most obvious influences being Wagner, Tchaikovsky, and Franck.

But since 1930 the influence of Parry has largely disappeared. Now the Elgarian approach, with its direct admission of continental contemporary influence, has asserted itself. The great success of Walton's *Façade* and Lambert's *Rio Grande*, both with the public and the intellectuals, left no doubt in the minds of the younger composers as to which was the more profitable path to follow.[1] Elizabeth Maconchy owes much to the strong rhythms and acidulous harmonies of Bartok; Lennox Berkeley to the later works of Stravinsky and the younger French school; Christian Darnton and Elizabeth Lutyens have adopted a modified version of the twelve-tone system, as used by Webern and Berg; Alan Rawsthorne's general intellectual approach and his avoidance of tonal centers remind one of Hindemith; Howard Ferguson and Edmund Rubbra derive largely from those heavy-handed late-romantics, Brahms and Sibelius (which, I admit, is a criticism).

Source: *Modern Music* 18/2 (Jan./Feb. 1941), 71–5.

[1] *Façade* (1922–9, rev. 1942, 1951, 1977), words by Edith Sitwell (1887–1964); *Rio Grande* (1927) with words by Sitwell's brother, Sacheverell (1897–1988).

The failure of folksong to provide contemporary England with an adequate basis for organized music is due to many factors, some general, some local. The chief attractions of English folksongs are the sweetness of the melodies, the close connection between words and music, and the quiet, uneventful charm of the atmosphere. This uneventfulness however is part of the weakness of the tunes, which seldom have any striking rhythms or memorable melodic features. Like much of the English countryside, they creep into the affections rather than take them by storm. This amiable feature of the English landscape has had also a practical effect on folksong. For a very long time communication over the island has been easy, and so access to more organized music has also been easy. Most people will admit that the more highly organized, the more interesting the music. Folksong in England had practically disappeared, and only fairly recently has it been brought to light by the energies of collectors. These worthy people have made strenuous efforts to re-establish it, but their efforts were doomed to failure, since folksong is no longer part of the social life of the people.

* * * *

English folk-art as we know it has probably been static for about three hundred years. It has not continued to evolve like that of many Central European countries, or the songs of the Appalachians, or of Scotland almost up to the present day—at any rate until the advent of radio. Incidentally, even I can remember Scottish fisher-girls who visited my home town of Lowestoft to gut the herrings every fall, singing their lovely, lilting Highland tunes. Nowadays they sing the latest song from the weekly hit-parade.

This decline raises the whole general problem of the nature and origin of folk-art. The nearest approach to folk-music today is swing and the Negro spiritual. People have different opinions on the origins of the former, but to me the line seems clearly to proceed through jazz, rag-time, Victorian popular song back to the lighter Italian operas (Rossini, Donizetti, and early Verdi, with their frequent dotted rhythms) and Johann Strauss, to be colored by the luscious harmony of Debussy, Franck and Delius. The Negro spiritual has some of its roots obviously in Methodist hymns. It is important to realize that what we call folk-music is no product of primitive society, in the sense that a homogeneous and segregated tribe is primitive. Since the Roman Empire, all culture, folk or sophisticated, has been under international influence. Indeed the whole conception of folksong as a germ from which organized music grew may prove to be a false one. Literary research into the origins of the folk-ballad shows that it is an end-product of an aristocratic art form, the epic. (There is a Yorkshire version of the Mummers' play which has incorporated a whole scene from an eighteenth-century opera.) Folk-music most probably has likewise been evolved from conscious art-forms, such as church music or the art of the Minne-singers.[2] And to come to the present time, compare the wholesale borrowing from the popular classics by swing musicians. Creation is always the work of an individual although works may be modified by the performers to suit their own skill or the audience's preferences.

Whatever its origins, there are, moreover, serious difficulties in the way of making folksong the basis of contemporary art-forms. Since the form of a work is dictated by the material, the characteristics of English folksong mentioned above are bound to have a weakening effect on the structure of music founded directly upon it. Folksongs are concise and finished little works of art. When used as raw material they tend to obstruct thinking in the extended musical forms. Works founded on them are usually little more than variations or potpourris. Again, each folksong has a completely suggested harmonic scheme—so that it should sound satisfactory when sung unaccompanied—and much deviation therefore tends to produce a feeling of irritation. A work like the *Sacre du Printemps* of Stravinsky is unsatisfactory because it disregards this fact and suggests in some places a row-boat rocking uneasily on oblivious waves of extravagant harmonies. Later, in *Les Noces*, Stravinsky is far more controlled and the harmonies are closely related to the tunes. In this fine work he breaks up his folk-themes into small phrases, and is consequently freer to develop the form.

All these characteristics tend to make folksong a most restricting influence, which, as a matter of fact, is no doubt what many composers have wanted. Lacking the necessary discipline they forget that discipline must come from within. No one would dream, for instance, of founding a school upon the music of a composer like Donizetti; whereas folk-art is infinitely narrower than that delightful but limited master.

* * * *

Those circumstances which prompted the whole movement of Nationalism in England have been not above suspicion. Any cultural 'movement' (especially if it ends in 'ism') is more often than not a cover for inefficiency or lack of artistic direction. If one is unsatisfied with a piece of work it is useful to have some theory to shield it, and Nationalism is as good as any other—especially when one is dealing with foreigners! But there is another more sympathetic aspect of the picture. For nearly two centuries English music had been second-rate, with no more than local importance. The composers had been too ready simply to

[2] Minnesang, the German tradition of courtly monophony, dating from the 12th to 14th centuries.

imitate their European (and especially Viennese and Italian) colleagues. The fault lay not in the influences but in the lack of talent and inability to assimilate them. It should be obvious that the national character of a composer will appear in his music, whatever technic [*sic*] he has chosen or wherever his influences lie, in the same way that his personal idiosyncrasies cannot be hidden. The case of Elgar we have mentioned above. Perhaps the piece of music that brings tears most easily to the eyes of an expatriate Englishman is Delius' *On Hearing the First Cuckoo in Spring*, which is founded on a Norwegian tune and written by a man who spent most of his life out of England, who responded most to the influences of Grieg and Liszt, and whose publishers were Viennese. To push the argument further, would anyone really mistake the Italian or Spanish *Capriccios* for anything but Russian, or *Iberia* and *Carmen* for anything but French?[3] People often cite the Russian school in defense of Nationalism, but it is worth noting that the composer who immediately strikes one as the most Russian of Russians is Tchaikovsky who all his life was berated for being too occidental. And it was the influence of Mozart on Tchaikovsky which helped to make the texture of his music so marvelously clear and his form so much more satisfactory than that of his Nationalistic compatriots.

The attempt to create a national music is only one symptom of a serious and universal malaise of our time—the refusal to accept the destruction of 'community' by the machine.

However we decide to Act
Decision to accept the fact
That machine has now destroyed
The local customs we enjoyed,
. . . .

And publicized among the crowd
The secret that was always true
But known once only to the few,
Compelling all to the admission
Aloneness is man's real condition,
That each must travel forth alone
In search of the Essential Stone,
'The Nowhere-without-No' that is
The justice of Societies.[4]

[3] Debussy's *Ibéria* (1905–8), is one of his *Images*; Bizet's *Carmen* was composed in 1873–4.

[4] Original footnote: From *A Letter to Elizabeth Mayer*, by W. H. Auden, to be published in March by Random House. [See 'New Year Letter (January 1, 1940)' in W. H. Auden, *Collected Longer Poems* (London: Faber & Faber, 1988), 125–6. There are minor differences in punctuation and capitalization in the published version.]

The English composers of today have consciously or unconsciously seen the danger-signals ahead. They are avoiding the pitfalls that some of their musical fathers and uncles have dug for them. It is only those who accept their loneliness and refuse all the refuges, whether of tribal nationalism or airtight intellectual systems, who will carry on the human heritage.

9 Au Revoir to the U.S.A. (1942)

Since I am about to leave America and cannot expect to return for some time, let me set down briefly some of the impressions I shall take away with me, after a visit of nearly three years.

One of the first was perhaps an obvious one, but it was strong and it persists. The abundance of musical activities in this country cannot surely have been equalled within the memory of any European musician. Although it is unfair to compare conditions here with those of Europe in recent years, I am sure there never was so much music-making even in Imperial Vienna as there is here now. The number of concerts and concert-goers in this country is prodigious. (I am not now considering the value of these activities, about which opinions may differ.)

Apart from the rather conservative treatment of opera, there is no field neglected. Programs are usually pretty catholic in make-up, and they also show general signs of improvement. For my taste, there is still too great an insistence on the nineteenth century in the orchestral repertory, but that is to be expected and will probably continue, since people who go to hear a symphony orchestra usually like to hear everyone playing all the time, and most music before Beethoven was written for fewer players.

The standard of performance generally is very high, particularly that of the symphony orchestra, which has become to the twentieth century what the virtuoso singer was to the eighteenth. In skill and quality of sound, as is now universally recognized, the great American orchestras have no superior.

The general encouragement given to living composers, old and young, is remarkable. I still maintain that, compared with their contemporaries in Europe during the years that I have been around, composers here have very rosy opportunities, what with commissions, prizes, performances as well as the work in the commercial fields of radio, film and theatre. I do not say that this has always been the case or that the composer's lot is now a perfectly happy one. But even during the last three years, I seem to have noticed an increase of general interest in contemporary music. Owing perhaps to the radio-education of the public, audiences begin to prefer less hackneyed pieces—an interest not always so well catered to as it has been by one great Midwestern orchestra which, in response to public demand, played the *Mathis der Maler* suite ten times on tour.[1]

How much this interest in music is founded on genuine taste and knowledge, and how much on the desire to be au courant, to hear the latest thing, it

Source: *Modern Music* 19/2 (Jan./Feb. 1942), 100–1.

[1] Hindemith's *Mathis der Maler* (1934).

is hard to say. One of the most serious dangers to the future of American music seems to me to lie in the crop of interpreters, commentators, explainers and synthesizers, who make such comfortable livings telling the public that music is really very simple and easy to understand and available to anyone who absorbs this or that easy approach. (Whereas any honest musical craftsman can tell you it is not. Like any other art, the true understanding of music requires great labor and patient concentration, as well as a good deal of humility.) Those who sell music as if it were a kind of breakfast-food merely function as part of the big business machine which runs so much of the music in this country, and on whose future development the future relation between music-producers and consumers depends. What will happen, for instance, if the public gets tired of this particular kind of cereal?

Three years ago, it seemed to me that a self-conscious wave of musical nationalism was sweeping this country, and I was sorry to see it. Perhaps I am wrong, but I think that in the last year this has started to recede. If so, it is good, as now, more than ever, nationalism is an anachronistic irrelevance.

What will happen to music in this exhilarating country in the next few years? I myself would like to see it much more decentralized, and the scene dominated by vital young artists who are concentrating more on music rather than on personalities. I should like also to see more small groups of players, on the lines of the dance bands, so that people may learn that a hundred players are not essential to every orchestral concert. Perhaps opera will be financially successful away from the Met. Perhaps by the time I return to America, the successor to *Das Lied von der Erde* and the *Symphonie des psaumes* will have been written by an American. Scope, spirit, enthusiasm, skill—in America the stage is all set.

10 On Behalf of Gustav Mahler (1942)

Most young American and English musicians have been encouraged, I think, to disregard Mahler. At least I myself was. Always coupled with Bruckner, he was supposed to be a purely local composer. For Germans, I was told, he had a certain sentimental attraction, though even on the Rhine and the Danube, the academicians preferred Brahms, the glamour-seekers Strauss, and the modernists Schönberg and Berg. He was long-winded and formless—the bright intellectuals cited him as an example of a romantic self-indulgent, who was so infatuated with his ideas that he could never stop. Either he couldn't score at all, or he could only score like Wagner, using enormous orchestras with so much going on that you couldn't hear anything clearly. Above all, he was not *original*. In other words, nothing for a young student!

And so, when I was at a concert soon after leaving school, specially to hear an exciting new piano concerto, and saw from the programme that I had first to hear a symphony by Mahler, I naturally groaned in anticipation of forty-five minutes of boredom.[1]

But what I heard was not what I had expected to hear. First of all, in spite of a slack, under-rehearsed and rather apologetic performance, the scoring startled me. It was mainly 'soloistic' and entirely clean and transparent. The coloring seemed calculated to the smallest shade, and the result was wonderfully resonant. I wasn't bored for one of its forty-five minutes, whereas I was for every one of the fashionable new concerto's twenty-three. The form was so cunningly contrived; every development surprised one and yet sounded inevitable. Above all, the material was remarkable, and the melodic shapes highly original, with such rhythmic and harmonic tension from beginning to end. After that concert, I made every effort to hear Mahler's music, in England and on the continent, on the radio and on the gramophone, and in my enthusiasm, I began a great crusade among my friends on behalf of my new god,—I must admit with only average success.

For one thing, owing to the size of the orchestra required, performances were few and far between.[2] And then, of course, no complete Mahler symphony

Source: *Tempo* (American edn.) 2/2 (Feb. 1942), 5.

[1] The symphony was Mahler's fourth, performed on 22 September 1930 at the Queen's Hall, which Britten thought 'Much too long, but beautiful in parts' (as his diary states).

[2] Of the many differences between published article and autograph draft (*GB-ALb* 1–02053790), those here are worth detailing: 'For one thing, the performances were so infrequent, mainly owing to the size of the orchestra required, & those locally were usually so bad—at that time English orchestras were known more for their stamina (vide the Promenade season), than for their quality. For another thing, this I admit "heavenly-length" was rather a stumbling block. So few people seemed to be able to concentrate—& I was the first to insist that complete

lasts less than three quarters of an hour, and many of them a great deal more. Now these two difficulties, of size and length, are bound to limit the number of orchestras that play Mahler and of audiences that hear him. And this is most regrettable. Once people have learned to take Mahler, as they did, for instance, in Holland, they have also learned to love him, and his music has drawn full houses. His influence on contemporary writing, too, could only be beneficial. His style is free from excessive personal mannerisms, and his scores are models of how the modern virtuoso orchestra should be used, nothing being left to chance and every note sounding. Besides, how wonderful it would be for all those over-worked nineteenth-century symphonic masterpieces to have a rest now and then.

It will be realized therefore how glad I was to hear that Messrs. Boosey & Hawkes were considering bringing out several of the movements from the Symphonies of Mahler in separate editions and for slightly reduced orchestras, and how anxious I was to co-operate.

The reduction of the scoring will not make as much difference as might at first be thought, as the movements chosen for this edition are mostly the middle ones, in which the extra instruments (such as 4th Flute, E flat Clarinet, and Double Bassoon) are only very occasionally introduced, and so may be omitted with small loss of effect. The complete orchestra is usually reserved for the big first and last movements. Mahler himself set the precedent of performing the movements out of their contexts, giving in fact titles to some of them. And though one has to admit that these movements must lose something of their special significance when performed thus, I am convinced that it is an excellent way of introducing Mahler's music to more orchestras and a wider public, and of helping to remove his 'hard-dying' bad reputation.[3]

concentration was necessary—for such a time—and many was the time I was driven frantic by restless companions during the Mahler session at a concert. (Even to this day I prefer to hear big Mahler works undistracted, in the seclusion of the home.)'

[3] Britten's draft concluded with the following paragraph: 'The movements under consideration, & in some cases in the process of being printed & published are the Minuet & Funeral March from the 1st Symph, the 2nd movement (Andante con moto) of the 2nd Symphony & the several short movements which make up the 2nd half of the Third Symphony. If the present extraordinary conditions permit, it is hoped to continue the series with some of the movements of the later Symphonies, of which the Alla Burlesca of the 9th is an outstanding example.'

11 Statement to the Local Tribunal for the Registration of Conscientious Objectors (1942)

Since I believe that there is in every man the spirit of God, I cannot destroy, and feel it my duty to avoid helping to destroy as far as I am able, human life, however strongly I may disapprove of the individual's actions or thoughts. The whole of my life has been devoted to acts of creation (being by profession a composer) and I cannot take part in acts of destruction. Moreover, I feel that the fascist attitude to life can only be overcome by passive resistance. If Hitler were in power here or this country had any similar form of government, I should feel it my duty to obstruct this regime in every non-violent way possible, and by complete non-cooperation. I believe sincerely that I can help my fellow human beings best, by continuing the work I am most qualified to do by the nature of my gifts and training, i.e. the creation or propagation of music. I have possibilities of writing music for M.O.I. (Ministry of Information) films, and for B.B.C. productions, and am offering my services to the Committee for the Encouragement of Music and Art. I am however prepared, but feel completely unsuited by nature & training, to undertake other constructive civilian work provided that it is not connected with any of the armed forces.[1]

Source: Typescript (carbon copy), 4 May 1942 (*GB-ALb* 1–02053791). Reproduced in Mitchell and Reed, ii. 1046.

[1] The Tribunal's report on Britten's hearing was as follows: 'Mr. [Canon] Stuart Morris represents the applicant. Applicant says:—I cannot destroy a man's life because in every man there is the Spirit of God. I was brought up in the Church of England. I have not attended for the last five years. I do not believe in the Divinity of Christ, but I think his teaching is sound and his example should be followed. I believe in letting an invader in and then setting him a good example. Denmark has allowed the Germans in and has not yet got them out, but time is short so far. I do not object to the civil defence forces. I object to joining the forces and helping in the killing. I will join the R.A.M.C. [Royal Army Medical Corps]. I do not know what the other non-combatant services are. I think with the Quakers I might find a spiritual home. I have written music for a pacifist song [*Pacifist March* (1937)], and a pacifist film [*Peace of Britain* (1936)]. There would be no non-combatant corps if it were not for the Army.'

12 Appeal to the Appellate Tribunal (1942)

That the local Tribunal failed to appreciate the religious background of my conscience trying to tie me down too narrowly to a belief in the divinity of Christ. I don't seek as suggested to pick & choose from his teaching, but I regard the whole context of his teaching & example as the standard by which I must judge. It is for this reason that my conscientious objection covers non-combatant as well as combatant service in the army. The reference to the RAMC & non-combatant service in the summary of further evidence does not fairly represent what I tried to convey to the Tribunal. I could not conscientiously join the RAMC or the non-combatant corps, because by so doing I should be no less actively participating in the war than if I were a combatant against which service the Tribunal recognised the validity of my objection. I realise however that in total war, it is impossible to avoid all participation of an indirect kind but I believe that I must draw the line as far away from direct participation as is possible. It is for this reason that I appeal to be left free to follow that line of service to the community, which my conscience approves & my training makes possible.

Source: Autograph draft, n.d. [June 1942] (*GB-ALb*, 1–02053792). Reproduced in Mitchell and Reed, ii. 1058.

13 How a Musical Work Originates (1942)

The actual origin is usually very difficult to define. Personally, I always have a number of ideas floating around: ideas of either a tune or a rhythm or a particular timbre (what the Americans call 'sonority'), or most usually ideas of the form of a work. The incentive which makes one develop or extend these ideas may originate from many different sources. It can come quite simply from a conductor or performer saying that he can use a certain kind of work, in which case one would hunt around in one's idea box to see what would be suitable. Or a great personal experience can set one going, or even sometimes one may feel the need of celebrating either a private or a public event. I do not say for a moment that some external reason is essential, that the ideas may not develop into a complete work of their own accord; but in my experience it is usually some such incentive as those I have mentioned that is necessary.

Here I must make one little observation. For me to produce my best music it is always essential for the purely musical idea or germ to precede the external stimulus. In the case of the *Sinfonia da Requiem* this external stimulus was the death of my mother a few years ago.[1] It had an especially powerful emotional effect on me and set me, in self-defence, analysing my feelings in regard to suffering and death. To this personal tragedy were soon added the more general world tragedies of the Spanish and the present wars.

Source: *The Listener* (30 July 1942), 138. A version of this was originally broadcast 19 July 1942 in Alec Robertson's Home Service programme, *This week at the Proms*.

[1] The UK premiere of the *Sinfonia da Requiem* took place on 22 July in a Prom performance with the London Philharmonic Orchestra conducted by Basil Cameron. It was broadcast by the BBC.

14 Conversation with Benjamin Britten (1944)

Question. You have written works in many forms and combinations, but you seem to prefer certain mediums to others. For example, you have written a great deal for string orchestra, but comparatively little for full orchestra. Why is that?

Answer. I am attracted by the many features of the strings. For instance, the possibilities of elaborate *divisi*—the effect of many voices of the same kind. There is also the infinite variety of colour—the use of mutes, pizzicato, harmonics and so forth. Then again, there is the great dexterity in the technique of string players. Generally speaking, I like to think of the smaller combinations of players, and I deplore the tendency of present-day audiences to expect only the luscious 'tutti' effect from an orchestra. I think this has been engendered by a 'Hollywood' method of scoring—both here and abroad—and also by the modern radio sets and electrical gramophones, which tend to cut off the upper partials and give the orchestra a constant rounded, booming and 'fat' sound. I've always inclined to the clear and clean—the 'slender' sound of, say, Mozart or Verdi or Mahler—or even Tchaikovsky, if he is played in a restrained, though vital, way. But I also write for string orchestra because I don't like writing music in a vacuum. To my mind, actual contact with performance is very important. String orchestras are more enterprising in their programmes than symphony orchestras and I have often been asked to write for them. I feel grateful if artists take the trouble to be interested in my music and ask me to compose something. In this way, I have been glad to write for soprano and tenor voices, for the horn and oboe, and string orchestra—and even for the opera-house.

Q. You are said to be writing an opera now, commissioned by Koussevitzky. Have you a particular liking for the stage?

A. I am passionately interested in seeing a successful, permanent, national opera in existence—successful both artistically and materially.[1] And it must be vital and contemporary, too, and depend less on imported 'stars' than on a first-rate, young and fresh, permanent company—Sadler's Wells have made a good beginning. I feel that with the advent of films, opera may turn its back on realism, and develop or return to stylisation—which I think it should. It is an art and it should be 'artificial,' for, after all, people don't use

Source: *Tempo* 1/6 (Feb. 1944), 4–5. Interviewer unknown.

[1] At this stage arguments about the future of the opera house at Covent Garden were filtering through the London political and arts worlds, especially given its temporary wartime use as a dance hall. The lease signed by Boosey & Hawkes in December 1944 ensured that Britten was kept particularly close to the various arrangements and arguments.

singing as their usual method of communication in real life. I don't mean to suggest that the production side of opera is unimportant: in fact, one of the worst features of the old 'grand' opera was the *laissez faire* attitude towards the movements and costumes of the singers, and the *décor*.

Q. It seems that you don't think that opera is outmoded by the film. But what about the musical film itself?

A. I think there are great possibilities in music for the films, but it must be taken seriously by the director and the composer, and used as an integral part of the whole thing—not just as a sound-effect, or to fill up gaps during the talking. The nearest approach to this I've seen has been in the Disney cartoons and a few French films. The position of music in radio drama is very similar.

Q. You have arranged some Rossini pieces for ballets and orchestral suites.[2] What is your general attitude towards arrangements and transcriptions?

A. I don't believe in the 'copyright' of the material of music. A work of art is more than just a tune, or a rhythm, or a sequence of harmonies. If Tin-Pan Alley wishes to use a tune of Tchaikovsky's, it doesn't affect the original work—it just makes a new one. The trouble is that general criticism of originality in music is entirely built on melody and occasionally harmony—in spite of the well-known case of the first tune of the *Eroica*, which you find note for note in the overture to *Bastien and Bastienne*, written by Mozart when he was twelve. Transcribing music from one medium to another is a complicated matter, because you have to try and place yourself in the position of the composer conceiving the music for a different medium. You can see how this may be done in Liszt's many piano transcriptions, especially of the Beethoven symphonies. I also support the idea of transcription against many who think it inartistic, because it can extend the possibilities of hearing the music. It is difficult to generalise, and you can only judge by the value of the transcription. But I could easily imagine that a transcription by a master of a work by a minor contemporary could be better than the original.

Q. You seem to be devoting a great deal of your time to performing. Is there a special reason for this?

A. I like performing for several reasons. I enjoy the contact with the audience, and I find it valuable for my activities as a composer to see how listeners react to the music. I also enjoy rehearsals—especially if I am working with sympathetic and intelligent musicians—delving deeper and deeper into the great music of all ages, and learning a lot from it. There are some composers whose music I do not like, but performing it makes me analyse my reasons for the dislike, and so prevents it from becoming just habit or prejudice.

[2] *Soirées musicales* (1936) and *Matinées musicales* (1941)—each a 'suite of five movements from Rossini'.

15 Speech to the International Arts Guild (*c.* 1944)

Ladies & Gentlemen—I must say it feels very odd standing up here talking to you. My usual place is sitting over there at the piano there [*sic*], & its the other chap who stands here with his mouth open!! But I can assure you that I wouldn't have undertaken such an unusual & (I admit) terrifying job unless it was a very important occasion. And such I believe this to be.

I believe Contact with other countries, which means other styles, other schools of thought, to be essential to art. Music, I'm sure about—& I think that my colleagues on the platform would agree as to the other arts. In the finest periods of music contact with the continental schools has always been close. John Dunstable in the 14th Century had pupils from Burgundy—who took his ideas abroad, & gave an enormous impetus to the growth of music.

In the 16th Century—the Italian madrigals & canzonetta were brought here—and these forms were borrowed by the great English composers of that time, with most amazing results as we all know. Perhaps greatest of all—Purcell borrowed enormously from abroad, many forms, new ideas in instrumentation, digesting them, & making them his own—& this is an important point. Foreign influences must be assimulated—& not just blindly accepted—we know only too well the little Mendelssohns of the 19th Century, & little Brahmses, Hindemiths & Debussys of a later date. But to go back to my original point—we in England need the stimulus of the foreign country in music—think of what we can learn from say—France—consciousness of sound, perfection of detail. From Germany, intellectual control, formal balance, & seriousness. From Italy, that wonderful sensuous melodic line—born of a country of fine voices. From Russia, a vividness of colour & lack of inhibitions; & from Austria what I can only describe as the sex-appeal of music. And the reverse side of the coin too—the Guild plans to bring students here. We in England have a few things we can teach our visitors [–] things that maybe have lain dormant for some time, but which are I feel stirring again. A strong

Editor's title.

Source: Autograph draft, n.d. (*GB-ALb* 1–02053793). Britten had been sent a prospectus of the International Arts Guild: 'A group of musicians, actors, writers and artists of various nationalities now here in London considers the present moment opportune for making plans whereby contacts which have grown up during the last five years in this great metropolis of freedom can be maintained, strengthened and developed after the war. With this purpose in mind, an International Arts Guild has been formed in London, in association with the London Philharmonic Arts Club, this centre to be the first of many, to begin the work which will later spread and have its branches in the U.S.A., Australia, Canada, South America, China, India, etc. . . .'.

melodic line—rhythmic ingenuity, & above all a free & ruthless harmony, enjoying clashes & full of intensity.

In conclusion I should like to say that I have had a letter from the American League of Composers—representing composers of every age & fashion. They had heard of the founding of this Guild, & write offering every kind of help. I was delighted to receive this letter because the American composer has been going through an intense period of Isolationism—and this was a sign that that is now over, because America needs Europe just as much as Europe needs America—and that is quite abit. I hope many young artists will be allowed to travel to the U.S.A.—to study with the great artists now living there, and to experience the enormous vitality & enthusiasm which characterises the art-life of that great country. So I hope that as soon as this terrible war is over, & we can break this enforced isolation of five years, that young performers will be able to travel & study, & that we in our turn will be able to welcome those coming from abroad, with enthusiasm tempered by really discriminating criticism.

16 Vienna (1945)

To a musician, of all cities in the world, Vienna must surely be the best beloved. From the day when one's childish fingers stumbled through the sonatas of Mozart, or the Moments Musicales of Schubert, to the exciting day not long before this war when one heard the Violin Concerto of Alban Berg for the 1st time, Viennese music has played a dominating part in one's life. In that great and lovely city there has flourished a musical tradition which nothing has yet supplanted. For two hundred years every kind of music has flowered there. Masses, Operas, Symphonies, Concertos, all sorts of dance music, songs, chamber music and so on.

For two hundred years, Vienna has been the spiritual home of the most extraordinary number of great composers. If they weren't lucky enough to be born there, they emigrated there. Gluck, Haydn, Mozart, Beethoven, Schubert, Lanner, all the Strausses, Brahms, Bruckner, Mahler, Schönberg, Berg and Webern, and the rest of that glorious list. Sometimes they cursed Vienna for her laziness; despised her for her narrow-minded-ness: Figaro was a flop: Schubert never heard his C-major Symphony: Mahler had unending battles with the press: Berg was never officially recognised: but always her sweetness, and charm, her gaiety and her warmth, coaxed out of composers the best they had to give.

After I left the Royal College of Music, I wanted to go to Vienna to study under Alban Berg. It was a bitter disappointment to me that I was not allowed to do so.[1] But I did go there for a few weeks in 1934, when I looked round the birth places of the great ones, and payed [*sic*] tribute at their graves.

Now for some years little has been heard of her musical life, but I suspect that under the surface the stream has continued to flow. It is hard to believe that even in Vienna's direst distress lovely music is not being written there. Music in Vienna must not, cannot die.[2]

Source: Posthumous typescript of Britten's autograph draft (now missing) of BBC radio talk (*GB-ALb*). This broadcast talk, pre-recorded on 7 April 1945, was first read in English, then translated into French and German and read and recorded in those languages by Britten on the same day. The English version was broadcast on 14 April, at 3 p.m., on European Service (London). At 7.30 p.m. it was sent out in French on the French Service, and on 15 April at 12.15 p.m. it went out in German on the Austrian Service. The talk formed part of a longer feature, *The Liberation of Vienna*. For the French Service the feature was introduced with the following announcement: 'Vienne, capitale de l'Autriche, vient d'être libérée par les armées russes. Cette victoire ne constitue pas seulement un évènement militaire de première importance; elle est aussi le gage de la résurrection de la civilisation occidentale, dont Vienne fut longtemps un des joyaux.'

[1] See Essay 52 for more on this.

[2] At this stage in the war, Vienna was once more under siege, this time from Soviet troops, who captured the city from the Germans on 13 April 1945, following a battle lasting four

weeks. Hitler committed suicide on 30 April; VE Day was celebrated on 8 May. Britten made another startling intervention into the politics of war and peace when he called a press conference to discuss the Potsdam Conference—the meeting of Harry Truman, Josef Stalin, Winston Churchill, and Clement Attlee, from 17 July–2 August, to discuss the future of Germany. The press conference was reported in *Peace News* (27 July 45):

> 'Mr. Churchill's high living at Potsdam is an offence that stinks to high heaven. It is a political indecency—a moral crime.' This was the verdict of Benjamin Britten, the eminent composer and a Sponsor of the PPU [Peace Pledge Union], on 'the fleshpots of Potsdam' at a Press conference which he called in London on Friday last.
>
> Mr. Britten said that he had been 'provoked into this by the news from Potsdam—and elsewhere—earlier this week.' The conference took the form of a foodless lunch, as a 'small gesture.'
>
> He wanted to encourage or shame those whose job it was to lead public opinion into treating our responsibility towards the hungry peoples of Europe as the terribly urgent problem it was.
>
> What little we knew of actual conditions in Europe now justified the judgment of Herbert Lehman, Director-Gerneral of UNRRA:
>
> 'Europe must depend heavily upon food imported from abroad. The alternative is starvation. Nor is starvation the only danger. For with famine must inevitably come pestilence.'
>
> Benjamin Britten recalled Mr. Churchill's pledge of 1940 to 'arrange for the speedy entry of food into any part of the enslaved area . . . so that there will always be held up before the eyes of the people of Europe—including, I say it deliberately, the German and Austrian peoples—the certainty that the shattering of the Nazi power will bring to them all immediate food, freedom and peace.'
>
> No British statesman had disavowed that: it remained an obligation which we were bound to do our utmost to carry out.
>
> 'Now it is in this wrecked, beaten, hungry country,' went on Mr. Britten, 'that the United Nations leaders have met. And the first news we get is that they are gorging themselves on turkeys, hams, fresh eggs, juicy steaks, melons, strawberries, wines and whiskies.
>
> 'All around is the stricken enemy people, hungry and facing greater hunger; not far away are the people of France, Belgium, Holland, Norway. They have been hungry for years and are still hungry.'
>
> Large numbers of people in the liberated countries were getting about half of our present food value and less than half of the Americans. In fact, nationally we and the United States were guilty of what outraged us when done on a grander scale at Potsdam.
>
> Would we share what there was according to need? Or cling desperately to a privileged position—feed well at the expense of hungry friends? 'I'll take the risk of expressing England's answer,' Mr. Britten concluded. 'We're ready to share.'

17 *Peter Grimes* (1945)

During the summer of 1941, while working in California, I came across a copy of *The Listener* containing an article about George Crabbe by E. M. Forster. I did not know any of the poems of Crabbe at that time, but reading about him gave me such a feeling of nostalgia for Suffolk, where I had always lived, that I searched for a copy of his works, and made a beginning with 'The Borough.' Mr. Forster's article is reproduced in this book: it is easy to see how his excellent account of this 'entirely English poet' evoked a longing for the realities of that grim and exciting seacoast around Aldeburgh.[1]

Earlier in the year, I had written the music of *Paul Bunyan*, an operetta to a text by W. H. Auden, which was performed for a week at Columbia University, New York.[2] The critics damned it unmercifully, but the public seemed to find something enjoyable in the performances. Despite the criticisms, I wanted to write more works for the stage. 'The Borough'—and particularly the story of 'Peter Grimes'—provided a subject and a background from which Peter Pears and I began trying to construct the scenario of an opera.

A few months later I was waiting on the East Coast for a passage back to England, when a performance of my *Sinfonia da Requiem* was given in Boston under Serge Koussevitsky [*sic*]. He asked why I had not written an opera. I explained that the construction of a scenario, discussions with a librettist, planning the musical architecture, composing preliminary sketches, and writing nearly a thousand pages of orchestral score, demanded a freedom from other work which was an economic impossibility for most young composers. Koussevitsky was interested in my project for an opera based on Crabbe, although I did not expect to have the opportunity of writing it for several years. Some weeks later we met again, when he told me that he had arranged for the commissioning of the opera, which was to be dedicated to the memory of his wife, who had recently died.[3]

Source: Introduction to Sadler's Wells Opera Guide, *Peter Grimes* (London: John Lane The Bodley Head, 1945), 7–8. This article was written prior to the opera's first performance.

[1] See Philip Brett (comp.), *Benjamin Britten: Peter Grimes* (Cambridge: CUP, 1983) for a reprint of this article.

[2] W. H. Auden (1907–73), influential English poet, writer, critic, and librettist. Britten's relationship with him is discussed in Donald Mitchell, *Britten and Auden in the Thirties* (2nd edn., Woodbridge: The Boydell Press, 2000), and Paul Kildea, 'Britten, Auden and "otherness" ', in Mervyn Cooke (ed.), *The Cambridge Companion to Benjamin Britten* (Cambridge: CUP, 1999).

[3] Nataliya Ushkov (Konstantinovna) (d. 1942), whom Serge married in 1905. With her he founded a publishing firm L'Édition Russe de Musique in 1909, which directed all profits to Soviet composers and which had contracts with Skryabin, Prokofiev, Stravinsky, and Rachmaninoff. The Koussevitzky Music Foundation was founded in 1943.

On arrival in this country in April 1942 I outlined the rough plan to Montagu Slater, and asked him to undertake the libretto.[4] Discussions, revisions, and corrections took nearly eighteen months. In January 1944 I began composing the music, and the score was completed in February 1945.

For most of my life I have lived closely in touch with the sea. My parent's [*sic*] house in Lowestoft directly faced the sea, and my life as a child was coloured by the fierce storms that sometimes drove ships on to our coast and ate away whole stretches of the neighbouring cliffs. In writing *Peter Grimes*, I wanted to express my awareness of the perpetual struggle of men and women whose livelihood depends on the sea—difficult though it is to treat such a universal subject in theatrical form.

I am especially interested in the general architectural and formal problems of opera, and decided to reject the Wagnerian theory of 'permanent melody' for the classical practice of separate numbers that crystallize and hold the emotion of a dramatic situation at chosen moments.[5] One of my chief aims is to try and restore to the musical setting of the English language a brilliance, freedom, and vitality that have been curiously rare since the death of Purcell. In the past hundred years, English writing for the voice has been dominated by strict subservience to logical speech-rhythms, despite the fact that accentuation according to sense often contradicts the accentuation demanded by emotional content. Good recitative should transform the natural intonations and rhythms of everyday speech into memorable musical phrases (as with Purcell), but in more stylized music, the composer should not deliberately avoid unnatural stresses if the prosody of the poem and the emotional situation demand them, nor be afraid of a high-handed treatment of words, which may need prolongation far beyond their common speech-length, or a speed of delivery that would be impossible in conversation.

The scarcity of modern British operas is due to the limited opportunities that are offered for their performance. Theatre managers will not present original

[4] Montagu Slater (1902–56), English writer and librettist. Britten had set only one piece by Slater, 'Mother Comfort', before asking him to write the libretto of *Peter Grimes*. The writer's left-wing politics, though, were clearly part of the attraction. Britten dedicated his *Temporal Variations* (1936) to Slater, and his *Ballad of Heroes* (1939) to Slater and his wife, Enid.

[5] cf. Stravinsky's much later note on *The Rake's Progress*: 'Rather than seek musical forms symbolically expressive of the dramatic content (as in the Daedalian examples of Alban Berg), I chose to cast *The Rake* in the mould of an eighteenth-century "number" opera, one in which the dramatic progress depends on the succession of separate pieces—recitatives and arias, duets, trios, choruses, instrumental interludes . . . as the opera warms up, the story is told, enacted, contained almost entirely in song—as distinguished from so-called speech-song, and Wagnerian continuous melody, which consists, in effect, of orchestral commentary enveloping continuous recitative.' August 1964, reproduced in Paul Griffiths, *Igor Stravinsky: The Rake's Progress* (Cambridge: CUP, 1982), 2. See notes to Essay 30 for Britten's and Stravinsky's further thoughts about number operas.

works without a reasonable hope of recovering their costs of production: composers and writers cannot thrive without the experience of seeing their operas adequately staged and sung: the conservatism of audiences hinders experimental departures from the accepted repertory.

In my own case, the existence of Sadler's Wells has been an incentive to complete *Peter Grimes*: the qualities of the Opera Company have considerably influenced both the shape and the characterization of the opera. Whatever its reception may be, it is to be hoped that the willingness of the Company to undertake the presentation of new operas will encourage other composers to write works in what is, in my opinion, the most exciting of musical forms.

18 250th Anniversary of the Death of Henry Purcell (1945)

Henry Purcell was the last important international figure of English music. Ironically the continent of Europe has been more aware of his greatness than this island which produced him. But that he should be to the English public little more than a name in history books is not altogether strange, for he is the antithesis of the music which has been popular for so long in this country. Think of his unfettered rhythms, boldly discordant harmonies, his long soaring melodies without automatic repetitions of 'memorable' phrases, and especially his love of the virtuoso, the operatic, and conscious exploitation of brilliant sounds; then remember the bulwarks of music in 19th century England! One obvious reason for his neglect has been the lack of accurate (unexpurgated) convenient and vital editions of his work. The great majority of his music has, as an integral part, the thoroughbass which must be 'realised' before it comes to life. When one considers the problems of this realisation, one has to admit that the creative imaginations of critics, musicologists, or musical historians (who have exclusively tackled it) are scarcely adequate for the task. Each work must be re-thought in order to evolve textures and figurations to express its mood, remembering all the time the effect of those instruments for which it was conceived. The figuring of the basses is often spasmodic, and the realiser must soak himself in the composer's idiom in order to provide natural Purcellian harmonies for the melodies. Nor must he be afraid of those very Purcellian qualities of clarity, strangeness, tenderness and attack. But what a rewarding task it is! One can learn endlessly by becoming intimate with such a gift as his. There seems to be nothing this composer cannot do. But almost the greatest importance of Purcell for us to-day is the example of his prosody. Here surely is the way to make the English language live again in song. He is successful in every kind of prosody:—the natural declamations (as in the recitatives of Saul at Endor); the elaborate and artificial coloraturas (as in If Music be the Food of Love) and the simple regular tunes (such as Fairest Isle). No composer can ever have loved his native tongue as Purcell did. He was indeed the Orpheus Britannicus.[1]

Source: Pamphlet issued concurrently with a series of two concerts at Wigmore Hall on 21 and 22 Nov. 1945 (*GB-ALb* 1-9600094). (Pamphlet title: '250th Anniversary of the Death of Henry Purcell (Nov. 21st, 1695–Nov. 21st, 1945), Homage by Benjamin Britten and Michael Tippett'.) Britten's tribute to Purcell, his String Quartet No. 2, was premiered at the former, his *Holy Sonnets of John Donne* at the latter. The note is signed by Britten alone.

[1] i.e. the British Orpheus. This was the name given to two posthumous collections of Purcell's songs. See *Benjamin Britten: A Catalogue of the Published Works* (Aldeburgh: BPL, 1999), 173–84, for a complete list of Britten's Purcell arrangements and editions.

PART II

*

1946–1955

'This region of sin that you find you in,
But are not of'

INTRODUCTION AND CHRONOLOGY

There is something eerily calm about the penultimate article in Britten's 'first period' of writing (Essay 17). It is modest, unassuming, and totally unprepared for the way the opera it describes would change his life and the direction of British music. Simple facts concerning the origins of *Peter Grimes* are relayed; modest (and not so modest) hopes for the future of English opera are established; cogent ideas about prosody and opera in English are delivered; and economic arguments about staging native works are incorporated with the easy logic that anticipates the post-war composer-impresario. Yet whatever hopes Britten had for his opera and for a cultured, humane, post-war society, they were at the time of writing unrealized.

After *Grimes*, Britten's public role was greatly elevated; yet fame muted him, much as pacifism had done in wartime England. And the seeds of paradox were sown; for now Britten was given a forum, a platform, but chose instead to address the issues of his heart and conscience through his music. Thus his prose writings in this second period are less brash, more cultivated than those in the previous one. His opera *Gloriana* (1953), probably not coincidentally, deals precisely with this conflict between public responsibility and private passion. Essex's second lute song, in which he longs for a place 'obscure from all society' is little different from Grimes's search for a harbour sheltering peace, yet the difference in Britten's status as a composer in early 1945 compared to 1953 could scarcely be exaggerated. In part, his journey was that of the boy in Hardy's 'Midnight on the Great Western', one of Britten's *Winter Words* (1953), taken to realms beyond his expectation: 'This region of sin that you find you in, | But are not of'. Fame gave him entrée to aristocratic English society; yet his homosexuality, or more precisely the sexual expression of his relationship with Peter Pears, was illegal until 1967. Whatever was his enjoyment of this elite society (and he retained royal connections and privileges throughout his life), he was never really part of it, unable to conform to conventional sexual mores.

Apart from a few exceptions, his writings of the period do not display this paradox or conflict. They are mostly contemporary, dealing with works then being produced at a great rate; or laudatory (Essay 28 on Boyd Neel or Essay 38 on Kathleen Ferrier); or responsible—an address on being made an honorary freeman, or an interview with the Arts Council about the future of English opera (Essay 29), for example. Yet the few transgressions are terribly revealing: a public spat about Arts Council funding of *The Rape of Lucretia* (1946), early on in the evolution of his public persona (Essay 20); a pacifist plea on behalf of UNESCO on the eve of the cold war and the atomic arms race (Essay 27); a gauntlet thrown down on music criticism in the months following the 1951 premiere of the perplexing *Billy Budd* (Essay 36), and his own attempt to demonstrate what such criticism could be in the right hands (Essay 37); his thoughts on the importance of celebrating and contributing to British culture, particularly in 1951, the year of the Festival of Britain (Essays 31, 32, 33, 34). In these few examples, Britten's new public role and private convictions clashed, and the writing evokes the style of his essays in the first ten years of his life as a cultural commentator.

1946 Composes *The Rape of Lucretia*, Op. 37, which reopens Glyndebourne following the war, and which launches the Glyndebourne English Opera Company, founded by Britten, Eric Crozier, and John Piper; *Lucretia* is toured in Europe; realizes more Purcell songs; composes *Occasional Overture*, Op. 38, to inaugurate the BBC Third Programme, before the piece is withdrawn by the composer; completes his second volume of folksongs.

1947 Completes *Albert Herring*, Op. 39, which launches the English Opera Group following the fallout between Britten, Eric Crozier, and John Christie of Glyndebourne; moves with Pears from Snape to Crag House, on the seafront in Aldeburgh; EOG tour of *Herring* to Holland; plans with Pears and Crozier the first Aldeburgh Festival; composes Canticle I 'My beloved is mine', Op. 40, *A Charm of Lullabies*, Op. 41, and completes third volume of folksongs.

1948 Completes *Saint Nicolas*, Op. 42, which is given its premiere in the first Aldeburgh Festival of Music and the Arts; completes his realization of Gay's *The Beggar's Opera*, Op. 43, which is premiered by the EOG in Cambridge; EOG tours throughout England, Holland, and France.

1949 Composes *The Little Sweep*, Op. 45, in two weeks, which helps reverse the fortunes of the EOG; attends premiere of *Spring Symphony*, Op. 44, in Holland; composes *A Wedding Anthem*, Op. 46, to celebrate the marriage of the Earl of Harewood and Marion Stein, a close friend.

1950 Commences work on *Billy Budd*, Op. 50, his Festival of Britain commission, with librettists E. M. Forster and Crozier; composes *Five Flower Songs*, Op. 47, and *Lachrymae*, Op. 48, written to entice William Primrose to the third Aldeburgh Festival.

1951 Rekindles his 1930s interest in the oboe with *Six Metamorphoses after Ovid*, Op. 49, premiered in the Aldeburgh Festival; completes a realization of Purcell's *Dido and Aeneas* in time for an EOG season as part of the Festival of Britain; conducts premiere of *Billy Budd* at Covent Garden.

1952 Composes Canticle II 'Abraham and Isaac', Op. 51, for Kathleen Ferrier and Pears; *Billy Budd* is premiered in America in a television production; EOG tours Europe; commences work on his coronation commission; offered post of Music Director of Covent Garden, but declines; Donald Mitchell's and Hans Keller's *Benjamin Britten: A Commentary on his Works from a Group of Specialists* is published, provoking a critical backlash against Britten.

1953 Created Companion of Honour in Coronation Honours List one week before the premiere of *Gloriana*, Op. 53, at Covent Garden; composes *Winter Words*, Op. 52; records *A Ceremony of Carols* and *Sinfonia da Requiem* for Decca.

1954 Composes *The Turn of the Screw*, Op. 54, which he conducts at its premiere in Venice; records *Winter Words*, *Michelangelo Sonnets*, *Diversions*, and assorted folksongs for Decca; composes Canticle III 'Still falls the Rain – The raids, 1940, Night and Dawn', Op. 55.

1955 Records *The Turn of the Screw*, his first complete opera to be committed to vinyl, *The Little Sweep*, and *Saint Nicolas* for Decca; composes *Hymn to St Peter*, Op. 56a; following a recital tour in Yugoslavia, embarks on tour of the Far East with Pears.

19 *Sinfonia da Requiem* (1946)

In the early autumn of 1939 I was approached by the Japanese Government through the British Council to compose a work to commemorate the two thousandth anniversary of the Japanese dynasty. I replied that I would be willing to do so on condition that I was left free in the choice of subject and medium, and specified that I was unable and unwilling to provide any jingoism.

The reply to this was definitely in agreement to my conditions, but for six months I waited for the actual contract. When this finally arrived I was working on the 'Sinfonia da Requiem,' which was a tribute to the memory of my parents. Owing to this delay I was left with something like six weeks in which to complete the required symphony, and I replied that the only work I could provide in the time would be the said 'Sinfonia da Requiem.' I discussed the suitability of the work with the local Japanese consul, indicating its nature, and telling him that each movement had a Latin title—Lachrymosa, Dies Irae, and Requiem Aeternam. He communicated, I presume, with his ambassador and I was notified that the work was considered entirely suitable. I accordingly completed the score, delivered it to the consul, and for at least six months heard no more.

In the autumn of 1940 I was summoned to the consul. He then read, with gradually mounting passion, a long letter from Prince Konnoi, brother of the then Prime Minister of Japan, who was organising the festival. This letter accused me of insulting a friendly power, of providing a Christian work where Christianity was apparently unacceptable, that the work was gloomy, and so on. I replied to this letter in as dignified a manner as possible, saying that since I was a Christian and came from a Christian country, the work was (not surprisingly) Christian, denying that it was gloomy, denying the insult, and so on. This letter was sent for approval to the local British consul and other British officials, and sent off to Tokyo. I awaited the next move.

Owing to the steadily worsening relations between England and Japan, and finally the incident at Pearl Harbour, it is perhaps not surprising that I never heard any more about it, but I am told that in several books there are descriptions of the arrival of the score in Tokyo and its subsequent rehearsal.[1]

Source: *Radio Times* (18 Jan. 1946), 3.

[1] Britten's letter was prompted by correspondence in the 28 Dec. issue of the *Radio Times*, in which reference was made to a book by John Morris, *Traveller from Tokyo* (London: The Book Club, 1945), 91: '. . . the letter . . . was apparently badly worded in that he was asked to write something in memory of the defunct Emperor, and no hint was given that the occasion was a joyful one. Not unnaturally, Mr. Britten submitted a dirge . . . in order to save the face of all concerned it was made known that the English offering had not been received in time to permit of adequate rehearsal. In fact it was the first to be received.'

20 *The Rape of Lucretia* (1946)

Sir, Two leading members of the Arts Council have now stated that Glyndebourne is 'lending' or 'letting' its opera house for the production of *The Rape of Lucretia*.[1] This is a complete misrepresentation of facts. When some eight months ago the Glyndebourne management became aware of my plans for opera I was approached by Mr. Bing,[2] Glyndebourne's general manager, and was offered the production of my new opera at Glyndebourne for the reopening of the Glyndebourne festival—an offer which I gladly accepted. The engagement of all artistic personnel, and the whole organization of the production, carried out in closest collaboration and agreement with myself, was and is in the hands of the Glyndebourne management, who are presenting the opera and are financially and otherwise solely responsible for it.

The purpose of this letter is to inform the Arts Council, who from the start were asked to collaborate, and those who may be interested in the vicissitudes of English opera of the facts.[3]

Yours faithfully,
BENJAMIN BRITTEN
Glyndebourne, Lewes, Sussex, July 8.

Source: *The Times* (11 July 1946).

[1] Ralph Vaughan Williams (1872–1958) was one of them.

[2] Rudolf Bing (1902–97), Austrian-born impresario, manager of Glyndebourne (1935–9; 1946–9), the first director of the Edinburgh Festival (1947–9), and general manager of New York Metropolitan Opera (1950–72).

[3] Steuart Wilson of the Arts Council disagreed with Britten's interpretation of events, provoking a furious response from the composer. Vaughan Williams wrote to Wilson, apologizing for being unaware of the circumstances surrounding the first performance of *Lucretia*. Wilson replied on 18 July 1946: 'Pity Ben should write to the Times when he should have been attending to his score!' (ACGB).

21 The Artist and his Medium: Composer and Listener (1946)

I expect most of you have read about composers of the past and know something about the kind of lives they lived. You will have noticed how in each country and in each period these lives varied—how some composers were attached to courts and their works were written to order to please the taste of their rich patrons; how some were attached to famous churches and had to compose cantatas each week to fit the calendar of church festivals; how some were attached to theatres and had to produce operas to the taste of the theatre directors. If you feel that such harnessing of the creative vision is all wrong just let me remind you that these systems produced such giants as Bach, Haydn and Mozart.

Perhaps also you have noticed that in the 19th century another kind of composer sprang up, who was more independent and composed music to please himself only and who sometimes, as a result of this, had a very hard life and often chose to starve in a garret rather than pander to the whims and fancies of other people. The 19th century also produced great composers.

I should like to talk to you this morning about the kind of life the composer leads in the 20th century so that you can compare this with the lives of earlier composers.

Now today the composer doesn't usually have the court, the church, or a regular theatre to work for, but compared with the Romantics, he is a much more practical chap; he is less likely to go his own way, less likely consequently to have long hair, and I hope, less likely to starve in a garret.

What is he like, the composer of today? To answer that, may I take myself as an example—because then, of course, I can talk from first-hand knowledge of the subject. If you want to know why I started writing, it was because I liked music in a big way. I remember the first time I tried composing, I was an extremely small boy. The result looked rather like the Forth Bridge, in other words—hundreds of dots all over the page connected by long lines all joined together in beautiful curves.[1] [Excerpt 1: illustration on piano] I am afraid it

Source: Original script (BBCWAC microfilm, Schools, Talks for Sixth Forms, 18 Oct. 1946). Broadcast 18 Oct. 1946, BBC Schools Home Service, 11.40 a.m., in the series *Talks for Sixth Forms*. (Pre-recorded 15 Oct. 1946.) This talk was commissioned by Grace Williams (1906–77), the composer and friend of Britten's. Various versions were transcribed and published, including: John Pringle (ed.), *The Radio Listener's Week-end Book* (London: Oldhams Press, n.d.); *The Listener* (7 Nov. 1946).

[1] Firth of Forth Bridge, Scotland, completed in 1890, with a cantilever design to which Britten alludes.

was the pattern on the paper which interested me and when I asked my mother to play it, her look of horror upset me considerably. My next efforts were fortunately much more conscious of sound. I had started playing the piano and wrote elaborate tone poems usually lasting about 20 seconds, inspired by terrific events in my home life such as the departure of my father for London, the appearance in my life of a new girl friend, or even a wreck at sea. My later efforts luckily got away from these emotional inspirations and I began to write sonatas and quartets which were not connected in any direct way with life. In short, I began to write what is usually called abstract music and I feel it is important to say here that those of you who want to be either good composers or good listeners (or both) should be able to think of music in this abstract way. Music is a world of its own. One should enjoy music, not so much because it is connected with actual life, but because of the way it shapes itself; one gets fascinated by its tunes, rhythms, and harmonies for their own sake.

Well now—to complete my brief autobiography: At school I somehow managed to be able to fit in a great deal of composing with the extremely full life that every schoolboy leads. (I don't think my school work suffered nor my games, which I was passionately keen on.) Anyhow, I wrote symphony after symphony, song after song, and a tone poem called 'Chaos and Cosmos' although I fear I was not sure what the words really meant. Some of these pieces I later arranged for string orchestra and published, and this is the first illustration that I should like to play you. It is a movement from my 'Simple Symphony' and was arranged from a movement of a sonata which I wrote when I was about 10.[2] [Excerpt 2: *Simple Symphony*]

This was all very well, and I enjoyed writing music in a very childish, carefree manner. But one has to grow up, and I was extremely lucky at this age to meet a composer whose pieces I hope you know, because they are so good; he was Frank Bridge.[3] This started many years of long study and very hard work. Not only did he keep my nose to the grindstone, but he criticised my work relentlessly, and I, who had thought that I was already on the verge of immortality, saw my illusions shattered and I felt I was very small fry. Now I can see that this period of my life which then seemed to be worrying and depressing was the best possible thing for me and a thing which every young composer must undergo. When I grew up I wrote a work for String Orchestra as a tribute to Frank Bridge.[4] [Excerpt 3: Variation 8 'Funeral March' from *Variations on a Theme of Frank Bridge*]

[2] Most likely the fourth movement, 'Frolicsome Finale', which is based on the Finale of his Piano Sonata No. 9, Op. 38 (Mar. 1926), and an unidentified song (1925).

[3] Frank Bridge (1879–1941), English composer, conductor and teacher. Britten became a pupil of his in 1927.

[4] *Variations on a Theme of Frank Bridge* (1937).

When I was 19, I had to set about earning my living. I was quite determined to do it through composition, it was the only thing I cared about and I was sure it was possible.

My first opportunity was the chance of working in a film company.[5] This was very much to my taste although it meant a great deal of very hard work. I had to work quickly, to force myself to work when I didn't want to, and to get used to working in all kinds of circumstances. The film company I was working for was not a big commercial one, it was a documentary company and had very little money. I had to write scores not for large orchestras but for not more than six or seven players, and to make these instruments make all the effects that each film demanded. I also had to be very ingenious and try to imitate, not necessarily by musical instruments, but in the studio, the natural sounds of every-day life. I well remember the mess we made in the studio one day when trying to fit an appropriate sound to shots of a large ship unloading in a dock. We had pails of water which we slopped everywhere, drain pipes with coal slipping down them, model railways, whistles and every kind of paraphernalia we could think of.

As well as music for films I discovered that radio and theatres sometimes wanted incidental music for their plays. It was also extremely good practice for me as a young composer to take exact instructions from the directors and producers of those plays and to try to please them. Now when I say 'try to please them' I don't for one moment mean that I went against my own ethics of self-criticism which were steadily developing all through this period. I maintain very strongly that it is the duty of every young composer to be able to write every kind of music—except bad music. That has nothing to do with high-brow or low-brow, serious or light music. It is a very good thing for a young composer to have to write the lightest kinds of music. I knew, at that time, a very good cabaret singer who asked me to write some songs for her. I obliged and wrote to the best of my ability some 'blues' and a calipso of which I am not at all ashamed and which I often play for my friends' amusement.[6] It had an accompaniment like this . . . [Excerpt 5: illustration on piano]

I was very lucky before I was very much older to find a publisher for some of my music. And that is another way for a young composer to keep himself alive, by writing the kind of pieces that a publisher likes to have—pieces that are not too difficult to understand and easy enough to perform.

I said at the beginning that I wanted to earn my bread and butter by

[5] General Post Office Film Unit.

[6] The singer was Hedli Anderson (1907–90), later the wife of Louis MacNeice; the works were Britten's so-called *Cabaret Songs*, the first of which ('Funeral Blues') was written as incidental music for Auden's and Isherwood's play *The Ascent of F6* in 1937. Other songs followed over the next two years.

composing, and that is roughly what I did, although I have from time to time earned myself a little jam and occasionally cake as a pianist. I started giving recitals with a friend of mine, a singer whose name is Peter Pears. We worked hard together at the great classic songs, and in this way I learnt more than I can say about the structure of songs and above all, how to write for the voice and the setting of words of all languages. Also, I started writing songs myself and arranging folk songs for these recitals. Here is a short record of one of the folk songs I arranged. [Excerpt 6: 'The Salley Gardens']

I do not want to give the impression that the whole of one's musical life is dictated solely by the need to keep alive in as comfortable a manner as possible. One has certainly got to keep the wolf from the door, otherwise one can't do one's best work. At the same time the composer's mind does want to go off on its own track sometimes, getting ideas for works such as quartets and symphonies, which have nothing to do with popular demand. These works, I admit, mostly lie around on shelves until the occasional Contemporary Concert, when the dust is knocked off the scores and the work is given a brief airing—usually, I regret, under-rehearsed and played with a lack of energy and interest which so often colours the orchestral playing of contemporary music, especially by unknown and unimportant young composers. A word of warning about this. If you hear at a concert or on the radio a performance of a work by a composer you know nothing about, which sounds to you a pretty grim affair, remember that occasionally the performance might be slightly to blame—often not out of any reasons of sabotage, but because the style may be a new one and the orchestral player may not have time to absorb it, especially if he is, as most orchestra players are today, grotesquely over-worked. All I say is, do not dismiss any composer until you have given him a fair chance. Remember that the first rehearsal of one of Schubert's greatest works, the C major symphony, had to be abandoned because the orchestral players laughed so much at what they felt was ridiculous writing. [Excerpt 7: Schubert, Symphony No. 9, D. 944 'Great']

Now let me tell you something about opera-composing. I had a great piece of luck when a very famous conductor asked me whether I had ever written an opera.[7] I wonder if you realise what a labour writing an opera is—even one of moderate length like my 'Peter Grimes', lasting about two and a half hours. It means writing by hand nearly 1,000 pages of orchestral score. I was once told that there are more notes in one Wagner opera than words in all the plays of Shakespeare. If you want to prove me wrong—count them yourselves.

Now to return to the conductor who wanted me to write an opera. I had to tell him that I was so busy writing incidental music and shorter works that

[7] Koussevitzky.

I could not afford to take the time off to write an opera. He then said: 'Well if I give you the money, will you take time off, and will you do it?', to which I obviously agreed at once, and 'Peter Grimes' was the result. Then followed many months of planning the work and then the excitement of actually sitting down to write the music. My luck still held. The problem of finding an opera company to perform 'Peter Grimes' was soon solved by Joan Cross, who was the director of Sadler's Wells.[8] With great courage she decided to put it on at the Wells last year. This really was a piece of enormous luck for me. I had a first-rate young producer[9] to work with who criticized every detail of the work relentlessly, I had first-rate young singers to sing the opera, and I attended every single rehearsal and learned from this an enormous amount about what not to write in operas in future. Some of these things, of course, I was able to alter in rehearsal.

To sum up briefly, the composer's life today is a mixture of working to order and working for himself. The older and more independent he becomes, the less he need work to order, but I believe it is always a good stimulus for him to have to write something that he doesn't feel like writing, because it keeps his technique in first-class order. I can't over-estimate this importance of technique. It is the same in every walk of life. It is no good having ideas unless you can carry them out. In tennis you may have a superb scheme for bringing your opponent up to the net and then lobbing over his head, but this scheme is useless unless you can make drop-shots and lobs. Obviously it is no use having a technique unless you have the ideas to use this technique; but there is, unfortunately, a tendency in many quarters today to believe that brilliance of technique is a danger rather than a help.[10] This is sheer nonsense. There has never been a composer worth his salt who has not had supreme technique. I'll go further than this and say that in the work of your supreme artists you can't separate inspiration from technique. I defy anyone to tell me where Mozart's inspiration ends and technique begins in such a work as this. [Excerpt 8: Mozart, Symphony No. 41 in C, K. 551 'Jupiter']

This talk was supposed to be about the Composer and the Listener. I am afraid it may seem to have been mostly about the composer. But I hope that this taking you behind the scenes will have stimulated you into becoming better listeners—listeners not only to the older music but also the music of today—your music.

[8] Joan Cross (1900–93), English soprano, teacher, and producer. She created five Britten operatic roles—Ellen Orford (*Peter Grimes*, 1945), Female Chorus (*The Rape of Lucretia*, 1946), Lady Billows (*Albert Herring*, 1948), Elizabeth I (*Gloriana*, 1953), and Mrs Grose (*The Turn of the Screw*, 1954).

[9] Eric Crozier (1914–94), English writer and producer, librettist of Britten's *Albert Herring* (1947), *Let's Make an Opera* (1949), and, with E. M. Forster, *Billy Budd* (1951). He also wrote the text for *Saint Nicolas* (1948) and produced the premieres of *Peter Grimes* and *The Rape of Lucretia*.

[10] This was a criticism constantly levelled at Britten throughout the 1930s and early 1940s.

And now there are a few general things I should like to say. I know that among you young listeners there is not the prejudice against new music that there is among older people. I do not mean that you always like it, but there is a certain topical quality about it which is exciting for you. Of course not all of it; much of it is very bad and will not live very long, but there is a great deal of fine and lasting music being written today.

One other thing. Don't give up after the first hearing of a new piece. Very little music can be appreciated at once. And remember, music is not all easy entertainment (although much of the lighter kind is). Don't just day-dream when listening to it, but listen seriously to the music that you feel one day you may like. I am afraid many people like music only for the ideas it gives them. They imagine wonderful scenes, or themselves involved in some romantic situation. They may enjoy this, but it is not the music they enjoy but the associations stirred up by this music. The fullest benefit and enjoyment to be got from listening to music is a much deeper thing—the appreciation and love of the tunes for themselves, the excitement of the rhythms for themselves, the fascination of the harmony and the overwhelming satisfaction which a well-constructed piece of music gives you. These are the things which the good composer offers you. The good listener is ready to receive them.

22 An Opera is Planned (1947)

McKechnie: Was it you, Eric Crozier, who thought of the theme first?

Crozier: Yes I think it was originally, wasn't it, Ben?

Britten: How it happened was that we were looking for a subject for a light opera comedy to go with *Lucretia* which was serious and pretty gloomy. We originally picked another subject which we worked on for a short time.

McKechnie: Was that the Jane Austen subject?

Britten: Yes, *Mansfield Park.*

Crozier: That didn't work out too well.

Britten: We'd thought of it and actually worked on it a bit but we'd an awful lot of office work on the formation of the new company, the English Opera Group, and the work itself had to be done rather quickly and *Mansfield Park* was obviously going to be a long, subtle, and complicated job.

We liked this de Maupassant theme first of all because it fitted our singers. There was a good part for Joan Cross and Peter Pears, probably for Nancy Evans and Jimmy Sharp as well.[1]

Crozier: Oddly enough, it was the English possibilities of the French story which attracted us.

Britten: In a way that was the first snag.

Crozier: Yes, there was trouble about the feast. You see, in the French story, the young man gets drunk at the feast on red wine at supper. Well in England, of course, you wouldn't have red wine for supper.

Britten: Yes exactly. We soon decided that just translation wouldn't be enough and that if it was to be sung in English it must be English entirely, setting and everything.

Crozier: And England for us meant Suffolk, but I don't remember how we pinned it down to the actual place in Suffolk?

Britten: Well, we looked for the right-sized town.

Crozier: Oh yes, that was it.

Britten: It was a town large enough to have a mayor—a town about the size of Woodbridge.

Source: Editor's transcript of recording (NSA 10727–8/9CL0009198–9). Broadcast 19 June 1947, BBC Third Programme, 8 p.m.: discussion between Britten, Eric Crozier, and John Piper, with James McKechnie, written and produced by Stephen Potter. (Discussion pre-recorded 16 June 1947; music examples pre-recorded 10 June 1947.) First reproduced in Rosie Sinden-Evans, '"The Making of a May King" or The Creation of Albert Herring: A Comic Opera by Benjamin Britten and Eric Crozier' (M.Mus, University of London, 1995).

[1] Frederick Sharp (1911–99), English baritone, who shared the role of Junius (with Edmund Donlevy) in the first production of *The Rape of Lucretia* (1946) and who created the role of Sid in the first production of *Albert Herring* (1947).

CROZIER: It was John Piper who thought of the name Loxford.[2]

MCKECHNIE: Did you at this point, Ben, think that the story had musical possibilities?

BRITTEN: Well I might say quite simply that any story has musical possibilities—as long as one can think of the right music to go with it. In this case I thought rather of the dramatic possibilities and this question of the story and the characters fitting our company.

MCKECHNIE: I see. And writing as you say to fit a cast, do you find that a help or a hindrance?

BRITTEN: For me it's a great stimulus, having actual people to write for and to think for.

CROZIER: One real difficulty with this story was that we couldn't count on a chorus to suggest the townsfolk.

BRITTEN: In most opera companies, there would be an enormous chorus available for villagers etc. In this case we invented Sid and Nancy and of course the horrid village children to suggest the background of village life.

CROZIER: I think eventually those limitations are a source of strength, aren't they? They were in this case. You see, if we'd been able to count on a chorus the whole thing might have demanded a much wider canvas and perhaps it wouldn't have fitted the particular situation or the story so well.

MCKECHNIE: In writing the music, Ben, did you start at the beginning or with one particular scene or theme or what?

BRITTEN: Well of course I couldn't start with the music until the libretto was planned and partially written, and the first thing we had to do was to sit down and plan the rough shape of the new opera and then we made preliminary sketches of the details, and then one morning last November, Eric got going and then when the first scene—or actually the first act—I think it was, was completely written, we discussed it.

CROZIER: After we'd talked and talked about it, I rewrote my first draft of the first act, and it was considerably changed from what I'd originally written. It fell into much more of a musical shape from our discussion.

BRITTEN: On the first reading it read much more like a straight play.

CROZIER: Yes, it did.

BRITTEN: We came to the conclusion that we should leave out a great deal of the detail which would have to go into a straight play.

MCKECHNIE: Because you have room for so much less?

BRITTEN: Because one can suggest so many details in music that you'd have to say in full in a straight play. And another thing was recitative. We

[2] John Piper (1903–92), English painter and opera designer, who created many Britten stage works. He was married to Myfanwy Piper (1911–97), librettist of *The Turn of the Screw* (1954), *Owen Wingrave* (1970), and *Death in Venice* (1973).

had many discussions on recitative. Originally it was in straight prose I think.

CROZIER: That was a queer business, wasn't it?

BRITTEN: I found it extremely difficult to set it. It didn't work out at all. So you, Eric, rewrote it in verse—controlled verse—the whole recitative, I think.

CROZIER: Yes, and then you broke it down more or less into prose again in the actual setting. If you're writing a form of verse, you tend to eliminate details and concentrate on essentials and that's rather what's wanted for writing in music, isn't it?

BRITTEN: Yes; but there is the lyric quality of verse too.

MCKECHNIE: Now what happens, then, is that you passed script and music backwards and forwards between you. What you said to me, Eric, is that ideally you're working in the same house during this period, though perhaps at opposite ends of it.

CROZIER: Yes, that's it. But if you're talking of ideal conditions, it's really just as important that the designer should be working with the composer and librettist, and fortunately, in the case of *Albert Herring*, he was able to work with us from a very early stage.

PIPER: If the artist is to understand the problems of the stage he must work with the people of the theatre.

CROZIER: What I don't think I'd ever realized before was that the actual visual shape—the visual development scenically—should be an element in determining the construction of the story.

PIPER: Well yes, you see if you have a series of indoor scenes and then one outdoor scene—you go out into the open—it might be possible and better to plan it differently. You'd possibly lose nothing practically, and you might gain quite a lot visually. So you have a visual element brought into play from the start, and the designer could make suggestions about that perhaps and he might say 'Hey! you've got three indoor scenes, when are we going to get some breathing space? You've all that space to play about with, why not use it before the last act?'

CROZIER: The point is that working in the theatre the artist finds himself grappling with a very complex machine which has an awful lot of laws of its own, and it's awfully difficult for him to have time to learn how to tackle it.

PIPER: It's a very arduous undertaking indeed, for the artist to go to the theatre and learn the ropes. The point really is that the artist is a man used to working by himself and therefore he's a very much worse mixer with chaps who are working all together on a job, because he always tends to think he's the only one that counts, simply because he works at home on his easel all the time and when he gets down to working with a producer and so on in the theatre he's not a single chap at all any more, he's a chap working for a unity.

CROZIER: That boils down to the fact that opera is a cooperative art.

PIPER: Which doesn't take away from the need to keep a personal style all the time and a personal interest in the work as a contribution to the whole. It's a question really of personalities uniting without sinking.

MCKECHNIE: When you're writing, Ben, do you consciously make a change from the style you used in say, *Lucretia*, or do you remember to avoid some snag, or follow some promising development in your previous writing?

BRITTEN: That's a frightfully difficult question to answer that, because, as we were saying last night, weren't we, one carries on a lot of dos and don'ts from one work to the next and yet I think it is dangerous to go on to a new work with a lot of preconceived ideas. One has to take every opera as an entirely new problem and work at it afresh. All the same, there are certain practical things that one learns about opera writing—the whole time one is writing operas—things like allowing enough time for the scenery and for the sets to be changed.

MCKECHNIE: You're using the same small orchestra?

BRITTEN: Yes—partly from necessity and partly because I find that the sheer challenge or writing for an orchestra of twelve, as opposed to one of seventy, extremely exciting. Writing music is such a complicated thing that one can say that limitations like this have advantages as well as disadvantages. They limit you and yet excite you at the same time. You think of an orchestra of twelve. Well, I had a big solo for the bassoon in this scene, in the next scene I must obviously leave out the bassoon—it needs a rest for the ensemble later. Therefore I shall not have four woodwind in the next scene, I shall only have a flute, oboe, and a clarinet. What can they do? Well, they can play solos or duets which immediately suggest various combinations. For instance, in the second scene of the second act, I was anxious to use instruments of a dark quality: bass flute and bass clarinet were the obvious ones. There was an interlude just before that. I had to avoid these instruments so as to enable the flute to change over to the bass flute and the clarinet to a bass clarinet, and they have to have at least a minute's rest to do that, and therefore that limited and gave one ideas for that particular piece beforehand.

CROZIER: If there were a superb orchestra and superb opera company available, then I suppose your tendency would be to write works for them, but in the present circumstances, if you want high standards of performance, you have to create an ensemble yourself and that has to be a small one.

BRITTEN: I think I should say, in existing circumstances, I would always choose a small orchestra.[3]

[3] See Essay 29 for Britten's views in 1950 on grand opera and chamber opera.

CROZIER: You know I think this is an important point. When he writes the first draft of his libretto, the author has to write his dialogues out in full. If the composer likes what he's done, he takes the idea but perhaps he won't take the whole sentence.

MCKECHNIE: Do you agree with that Ben?

BRITTEN: Yes, I think it's true.

CROZIER: But if the librettist is so proud of his original sentences that he doesn't want any of the words altered and the composer has to take the whole of what he's written, the thing becomes constipated and you get a fight between the literary and the musical. It seems to me important for the author of an opera to remember that the composer has short cuts. He has all sorts of devices by which he can say in a twentieth of the time what the librettist has to say in a great many words, and it seems to me that the librettist's job is to realize that fact and to learn to write simple words in very simple forms.

BRITTEN: The one point I should like to make about *Albert Herring* is that it is extremely exciting to set everyday language, to try and cope with the problem of setting things like 'Well, come and serve me. I'm in a hurry . . .'—trying to find a musical equivalent for it. This is a fascinating problem and a thing I've always wanted to do. We haven't yet quite faced the problem of setting absolutely contemporary pieces, which I think we must soon do. *Herring* is 1900 and if you think of the famous Loder operas—well![4] *Butterfly* is about middle-class people, but the words creak a bit!

CROZIER: 'Round his seat a garland let us twine'—that's my favourite line from *Butterfly*![5]

BRITTEN: Yes, we decided fairly early on that it would be a nice point for Albert to arrive back in the middle of his own funeral. Obviously the reason for their presuming him to be dead was the discovery of the wreath which belonged to Albert, crushed by a cart.

CROZIER: I remember very well asking you how you wanted that actual funeral dirge written. You said you thought it would be a good idea to have an individual quatrain for each person and then a chorus for them to sing all together, and when I got down to writing it, that's what I wrote. I wrote a triplet for each of the characters and then a quatrain for all of them to sing, and gave it to you. Well, you looked at it and then—what was the next stage?

[4] Edward Loder (1813–65), English composer and conductor, whose operas include *Raymond and Agnes* (1855), and *Francis the First* (1838).

[5] Possibly an early poetic translation of Puccini's *Madama Butterfly* which Crozier may have encountered at Sadler's Wells.

BRITTEN: Then when I began thinking about it and decided what I really wanted was to have a sort of background chant for them all, out of which each individual could emerge for a solo and then drop back again.

CROZIER: That was even more complicated because first of all I wrote that chorus in seven lines, but you found that you wanted only four lines of the chorus at the beginning, and then later on you'd want all my seven lines. So my chorus had to be rewritten again to allow for that.

BRITTEN: Yes, that's right.

CROZIER: We began with a greengrocer's shop. Do you remember that little greengrocer's shop in Aldeburgh High Street? We had tea opposite one day and then we went over there to see what it was like inside. Do you remember that, John?

PIPER: Yes, and that definitely was the shop for me, before the script was written down at all.

MCKECHNIE: You mean in colour, shape, or what?

PIPER: Oh no, in the character of a small-town greengrocer's shop in Suffolk which, after all, has a definite shape and colour and so on, for me.

CROZIER: We had to think of the practicalities of it too. First we wanted the feeling of smallness in the greengrocer's shop. We had to be able to see through the window what was going on outside in the street and we had to get eight people into it. All those factors had to be taken and put together.

MCKECHNIE: So you discussed that with John?

CROZIER: Yes.

MCKECHNIE: And you, John, you'd make counter-suggestions?

PIPER: Yes, but there weren't many counter-suggestions to be made.

CROZIER: Well, your roof was one, wasn't it?

PIPER: Oh yes, I invented a roof over the counter to give a suggestion of the ceiling closing in rather low-down—thinking of a big stage, you know, and having to bring it down to the ordinary level of a shop.

CROZIER: That's important because that roof is the artist's contribution to the idea of a greengrocer's shop.

PIPER: And it had the great advantage from my point of view also of not being naturalistic. It was a positive virtue that, because it took one away from realism largely.

CROZIER: Another thing we decided was that if we had a sack or vegetable basket on the stage in the shop, it mustn't be a real one. It had to be designed, because that was part of John's contribution to the whole business.

PIPER: Yes, the box or whatever it was mustn't start as a real one but must be painted back, if you see what I mean, to being a real one.

MCKECHNIE: Was there anything you'd wanted to do in theatre design in this opera—something you hadn't done before?

PIPER: I'm sure the answer to that is a very definite one really, because the thing I always enjoy about working for the theatre is seeing a work of mine carried out on a big scale and that one doesn't get an opportunity of doing, except really on a front cloth.

CROZIER: Actually, John went off to Woodbridge a few weeks ago to look around for ideas for the front cloth. We originally thought of a view of Loxford with Loxford arms up in the sky, you know, like one of those old maps.

PIPER: Or a cloth by Rex Whistler, that's actually what I thought Ben must have had in mind.[6]

MCKECHNIE: Yes, but it wouldn't fit in with the rest of the design?

PIPER: No, I don't think it would help the music either. With costumes there are just as many things to look out for too—just as many reefs to be wrecked on—the blue of the butcher boy's apron, now for instance, that blue has to be visually right with all the other colours. So that there's a double thing with costumes working all the time, and once you begin to think of your shop as something, well for instance, like a painting by Braque, then you have to think of putting people into that Braque and your costumes have to belong to the human beings inside and to the surroundings of the shop.

CROZIER: That's very much the same thing with the production. The behaviour of the people on stage must match up with the artist's conception and with the style of the music.

PIPER: It's all a question really of finding some parallel on the same level isn't it—of human action, dress and behaviour.

CROZIER: That sounds very formidable!

MCKECHNIE: One thing I notice I miss and, if I may say so, am delighted to miss, that is the old operatic clichés of acting: the convulsive downstage walk, the enormous gestures, the stumble forward.

BRITTEN: I think that apart from the D'Oyly Carte opera tradition, which has perhaps been allowed to die on its feet because it's never changed or been added to, we have no English tradition of opera acting at all.[7]

MCKECHNIE: Well to me the effect is that the acting is quieter. It's more naturalistic.

[6] Rex Whistler (1905–44), English artist and illustrator, who became famous following a mural he painted for the Tate Gallery. He enjoyed a vogue as a country house decorator before being killed in action in Normandy.

[7] Richard D'Oyly Carte (1844–1901), English impresario and producer, who put together the team of Gilbert and Sullivan for *Trial by Jury* and thereafter produced the many operettas resulting from this collaboration at his new theatre, the Savoy. His company's exclusive control over these works lasted until 1950.

Crozier: Certainly in *Peter Grimes* we tried to give a naturalistic impression of small-town life. We didn't do it by imitating naturalism but by suggesting a kind of naturalism, and trying to create a stage truth which did, I think, at certain points, come off. But so often in the operas that you see, masses and masses of people come on the stage and they are arranged in patterns and they stand about and they sing and then suddenly they all scramble off into the wings for no reason at all. One sees that in opera houses not only in England but all over the continent.

Britten: I suppose in a way we've tried in this opera to make every element in it as good as every other—to treat the scenery, the libretto, the acting, the production, the orchestral playing, and the singing, equally seriously.

23 Frank Bridge and English Chamber Music (1947)

A highly intelligent & open-minded conductor made an interesting remark to me the other day.[1] It was after a concert in London when the Divertimenti for Wind Instruments of Bridge were played—'Why,' he said to me, 'I had no idea that Bridge was an 'interesting' composer.[2] I had always connected his name with salon music.' And so would have 90% of other highly intelligent and open-minded musicians & music lovers in this country, if they connected his name with anything at all—so neglected has his music become recently. In these few moments before the concert tonight I should like to try and do two things: one; to correct the impression that Frank Bridge only wrote Salon music; two; to try and defend him, from those who are prejudiced against Salon music, for having written it at all.

When Frank Bridge matured at the turn of the century—the school of chamber music was really in the doldrums. The headmaster was Brahms, chief assistant masters, Schumann and Mendelssohn; the dancing-master, Dvorak, and of course above all, the Chairman of the Governors—Beethoven.[3] Not much notice was taken of those rather dull, superannuated professors Haydn and Mozart—and though the occasional visits of the Art master Schubert gave pleasure, his character was highly suspect. Not as suspect, however, as the masters of that dreadful neighbouring coeducationalist school, Debussy and Faure. But what an atmosphere of romantic gloom for the poor boys to be brought up in—think of all that hideous, if worthy, striving! How much more so for a Frank Bridge, who was not only a listener and composer, but a player too. Little wonder that he wanted to write the Idylls and Novellettes and gay folksongs, music grateful to play and easy to listen to, which some people label and dismiss as salon music, people who only want fateful quartets in C minor or philosophic 'Muss es sein's.[4] His inclination was instinctively towards the French tradition of skill, grace and

Source: Draft (typescript), n.d. (*GB-ALb* 1–02053794). Broadcast 9 Nov. 1947, BBC Third Programme, 7.50 p.m.: talk introducing recital of works by Frank Bridge, performed by Britten and members of the Zorian Quartet.

1 Not identified.

2 Divertimenti (1934–8). Frank Bridge began teaching Britten in 1927, a practice that continued beyond Britten's acceptance into the Royal College of Music in 1930. He remained a vitally important role model and father figure to the young composer.

3 Dvořák is listed as the bursar in Britten's draft.

4 Reference to Beethoven's String Quartet in F, Op. 135, which includes as an epigraph to the Grave section of the final movement the phrase 'Muss es sein?' ('Must it be?'). The following Allegro is prefaced by the phrase 'Es muss sein!'.

good workmanship, and away from 19th-century German decadence. I'm not saying that the Frank Bridge of 1900 wouldn't have been as shocked, as some of <u>you</u> may be, at what I've been saying—but subconsciously then, as consciously later, he rebelled at having to play and listen to music that was excused as being Philosophic because it was simply ineffective, badly written and poorly worked out. To such a reaction belongs the first piece in the programme to-night, a Phantasy for piano quartet, published in 1910. It is beautifully written for the instruments and, tho' in a free form so easily and often abused—it is far from being sloppy or accidental. It is perhaps slight in content, and certainly without any deep emotional pretentions—but there is one moment after a big climax towards the end of the piece when something bigger and more <u>uncomfortable</u> occurs. There comes a kind of nostalgic surge, with a passion outside the scope of the piece and, I think, slightly <u>marring</u> it. It is this tendency which I believe was important in Bridge's early music, if disturbing, and led to his development which I now want to go on to.

I didn't meet Frank Bridge until I was twelve—fifteen years after the <u>1914–18</u> War had shattered the easy-going, self-confident Edwardian life.[5] But the many talks I had with him, indeed everything about him, told me of the utter horror and revulsion that he felt about that catastrophe. The seed of discontent, or whatever it was, at the end of the Phantasy, grew and grew until the horrible protest of his Piano Sonata, written in memory of Ernest Farrar[6] a young composer killed in that war. Some people think that the protest in that sonata is too subjective, too near the surface, not <u>digested</u> enough. But whether they are right or not, the whole of Bridge's musical horizon was now shattered—unlimited possibilities, harmonically and texturally especially, became possible. As he <u>was</u> exploring territories unknown to him, he had to go slowly and sometimes went a little off the path. But always his instinct for form and workmanship and unerring ear brought him back, and occasionally, as in the second work, the big <u>Piano Trio</u> dating from 1929, he reached great heights.[7] How great those heights really are is difficult for us in 1947 to assess. There are not many moments of repose or relaxation in these later works. Nowadays, we are concerned with other problems than his and we are not so worried about expressing our personalities. But many of these works I have lived with for years, and learned to love dearly. The quartets, the touching and intimate Willor, Grassland and Brook [i.e. 'Willow

[5] Britten met Bridge in 1927, a little before his fourteenth birthday and thirteen years after the beginning of the First World War.

[6] Ernest Farrar (1885–1918), English composer and organist, pupil of Stanford's at the Royal College of Music.

[7] Piano Trio No. 2 (1929).

Grows aslant a Brook'], the impetuous 'Enter Spring,' and the athletic and witty Divertimenti. These works have a quality of seriousness, of pure and logical harmony and of clear and complete workmanship, all too rare these days. I am <u>not</u> sure that this Trio is not one of the finest pieces of extended musical thinking of our time.

24 *The Rape of Lucretia* (1948)

Many people think that composers can set any old kind of poetry to music; that any pattern of words may start his imagination working. In many cases that is true. Some of the greatest composers have found inspiration in very poor verse (see Schubert in many places), although not many have gone as far as Darius Milhaud in his 'Machines Agricoles'—which is a setting of a catalogue. But I believe that if the words of a song match the music in subtlety of thought and clarity of expression it results in a greater amount of artistic satisfaction for the listener. This applies equally to the larger forms—oratorio, cantata and opera. In many oratorios, of course, where the words come from the liturgy or the Bible the composer has the greatest possible inspiration for his music; but with a few exceptions, like Metastasio, Dryden, Da Ponte and Boito, few serious poets have provided libretti for these kinds of works.[1] There may be many reasons for this. Opera composers have a reputation for ruthless disregard of poetic values (in some cases rightly)—and all they need is a hack writer to bully, and serious poets won't stand for that. Besides, it takes a great deal of time to learn the operatic formulae—the recitatives, the arias and the ensembles. The bad enunciation of many singers doesn't seem to provide a suitable show place for a poet's finest thoughts. One of the most powerful reasons for a poet's operatic shyness I suspect to be this. To be suitable for music, poetry must be simple, succinct and crystal clear; for many poets this must be a great effort, and the psychological epic poem to be read (or not read) in the quiet of the study is more attractive. I think they are wrong. Opera makes similar demands of conciseness on the composer. He must be able to paint a mood or an atmosphere in a single phrase and must search unceasingly for the apt one. But this is everlastingly fascinating and stimulating, as it must be to the poet. Similarly fascinating to him should be the problem of continuity, or degrees of intensity, development of character and situation. Also, if he is working together with a sympathetic composer, then the timings and inflections of the dialogue can be fixed exactly and for ever—a thing not possible in any other medium.

This 'working together' of the poet and composer mentioned above seems to be one of the secrets of writing a good opera. In the general discussion on

Source: Foreword to *The Rape of Lucretia* [ed. Eric Crozier] (London: The Bodley Head, 1948), 7–8.

[1] Pietro Metastasio (1698–1782), Italian poet and librettist, whose libretti were set by Caldara, Handel, Gluck, Mozart, and many others. John Dryden (1631–1700), English writer and dramatist, author of, among other important works, *King Arthur* (Purcell). Lorenzo Da Ponte (1749–1838), Italian librettist, who collaborated with Mozart on *Le nozze di Figaro*, *Don Giovanni*, and *Così fan tutte*. Arrigo Boito (1842–1918), Italian librettist, poet, critic, and composer, best known for the libretti set by Verdi, *Otello* and *Falstaff*.

the shape of the work—the plot, the division into recitatives, arias, ensembles and so on—the musician will have many ideas that may stimulate and influence the poet. Similarly when the libretto is written and the composer is working on the music, possible alterations may be suggested by the flow of the music, and the libretto altered accordingly. In rehearsals, as the work becomes realised aurally and visually, other changes are often seen to be necessary. The composer and poet should at all stages be working in the closest contact, from the most preliminary stages right up to the first night. It was thus in the case of 'The Rape of Lucretia.'[2]

[2] See Essay 57.

25 Piano works by Frederic Chopin and Gabriel Fauré (1949)

A great virtuoso pianist of the nineteenth century did not, as today, only give recitals in mammoth concert-halls with delirious audiences of thousands; he also appeared in the exquisite drawing-rooms of elegant and discriminating patronesses. For these delicate occasions, very extended or strenuous compositions were out of place—being wearisome and rather embarrassing at such close quarters. So a kind of short, decorative and evocative music has come to be called *Salon* music. We have *nocturnes*, *impromptus*, *fantasias*, *barcarolles*, *scherzos*, and every sort of dance music—though never to be danced to.

All the best ideas of Chopin were cast in this form, and with his superb melodic gift, and his vivid and original imagination for colours, many small masterpieces were created.

Half-a-century later Fauré was writing for the Paris Salons. At first his little pieces were closely modelled on Chopin, but soon he developed a highly original style of his own—most personal melodies, with daring and surprising harmonies, and always beautifully imaginative textures. One often feels that his audiences must have been bewildered by the strangeness and apparent vagueness of some of his later pieces, especially the great *Nocturnes.*

Source: AFPB (1949), 31–2.

26 A New Centre for Music (1949)

For a long time London has suffered from the over-centralisation of her art and entertainment. The destruction of Queen's Hall by the enemy during the war certainly hastened a most welcome spreading of musical activities throughout the capital, and there is no reason why this diversity should cease when London has at last a new central concert hall.

In this movement Chelsea has played a most notable part. For long a centre of art, it was only perhaps to be expected that music would establish itself sometime. What has in fact happened is both significant and encouraging.

The admirable series of concerts under the auspices of Boyd Neel have maintained the high standard set by his own orchestra over the years and have introduced many unfamiliar works to Chelsea, as well as providing superb performances of music in the standard repertory.[1]

I was happy to conduct the Boyd Neel Orchestra at the Town Hall recently.

Again, when Norman del Mar formed his orchestra of students and amateurs for the performance of symphonic music outside the normal curriculum of study he chose to play in Chelsea, where he has revived much neglected music and given a number of important first performances.[2]

It was to Chelsea that the reconstituted Philharmonic String Quartet came, as have many other distinguished consorts, while only recently that fine artist Flora Nielsen[3] gave the first public entertainment in the newly opened Chenil Galleries.[4]

T. B. Lawrence, who himself belongs to Chelsea, has let us hear his Fleet Street Choir, which has earned for itself a European reputation, and his son, A. H., is doing yeoman work with his Chamber Orchestra, which we can sometimes hear at the Polytechnic.[5]

Source: *Chelsea Week* (1949).

[1] Boyd Neel (1905–81), English conductor, who founded the Boyd Neel String Orchestra in 1933.

[2] This was the Chelsea Symphony Orchestra, founded by the English conductor Norman Del Mar (1919–94) in 1944.

[3] Flora Nielsen (1900–75), soprano, who created the role of Mrs Peachum in Britten's realization of *The Beggar's Opera* (1948), and shared the role of Female Chorus with Joan Cross in the first production of *The Rape of Lucretia* (1946), later playing Bianca. She performed the role of Sorceress in Britten's and Imogen Holst's version of Purcell's *Dido and Aeneas* (1951). She was professor of singing at the Royal Academy of Music.

[4] A gallery in King's Road, Chelsea, with a long history of exhibitions and concerts. The young John Barbarolli conducted an orchestra of his own making at the gallery in the mid-1920s. *Façade* was presented there in June 1926.

[5] Thomas Bertie Lawrence (1880–1953), founder and conductor of the Fleet Street Choir, who directed the first performance with the women of this choir of *A Ceremony of Carols*

A recent development has been the series of Sunday afternoon recitals organised by May Harrison,[6] the violinist member of that remarkable family of musicians, at Nell Gwynn House, where we have been able to hear a succession of eminent artists in informal surroundings.

But with all this, an enormous debt is owed to the Chelsea Music Club, which blazed a trail many years ago, and which seems to go from strength to strength as the years go by. It is, indeed, fitting that the Club should be holding one of its concerts during Chelsea Week,[7] and it is a typical gesture that they have surrendered a number of seats to the public on this occasion.

If what I have written is no more than a catalogue, it is surely remarkable that such a catalogue is possible—and, of course, I have only touched on one or two important developments.

With such brilliant achievement, music certainly deserves a prominent place in the varied arrangements for Chelsea Week, and the programmes should attract many visitors to come to Chelsea.

(1942). His son, H. Arthur Lawrence (d. 1953), was, amongst other things, conductor of the Banstead Musical Society.

[6] May Harrison (1890–1959), English violinist, whose sister was Beatrice Harrison, the cellist.

[7] Chelsea Week, a celebration of spring gardens, occurs each year in late May.

27 UNESCO (1949)

The governments of the world have declared in the Charter of UNESCO: 'Since wars begin in the minds of men, it is in the minds of men that the defenses of peace must be constructed.'[1]

One of our leading English writers, the historian of art, Mr. Herbert Read,[2] has pointed out what the scientists and the military also in effect declare, namely, that with the advent of atomic and biological weapons, war and armaments no longer provide any defense. Power in the military sense has become an illusion and it is indeed 'worse than an illusion—it is an hallucination which invites suicide.' Herbert Read says that under these circumstances young Englishmen who agree to be drafted 'are engaging in a gigantic conspiracy which can only end in the obliteration of their island home' and adds that 'the case is not different for young Americans, young Frenchmen, young Russians—for the youth of any nation.'

Not only is modern war completely irrational and suicidal; it is also completely immoral. Recently Rear Admiral Ralph A. Offstie, U.S.N., at a Congressional hearing, raised the question, in a denunciation of atomic and 'obliteration' bombing, what people mean by 'survival.' He declared: 'If we mean the survival of the values, the principles and traditions of human civilization, we must insure that our military techniques do not strip us of our self-respect.'

In these circumstances the first act of sanity for any nation is to break with war. The first patriotic, sane, morally decent step for the youth—any youth of any nation—is to withhold himself from military service.

Once we have decided not to slip over the precipice into atomic war, we can train ourselves to use higher and truly effective means to resist evil and possible aggression. If our democratic peoples maintain a vigorous health in their economic life, in relations between the nations, in education and art, health will gradually be instilled into the whole community of nations. Gandhi has shown how nonviolent resistance can be 'a living reality among the practical policies of world politics.'

It is because we believe these things and have in our own country been connected with movements which promote these pacifist ideas that we gladly give this performance under the sponsorship of two organizations which in

Source: Unidentified programme note, 8 Dec. 1949 (*GB-ALb*). Written by Britten and Pears.

[1] UNESCO: United Nations Educational, Scientific and Cultural Organization, formed in 1945.

[2] Sir Herbert Read (1893–1968), English poet, writer, and art critic. See Essay 43 in which Britten and Read cross swords.

this country seek to advance the same course—the Fellowship of Reconciliation and the War Resisters League.[3]

[3] Fellowship of Reconciliation, English organization formed in 1914. It brought together people of many different faiths, 'For Peace, Justice and Nonviolence'. An international FOR was formed in 1919. War Resisters League, American organization, founded in 1923 by individuals who had been opposed to the 1914–18 war.

28 Boyd Neel: *The Story of an Orchestra* (1950)

It gives me great pleasure to introduce this account of the Boyd Neel Orchestra by its gifted and energetic founder and conductor. Such an account is welcome, for in its seventeen years of existence this orchestra has gained an important position in our musical life.

The Boyd Neel Orchestra was the first in Great Britain and among the first in the world to establish on the musical scene the small self-contained orchestral ensemble.

To their efforts largely is due the fact that the public nowadays will accept the distinction between Great music and Big music, will realize that importance is not achieved by a large, thick sound and that a band of hundred is not five times as good as a group of twenty. And what a repertoire the orchestra has made known to us—not only music foreign to the limited, nineteenth century-ridden orchestral programmes of to-day, but also much familiar music which yet needs the thin clear lines of a small ensemble to make really musical sense.

Let us composers, too, remember what Boyd Neel has done for us. Not only has he asked for and used new music but—here's the difference—he has used it many times.[1] If Boyd Neel and his orchestra like and believe in new music, they play it over and over again until the audience get used to it and begin to like it too; not for it a first performance and then the dusty shelf.

This account is honest enough not to minimize the difficulties and worries which Boyd Neel and his young group have had to face. And even now these troubles are not over. Though firmly established in the lives of serious music lovers, the great general public, still attracted by the Big at any cost, often fails to respond, as Boyd Neel himself points out.

I suggest it is our pleasure, privilege and duty to support this gallant enterprise, whether as players, composers, or members of the audience.

Source: Introduction to Boyd Neel, *The Story of an Orchestra* (London: Vox Mundi, 1950), pp. i–ii.

[1] *Variations on a Theme of Frank Bridge* (1937) was commissioned by Boyd Neel and given its first performance in the Salzburg Festival of that year.

29 The Arts Council and Opera (1950)

POOLEY: What we are trying to do, Mr. Britten, is to make up our minds what are the real requirements in regard to opera and ballet during the next five years, and what funds will be needed to sustain them on the basis of building up a national opera and a national ballet. Those requirements will then be put before the Arts Council, and they will put them before the Treasury, and we shall see what happens. We have asked a number of people to consult with us, and it is very nice of your [*sic*] to come this morning. We would, of course, like to hear anything that you wish to say, but what we are especially interested in is the English Opera Group, which you largely founded and of which you are now the mainstay.

BRITTEN: More or less, I should like to say; because at the beginning, since we had to found a new style, my task was greater than I hope it will be in the future. Until one established a style such as this, other composers will not write for it, but now, happily, other composers are writing for it, and so I think my part in it will probably be less in the future than it has been in the past.

DENISON: As you will see from the notes for consultation which have been sent to you, we have been talking about the needs not only of Covent Garden and Sadler's Wells and other companies, such as the Carl Rosa, but also about the demand in the provinces and the resources we are to provide to meet it.[1] A fairly clear view seems to have emerged that the provinces do require new resources to deal with the standard operas, as, for example, a reconstituted Carl Rosa of a better standard and designed specifically to meet the needs of the provincial theatres, related financially to the amount of money that could be taken over a week in a given theatre.

What we should like to hear from you is your views as to how the work of the English Opera Group can be related to the work of the companies playing the normal repertoire of operas. Do you, for instance, see it being established on a permanent basis with an all-the-year-round contract, touring in part and playing festivals in part; or do you see it in a more limited sphere, at any rate for the next five years? There is the problem of its repertoire, the

Editor's title.

Source: The Arts Council of Great Britain Opera and Ballet Sub-Committee thirteenth meeting, 5 July 1950. Consultation with Mr. Benjamin Britten. Original document held in the archives of the Arts Council of England. The committee consisted of Sir Ernest Pooley (Chairman), Dr B. Ifor Evans, Viscount Esher, Dr T. Wood, W. E. Williams, John Denison (Music Director), Eric Walter White (Music Officer).

[1] Presumably all those participating in this consultation were sent notes outlining areas of discussion. These have not been traced.

extent to which the public could be persuaded to attend all the year round, and so on. Could we perhaps take that line of thought first?

BRITTEN: Eventually—how soon this will come, I cannot say, but eventually—we should very much like to be on a permanent basis, simply because we have discovered from experience that the more we perform the better we are. The young singers, we have discovered, need the performing experience. We have had with us for the last three or four years some extremely young singers, and we have proved that, even performing the same piece for, say, two or three months running, their performances and their whole attitude towards the stage have become infinitely better, and they have become real performers. So eventually we want to perform permanently; and of course, the more we perform the better known we become and therefore the more composers will write for us.

With the composers, we have discovered that in our kind of company if we can perform the same opera many times it gives the composers a chance to see where the mistakes in their works lie, what things are good and what things are bad, and to profit from that knowledge. I have discovered in my own case that it is not enough to see an opera once or twice, such as is necessarily the case in the big companies that have a large repertory; but that one wants to see the work gradually run in, with the performers becoming confident and performing with authority, which is difficult in the case of a new work.

To take the example of my first two operas: *Peter Grimes*, at Sadler's Wells, was performed I think (I have not the figures before me) in the first season perhaps twelve times, and *Lucretia*, which was given by our Opera Group, with a small orchestra and a small company, had one hundred performances in the first two years.

POOLEY: It was given at Glyndebourne, was it not?

BRITTEN: It was given first at Glyndebourne and then we toured and took it abroad; and in the second year we played more often. *Lucretia* had not the success that *Grimes* had, but now it is one of our big drawing cards simply because it is so familiar that people are used to it and say, 'Oh, yes, we have heard about that; we will go and see it.' But the point is that with *Grimes* I did not have a chance to find what the mistakes were because of the small number of times it was performed in the first year. With *Lucretia*, where we had time to experiment, I made a completely changed and revised version of it in the second year because I discovered in the performances that I had made some bad mistakes. Therefore, for composers as well as for the singers I think that many performances are essential.

DENISON: Do you see the Group continuing to be formed on this specialised basis of a limited orchestra, of solo players and no chorus in the accepted sense but a number of principals of varying grades?

BRITTEN: It would be very difficult for us completely to change the style of the work of our company. We could not have a symphony orchestra, but next year for Dido, which we hope to do, we shall have a string orchestra of, say, fifteen. We can just afford that, I think. For the Easdale opera, which we have commissioned and are going to put on next year, we shall have a slightly larger orchestra.[2] We do not say that we have an orchestra of twelve and no chorus, and that we must stick to that; but within limits we must remain a small opera company.

WHITE: On the question of the orchestra, I wonder whether I am right in thinking that the average size of the English Opera Group orchestra is very similar to that used by the Old Vic in the early days of the Vic Opera Company, when a number of operas were scored for an orchestra of not more than twenty—and probably less.

BRITTEN: We have discovered that this sized orchestra can sound good even in quite a large theatre if it is treated with wisdom, but as I said at the beginning of my remarks, the composers shied off it a little at the beginning until they were quite convinced that it could be done. But other composers are now definitely writing for us.

POOLEY: When you speak of composers, do you mean English composers?

BRITTEN: Yes.

POOLEY: That is what you aim at—to get new operas by English composers which are suitable to be put on by your company?

BRITTEN: Yes.

POOLEY: But not necessarily to be confined ultimately to your company—they might be suitable for other companies as well?

BRITTEN: Oh, yes. My own experience is that the operas Lucretia, Albert Herring, Let's Make an Opera and Beggars' Opera [*sic*] are all being done abroad now in quite a big way. There is no reason at all why they should not be done by other companies in England, granted that they are of suitable size.

ESHER: Do you consider that there are certain operas which are suitable for Covent Garden and others that are suitable only for Sadler's Wells?

BRITTEN: I believe that very strongly.

ESHER: Would you consider that your own operas are totally unsuitable to be played at Covent Garden?

BRITTEN: I think I would say that now. At one time I was not quite sure whether that was so, but I think that the lack of impact in a theatre the size of Covent Garden with an orchestra of twelve is a great disadvantage.[3]

[2] Brian Easdale (1909–95) composed *The Sleeping Children* (1951) for the English Opera Group. Like Britten, he composed scores for the GPO and Crown Film Units.

[3] The English Opera Group season at Covent Garden in 1947 was neither financially nor critically successful. See Paul Kildea, *Selling Britten* (Oxford: OUP, 2002). Covent Garden's seating capacity in this period was 2,022, compared to the Jubilee Hall's of 290.

ESHER: But if scored for a larger orchestra, there is no reason why, in your opinion, the opera itself should not be played at Covent Garden?

BRITTEN: Well, I could not conceive of the opera being re-scored. You see, it is planned for that kind of medium. There is not only the sound of it, but also the visual side of it. If there is a large stage the size of that at Covent Garden with never more than eight people on it, I think the eye becomes a little inadequately treated. Similarly, when one is planning an opera for an orchestra of twelve, one deliberately avoids the kind of music which demands a great deal of volume.

ESHER: Do the English composers, of whom you now stand at the head, contemplate writing what I may call the large scale of opera, or will they confine themselves to the smaller operas, what I might call the opera comique standard?

BRITTEN: I do not quite see why they should choose one or the other. I believe that one wants at times to write for a full symphony orchestra and one wants at other times to write for a string quartet. Perhaps I am wrong and I say this with hesitation, but I feel that in the future the emphasis will be more on the string quartet than on the symphony orchestra because of the way in which music seems to me to be going; and also—again I say this with hesitation—our English character rather inclines towards the small than to the very big. That is my personal opinion. Certainly that is the way I feel now. Although I am planning for next year a full-sized opera, I can see myself writing in the future one big opera to, say, six small ones.

ESHER: You would not say that it is more difficult to write the big scale of opera than the small one, would you?

BRITTEN: I should just say that it is harder work! There are more notes to write.

POOLEY: Your Peter Grimes was intended for a full-sized orchestra, was it not?

BRITTEN: Yes, it was. I would not suggest for a moment that I am trying to stop the big kind of opera. That would be nonsense. I want to add the small type to the big type, and to have two kinds.

DENISON: Do you think we are going to find theatres in the provinces in all the different towns and cities which will be suitable for the size of the English Opera Group? If you are thinking of it becoming a permanent organisation, it is necessary to find a year's work for it playing in different centres.

BRITTEN: Although not speaking with specialist knowledge, I think it would be easier for us to find room in theatres than it would be for the big companies. We all know the difficulty of a big company going into a theatre that has room for an orchestra of twelve.

Denison: There is difficulty about a company of the size of the Covent Garden company going to cities outside London, except for three or four of them, but the size of the Sadler's Wells company is about right.

Britten: The English Opera Group can easily perform in a theatre like Sadler's Wells; therefore, the theatres to which Sadler's Wells go would be suitable for us. We have found that in London our most suitable theatre for performing in is Sadler's Wells. At the Lyric, for opera one is perhaps in too close contact with the stage. One needs a little more room. The stage is also very small. But we are grateful to the Lyric for existing; otherwise we would be hard put to it to find a theatre.

Pooley: Most people with whom we have consulted have led us to believe that the right thing to do, if it can be done, would be to have Covent Garden, including one international season, and otherwise to build up a national opera (I do not mean British music necessarily) with Sadler's Wells and a company to be based in the provinces—Manchester being the place suggested—which could be a resuscitated Carl Rosa or could be something else.[4] Supposing that were the right set-up—and other people have suggested more than one opera based on [*sic*] the provinces, and even two or three if the sinews of war were there—how would your English Opera Group dovetail into any scheme of that sort, or would it be completely outside, travelling round on its own?

Britten: We should not have a permanent centre. I do not think our function would be only to perform in London or Aldeburgh. I think our real purpose is to get new works from English composers, to get young singers and actors, and to travel extensively rather than to stay in one place, because our organisation is not big enough to have a large repertory which would enable us to stay in one place. I feel that very strongly. Supposing we had a successful opera by composer X, I think one of our main advantages would be that we could take that into places where, because of the size of the theatre and the public for opera generally, the big operas could not go. If you have a popular company playing Boheme, you can go to almost any town in the British Isles probably; but with a modern English work you could not go because the risk would be too great with the big-sized company. With our size of company, although there is a risk financially, the figures are just so much smaller than with a full-sized company.

Pooley: You will correct me if I am wrong, but you would contemplate being quite on your own? What would be the financial requirement to enable you to sustain that position? Have you worked that out at all?

[4] Karl Rosa (1842–89), German conductor, violinist, and impresario, who formed the Carl Rosa Opera Company in 1874 (anglicizing his name in the process), which was based in England from the following year.

BRITTEN: We have worked out what we can exist on. I think you have talked to our ex-Chairman about that.[5] We originally had five thousand pounds a year from the Arts Council, which was a very generous amount, and we did perform satisfactorily on that; but, alas, we took one or two risks in the first year or so which led us rather heavily into debt. The result was that in the following two years we had to economise and perform much less, therefore rather minimising our uses, because, as I said at the beginning, we need to perform a great deal to give these people experience. When the Arts Council had to cut our grant to three thousand pounds, our position was very difficult; but we managed to keep going, and with our little children's opera, which can tick over and not lose money, we have been able this year to perform, or shall have been able to perform, about one-third of the year.

If in the future you could see your way to increase our amount to, say, six thousand pounds, that would mean that we would be full on the way to becoming a permanent company. We could go to some of these northern cities that want us and cannot afford to give us a guarantee; we could afford to take a risk. At the moment, with the three thousand pounds subsidy, we cannot afford to take a risk; that is our drawback. At the moment we can perform only in those places which can give us a guarantee. We cannot afford to lose three or four hundred pounds a week, because three thousand pounds is easily used up in that way.

POOLEY: When you say 'become a permanent company', do you mean you would have singers who would really remain with you for an indefinite period of time, or would you contemplate a continual change, with singers going off to Sadler's Wells, and so forth?

BRITTEN: Oh, yes, we would make arrangements with singers. Most of the singers that sing for us do other things as well. But we could easily play for the whole year with one lot of singers for the whole year, another lot for half the year, and some even, like Kathleen Ferrer [*sic*], whom we hope very much will come back to sing with us next year for a few performances—just for those performances with which she has been associated in the past.

WOOD: With six thousand pounds a year, you feel reasonably happy that you could keep the young singers, attract players, and generally feel yourselves to be in good clear waters?

BRITTEN: That would be the sum we would feel entirely happy with. Then I think it would be up to us to exploit that amount of money in the best possible way. That is the sum that we have been roughly working on.

[5] Oliver Lyttleton (1893–1972), later Viscount Chandos, active in business and government, including membership of the War Cabinet (1941–5).

Denison: Looking at some of your figures in the past, the cost of running the English Opera Group, small though it is, has been relatively high because of the high cost of the individual players and the orchestra, and so on; and that is a very real problem about day-to-day administration. I do not want to go into finance very closely. It seems to me that is one of the things we have to look at very carefully. If you say that six thousand pounds is, fairly definitely, the sort of figure, we know where we are.

Britten: I feel immensely conscious of the fact that you have given us three thousand pounds a year for the last two years and we have done performances for only about one-third of the year on it, but that was because of the risks that we took in the earlier period which landed us in a bad financial situation, and we had to recoup, otherwise we would have had to close.

Pooley: Do you regard the English Opera Group as your own personal central activity, or do you regard it as one of the many things you are concerned with?

Britten: If you would include with the English Opera Group the Aldeburgh Festival, which after all was started by the Group and run entirely by it, I would say Yes, definitely.

Esher: How long can you run on six thousand pounds—how many months in the year?

Britten: It is difficult to answer that question exactly. I should hope eventually that we could run permanently on that.

Esher: Would that mean that your company would be then out of a job for a certain number of months, and if so, what would you do with them?

Britten: We would only engage the people for the periods that we were sure of playing for in the first year or so; but we would hope to find ways of playing for the whole year. I do not mind so much about the older members of the company; they can look after themselves and are busy enough. It is the younger ones that worry me very much. I hate the idea of young singers keeping themselves free for us, as they do at the moment, and then not being able to use them quite enough.

White: Would it be right to suggest that the English Opera Group is a good article of export, and that you have already appeared abroad at festivals in Holland and Switzerland, and did a small tour to Scandinavia;[6] and that that side of the work is likely, if anything, to increase in the future? Is it likely that the demand for what you can present is going to increase from abroad, mainly from the Dominions?

[6] Ten performances of *The Rape of Lucretia* (1946) and *Albert Herring* (1947) in Copenhagen and Oslo, 12–23 Sept. 1949.

BRITTEN: That is very real. For next year we have been approached to go to Germany, and quite strong pressure has been put on me personally from the Foreign Office that it is our duty at the moment to go to Germany.

ESHER: When you speak of the Foreign Office, do you mean the Foreign Office or the British Council?

BRITTEN: The Foreign Office direct.

POOLEY: Supposing the Almighty decreed that you should be run over by a tram tomorrow morning, I suppose the English Opera Group would virtually come to an end?

BRITTEN: No, I do not think so. Actually, if I may say it with all modesty, the same problem has occurred to me once or twice; I take great care in crossing streets at the moment!

ESHER: The same point would apply to the Aldeburgh Festival, would it not?

BRITTEN: I do not think so, now.

WOOD: I do not want to get away from the main stream of question and answer, but I should like you to link up the mention of the North of England, Germany and other parts of Europe: do you find in your experience that there is a growing demand for what might be called the intimate opera spreading through a wide area?

BRITTEN: I would say so definitely.

WOOD: As opposed to the more grandiose grand opera?

BRITTEN: Our experience is that perhaps we can, with our small size, take more care over the way things look and the way things are acted. We can afford to rehearse much more. By using young singers (this sounds disrespectful perhaps) we can use people who perhaps look better; and also, because we do not have an orchestra of 100 in the pit, we therefore need not develop bodies which produce a certain—no matter how you measure sound—a certain number of kilowatts of sound to override that orchestra, and they need not all be very big. That is rather a real point, in the provinces especially. I was told at the beginning that we would find great resistance to the smaller kind of opera, especially in the provinces, and I think that was true at the beginning; but I think now, from the audiences that we got, that it is no disadvantage to have a small orchestra. Obviously the people who only like the Drury Lane sized shows do not like us, but if a person is moderately disposed towards opera and modern opera in particular, I do not think there is any initial resistance to us.

DENISON: What is your latest experience, and in which city, of that sort of thing? It would be very interesting to know.

BRITTEN: In Cambridge, Oxford, Aldeburgh itself; and there is the way that Lucretia and Herring have gone on the Continent. One can measure it by the number of performances that occur.

DENISON: We have still to crack the citadel of the Wigans and Manchesters, and so on.

ESHER: Did not Mr. Britten say that he had cracked it?

BRITTEN: In the Industrial North we had a very good success two years ago with Beggars' Opera [*sic*] and Herring, whereas two years previous to that we had had a very difficult time with Lucretia.

WOOD: I think that is a real achievement. I can recall in my youth going to hear a performance, for which there was an enthusiastic reception by a vast audience, by an orchestra which consisted of a harmonium, a fiddle, a trombone and a piano. If you can induce people to hear your small, delicately poised and immaculate playing, I think that is a very real achievement.

BRITTEN: It is one of our aims to achieve that.

DENISON: It does seem that you ought to be outside this main scheme of a ladder of opera companies playing the standard repertoire. You yourself, I think, indicated that you ought to be more or less independent. One of the points that has arisen as a result of that conception of a ladder system of companies playing the standard repertoire is that there must be a much closer integration between those companies in many things, such as the exchange of singers and having singers on joint contracts, for example, as between Sadler's Wells, Covent Garden and, it may be, a third company, and appearing in different companies in their own special rôles. Is there any field in which the English Opera Group could be drawn, advantageously from its point of view, into such a scheme in regard to the use of artists? I imagine Sadler's Wells would be the most likely theatre to be near your kind of work and weight of singers, and so on.

BRITTEN: We are at the present moment in very close contact with Sadler's Wells. For instance, next week at the Cheltenham Festival, Norman Tucker[7] has very generously made one of their principal singers available to us for performances. I think that sort of thing should be extended. But I do not think there should be one central engaging bureau for all the opera companies, because singing is a thing about which people disagree passionately. One person is inclined to think that Mr. A is the best singer in the world; the next person will think that Mr. A is the worst singer in the world. Therefore, I think there should be always the possibility of decentralisation.

DENISON: Oh, yes; I do not think we envisage one vast central bureau; but there are singers of reputation who are wanted by all the companies, and it has been suggested that they could be engaged on an agreed basis for work in all the companies.

[7] Norman Tucker, pianist, civil servant, Treasury officer (1939–45), appointed director of opera at Sadler's Wells (1947), later becoming director of Sadler's Wells (1951–66).

BRITTEN: Yes, I think I would agree to that.

DENISON: That applies particularly to people who play character parts and make a speciality of that kind of thing.

ESHER: I am very ignorant about what you do, Mr. Britten: do you only produce your own operas, or do you produce other people's operas as well?

BRITTEN: If I may give you just a minute history, I would say roughly that we had to start with my own pieces simply because no one had yet written operas for that kind of medium. For two years I did that. The third year I was getting a little bored with always doing, and I felt the public also might be getting a little bored with only hearing, operas by me. So I rearranged the Beggars' Opera [*sic*], sticking exactly to the tunes that Gay had arranged and making no changes at all. That was in the third year. By the fourth year people were starting to write operas for us—there was one person in particular[8]—but they were not yet ready, so we had to fill in with something; I wrote the little children's opera. But I hope that will be the end of my exclusive domination of that particular scene.

ESHER: You considered Mr. Benjamin's Prima Donna, for example?[9]

BRITTEN: We have discussed with him the possibility of his rearranging that for our company; but in confidence I should like to say that he is considering at this moment writing an opera specially for the company and not rearranging something from the past. He is a person who has a gift which I admire very much, and with whom we have discussed in the past his working with us. For next year we have the opera by Easdale, which is just nearing completion. There is no reason at all to stick to just me. I regret that in the past it has been necessary for this to happen, but in the future I can assure you it will not be such a narrow sphere.

May I say, with regard to the second point in the notes, that I think the present methods of encouraging the composition of new English operas have been in this last year adequate, but on the second part of that item (the production of new English operas) I do not think they have been adequate. That is another reason why we should continue to exist as a Group—that we are trying to devise now a way of trying out new operas; we are trying to arrange for private concert performances of new operas. For instance, some of those that have been commissioned or suggested for the 1951 Festival we should like to present, without costumes but with singers, and performed with the piano in order to see whether there is the possibility in the future of making them into productions.

There is an Association which is run by the Group which helps to keep us

[8] Not identified.

[9] *Prima Donna* was composed in 1933 and first performed in 1949 at the Fortune Theatre, London.

going and it has, in fact, commissioned our next opera. We want to organise through our association and in collaboration with the Sadler's Wells association, that in their theatre on Sunday evenings regularly during the season we should present concert performances of opera with a view to future production.

It is awfully important, under heading no. 2 of the notes, that we should not only encourage the writing of operas but, having encouraged the writing, we should find some way of showing to the composers roughly what their operas are like. In my own experience, there is all the difference in the world between writing notes on paper and hearing notes sung and seeing them acted. Theories that one has can become exploded by a wrong timing, a wrong calculation of the time of a person crossing the room. What makes Puccini a greater composer of operas than, in my humble opinion, a great composer, is that he knows how long it takes a person to cross the room. That can only come from hearing the operas produced.

WOOD: There is a tiny practical question I should like to ask. In these productions on Sunday nights, would the singers sing from the copies? Would you have a rehearsal kind of production with the people not necessarily memorising?

BRITTEN: We thought of two different kinds of experiment. We thought of one which would be done with copies, with the piano, with a minimum amount of movement to give an illusion. If the opera seems to stand up under that kind of production, we then thought of going to the next stage, later in the same season, of getting the singers to memorise it and do it with curtains and the bare minimum of costumes.

WOOD: If the opera passes the first test, there is some hope that it will pass the second.

BRITTEN: It is too much to ask a singer to learn something which probably will be thrown away afterwards. But we have—I say in parenthesis—the goodwill of a large number of singers now who will come and will study a thing, not to memorise but from the copy, with the vague possibility that in the future there may be a chance of doing it, and will even appreciate the chance of learning the work with the composer.

POOLEY: Have you anything to say about point no. 3 in the notes—operatic training?

BRITTEN: This really is outside my province, except that, as I think you know, we have started under the Group's auspices, an Opera Studio under Miss Joan Cross.[10]

[10] Joan Cross formed the Opera School with Anne Wood in 1948, which became the National School of Opera in 1955.

POOLEY: Yes, she has talked to us.

BRITTEN: That has been, speaking selfishly as an opera administrator, of extreme value to us in this last year because she has filled with her students quite a lot of our smaller parts, which has been of value to her in that it has given her students experience, and it has been of value to us in that we have had people who were already trained and therefore were much easier to rehearse. Is there any particular thing you wish to ask on this matter?

POOLEY: We have, for instance, considered whether Glyndebourne could be used in this building up of the national opera; have you?

BRITTEN: I think it could be. It has a magnificent theatre which is empty for fifty weeks of the year—perhaps I am exaggerating and should say forty-six weeks of the year. If arrangements could be made with Mr. and Mrs. Christie, it would be extremely valuable for schools, I think; but, if I may say so, it is awfully important to find the right person to run the school before we decide that a school is necessary.

DENISON: Within the confidence of these four walls, have you any views on the quality of the product being turned out from the College and the Guildhall?

BRITTEN: If I may answer that question generally, we hear a large number of people during the year. We have a large number of letters from people applying for auditions, and we always make a point of listening to them. The standard is shockingly low. I regret to say that many of these people do come from those two institutions that you have mentioned. I believe that at the Guildhall (I am only speaking from the outside and have not expert knowledge) they have a great deal of enthusiasm, but I have been given to understand that the actual training from the production side is not perhaps as intelligent or as experienced as it might be. But I should hate to make that public.

ESHER: Sir Thomas Beecham told us that the dampness of our climate must always make it impossible for English people to sing, and that it does something to the throat.[11] Do you believe in all that?

BRITTEN: I think it is extremely witty and I think it is absolutely untrue. For one thing, I think that that gentleman himself would admit that the most resonant voices come from Wales, and Wales, I should have thought, was one of the dampest parts of this country.

ESHER: I remember that at a meeting of the [Arts Council] Drama Panel you once said that you did not think that a voice had to be of a different quality to sing at Covent Garden as compared with Sadler's Wells, and that it was only a question of training. Do you adhere to that?

[11] Sir Thomas Beecham (1869–1961), English conductor and impresario.

Britten: I believe very strongly that if the orchestra plays well enough in a big theatre—in other words, if it can play quietly enough—a gigantic, wopping great voice is not necessary. In fact, I have heard many singers who sound very loud in a small room sound very soft at Covent Garden because of the faulty training. I would not put it past the realms of possibility that a singer like Margaret Ritchie,[12] who has a tiny voice, given suitable conditions could sing extremely beautifully and effectively at Covent Garden. There are many singers very famous in this country who have not big voices but have good voices to sing at Covent Garden. The trouble, in my humble opinion, is that often at Covent Garden they are encouraged to sing more loudly than they can. They start forcing, and therefore the sound does not carry. They should not be encouraged to sing always louder, but to sing better. I have travelled quite extensively in the past few years and heard many operas and opera singers in other countries. The enormous voice is an exception in any country. Opera singers in Italy, for instance, do not always have gigantic voices. One does, of course, get the exceptional voice. But we have produced voices in this country in the past comparable in volume with voices anywhere.

Esher: I suppose you think it would be true to say that in this country our best voices are inclined to go into oratorio rather than into opera?

Britten: Yes, I should think that is true if only for one reason—that there has been more oratorio for them to go into.

Esher: There is one other question. Mr. Frank Howes[13] said that the dislike of the English language for singing was based on one or two words, like 'love', which are very inferior for singing in English to their equivalents in foreign languages; but that on the whole there was no real reason why English should not be sung and sound just as beautiful when sung as any other language. What is your view on that?

Britten: I would entirely agree with Mr. Howes that there is absolutely no reason why English should not be sung as beautifully; whether it can be sung as resonantly as Italian is a thing which is open to discussion, because the Italian language has fewer diphthongs than English has, and also a word like 'all', which is very frequent in English, is difficult to manage. But I believe it can be sung extremely well, otherwise I would not have spent my life writing vocal music and setting it in English words.

Wood: I think there are two technical problems there. One is that the singer far too rarely gives enough attention to diction. The second is that often composers do not take enough care with the beauty and subtlety of their own language. You, sir, are an exception.

[12] Margaret Ritchie (1903–69), English soprano, who created the roles of Lucia (*The Rape of Lucretia*, 1946) and Miss Wordsworth (*Albert Herring*, 1947).

[13] Frank Howes (1891–1974), English music critic, principally with *The Times* (1925–60).

POOLEY: Plunket Green[14] always gave much attention to it, even if he sang out of tune.

WOOD: He had no voice at all, but no man ever spoke English so beautifully and nobody was better heard in any condition.

BRITTEN: I agree.

ESHER: Do you feel that this opposition to the English language which one hears expressed is a prejudice?

BRITTEN: I believe that it is a prejudice, but also partly it is an experience, because the operas that have become popular in the past have been either sung in a foreign language or in a bad translation. Often a very beautiful musical phrase is sung to a very stupid verbal phrase. Therefore it is not only prejudice but experience which makes people say that they would rather hear the opera in a foreign language. I do not believe there is any fundamental reason why English should not be, as I think it always has been, a very beautiful language to sing. The vocal works of Purcell are a living protest against the other point of view.

WOOD: But the singing teacher must do his job and the composer must do his—two fundamental things which are so often forgotten. Forgive this slightly paternal attitude!

DENISON: Going back to training, have you any specific ideas of the way the Council could help to improve opportunities for training? You expressed just now views about the R.C.M. and the Guildhall, which are also the same as those which we have heard expressed on earlier occasions. It does seem a pity, because they have far better resources than a smaller organisation, like the Opera Studio—a better theatre and an orchestra, which is very important. Do you think there is any particular way in which the Council could help? We all agree that the time has not come for a big opera school.

BRITTEN: I am glad you feel that.

My feeling, again, is that if you were quite convinced in your own minds that A, B and C were ideal teachers and organisers of the school, you should go straight ahead and help it as far as possible; but if we are right in our opinions about these two institutions—that they are inadequate—it is a case where, unless you have the right person, however much help you give, the result is not satisfactory.

I believe firmly that there should be more training, because it is deplorable, often when one has a really famous or excellent singer coming to one, to find that he or she has no operatic experience and training at all. One has

[14] Harry Plunket Greene (1865–1936), Irish bass-baritone who gave premieres of works by Vaughan Williams, Stanford, Parry, and Elgar.

to start from the very beginning and teach them the acting equivalent to crotchets and quavers. One says to a person, 'Come into the room as if you are going to commit murder,' and the person will often come into the room as if he or she were going to order tea. They have not been taught. It is not only a matter of a gift; they can be taught it. There are people who are acting-deaf, or whatever you call it—resistant to the stage. But these are very rare cases. They may not always become great actors, but most people who have a feeling for music and drama can be, with training, given experience and made to be adequate.

POOLEY: That is what the Opera Studio is trying to do, is it not? The Opera Studio does not teach singing?

BRITTEN: No. We do not do that at all, although often, I am afraid, as Dr. Wood said, we wish that we could, because the teaching is so poor. It is so ignorant. The harm that is done is really deplorable. Fine voices are ruined by eccentric teachers.

WOOD: That is completely true. The singer so often wants to get pure tone without thinking of the words that the tone has to convey.

BRITTEN: I believe that fundamentally.

ESHER: When a singer sings as well as Melba did, some people say that it does not matter whether she can act or anything else.[15]

BRITTEN: Surely we agree that if Melba had been able to act, it would not have been worse; it would have been better. I do not know; alas, I was not privileged to see her.

POOLEY: Whatever the public may have stood for when you were young, Lord Esher, I do not think they would stand for these big singers just strolling about and not acting at all; do you, Mr. Britten?

BRITTEN: Whether they would or not, I do not know, but I think they should not, any more than I think they should stand for bad playing or bad scenery or bad production. I think it is our job to teach them not to stand for it.

WOOD: There is growing intelligence in these things. Melba and Clara Butt could stand up and sing 'Home Sweet Home' and the tears would run in rivulets.[16] I do not think they would run in the same way now. People have been taught something.

POOLEY: They are not so sentimental. Are there any other questions? Is there anything more you would like to tell us, Mr. Britten?

BRITTEN: Is there anything more you want to ask me, Sir?

POOLEY: I do not think so.

[15] Dame Nellie Melba (1861–1931), Australian soprano, famous for roles such as Gilda, Violetta, Mimi, and Marguérite, who appeared often at Covent Garden.

[16] Dame Clara Butt (1872–1936), English contralto, who left opera for the concert platform, giving the first performance of Elgar's *Sea Pictures* in 1899.

BRITTEN: I am a very bad speaker. I always think of what I wanted to say afterwards.

POOLEY: You have been very helpful and we are very much obliged to you.

ESHER: I do not believe you are a bad speaker. You have been very clear.

WOOD: I second that compliment.

BRITTEN: Thank you very much.

30 Verdi—A Symposium (1951)

Several years ago I had the occasion to hear a series of performances of those two old favourites, *Traviata* and *Bohème*.[1] At the time my feelings towards Verdi and Puccini were about the same—both of them efficient, with routine and apt stage-craft, but not very interesting musically. So I was not surprised when after four or five performances I never wanted to hear *Bohème* again. In spite of its neatness, I became sickened by the cheapness and emptiness of the music. On the other hand, I was surprised to find myself looking forward with excitement to each successive performance of *Traviata*. In fact, after at least a dozen performances I felt I was only just beginning to know it, to appreciate its depths of emotion, and musical strength. That was the beginning of a devotion to the music of Verdi which grows greater as I grow older, as I get to know fresh works of his, and deepen my understanding of the ones I already know.

To analyse a devotion to an art is beyond me, but here are a few observations, which I hope will explain a little why I love the music of Verdi so much.

The variety and strength of his melodies. Verdi can, of course, write the obvious square tunes, which use many repetitions of the same little phrase and work to an effective climax. These abound in the earlier operas, and are immediately endearing: I think particularly of *Parigi o cara* in *Traviata*. But he can also write the long casual lines, a succession of apparently unrelated phrases, which repeated hearings discover to have an enormous tension deep below the surface. The wonderful 'conversational' duet at the end of Act I of *Otello* is a case in point.

The perpetual 'unobviousness' of his harmonies. Verdi has the gift, which only the very greatest have had: that of writing a succession of the simplest harmonies in such a way as to sound surprising and yet 'right.' The accompaniment to the Egyptian trumpet tune in *Aida* is an extreme example of this. Then later in his life he developed a new kind of harmonic originality, which I can most easily describe by reminding the reader of the astounding string accompaniment to the Bell strokes in the last scene of *Falstaff*, and the obscure *Ave Maria* 'on an enigmatic scale' from the *Quattro Pezzi Sacri*.

His attitude to the voices on the stage and the orchestra. This seems to me to be perfectly right. The voices dominate, and the orchestra is the background—but what a background! In the later works especially, the orchestra has a range of colours wider than with any other composer. For soft shading,

Source: *Opera* 2/3 (Feb. 1951), 113–15.

[1] These were the Sadler's Wells seasons in 1943 (*La traviata*, with Pears as Alfredo) and 1944 (*La Bohème*, with Pears as Rodolfo).

the *Nile* scene in *Aida* is inimitable, and no one has ever made the orchestra roar so terrifyingly as at the beginning of *Otello*.

In the construction of his later works Verdi seems to have discovered the secret of perfection. At the beginning of his life he accepted the convention of the times in the sharp definition of the numbers, and he balanced these numbers brilliantly. Fundamentally, he never changed this attitude, but later on the numbers melt into each other with a really astonishing subtlety. The fact that the most famous composer alive to-day dismisses *Otello* and *Falstaff* 'because they are not written in numbers' shows, it seems to me, that he does not know the works very well.[2]

And so on. I have no space to write about his vitality, his breadth of humanity, his courage, his extraordinary career which developed into an almost divine serenity. I should like to end with a personal confession. I am an arrogant and impatient listener; but in the case of a few composers, a very few, when I hear a work I do not like I am convinced it is my own fault. Verdi is one of these composers.

[2] Stravinsky had talked about Verdi's 'Wagnerian' late operas in *Poetics of Music*, six 'lessons' on music delivered at Harvard College in 1939–40, which were translated into English and book form in 1947, a copy of which Britten possessed:

> Think how subtle and clinging the poison of the music drama was to have insinuated itself even into the veins of the colossus Verdi.
>
> How can we help regretting that this master of the traditional opera, at the end of a long life studded with so many authentic masterpieces, climaxed his career with *Falstaff* which, if it is not Wagner's best work, is not Verdi's best opera either? . . .
>
> Wagner's work corresponds to a tendency that is not, properly speaking, a disorder, but one which tries to compensate for a lack of order. The principle of the endless melody perfectly illustrates this tendency. It is the perpetual becoming of a music that never had any reason for starting, any more than it has any reason for ending. Endless melody thus appears as an insult to the dignity and to the very function of melody which, as we have said, is the musical intonation of a cadenced phrase. (pp. 61–2)

Stravinsky was at this time composing his own 'number opera', *The Rake's Progress*. In Robert Craft's *Conversations with Igor Stravinsky* (1959), when asked about whether he still held his earlier views, he replied: 'No. In fact, I am struck by the force, especially in *Falstaff*, with which he resisted Wagnerism, resisted or kept away from what had seized the advanced musical world' (p. 83).

31 *The Rape of Lucretia* (?1951)

In 1946 in England there was in all-the-year-round use one Opera House—Sadler's Wells (the present permanent Covent Garden Opera Company had not yet been formed[1]) and although 'Peter Grimes' had been well received the year before, it seemed unlikely that other new Operas would be put on. To some of the singers, writers and musicians involved in 'Peter Grimes' this appeared to be the moment to start a group dedicated to the creation of new works, performed with the least possible expense and capable of attracting new audiences by being toured all over the country.

We, in this group, could not afford to risk the expense of a large chorus, orchestra and heavy elaborate scenery. We had no theatre of our own and very limited financial backing, so we determined to experiment and write an Opera with only eight characters, a tiny orchestra of twelve and a simple production. John Christie of Glyndebourne generously underwrote the venture with the backing of the newly formed Arts Council. Ronald Duncan,[2] a poet with whom I had worked before, and I chose the suitable classic story of 'The Rape of Lucretia' by Tarquinius Sextus and set to work. We borrowed from many sources but principally from André Obey's fine play 'Le Viol de Lucrèce' which made great use of two choruses, male and female, acting as commentators on the action throughout, situated on thrones on either side of the stage. In the original production these were sung by Joan Cross and Peter Pears, who had sung in the original production of 'Peter Grimes' the previous year and were among the leaders of this group. The scenery and costumes were designed by John Piper, one of our best English painters. It was produced by Eric Crozier, who is also concerned in the 'Peter Grimes' performance, and conducted by Ernest Ansermet.[3]

Although the work had a mixed reception, a section of the public, hoping for a work on the grand scale and not understanding its style, the group was sufficiently encouraged to continue its work, now independently under the title of English Opera Group. The next year I wrote for it a comedy 'Albert Herring', a new version of the eighteenth century ballad opera 'The Beggar's

Source: Typescript draft, n.d. (*GB-ALb*). Possibly intended for 1951 EOG prospectus.

[1] This only occurred following the establishment of the Covent Garden Opera Trust in 1944. The first performance of this new company, *The Fairy Queen*, took place in 1946. The Covent Garden Opera Company became the Royal Opera in 1969.

[2] Ronald Duncan (1914–82), English poet and dramatist, who first collaborated with Britten in 1937 on the *Pacifist March* and later on *This Way to the Tomb* (1945), *The Rape of Lucretia* (1946), and a few smaller works.

[3] Ernest Ansermet (1883–1969), Swiss conductor who gave the first performance of *The Rape of Lucretia* at Glyndebourne and, later (1959), *Cantata academica, carmen basiliense.*

Opera' in 1948 and in 1949 an Operatic entertainment for young people, 'Let's Make An Opera!'; all these for the same kind of resources. This year we are presenting for the first time an Opera by another composer, Brian Easdale, and there are indications that other writers and composers see in the medium not a pale reflection of a great and operatic style, but something in its own right, with its own individual qualities and problems.

The form of the orchestra I originally selected and only varied very slightly since, was a quintet of wind (flute, oboe, clarinet, bassoon and horn), a quintet of strings (2 violins, viola, 'cello and double bass), harp and percussion (one spare playing many different instruments including tympani). Early on, I saw that the listeners would demand some relief from the sharp quality of the solo instruments and so I decided to use a piano to accompany the 'secco' recitatives. The piano is never used as part of the orchestra and is in fact played by the conductor. It will be seen that this will make the division into recitative and numbers clearer than has been the custom in the last hundred years or so.

One of the chief problems in performing works of this calibre is the enormous responsibility that falls on the shoulders of the individual performers. It demands a great quality of seriousness and team spirit. Luckily the English singer has this quality to a marked degree and that is the reason that this Group (in spite of its limited financial backing) has been able to exist so long, giving more than number of performances of 'Lucretia' including the Lucerne and Holland Festivals.

32 *Dido and Aeneas* (1951)

Sir,—In his letter of May 3 Dr. Geoffrey Bush states that Purcell's music to *Dido and Aeneas* has been 'carefully preserved.'[1] That is not quite the case. The only surviving manuscript of the music seems to be one written by John Travers 25 years after the death of Purcell and 40 years after the only contemporary performance of the work. Travers was not born at the time of this performance, and judging by obvious copying errors in the manuscript he cannot have been very familiar with the work, and it can never have been used for performance. The source for Dr. W. H. Cummings's Purcell Society edition was written 'probably in Purcell's time' (Dr. Cummings's words).[2] This came to light in the 1880s and has since disappeared (according to Professor E. J. Dent).[3] It differs widely from the above Travers manuscript which is preserved in the library of St. Michael's College, Tenbury. There was apparently yet another manuscript consulted by MacFarren for his edition of the work for the Musical Antiquarian Society in 1841, which again differs from the above version, actually being considerably shorter.[4] It seems that there is no trace of this manuscript to-day. 'Carefully preserved' is, therefore, a scarcely accurate phrase to use.

The musical scheme of *Dido and Aeneas* is remarkable: each scene is a complete unit containing many numbers in closely related keys following each other without pause, and ending in the same tonality or its relative major or minor as it started in (very much like his own verse-anthems and sonatas in fact). That Purcell, as Dr. Bush suggests, should suddenly at the last moment abandon this plan for one of the scenes seems to me inconceivable. For one thing, it is completely foreign to the aesthetic attitude of the time. For another, it suggests that he rated the part played by tonality in form as low as many composers do to-day. No, I am afraid that I accept the verdict of the one piece of contemporary evidence we have—the libretto—and judge that the work still remains, alas, incomplete. Until such a happy event as the discovery of the missing numbers occurs, I believe it is better to restore the original symmetry

Source: *The Times* (8 May 1951).

[1] Geoffrey Bush (1920–98), English composer, lecturer, and writer.

[2] William Hayman Cummings (1831–1915), English organist, singer, and musicologist, who was a founder of the Purcell Society for whom he edited a number of volumes of Purcell's music.

[3] Edward Dent (1876–1957), English musicologist and lecturer, professor of music at Cambridge University (1926–41).

[4] Sir George Macfarren (1813–1887), English composer and lecturer, professor of music at the Royal Academy of Music (1837–87), and editor of works by Purcell and Handel.

of the work with Purcellian material than to leave this wonderful musical building with a large hole in it.[5]

Yours faithfully,
BENJAMIN BRITTEN.
Lyric Theatre, Hammersmith.

[5] See the preface to Britten's and Holst's edition, published by Boosey & Hawkes (and reproduced below in Part V) for a discussion of Britten's solution. Britten further discussed *Dido and Aeneas* with John Amis; see Essay 50.

33 Freeman of Lowestoft (1951)

Your Worship, members of the Council, ladies and gentlemen: when I was first told that I was going to receive this great honour today, I was flattered, thrilled and touched—but also, I must confess—rather surprised. I am afraid that in my ignorance I had always imagined that Freedoms of Boroughs were given to people like politicians, statesmen and warriors—eminent and highly respectable people—and not at all such dubious creatures as artists or composers.

But although I feel myself quite unworthy of the wonderful things you've heard said about me, or read about me, this afternoon, in one way I feel I must congratulate this Borough of Lowestoft for having chosen to honour a composer to-day rather than a statesman! If a composer made such a mess of *his* work as most politicians here and abroad make of *theirs*,—well . . .

But seriously, I should like to thank the Borough of Lowestoft for the great and rare compliment it pays to Art generally, by so honouring me, a humble composer, this afternoon.

To be made Honorary Freeman of the Borough of Lowestoft is one of the loveliest things that could ever happen to me. It puts, as it were, an official seal on my connection with this little corner of England—where I was born, and where I have spent so many years of my life.

Suffolk, the birthplace and inspiration of Constable and Gainsborough, the loveliest of English painters;[1] the home of Crabbe, that most English of poets;[2] Suffolk, with its rolling, intimate countryside; its heavenly Gothic churches, big and small; its marshes, with those wild sea-birds; its grand ports and its little fishing villages. I am firmly rooted in this glorious county. And I proved this to myself when I once tried to live somewhere else. Even when I visit countries as glorious as Italy, as friendly as Denmark or Holland—I am always home-sick, and glad to get back to Suffolk.

I think that my work shows this too, for of the five operas I have written, three actually take place in East Suffolk. *Let's Make an Opera* is set in Iken, not far from Saxmundham,—*Peter Grimes* in what is called in the opera the Borough, but is really Aldeburgh, where Crabbe worked,—*Albert Herring* in a nameless Suffolk town which could be anywhere where there are dictatorial old ladies or backward boys—perhaps even in Lowestoft.

Source: *Tempo* 21 (Autumn 1951), 3–5. Speech given in Lowestoft, Britten's birthplace, on 28 July 1951.

[1] John Constable (1776–1837), English painter; Thomas Gainsborough (1727–88), English painter.

[2] George Crabbe (1754–1842), English poet, author of the poem 'Peter Grimes' (from *The Borough*).

I treasure these roots, my Suffolk roots; roots are especially valuable nowadays, when so much we love is disappearing or being threatened, when there is so little to cling to.

Ladies and Gentlemen, as you know, I lived here in Lowestoft for a long time. I am sure many of you knew me well, and I am sure I knew many of you. But I haven't actually lived in the town, nor, alas, visited it very often recently and I am sure I must have changed a great deal. Now, as you have elected me Freeman of your Borough, I think I'd better tell you a little of what I am like today—so that you should be quite clear what kind of responsibility you have undertaken!

When I say—tell you what I am like—I don't mean silly things like how I still enjoy swimming and playing tennis, how I still like my cold baths in the morning, or how old I am growing (you can see that for yourselves), but serious things, like what I think and believe my duty to be.

I am first and foremost an *artist*—and as an artist I want to serve the community.

In other days, artists were the servants of institutions like the Church, or of Society in the sense of private patrons. In these days, with a few notable exceptions, the Church seems indifferent to serious art, and taxation has largely ruled out private patrons. And the artist today has become the servant of the whole community. It is the State that commissions large paintings, and Grand Operas; it is the guarantors of five guineas or less who keep our Festivals or small Music Societies alive.

Today it is the community, or all of us in our own small ways, that orders the artist about. And I do not think that is such a bad thing either. It is not a bad thing for an artist to try to serve all sorts of different people.

I personally enjoy writing pieces for special occasions—music for children or amateurs, music for films, or the theatre, of [*sic*] the B.B.C.—trying to pour into these restricted bottles my best wine.

I should like to add here that—contrary to the general impression—it isn't a bad thing for an artist to have to work to order. Any artist worth his salt has always ideas knocking about in his head, and an invitation to write something can often direct these ideas into a concrete form and shape. Of course, it can sometimes be difficult when one doesn't feel in the mood, but perhaps that's good for one, too!—anyhow, composers, (like other people) can be horribly lazy, and often this is the only way that they can be made to produce something!

Anyhow, when you hear people saying that music written to order can't possibly be good, just remind them of *Dido and Aeneas* (written for a girls' school), the *Matthew Passion*, the *Marriage of Figaro*, *Aida*—and all the rest of them written to order.

For all these reasons, I can never manage to throw up my hands in horror quite as high as other people, when I hear stories of Soviet composers, ordered about by their government—in principle, it's just the same as Palestrina, ordered about all his life by the Church, Handel ordered about by kings and princes, Wagner ordered about by eccentric, if well-meaning patrons.[3] The rub comes when it is impossible to please these patrons when the artist sees beyond them, which often happened then, and often happens now.

Artists are artists because they have an extra sensitivity—a skin less, perhaps, than other people; and the great ones have an uncomfortable habit of being right about many things, long before their time. Think of the observations on life of Goethe, Milton, Leonardo, or Blake—the wonderful truths that are in the letters of Verdi, or Keats—or FitzGerald,[4] for instance. Some one once called artists the 'antennae' of Society—and I think they were right.

So—and this is the plea—when you hear of an artist saying or doing something strange or unpopular, think of that extra sensitivity—that skin less; consider a moment whether he may not after all be seeing a little more clearly than ourselves, whether he is really as irresponsible as he seems, before you condemn him. Remember for a moment Mozart in his pauper's grave; Dostoievsky[5] sent to Siberia; Blake[6] ridiculed as a madman, Lorca[7] shot by the Fascists in Spain. It is a proud privilege to be a creative artist, but it can also be painful. Great artists have been destroyed by their consciences.

But I don't want to depress you, so I will end my remarks on a gayer note. Some of you may remember, more than thirty years ago, a very small boy, dressed in skin-coloured tights, with madly curly hair, trying desperately to remember the lines spoken by Tom the water-baby, sitting on the lap of Mrs. Do-as-you-would-be-done-by (played on this occasion by his own mother)—*on this very stage*.[8]

That little boy never dreamed that he would ever appear again, on the stage of the Sparrows' Nest, and be honoured like this by his own townspeople. He cannot describe how touched and happy he feels to stand like this before you. I thank you all from the bottom of my heart.[9]

3 See Essay 66 and ensuing correspondence for English and Soviet responses to such views.

4 Edward Fitzgerald (1809–83), English writer.

5 Feodor Dostoevsky (1821–81), Russian novelist.

6 William Blake (1757–1827), English writer and artist. Britten set his texts in the *Songs and Proverbs of William Blake* (1965), written for Dietrich Fischer-Dieskau.

7 Federico García Lorca (1899–1936), Spanish poet and dramatist.

8 A picture of this is reproduced in Donald Mitchell (comp.), *Pictures from a Life* (London: Faber & Faber, 1978), pl. no. 15.

9 The speech was originally given on 28 July, part of which was recycled in an article for *Adam* 20 (1952) and which included these final two paragraphs which do not appear in the version printed above:

> Before Beethoven music served things greater than itself—the glory of God or the glory of the State, for example. After Beethoven the composer was the centre of his own universe. The romantics became so intensely personal that it looked as though we were

going to reach a point at which the composer would be the only man capable of understanding his own music. Then came Picasso and Stravinsky. They loosened up painting and music, freed them from the tyranny of the purely personal. They passed from manner to manner as a bee passed from flower to flower.

I do not see why I should lock myself inside a purely personal idiom. It is largely a matter of when one was born. If I had been born in 1813 instead of 1913 I should have been a romantic, primarily concerned to express my personality in music. Whereas now I am contented to write in the manner best suited to the words, theme, or dramatic situation I happen to be handling.

The Rise of English Opera

I welcome this finely detailed study of English Opera. English opera always seems to me, perhaps too hopefully, the Cinderella of the arts. This book makes it quite clear why the poor girl is having to wait so long for her handsome Prince. The three things English opera needs, as does any opera, are business organisation (including cash), public goodwill, and composers to write new operas. Never yet in this country have these three things coincided. Mr. White describes the launching of many admirable enterprises, good teams of singers engaged (there always seems to be good material available if not the good artistic direction to develop it)—and then the public response fails.[1] We read of good composers with exciting ideas for operas—and the backers are not impressed. And we read of flourishing seasons failing, because there are no new operas. It makes gloomy if fascinating reading!

But why should anyone mind?—who cares if there is English opera? We are told so often that Italian and German, even Russian and French, opera is superior to ours (true, in spite of *Dido and Aeneas*), and people have been known to say that the English language is ugly when sung (quite untrue, although it is more difficult to manage than, say, Italian). All the same, if we continue to perform opera, and to perform it in a language that most of the audience does not understand, one of the essentials of opera is lost. It is not enough to know *roughly* what is happening at a particular moment; if one thinks with what infinite precision a Mozart or a Verdi points the smallest word or tiniest shade of emotion, that will be clear. For this reason I am an unrepentant supporter of the regular seasons of opera in England being sung in English. But, however brilliant the translators' work may be, obviously it is not ideal; the composers' prosody must necessarily suffer, and the character of the opera change.

So ideally then we must have English operas, settings of English libretti by English composers. Although this book certainly records hundreds of such operas, it seems either that the composers were not very gifted, or that the more gifted were not wisely encouraged. Precious few of their operas are still in the repertoire. All the same, one wonders whether there may not be one or two satisfactory ones among them all. After all, the operatic repertoire of today is terribly narrow; only prejudice or undue box-office caution can be keeping out the masterpieces we already know exist. Let us hope, then, that people will

Source: Introduction to Eric Walter White, *The Rise of English Opera* (London: John Lehmann, 1951), 13–14.

[1] Quite apart from his association with Britten and the English Opera Group through the Arts Council, White was a music historian and early Britten biographer.

be encouraged by Mr. White's industry and persuasive power to explore some of these forgotten works, and that their efforts will not be wasted.

One final point, a selfish one, because I am going to speak for the composer. Writing operas is a very tricky business; only a great gift coupled with hard-won experience can produce enduring masterpieces. Today few composers can acquire the experience, even granted they have the gift. Therefore, let the managements and the public (not to mention the Press) be a little lenient about their early efforts. We have no small opera houses in the provinces in England where their immature works can be tried out—they must face the full glare of metropolitan publicity. Perhaps, in the feeble, gawky show we are watching, are hidden the seeds of some valuable operatic talent. Do not let us entirely crush them with damning criticism, and let us resist the opportunity for brilliant wit at their expense. After all, Mozart had to start with *Apollo and Hyacinth*,[2] and Verdi composed operas almost annually for fifty years before they achieved the dazzling perfection of *Otello* and *Falstaff*.

[2] *Apollo et Hyacinthus*, K. 38, was composed in 1767 when the composer was 11.

35 Arnold Schoenberg (1951)

I mourn the death of Schoenberg. Every serious composer today has felt the effect of his courage, single-mindedness, and determination, and has profited by the clarity of his teaching. The world is a poorer place now this giant is no more.

Source: 'Obituary: Arnold Schoenberg', *Music Survey* 4/1 (Oct. 1951), 314. Other contributors included Humphrey Searle, Hans Keller, Erwin Stein, Donald Mitchell, and Karl Rankl.

36 Variations on a Critical Theme (1952)

I can well remember my first contact with the critics. I was about 17 and three part songs of mine had been given at a London theatre concert.[1] They were written as a student's exercise, with the voice parts in strict canon. The first was amiably grotesque, the second atmospheric in a cool way, the third lumpily 'folky.' The only written criticism of this performance damned them entirely—as being obvious copies of Walton's three Façade Songs.[2] Now anyone who is interested can see for himself that this is silly nonsense. The Walton Songs are brilliant and sophisticated in the extreme—mine could scarcely have been more childlike and naive, with not a trace of parody throughout. It is easy to imagine the damping effect of this first notice on a young composer. I was furious and dismayed because I could see there was not a word of truth in it. I was also considerably discouraged. No friendliness—no word of encouragement—no perception. Was this the critical treatment which one was to expect all one's life? A gloomy outlook. I decided to avoid reading critics from that day onwards. And so I have as far as possible. Alas, there are always friends to send one press notices: 'Have you seen this; of course I don't agree but . . .'; or that amiable vagueness which sends one the most virulent attacks: 'Sure you would like to see this most interesting account of . . .'

In 20 years my critics do not seem to have changed much. Of course some have been more welcoming (about 50 per cent, at a guess) but practically all have been unobservant if not actually inane. I can say with honesty that in every piece I have written, in spite of hard work, there are still passages where I have not quite solved problems. Not once have these passages been noticed, nor of course suggestions made as to how I could have improved them. In the notices I have read I have been spared the classic cases of dishonesty (criticisms written when the writer was not present for instance), but I have had an opera of mine simultaneously reviewed well in an American paper and badly in an English—by the same critic; I have had a work enthusiastically welcomed, and then completely damned a few days later by the same writer (perhaps not dishonest this, but confusing for his readers); I have had a work and a performance judged on a dress rehearsal forgetting that it really *was* a rehearsal after which we made some changes, and forgetting that singers do not usually sing their best at 10 a.m.

Source: *Opera* 3/3 (Mar. 1952), 144–6.

[1] Three Two-part Songs (1932) were first performed at the Ballet Club (Mercury Theatre) on 12 December 1932 when Britten was 19. They were published by OUP in the same year.

[2] The critique was actually no worse than condescending: 'Benjamin Britten's setting of some of Walter de la Mare's poems for two-part female voices was good from one who, I believe, is only 19; even though they were reminiscent in a quite peculiar degree of Walton's latest songs which were heard recently elsewhere.' ('C.D.', *Music Lover*, 17 Dec. 1932.)

But these are not important, one gets riff-raff in any profession. It is the generally low level of competence that is worrying. What is one to say, for example, about a critic in these pages last month, who confessed he had been bewildered by his first hearing of my last two big scale works (The *Spring Symphony* and *Billy Budd*), works which certainly appeared to make no bewildering effect on the first night audiences.[3] Maybe that is honest; but if a critic cannot react as spontaneously as the average member of a large audience, he had better not be a critic.

Now does this all matter, does it affect the artist in any way? One remembers that Schnabel,[4] the greatest pianist I ever heard, usually had tepid reactions from the Press (even after his death)—and he did pretty well. But perhaps the standard of piano playing today might be a little higher if he had been recommended as a model instead of some tawdry virtuoso. We must remember that some of these phrases stick in the minds of people not *able* to hear or judge for themselves—we can't worry about the people who *won't* judge for themselves (incidentally I heard recently, of a woman who learned a certain critic's phrases off by heart in order to appear knowledgeable and witty herself—but that's an extreme case!) We are admittedly not quite as far gone as New York where, I gather, bad notices can kill a play or opera stone dead; here they can at least wriggle a little, though again one must remember that the damping effect of a notice can slow down the progress of a work considerably. I remember that the reactions of the *Times* critic to the first performance of one of my operas caused a foreign management who had booked the opera to try to cancel the contract.[5] Luckily we found a favourable notice in the *Daily Mirror* or *News of the World* which reassured him, so off we went with our opera and had a great success.

If it is necessary to have critics, as I am repeatedly assured it is, what is to be done about them? I have one or two suggestions. I do not think I need go into details why it is impossible to have reasoned judgment of a new work or

[3] Scott Goddard (1895–1965), English music critic. See his response below.

[4] Artur Schnabel (1882–1951), Austrian pianist and composer.

[5] Peter Diamand (1913–98), Dutch artistic administrator, director of the Holland Festival (1947–65) and Edinburgh Festival (1966–78), friend of Britten's, did try to pull out of presenting *Albert Herring* in Holland after reading Frank Howses's review in *The Times* (21 June 1947):

> . . . But the animation of the comedy does not communicate itself to the listener because the music does not engage his heart. Mr. Britten is still pursuing his old problem of seeing how much indigestible material he can dissolve in music. Last year in *The Rape of Lucretia* he tried ancient history as a sermon; this year he essays French farce and psychological caricature. A salacious French story of Maupassant is translated by Eric Crozier into a rustic English comedy of the way a bumpkin kicks over the traces, and the result is a charade. . . .

a serious performance in day to day criticism.[6] This being so, I suggest this function be passed to ordinary journalists, trained to give a straight-forward account of the concert—what it consisted of, the reaction of the audience, the size of it, and the dresses of the ladies, etc. The reasoned judgments should be written by a serious critic and must be allowed to wait for a week or a month (why not a *Times* Monthly Musical Supplement?), and then given adequate space. I think for instance there ought to be a gentleman's agreement that the critic has no less space than is taken up by the very expensive concert and opera advertisements (*Daily Telegraph*, please note). Adequate space is necessary for the critic to give himself away. Any idiot can get away with two sentences about a concert ('Miss X's interpretations of Schubert were all wrong. The new work by Mr. Y was brilliant but empty'), but eighteen inches will show him in his true colours.

Who are these serious critics to be? At the risk of appearing Irish, I say at once—not critics. There should be no such profession as criticism. Musicologists, of course, are quite different, and this is a sadly neglected profession in this country—but there should definitely be no regular critics. Criticism must be a side line. To go through life living off other people's work clearly has too degrading an effect. Therefore let the composers, the performers, the publishers, the concert promoters, the musical administrators, the intelligent amateurs too perhaps, take time off occasionally to write reasoned judgments on the work of their colleagues. I have no fear that it will lead to undue bias or jealousy; on the whole, the better the artist, the more he understands the problems of his colleagues and so will realise what they are trying to do, and be sympathetic towards it. There is much less risk of bias here than in the sourness of the *failed* artist who has had to turn to criticism to live. Again, in giving judgments the all important thing is 'truth,' and that can often fly out of the window if the critic is worrying about his career, about his editor's or seniors' reactions to his writings, about the memorable or witty quality of his phrases. Again, his reactions must remain fresh; he must continue to love the art he is writing about (my doctor has ordered me to give up the *Manchester Guardian* because of the lowering effect reading its London Dramatic critic has on me;[7] he clearly hates the theatre. And I wouldn't dream of buying *The Listener*: that ear is too withered).[8]

[6] Original footnote: How's a snap judgment to have critical value? On the other hand no amount of time spent by the musically blind, poring over scores will lead to anything but sure failure.

[7] Philip Hope-Wallace (1911–79), music and drama critic for the *Manchester Guardian* from 1946 to 1976.

[8] Dyneley Hussey (1893–1972), music critic for *The Listener* from 1946 to 1960, author of books on Mozart, Verdi, and opera.

Having decided on who should criticise, here are one or two requests. Please let us know by what *standards* we are being judged. 'For a first opera—a jolly good shot; but for an old hand—not so good.' 'For an amateur performance—very creditable', but let us be clear (for everyone's sake) that it was an amateur performance. Please, let us have *real* knowledge, not this half-learning which prevents a person reacting in the simple way, and yet doesn't give him technical assistance to understanding. Again, please let us have humility. We are not writing or performing for the critic, let him remember. Often his presence is a financial nuisance because his seat might have been sold to the public. And it is the public we are there for; they are open minded and, if we can deliver the goods and have the goods to deliver, friendly and sympathetic as well.[9]

[9] Scott Goddard replied in the *News Chronicle* (12 Mar. 1952), citing alongside Britten's complaints other articles in the edition of *Opera* that was dedicated to the topic of music criticism:

> Mr. Britten is angry and I am sorry. But the sorrow of a music critic is of less moment than the anger of a composer, and I will get as quickly as I can away from my side of the matter.
>
> Mr. Britten takes me to task for having owned I was bewildered when I first heard his Spring Symphony and his opera Billy Budd, and needed two tries at each before I could be sure of understanding them.
>
> 'Maybe,' he says, 'that is honest.' Maybe Mr. Britten will realise one day how honest. Then he may feel able to say so without that grudging qualification.
>
> I remember how moved I was by those two works of his. And how I felt the responsibility of writing about them. And I recall, too, that I told him this on one of the rare occasions we have met.
>
> That was in Amsterdam after a rehearsal of the Spring Symphony. He laughed; with me, I thought, though maybe he laughed at me. In any case I thought he sympathised in my dilemma. Maybe I was wrong.
>
> He pursues the matter further, saying: 'If a critic cannot react as spontaneously as the average member of a large audience, he had better not be a critic.'
>
> My spontaneous reaction to that, since I know nothing of this average member, is to quote from Lord Harewood's editorial: 'The *ex-cathedra* form of judgment . . . is one of the worst dangers which beset the critic.'
>
> Mr. Britten's judgment of our situation, his editor's and mine, when as critics we first hear a new opera, does not avoid that particular danger.
>
> He tells us further that he would like to have first nights covered by 'ordinary journalists, trained to give a straight-forward account of the concert . . . what it consisted of, the reaction of the audience, the size of it, and the dresses of the ladies.'
>
> I have no quarrel with that, but I pity the poor journalist. There are pitfalls even in describing the event.
>
> Size of audience means nothing unless you give the seating capacity of the theatre. As for the audience's reaction, I suppose Mr. Britten means the applause.
>
> What does first night applause mean? Relief that the show is over? An uneasy suspicion that one has to applaud because one was invited?
>
> A fellow-feeling for artists who have done their best with a weak work, or with a composer whose work has been let down by poor performance?

The journalist who has to assess the reaction of that audience will have his work cut out for him. There will be little time or energy left to describe the women's dresses.

A couple of pages further on the air clears in Sir Kenneth Clark's article dealing with the claims of the amateur upon the critic.

Sir Kenneth realises more clearly than Mr. Britten what the critic's task is and from his own experience in other arts he suggests how we should go about it.

Yet he, too, seems to have no idea of the crippling limitations imposed by a famine of newsprint.

And when he suggests 'quality of applause' as a means of gauging an audience's intelligence I must own I cannot follow his reasoning.

Nevertheless, his article deserves careful reading. It is good-humoured, it sets out to be helpful and it has the authority of a master among critics.

37 Opera Diary: *The Marriage of Figaro* (1952)

Covent Garden. *The Marriage of Figaro* (February 8).

I left this performance of *The Marriage of Figaro* overwhelmed anew by the enchantment of Mozart's score. What gaiety and brilliance, what passion and tension, what characterisation, what construction (I say this last deliberately because I for one can never understand comments on the inadequacy of the last act, even with the two clumsy cuts that are traditionally made—but more of that later). Now, I have attended many performances of this miracle in the last ten years or so, when I have been disappointed and irritated: Mozart is notoriously the easiest composer to spoil. My pleasure in this performance was caused principally by the extraordinary precision and beauty of the orchestral playing. The Covent Garden orchestra is now our finest orchestra (think of its playing in *Wozzeck* too), but obviously a conductor of genius and energy like Kleiber is essential for it to produce its best.[1] I must confess that once or twice I felt Kleiber curbed his natural reactions to the music, probably through a mistaken desire to be 'classical'; this deprived the overture of some of its delight and the last great aria of Figaro of much of its bitterness. Something also went wrong with the tempi relations of the last finale. But it is wrong to complain when so much of it was so right and so well studied. One quality which particularly delighted me was his treatment of the recitatives. I am so bored with the 'gabble' treatment they usually get (Glyndebourne, please note). These had real character and variety of tempo, and so one could hear the tunes which are embedded in them. It was a mistake, though, to put the accompanying piano away in a box, miles from the singers, so that occasionally the synchronisation was not as neat as it might have been.

So far we have only talked about what went on in the orchestral pit, and truly much of Mozart's genius lies there; but the stage is also important! Well, it was visually pretty drab; Gerard's sets had not been improved by having bits cut out of them,[2] nor had Peter Brook's production (which incidentally was not credited in the programme—no one had apparently produced).[3] But all the same there was energy and warmth in the acting, principally from Geraint Evans,[4] who was vocally and dramatically in every way a convincing Figaro: his

Source: *Opera* 3/5 (May 1952), 308–9.

[1] Erich Kleiber (1890–1956), Austrian conductor, father of Carlos.

[2] Rolf Gérard (b. 1909), British stage designer of German birth, Bing's principal designer at the Met from 1950 to 1970.

[3] Peter Brook (b. 1925), English director, famous Shakespearean, and director of productions at Covent Garden 1948–9.

[4] Sir Geraint Evans (1922–92), Welsh baritone, who made his Covent Garden debut in 1948. He sang Lord Mountjoy in the first production of *Gloriana* the following year.

voice and looks stole the show for me—one sympathised with Figaro throughout; and also from Sylvia Fisher,[5] whose beautiful voice and touching personality suffused the part of the Countess with great warmth. She was not at all helped by an unfortunate dress (a producer should have avoided this) but in spite of this her appearance was moving and sincere. Susanna (Ruth Guldbaek[6]) was, I suspect, having trouble in singing English, which may have accounted for her voice, especially on top, seeming not to be quite 'well placed.' Although her performance had charm and lacked most of the conventional Susanna whimsy, one would have thought an equally good performance might have been given by a regular member of the company.

Max Worthley[7] sang and acted brightly and neatly, but without a producer the part of Basilio cannot be expected to be convincing. Small parts like this must be worked out and dove-tailed with the bigger ones. The lack of a firm hand on the production side was clearly also the reason for the buffoonery which Bruce Boyce indulged in as the Count.[8] He had clearly misunderstood the part, and his buffoonery was not confined to his acting and make-up, because he so often distorted the musical line in an effort to be comic—a most dangerous practice in Mozart's music, which, like all serious art, evaporates when the line is lost. I was disappointed in this since I know how fine an artist Boyce can be, an opinion borne out on one occasion in this performance, at the supremely moving moment of *Contessa perdona* in Act IV, when he sang simply and beautifully. Another weakness was the Cherubino. I have admired Monica Sinclair's musicianship and style in the past, but I feel she was wrongly cast as the page.[9] Why a mezzo-soprano for this? Surely what is needed is a soprano who has a darkish voice with an edge to it to suggest the boyishness, and who can manage the high *tessitura* of much of the part. On this night I really suffered for Miss Sinclair during *Non so piu*.

Rhydderch Davies[10] (Antonio) was firm vocally and did not overdo the

[5] Sylvia Fisher (1910–96), Australian soprano, who made her Covent Garden debut in the same year as Evans, 1948, later becoming its leading soprano. She later sang in several Britten operas with the EOG (1963–71) and gave the first performance of the revised *Gloriana* (Elizabeth I) at Sadler's Wells in 1966.

[6] Ruth Guldbaek, Danish soprano.

[7] Max Worthley (1913–99), Australian tenor, who created the role of Clem in *The Little Sweep* (1949), Nimming Ned in *The Beggar's Opera* (1948) as well as a Sailor in Britten's and Holst's realization of *Dido and Aeneas* (1951).

[8] Bruce Boyce (1910–96), Canadian baritone and teacher, who gave the first performance in 1950 of *The Beggar's Opera* rescored for a baritone Macheath.

[9] Monica Sinclair (1925–2002), English contralto, who created the role of Lady Essex in *Gloriana* and who performed as a Niece in the 1949 Covent Garden production of *Peter Grimes*.

[10] Rhydderch Davies, Welsh baritone who created the role of the City Crier in *Gloriana* and the First Mate in *Billy Budd* (1951).

obvious comic business, as alas, did Edith Coates[11] as Marcellina, to the detriment of her often beautiful music. Howell Glynne[12] (Bartolo) sang well, but, as many of the others did, suffered from the lack of an intelligent producer. David Tree[13] (Don Curzio) produced miracles of stuttering, but I prefer (perhaps illogically) my stuttering confined to the recitatives.

In spite of these qualifications, the performance allowed the music to speak in no uncertain manner. Because it was so well studied musically and so beautifully played, the work shone with an unusual radiance. This opera is exactly considered from every point of view, I therefore distrust the tradition of cutting Basilio's and Marcellina's arias in the last act; they are both of them admittedly very difficult to sing (it would take an exceptional mezzo-soprano to sing *Il capro e la capretta*) and need tactful staging, but could we not once give Mozart the benefit of the doubt and include them? If not, I suggest we work out the cuts better. I found it embarrassing that both these characters came forward at the climactic points in the preceding recitatives and then . . . nothing . . . a hole. It felt like the old prep-school trick of having one's chair removed as one was about to sit down.

11 Edith Coates (1908–83), English mezzo-soprano, who created the roles of Auntie in *Peter Grimes*, and A Housewife in *Gloriana*.

12 Howell Glynne (1906–69), Welsh bass.

13 David Tree (1902–73), Welsh tenor, who created the role of Master of Ceremonies in *Gloriana* and Squeak in *Billy Budd*.

38 Three Premieres (1954)

It was in the last days of the war, at a performance of *The Messiah* in Westminster Abbey, that I first heard Kathleen Ferrier sing.[1] I was impressed immediately by the nobility and beauty of her presence, and by the warmth and deep range of her voice. It seemed to me (and seems so still) that hers was one of the very few voices that could tackle with success the low *tessitura* of that alto part. So, a few months later, in the autumn of 1945, when we were looking for a contralto to play the name part in a new opera I was writing, *The Rape of Lucretia*, and she was mentioned as a possibility, I enthusiastically welcomed the idea. Peter Pears, singing with her a few days later, suggested it to her, and she tentatively agreed. She was nervous about learning a new long, modern part; nervous, above all, about her acting—I think she had never been on the stage, certainly not the professional stage, in her life. She was persuaded, especially since the rehearsal period was going to be long and calm, and soon she was keenly involved, greedily absorbing each new bit of the score as it came along, and helping in the arrangements too; it was she, for instance, who suggested Nancy Evans to play the other Lucretia (we were preparing a 'run' of the opera, and so two alternating casts were necessary).[2] Thus in no time her warm friendliness and keenness on any serious artistic matter made her a member of the 'family' which was planning this operatic venture. The 'family' consisted of such as Ronald Duncan, who was writing the libretto of the opera; John Piper, designing the scenery and costumes; Eric Crozier, producing; Joan Cross and Peter Pears singing, with Kathleen, the principal parts; and myself writing the music.

As the rehearsals progressed during June 1946, at John Christie's little opera house at Glyndebourne in Sussex, Kathleen's diffidence as an actress began to disappear—not entirely, as she was easily crushed by a cutting remark. Vocally she was always secure, although the violent hysterics and the short transition to the long, soft line of the 'Flower Song' in the last scene of all had to be 'managed', and to be studied carefully under the devoted guidance of the conductor, Ernest Ansermet. I think we were all aware that a star was rising

Source: Neville Cardus (ed.), *Kathleen Ferrier: A Memoir* (London: Hamish Hamilton, 1954), 54–61.

[1] Kathleen Ferrier (1912–53), English contralto. She created the role (along with Nancy Evans) of Lucretia in 1946 and gave the first performance, with Peter Pears, of Canticle II 'Abraham and Isaac', 1952). The performance of which Britten speaks was her London debut, which triggered her career taking off.

[2] Nancy Evans (1915–2000), English mezzo-soprano, who created the role of Nancy in *Albert Herring* (1947) and gave the first performance of *A Charm of Lullabies* (1947), which Britten dedicated to her.

among us, although no one could have behaved less like a star than Kathleen did; in fact, her close friendship and friendly rivalry with the other Lucretia (Nancy Evans), remains one of the happiest memories of that time.

She was naturally nervous on the first night (12 July), and in the interval, in spite of the great beauty of her personality and her lovely singing, the act was considered to have gone to the male and female chorus. But at the end, her nobility and the deep pathos of her 'confession' brought Lucretia, the tragic Roman matron, right to the fore.

Many performances of the work were given that summer and autumn: two weeks (if I remember rightly) in Glyndebourne, then a tour of the provinces, with a week each in Manchester, Liverpool, Edinburgh, Glasgow and Oxford, and a season of two weeks back in London at Sadler's Wells Theatre. All this time Kathleen's Lucretia grew steadily in stature, always vocally richer, and her acting slowly more relaxed, until it became one of the most memorable of contemporary opera creations. She was always least happy about the 'hysterics' I mentioned before, partly because it was the least close to her own nature, and the part was in *tessitura* very high for her. One note at the climax, a top A, was quite out of her reach, so I wrote her an *ossia* of an F sharp. At one of the last performances at Glyndebourne, listening from the side of the stage, I was startled to hear her let out a ringing top A. Afterwards she confessed that she had got excited, forgotten her caution, and the F sharp, and was equally startled to hear herself singing an A (the first she had ever sung in public, I think I remember her saying). After that it was always the A, and I crossed the F sharp out of the score.

The season ended with a visit to Holland, with performances in Amsterdam, and The Hague. It was her first visit abroad and she enjoyed it all hugely. Everything fascinated her—the people, the food and drink (the Dutch gin!), the remarkable countryside, also some of the sanitary arrangements. She managed to project a stream of hot water from the hand-shower through the window of her bathroom into the street below. After this visit, in which she made such a deep impression, she was frequently to return to Holland. She eventually had almost as many friends in that country as in England, and her death caused widespread distress there.

In the summer of 1947 she again repeated her beautiful performance with us at Glyndebourne, but after that her concentration on oratorio and *Lieder* made her less available for opera. But she kept her affection for the part, and when, for the English Opera Group season at the Lyric, Hammersmith, in the Festival year, 1951, we asked her to play Lucretia again for us, she happily agreed. Alas, a few weeks before the season was due to start she had to have the first of the tragic series of operations, so Nancy Evans took over the part.

* * * *

During 1948, at the invitation of Serge Koussevitsky [*sic*], I was writing a large-scale work for voices and orchestra; this was the Spring Symphony, and it was commissioned to have its first performance at the Tanglewood Festival in New England the next summer. It was the first big non-operatic work I had written for many years. Therefore, since I was so keen to hear it and I could not go to the U.S.A. for the performance, Koussevitsky generously let it first be performed in Europe a few weeks earlier, on 9 July, at the Holland Festival.[3] There were three solo parts—soprano, contralto, and tenor—and I had Kathleen very much in mind when I wrote the long, serious setting of a poem by W. H. Auden, which is the central piece of the work.[4] Her beautiful dark voice and serious mien, together with her impeccable intonation, made a great impression in this sombre movement. Also memorable in this most wonderful of first performances (played superbly by the Concertgebouw Orchestra under Van Beinum[5]) was her gaiety in the trio of birds in 'Spring, the sweet Spring', along with Jo Vincent[6] and Peter Pears.

* * * *

The third and last close artistic association I had with Kathleen Ferrier was perhaps the loveliest of all, a kind of Indian summer. It was in the early days of 1952, the period after her first serious operation, and when we dared to hope that the miracle had happened, that she might possibly be getting well. It was a series of concerts organized for the funds of the English Opera Group—which, after all, she helped to launch by her wonderful Lucretia performances in 1946 and 1947—to be given in London and the provinces by her, Peter Pears, and myself. It was a programme which we all could enjoy: early English songs, including some of Morley's canzonets, ravishingly sung, some big Schubert *Lieder*, some folk-songs, grave and gay, ending up with the comic duet 'The Deaf Woman's Courtship', which Kathleen sang in a feeble, cracked voice, the perfect reply to Peter's magisterial roar. A masterpiece of humour, which had the audience rocking, but never broke the style of the rest of the concert.

To complete the programme I wrote a Canticle for the three of us, a setting of a part of one of the Chester Miracle plays—*Abraham and Isaac*.[7] It was principally a dialogue for contralto (the boy) and tenor (the father), although on occasions the voices joined together to sing the words of God, and there was a little *Envoi* in canon.

3 First performance was actually 14 July.

4 'Out on the lawn'.

5 Eduard van Beinum (1900–59), Dutch conductor.

6 Jo(hanna) Vincent (1898–1989), leading Dutch soprano, who along with Ferrier and Pears gave the first performance of the *Spring Symphony* (1949).

7 Canticle II 'Abraham and Isaac' (1952).

We performed this programme in Nottingham, Birmingham, Manchester, Bristol, and Liverpool, a broadcast, and at the Victoria & Albert Museum in London, the happiest of concerts. Everything seemed to go well, with big friendly audiences. *Abraham and Isaac*, when performed with such sincerity and charm, pleased the public. Only in Nottingham was there a cloud, but we did not realize the size of it. Kathleen seemed to trip and slightly wrench her back walking off the platform and she was in pain for some of the time. It turned out to be a recurrence of her terrible illness, but no one suspected anything—or perhaps she did and said nothing.

We all determined to repeat the concerts the next year, to write a companion piece to *Abraham and Isaac*, but operations and long and painful convalescences intervened and we had to give them up. But there was one more performance of the Canticle. Kathleen spent some days in Aldeburgh in June 1952, while the Festival was going on. She was convalescing but managed to go to quite a few concerts, lectures, and operas. Each morning my sister would walk along to the Wentworth Hotel, where she was staying, would go through the programmes with her, and she would make her choice for the day. She became a familiar and much-loved figure in the town. Finally, towards the end of the week, she joined Peter and me in our yearly recital in a touching performance of *Abraham and Isaac*. Many people have said they will never forget the occasion: the beautiful church, her beauty and incredible courage, and the wonderful characterization of her performance, including every changing emotion of the boy Isaac—the boyish nonchalance of the walk up to the fatal hill, his bewilderment, his sudden terror, his touching resignation to his fate—the simplicity of the Envoi, but, above all, combining with the other voice, the remote and ethereal sounds as 'God speaketh'. In the short run-through before the concert Kathleen failed to make her entry in one passage. Apologizing and laughing, she said she was fascinated by Peter's skill in eliding an 'l' and an 'm' in a perfect *legato*—'Farewell, my dear son'. She really must practise that, she said, she never could do it as well.

One of our most determined plans was to make a long-playing record of this programme. Several dates were fixed at the studio, but each one had to be cancelled because of new developments of her illness. Finally, the engineers inspected her bedroom—acoustically possible, they said. So we planned to go along one evening to record the Morley canzonets, the wonderful dialogue *Corydon and Mopsa* of Purcell, which we had all loved doing, the folk-songs, and *Abraham and Isaac*. This time it seemed that there could be no hitch; although bedridden, her voice had lost nothing; the record was even announced. But another operation, the last, intervened, and in a few months Kathleen was dead.

There seemed to be one more chance, even so, of perpetuating what was for me one of her most delightful performances. We had made a broadcast of this concert, and this had been recorded and repeated several times. Could this not be issued commercially? It seemed it could, with one or two permissions to be obtained (and eagerly granted), and the receipts would go to the Kathleen Ferrier Cancer Fund. But there was another 'but'. At the very last minute it was discovered that the recording had been destroyed 'in the course of events'. Not overmuch imagination here; for quite a time it had been common knowledge how ill Kathleen was, and everything she did had a more than usual significance.[8] Of course, there are many beautiful performances of hers recorded for our delight, but it is my own special selfish grief that none of my own music is among them—music that she sang with her own inimitable warmth, simplicity, and devoted care, as indeed she sang everything—as if it were the most important in the world.[9]

[8] Perhaps a jibe at bureaucratic incompetence rather than anything more malevolent.

[9] 'Representative excerpts' of Ferrier's performance of *Lucretia*, recorded in Holland in 1946, were released on disc in 1981. A private recording of the premiere of the *Spring Symphony*, made for the Earl of Harewood and only rediscovered in 1991, was issued by Decca in 1994.

39 *Serenade*, for Tenor, Horn and Strings (1954)

SIR,

Your review of the new Decca recording of my *SERENADE FOR TENOR, HORN AND STRINGS* has recently been shown to me. I should like, if you will allow me, to make a comment on it.

In the Prologue and Epilogue the horn is directed to play on the natural harmonics of the instrument; this causes the apparent 'out-of-tuneness' of which your reviewer complains, and which is, in fact, exactly the effect I intend.[1]

In the many brilliant performances of his part that Dennis Brain has given he has always I am sure, played it as I have marked it in the score.[2] Anyone, therefore, who plays it 'in tune' is going directly against my wishes!

If the critics do not like this effect they should blame me and not Mr. Brain.

Yours etc.,
BENJAMIN BRITTEN

Source: *Tempo* 34 (Winter 1954/5), 39. Letter dated 13 Dec. 1954.

[1] 'The same artists [Pears, The New Symphony Orchestra under Eugene Goossens] but this time with Dennis Brain perform the *Serenade*. The only disappointments here lie in the opening and closing horn solos; a curiously faulty intonation is apparent here and there which jars the magic of both the Prologue and Epilogue. Fortunately this disappears in the first song and from then on Dennis Brain's customary musicianship and brilliance are very much in evidence.' 'E.T.' in *Tempo* 33 (Autumn 1954).

[2] Dennis Brain (1921–57), English horn player, for whom, along with Peter Pears, Britten wrote the *Serenade*, and Canticle III. See Essay 47, in which Britten recounts his association with him.

40 *The Physician's Folly* (1955)

I SHOULD like to welcome most warmly into the exciting world of opera my young colleagues, Blythe and Collison. I have been working in that world myself for some ten years, and I know quite a bit about the excitements—and the difficulties too.

First, the planning of the work (that is all excitement), then the writing of the libretto and the music (some difficulties here). Then, when all that is satisfactorily accomplished, comes the production, and the excitements and difficulties *there* can hardly be exaggerated!

It is a triumph to achieve the production of a new opera, and I offer my young friends my sincere congratulations. And to you, the audience, I wish a happy and stimulating evening.

Source: Programme for first production of *The Physician's Folly*, music by David Blythe, libretto by David Collison, premiered at the Ipswich Art Gallery on 12 Apr. 1955 (*GB-ALb*).

41 The Aldeburgh Festival (1955)

Eight years of Festival making is a considerable period. After eight years, one may be allowed perhaps to take stock of the past and, in the light of the past, make plans for the future. Of the past, we think that our regular Festival patrons and visitors may be left to judge for themselves. They have shown their consistent interest at each Festival by suffering long hours in a stuffy hall or on hard pews to hear what we have offered them, and we deeply appreciate their loyalty. We had very much hoped by this, the eighth Aldeburgh Festival, to have announced confidently the plans for a small theatre in Aldeburgh which would be of real and permanent value to the town and would solve the perennial Festival bottleneck finances.[1] This plan has had, at any rate for the moment, to be postponed; expansion has had to yield to economy.

Last year's Festival budget was balanced only because we received some most generous gifts which we cannot expect every year, and because we cut expenditure on rehearsals to the very bone. The financial bottleneck remains the same, and since our expenses (like everyone else's) have swollen hugely since that first Festival of 1948, it became obvious that we must make some drastic reductions for the future.

As a result we shall have most regretfully to dispense with the services of a professional general manager. All Festival visitors will be very sorry to know that this present Festival is Elizabeth Sweeting's last.[2] Her tact and consideration for individual problems and wishes have been very much in evidence for eight years and she will be sorely missed. All good wishes will go with her.

In future, we shall have to rely much more on unpaid friendly (and Friendly!) help in many ways. It will be noticed that this year we have three local contributions to our programmes, two performances by the Aldeburgh Players, the Aldeburgh Music Club on the Meare, and (if Ipswich will allow us to regard it as local) the Ipswich Arts Theatre. This tendency will be carried over into the organising side of the Festival, and we trust that the saving effected will more than offset the dangers implicit in such a venture.

There have been rumours that this reorganisation means the end of the Festival. Let us dispel them here and now by saying that the Ninth Aldeburgh Festival will take place between 16 June and 24 June 1956, and that we shall do our best to ensure that Mozart's bicentenary is worthily celebrated here. His

Editor's title.

Source: Foreword to AFPB (1955), 7. Written by Britten, Pears, and Fidelity Cranbrook (b. 1912).

[1] A recurring theme until the creation of Snape Maltings Concert Hall in 1967.

[2] Elizabeth Sweeting (1914–99), English arts administrator.

piano concertos, chamber music and songs are well within our scope, and we shall give excerpts from his operas at our usual operatic concert. We plan too a repeat (in 1956) of that memorable 1954 *St John Passion* of Bach.

Lest it should be thought that we stop at 1956, we would like to assure our patrons that for 1957 there are two great composers waiting to be celebrated—Thomas Morley (born 1557) and Dietrich Buxtehude (died 1707). We have no lack of ideas (or enthusiasm) for future Aldeburgh Festivals. In 1959 there will be Purcell's tercentenary (for which we have already started a new edition of some of his unobtainable works) and in 1985 there will be Bach's!

But in the meantime, we welcome new covenanted subscribers for merely the next seven Festivals!

PART III

✳

1956–1965

'All a poet can do today is warn'

INTRODUCTION AND CHRONOLOGY

If Britten's journey in the period 1946–55 was metaphorical—a hurried elevation into a society he had spent his twenties openly disparaging or implicitly criticizing—his journey in 1956 to the Far East was as real as it was fruitful. Here he encountered sounds and cultures hitherto largely unknown to him. His reaction to Japan and Bali was registered immediately in his music, much as it had been for Holst, Bartók, Debussy, and Szymanowski in their encounters with the exoticism of the East. But there were philosophical and dramaturgical consequences as well. This trip was the beginning of a new phase in Britten's life, in which his retreat from the London performance scene, begun after the unsuccessful premiere of *Gloriana* and completed in the 1960s, directly affected both his music activities and the subject matter or narrative structure of the works he composed. Eastern sounds and dramaturgy shaped works as diverse as *Prince of the Pagodas* (1956), the Church Parables (1964, 1966, 1968), and *A Midsummer Night's Dream* (1960). His interest in the poetry and metaphors of night, latent since the *Serenade*, was reignited. His inversion of the balance between forest world and the courtly palace in *A Midsummer Night's Dream*—the former attracting his sympathies and most beautiful music, the latter depicted either fractiously or in the briefest of sketches—was a form of magical realism left largely unexplored in his previous stage works, one partly suggested by what he saw as the exotic/erotic promise of the East. Fantasy subtly depicting or celebrating otherness, so unlike the themes of his earlier operas (*The Turn of the Screw* included, which is more horror story than fairy tale), was a conscious retreat from the grim realism and obscured didacticism of his stage works from 1945 to 1953. It was a celebration of the power of the subconscious, a loosening of the shackles of the 1930s. Thus, the many 'night pieces' for different instruments in this period were an extension of Britten's fascination with hidden worlds, far from public gaze; this same feeling, after all, had led to his move in 1957 from Crag Path to the privacy of the Red House at the edge of Aldeburgh. And even a work as self-consciously 'public' as the *War Requiem* (1962) is remarkably intimate in places, almost as if the events depicted in many of the Wilfred Owen poems are overheard rather than recited.

Yet this search for a more private language and life was undermined by the very public success of the *War Requiem*, as unexpected as that of *Peter Grimes*. Designed as part memorial, part monument, it was also intended, in Wilfred Owens's words, to warn against the pity of war—a phrase Britten included as an epigraph to the score. Its quick recording by Decca (the gap between composition and commercial recording in this period closed dramatically) compounded its success, ensuring a vast worldwide audience. This success did not slow Britten's retreat into Aldeburgh, though, whereafter much of his live musical activity was centred, but it did establish him as a major composer with a *popular* following, and reaffirmed the power of his art as a mouthpiece for his beliefs. Yet, apart from *Voices for Today* (1965), his pacifist work written in celebration of the twentieth anniversary of the United Nations, Britten's music in this period is remarkably apolitical—almost as if he feared the consequences of such a public display of firmly held, nonetheless private, convictions.

His writings, though, reflect none of this search for privacy and intimacy; there were honorary degrees to collect, more boroughs to become Freeman of. They retain instead the themes of Establishment Responsibility that had marked his essays in the second period—without the occasional and revealing slips (or even irony, as in Essay 61, when he disparages 'the members of that favourite name today—the Establishment'). A new theme does emerge—that of Britten or his interlocutors surveying his life and output, rather than being concerned simply with the latest work (what Britten referred to time and again as his 'youngest child'). The theme that preoccupied him by far the most in this period, though, in his prose and interviews, is the responsibility of the artist towards society—something he first articulated in his Lowestoft address (Essay 33), some thirteen years before he made it the foundation stone of his Aspen speech (Essay 72): 'I am first and foremost an *artist*—and as an artist I want to serve the community.' Britten really did think that one element of this responsibility of the artist, this service, was to warn—in part because he had been indoctrinated in this way in the 1930s (Auden to Isherwood: 'So in this hour of crisis and dismay, | What better than your strict and adult pen | Can warn us from the colours and the consolations . . .'), but also because he believed in the prescience of the artist. He himself had spoken of this in his 1951 Lowestoft address: 'Artists are artists because they have an extra sensitivity—a skin less, perhaps, than other people; and the great ones have an uncomfortable habit of being right about many things, long before their time.' So although he was disinclined to maintain the role of public conscience in his music, he was happy to do this to a degree in his interviews and articles.

A devastating politeness descended upon most interviewers in this period—partly the result of the *War Requiem*'s extraordinary success, partly in recognition of Britten's fiftieth birthday—who each asked the wrong questions ('How does [*A Midsummer Night's Dream*] compare with your other major works?') or dumbly refused to follow up tantalizing answers ('The insinuation seemed to be that [Berg] was unsuitable on more than just musical grounds'). Yet when relaxed by people he knew (Crozier and Forster in Essay 57, John Amis in Essay

74, or the perceptive, cultured Earl of Harewood, five years away from the disintegration of his friendship with the composer, happily discarding his cue cards in Essay 53), or when writing passionately on subjects such as Purcell (Essay 51), the result is remarkably illuminating. And for each example of 'Britten Looking Back' (Essay 70), there is a paragraph or essay about the responsibility of the artist to society (Essays 60, 67, and 72). His use of the phrase 'the people' in the context of the Soviet Union earned him rebuke from the politically and linguistically astute Martin Cooper (Essay 66), although Britten's drafted response to this attack, impassioned and argumentative, is in some ways more revealing than his later, carefully sculptured Aspen speech (Essay 67).

1956 Continues tour in Far East with Pears; finishes *The Prince of the Pagodas*, Op. 57, upon his return; composes *Antiphon*, Op. 56b, and completes more Purcell realizations, this time for voice and orchestra.

1957 Conducts premiere of *Pagodas* at Covent Garden, and records a truncated version soon after for Decca, prior to its Italian premiere at La Scala; elected to the American Academy of Arts and Letters as an honorary member; tours with the EOG to Canada with *The Turn of the Screw*; moves to the Red House with Pears; composes *Songs from the Chinese*, Op. 58.

1958 Completes *Noye's Fludde*, Op. 59, which is premiered in the Aldeburgh Festival with a cast of Suffolk children; composes *Nocturne*, Op. 60, and *Sechs Hölderlin-Fragmente*, Op. 61; presents numerous song recitals with Pears; records *Peter Grimes*, one of the first opera recordings to use Decca's new stereo technology.

1959 Composes *Cantata academica, carmen basiliense*, Op. 62, and *Missa Brevis*, Op. 63; oversees publication of numerous volumes of Purcell realizations; Jubilee Hall is expanded, and a new opera is planned for its reopening in the 1960 Festival.

1960 Completes *A Midsummer Night's Dream*, Op. 64; revises *Billy Budd*, reshaping it into two acts, and conducts new version in a BBC broadcast; EOG now managed by Covent Garden; Pears stars in new production of *Grimes* at Covent Garden; meets Dmitry Shostakovich and Mstislav Rostropovich at Royal Festival Hall, London.

1961 Composes Sonata in C, Op. 65, for his new and admired friend Rostropovich; undertakes numerous recordings of his own music and that of others for Decca.

1962 Completes *War Requiem*, Op. 66; with Imogen Holst, revises 1951 version of *Dido and Aeneas*, a performance of which brings together Britten and Janet Baker (Dido) for the first time; composes Psalm 150, Op. 67; shares conducting of *War Requiem* with Meredith Davies at its premiere in Coventry Cathedral.

1963 Records *War Requiem*, and, with Pears, Schubert's *Winterreise* and Schumann's *Dichterliebe*; participates in British Council trip to Soviet Union for Festival of British Music; composes Symphony for Cello and Orchestra, Op. 68, *Cantata misericordium*, Op. 69, *Nocturnal after John Dowland*, Op. 70; celebrates fiftieth birthday with concert performance of *Gloriana* at Royal Festival Hall; is subject of BBC television profile and a book of tributes.

1964 Composes the first Church Parable, *Curlew River*, Op. 71, and the First Suite for Cello, Op. 72; conducts premiere of Symphony for Cello and Orchestra in Moscow, with Rostropovich and the Moscow Philharmonic Orchestra; receives first Aspen Award in America; tours EOG to Russia.

1965 Following deterioration of relationship with Boosey & Hawkes, changes publisher to the new Faber Music Ltd; awarded Order of Merit; composes *Gemini Variations*, Op. 73, *Songs and Proverbs of William Blake*, Op. 74, which he records with Fischer-Dieskau, *Voices for Today*, Op. 75, *The Poet's Echo*, Op. 76; revises Violin Concerto, Op. 15 (1939).

42 Britten's Method of Composing (1956)

BRITTEN: My method is quite simple. I plan my work away from the piano and away, moreover, from paper. I do 99 per cent of my work *thinking* about it—walking, or in trains, aeroplanes, if it's not too bumpy, and in buses and cars and so forth. Then when the music is fixed in my head I go to the paper and work out more precisely the details. I don't use the piano except at the very end when the work is more or less complete—more for confirming my ideas—if there's been a harmonic progression which was new for me—just to make sure it sounds, in sound, as it did in my head.

BIRCH: And do you usually write out all the parts—or part of the parts—yourself, or do you usually get someone to do that in detail?

BRITTEN: Oh no, one does everything oneself. Usually in orchestral work or a work for chorus or an opera which is an elaborate one, the first draft—which is in itself complete—it isn't a sketch in any way, but it is a simple way of writing it down in what one calls short score. In other words, instead of writing the thirty odd lines which one needs for a full score, I write it in two or three or four staves.

BIRCH: Indicating the instruments . . .

BRITTEN: Indicating all the instruments. And then I go to paper and do the full score and write out all the details of all the instruments. I must confess I occasionally have help in someone to put the key signatures in, the clefs, and to draw the bar-lines. And sometimes when the clarinet hobbles along in unison with the violins, I say 'with the violins' in the clarinet part, and someone later fills that in.

Editor's title.

Source: Editor's transcript of recording (NSA T9340R). Broadcast 13 Mar. 1956, General Overseas Service: Britten interviewed by Timothy Birch (Radio Hong Kong). (Pre-recorded 25 Feb. 1956.)

43 British Culture Abroad (1956)

Sir,

Having recently returned from a concert tour which took us through fourteen countries of the Far East and back, may we offer for your appraisal a few observations which are not entirely irrelevant to some recent correspondence in your columns?[1]

We went as British artists bringing mostly British music, and were soon made conscious of the tremendous interest in all branches of this country's art, and of the enormous goodwill towards us, at any rate on the cultural level. Our welcome was touchingly warm and enthusiastic, but our visit was as a drop of water in the desert. On a tour such as ours you will meet with musicians, dancers, actors from every country but our own; Russians in Delhi, Austrians in Tokyo, Poles in Madras, and Americans all over South East Asia. Every government but our own realises the importance of cultural propaganda—it must, we suppose, be called that. Four years ago the English Opera Group visiting the Wiesbaden Festival with a complete company of twenty-four was, absurdly enough, considered the most costly Festival Company, and that in competition with a full-scale performance of 'Aida' sent at Italian expense from Rome. In Tokyo, the Stuttgart Chamber Orchestra was being flown out by the German Government. This year at Aldeburgh the Dutch Government is offering us, entirely free, a famous Dutch male voice choir. Examples could be multiplied. In Djakarta they had had Martha Graham's Ballet Company and the Symphony of the Air, as well as a lot of similar stars, all at Uncle Sam's expense.

Source: Typescript (carbon copy), 30 Apr. 1956 (*GB-ALb*). Written by Britten and Pears. This letter was sent to *The Times* but was not published. A different, shorter version was sent to the *Manchester Guardian* and was published on 10 May.

[1] Herbert Read (see Essay 27) had written the following in *The Times* on 12 Apr.:

> The artists who have written to you to complain that their works, and the works of their friends, have not been exhibited abroad by the British Council should produce evidence of a demand for such exhibitions. . . .
>
> The Fine Arts Committee of the British Council, of which I am a member, does not act arbitrarily; it does not impose its own tastes on foreign countries. It is guided by an accurate knowledge of the conditions abroad, of the prevailing climate of public opinion, and it tries to satisfy the legitimate curiosity of its patrons. To send abroad unwanted works of art would be next to impossible, for no reputable gallery would give them houseroom; and even if exhibition space were to be hired at the expense of the British taxpayer there are no means of persuading the unwilling foreigner to go out of his way to view, for example, some tepid exponent of the English watercolour school. . . .
>
> As a nation we make ourselves internationally ludicrous by clinging to outworn fashions in art, as in everything else . . . but in the export of ideas (which is the sphere of the British Council) as in the export of goods it is only the new fashions that have the remotest chance of finding a market.

Indeed, we ourselves were invited in the first place to give thirty concerts in Indonesia by that admirable Dutch-State spirited organisation, the Association of Art Circles of Indonesia.

Now at last the British Foreign Office has sent a group of British musicians to Moscow. Will this be the thin end of the wedge? Dare one hope that the British Council, which started twenty years ago as a good idea and is now a national necessity, will soon be able to vote a less inadequate sum of money to the export of our cultural achievements?

Goodwill and enthusiasm are waiting, and in our experience the representatives too, representatives who, we would like to say, throughout our independent tour were models of efficiency, tact and kindness, and, shamed almost into despair at the amount they can do with the money they are given, and with continual carping from home, work themselves into near-illness, buoyed up presumably by missionary zeal and the desire to save their country's face.

We should by now have realised that the arts can play a valuable part in the export drive. Other countries which do so export their achievements, and hospitably await ours. Their goodwill should not be allowed to wither.

44 Britten and South-East Asia (1956)

HAMBLETON: *I now take you to South-East Asia, but not in actuality; only as seen musically by Benjamin Britten, whom I interviewed in his home in Aldeburgh in 1956, just after he and Peter Pears had returned from a concert tour of the world. I spoke to him generally about his tour and I found him a very accurate reporter, with the gift of recalling circumstantial details. For this programme I've taken the part where he speaks of the musicians, about the exotic music he heard, particularly in Siam. He began by telling me how his own music was received.*

BRITTEN: Many of the places you go to had quite a big European population. In Java, for instance, the audiences were predominantly Dutch, therefore the concerts were not at all unlike concerts in The Hague or Amsterdam. In Japan, of course, where the audiences were entirely Japanese, the reception to Western music is extremely exciting. It's highly cultured and extremely enthusiastic—very choosy. If they like you they like you very much; if they don't like you I don't think they mince matters at all. I conducted there an orchestra, which was a fascinating experience—a very technically highly developed orchestra, but with a quality quite unlike any European or American orchestra I've ever heard; and that is not a criticism—that's just a comment. Ah—where else? We had many Chinese in our audiences in Singapore and in Hong Kong, and one felt that the young Chinese particularly were extremely interested in Western music, but one must add that most of the orientals one played to were as bewildered by much of our music as one is bewildered by much of their music.

HAMBLETON: Did they put any of their bewilderment into words? Did you speak to any professional musicians there, for example?

BRITTEN: Oh yes, one did speak to quite a lot, and I think one can say that the sympathetic ones who came and spoke to one said that they were interested—deeply interested—in it. They found, I think, the classical Western music more difficult to assimilate than the modern music—I think because unconsciously in the last hundred years one has grown nearer together. The stylized eighteenth-century music of Haydn, for instance, or even slightly later of Schubert, bewildered them quite a lot. They couldn't quite see the harmonic background and of course if you miss that, you miss a great deal of it.

HAMBLETON: Well, I was wondering—is hearing foreign music in a foreign land different from hearing that same music in your own land?

Editor's title.
Source: Editor's transcript of recording (*GB-ALb* 3–02053904). Broadcast CBC, date unknown; rebroadcast 14 June 1962, CBC, in series *Worth Repeating*. (Pre-recorded 1956, Aldeburgh.)

BRITTEN: Completely different, and I can't emphasize that strongly enough. I have heard in London and on the continent quite a lot of oriental music, and seen also oriental dancing, and have been either mildly diverted or quite bewildered by it. I'm more and more convinced that art needs to be seen and heard in its own environment. Once you've done that maybe you can carry it away and reproduce the beauties and your excitement elsewhere; but the difference, for instance, between Balinese music played in the open, in the courtyard of a temple, in Ubud or some little village there—the difference between that and [it] being played in the cold light of a London theatre is quite a remarkable thing, not only in one's own reactions to it but in the spirit of the performers. There is *no* showing off at all in the dancing or the playing when it is done as a part of religious ceremony. You cannot avoid showing off a little if you are behind footlights; in fact you have to do so.

HAMBLETON: It has always seemed to me that oriental music has a very improvisatory nature. Is there really a formal structure behind it, do you think?

BRITTEN: Well there again, it's impossible to generalize between the various kinds. For instance, Indian music is largely—well, entirely—improvised. You are given a theme, a raga, a scale, or whatever, and on that theme you improvise. But further east, in Bali and further east still, in Japan, the music is highly organized and has been so for—well, in Japan, over a thousand years. A particular piece of music, a piece of the imperial court music I heard in Tokyo, called Bairo—I think it's pronounced like that—was brought to Japan in the seventh century from Siam, and so that shows there was nothing improvised about that.

HAMBLETON: Well when you hear music in these foreign lands, Mr Britten, do you hear it acquisitively? Do you hear it with the idea of in some way using it in the future?

BRITTEN: No, I never listen to it to that end. I listen to it simply out of interest because I am extremely interested in all different kinds of art, but I cannot say that one doesn't by accident acquire quite a bit of it. I'm not at all in favour of trying to copy it and trying to do a sort of pastiche, for a composer, nor am I enough of a musicologist skilled enough to be able to notate it accurately so that I can do a real study like so many people are in the Far East at the moment; but I cannot help being influenced by certain remarkable new things that even I with my small experience of oriental music cannot help but notice.[1]

[1] The first fruits of this Eastern tour were to be found in Britten's ballet *The Prince of the Pagodas* (1956), composition of which had been interrupted by the tour, and which he returned to with enthusiasm and great effect upon his return. See Mervyn Cooke, *Britten and the Far East* (Woodbridge: Boydell Press, 1998).

Hambleton: I had often wondered in what kind of a world does a composer move. He is a person who creates musical sounds and somehow you must either resist the musical influences from without or make a point of absorbing them and using them.

Britten: I couldn't do more than just give my own reactions to that remark. I couldn't generalize for other people—but I would say that, very briefly, one is trying to state certain things which you feel that you know, in the language that you use the best, in my case in music; and any material that you can use to that purpose is legitimate. If you want to express a mood and you are interested in a Balinese phrase, then, if you can assimilate that into your own style, well then I think you're quite—quite allowed—quite legitimate to do so. Briefly, you're trying to express something and you can use anything you like to express that something.

45 The Composer Speaks (1957)

COOPER: Today in our series *The Composer Speaks* I'm visiting Benjamin Britten, who is one of our most prolific and versatile composers. Benjamin Britten, I wonder if you could tell us a little of your early life. Would you say that your family was musical?

BRITTEN: Well my family wasn't professional musical at all. My mother sang very sweetly, and my mother—my mother sang, but my father was almost anti-musical I'm afraid, he liked tunes in the minor keys, he used to say.

COOPER: Did he walk out if anybody was playing in a major key?

BRITTEN: He was inclined to do that. But actually, she sang awfully well and my brother played the violin and I can—one of my earliest memories is not being able to go to sleep at night because of the musical party going on; I used to complain bitterly about that.

COOPER: Yes. When did you start yourself to write or to compose? Or did you go to the piano when you were aged four and finger things out on the piano?

BRITTEN: Yes, a family tradition is that I started playing the piano at an uncomfortably early age. My first actual efforts at writing music were about the age of five. I obtained from somewhere, I can't remember where, a piece of manuscript paper and started drawing curious rows of notes on this paper, looked more like the Forth Bridge than a piece of music—I was obviously more interested in the way it looked than in the way it sounded. I asked my mother to play this for me, would she please, and she was very cross and said: Don't be silly, of course I can't play that.[1] Well later—a little later when I started trying to connect that with the piano, and I really wrote quite a lot of music when I was—in the early—

COOPER: But did you actually improvise at the piano? Did you like sit down and make it up as you go along?

BRITTEN: Yes, I was—used to do that quite a lot.

COOPER: The thing that I always associate with you—I suppose everybody who knows you and knows of you is—associates you with the sea and the background of the sea.

BRITTEN: Well that I suppose is rather inevitable, because I was born in a house only a few yards from the sea, in fact all my life except for a few

Source: BBC transcript (BBCWAC microfilm, Composer Speaks, T88). Edited version broadcast 7 July 1957, BBC General Overseas Service, 11.15 p.m.: interview with Joseph Cooper in the series *The Composer Speaks*. (Pre-recorded 30 May 1957.) A recording of this interview exists (NSA T9340R).

[1] Clearly by this stage the story of Britten's origins as a composer was well rehearsed. Compare, for example, Essay 21.

years in the thirties, I lived as near to the sea as that, and I live now in Aldeburgh on the East Coast, my house is practically on the beach; in fact we've had the sea in the house on more than one occasion in the last few years.

COOPER: Would you say that the salt tang has got into your composition, or would you say that was a silly remark?

BRITTEN: Well it's [indecipherable] to talk about one's own music, but I'm told by my rather more frank friends that my *Peter Grimes* interludes are extremely salty.

COOPER: Well have you got an example of *Peter Grimes* you could just show us?

BRITTEN: Well there is this record of the interludes from *Grimes*—the first interlude, which is an Early Morning Scene—it preludes the first scene of the first act. It's perhaps the most suitably salty—here it is. [Excerpt 1: Sea Interlude, 'Dawn', from *Peter Grimes*]

COOPER: Just tell me, was your private school in view of the sea also, or was that—did you have to go inland for that?

BRITTEN: No, actually that school was as near to the sea as my home was, and I mean one used to bathe from the school and one was aware—equally aware of the sea there as one was at home. I had a very busy life, I enjoyed the school, it was a tough one but a good school.

COOPER: Did you play games, that kind of thing?

BRITTEN: Yes, I was frightfully keen on games, I was also quite good at work and worked as hard as I had to avoid getting into trouble. In fact when I think of these days I'm always amazed that I was able to write as much music as I did, as well as doing these other things.

COOPER: You wrote—really were writing a lot then were you, actually?

BRITTEN: Well, yes, I've got a list somewhere which says in great detail all the works that I wrote until about the age thirteen, when I left school, and it included something like twelve piano sonatas, four or five string quartettes, dozens of songs, two enormous symphonies, a tone poem called 'Chaos and Cosmos', etc. etc.

COOPER: Did you give them an opus number?

BRITTEN: Oh yes, I was well past a hundred by the age of twelve—yes.

COOPER: What happened to all those early things?

BRITTEN: Oh they're sitting in a cupboard. Actually there are some quite nice little tunes—very derivative of course as you might imagine, and a few years later I arranged some of these tunes into a little work for strings which I called *A Simple Symphony*—perhaps you'd like to hear one of the more harmless movements of this little work—this is called 'Playful Pizzicato'. [Excerpt 2: 'Playful Pizzicato' from *A Simple Symphony*]

COOPER: Well what happened after you'd left your private school; where did you go from there?

BRITTEN: Well I went on to Gresham School at Holt which was chosen because they didn't actively hate music, as so many other public schools did.

COOPER: Is that on the sea coast too?

BRITTEN: No, that is further inland, it's at least six miles from the sea so I was well removed. But it didn't—it wasn't really a great success as far as I was concerned. I think at that time I was already determined to become a musician and I felt it was rather a waste of time, my going on with general schooling—it was probably—that's untrue, that feeling, but I felt impatient and didn't really enjoy it.

COOPER: Did you have extra time to study music?

BRITTEN: No, I didn't—I didn't even play the piano there, I played the viola in the school orchestra and did that kind of thing. I sang in the school choir.

COOPER: But you felt starved in a way—

BRITTEN: Yes—

COOPER: —yes, frustrated a little bit.

BRITTEN: Actually I had a great stroke of luck, because when I was at my private school I had the chance of meeting Frank Bridge, whom I think is an excellent composer, very much underrated these days, but who was, as well as being a good composer, a first-rate practical musician. He took a great interest in me as a boy and I used to go and stay with him in the holidays, both from my private and public schools, and he would give me very rigorous lessons in composition, I would take him all my juvenile efforts and he would criticise them, really very severely indeed, and also open my eyes to another form of existence, the artistic existence, which I'd really honestly no idea existed before.

COOPER: It probably made you hate your school even more—

BRITTEN: It made the contrast greater.

COOPER: —getting back from the sort of holidays of sheer bliss must have been absolute hell.

BRITTEN: He was a very remarkable man and I can only hope that other young composers have as great a luck as I had in finding a person who was as gentle and yet firm as he was.

COOPER: You know those *Variations on a Theme of Frank Bridge* that you wrote: were they actually dedicated to him, were they for him or—

BRITTEN: Yes, they were written considerably later than that time when I was, I think, about nineteen or twenty, and as a tribute to him.[2] They start with

[2] Composed in 1937, when Britten was 23, and dedicated 'To F.B. A tribute with affection and admiration.'

a short introduction of mine and then the tune; the theme is played which is from one of his string quartets.[3] I'd like you to hear it because I think it is a very beautiful tune and typical of him as a composer, a sort of wistful sadness, and yet great originality. Can we play it? [Excerpt 3: either the second of Bridge's *Three Idylls for String Quartet* or the theme of Britten's *Variations on a Theme of Frank Bridge*]

COOPER: To make a horrible pun—what happened when you'd crossed the bridge?

BRITTEN: Well the next step in my life was the three years at the Royal College of Music. It was an interesting time in many ways for me—it was my first chance of getting to know London and I enjoyed meeting people and going to concerts and operas. I studied there for composition with John Ireland and with Arthur Benjamin, both of whom were very kind to me.[4]

COOPER: Arthur Benjamin surely for piano, was it?

BRITTEN: Yes, he was for piano; John Ireland was for composition. They were both kind to me and really nurtured me very gently through a very, very difficult musical adolescence which I was going through at that time.

COOPER: Did you—I make no secret at all, in fact I've always admired your piano playing very much ever since I can remember you, but did you—you're very modest about it I know, but did you actually study hard at the piano, or did you really rather treat it as a sort of—very much a second subject?

BRITTEN: I studied actually when I was at school pretty hard, when I was old enough, that was in my early school days, and also I forgot to say before, but at the same time I met Frank Bridge I also met Harold Samuel, who was a very fine pianist and he helped me a lot with my piano.[5]

COOPER: But at the College itself, I mean—you put it second presumably?

BRITTEN: I put it very much second, although I did stagger through the ARCM for solo piano—luckily there was—I had very gentle examiners and I was—I'm probably musical but as you say, I'm not very keen on my piano playing, I don't think.[6]

COOPER: And in your composition did you shock John Ireland with all your new ideas?

BRITTEN: No, he stood up to me manfully. I perhaps shocked him most of all in my prolificness. I used to come every week with a stack full of music, a

[3] The theme is taken from the second of Bridge's Three Idylls for String Quartet (1906).

[4] John Ireland (1879–1962), English composer and pianist, and Arthur Benjamin (1893–1960), Australian composer and pianist—both professors at the RCM.

[5] Harold Samuel (1879–1937), English pianist, composer of light music, and professor of piano at the Royal College of Music.

[6] ARCM: Associate of the Royal College of Music.

stack this high, and he used to get rather bewildered by this, and we only used to examine one or two of the top pieces, and I used to get impatient with him perhaps, but he was very nice.

COOPER: Now after the College I don't have to ask you what you did because I had the delight in meeting you for the first time, and that was in the thirties, when we both collided at the GPO Film Unit which took place, you might say, at Blackheath.[7]

BRITTEN: Yes, well that was a very—very remarkable and very, for me, very useful group of people. There were some remarkable people, don't you remember, in this—

COOPER: There was Cavalcanti wasn't there?

BRITTEN: Cavalcanti was a director of the film—actually the head of the whole Unit which was engaged in making films—propaganda for the GPO; [there] was John Grierson; then there were other people working along with us—you remember, there was Auden, now Professor of Poetry at Oxford; there was Bill Coldstream as we called him, now head of the Slade—

COOPER: Sir William—yes.

BRITTEN: And then of course there were other composers: Walter Leigh—do you remember—and Howard Ferguson used to come and help us.[8]

COOPER: Did you feel you learnt anything out of that?

BRITTEN: Oh I learnt a great deal.

COOPER: Did you?

BRITTEN: It was of the most—the utmost value to me in several ways. It made one practical as a composer; if one was asked to write a piece of music this length in twenty-four hours, one jolly well had to do it, ideas or no ideas. But I suppose the most useful quality of the Film Unit for me was this learning to handle small forces orchestrally.

COOPER: Why did they have to be so small? I've forgotten.

BRITTEN: I think it was just lack of money.

COOPER: Was it—or space—it was money was it?

BRITTEN: Perhaps a bit of both—I mean the studio was extremely small.

COOPER: And we worked in a tiny little sort of corner, yes. But that's been useful to you from having to scale your stuff down—

[7] The General Post Office Film Unit grew out of the Empire Marketing Board, which folded in 1933. It attracted many young talented writers, film makers, musicians, and artists, including John Grierson (1898–1972), Alberto Cavalcanti (1897–1982), William Coldstream (1908–87), W. H. Auden, and Britten, who started working for the company in 1935. Edward Clark had recommended Britten to Cavalcanti, at Frank Bridge's behest.

[8] Walter Leigh (1905–42), English composer, predominantly of light music for the London stage; Howard Ferguson (1908–99), Northern Irish composer, pianist, and teacher.

BRITTEN: I suppose it's partly a contemporary quality, but I think all art is tending towards—or serious art—towards the intimate, and especially in the opera world, one has to reduce one's orchestra to the minimum, and I have learnt, largely through my experiences in the Film Unit, I think, to handle—to make a small group of instruments sound not inadequate.

COOPER: Yes, I see. It's interesting: it sort of clarifies too—I mean it clarifies your whole scoring, instead of knowing you can just lay on things thick.

BRITTEN: Yes.

COOPER: What did you write immediately after that period—I mean that was all, if I may say so politely, hack work—I mean, very elegantly done, but it was—but once released from the Film Unit what did you—what was your first or one of your most interesting—

BRITTEN: Well I got more and more interested in the voice, I think that probably came from my love of English poetry, but I felt there was something wrong with my setting of English words; I didn't feel it had the freedom that the great vocal composers I admired had so beautifully, and curiously enough, although my interest in English poetry probably took me to vocal writing, my first big setting of words was of French words, and that was a work based on the poems of Rimbaud called *Les Illuminations*.[9] I suppose one could say that it was something in the setting of the foreign language which enabled me to have a freedom which set in my own language wouldn't have existed. I mean, there is a certain caution which goes with one's own language; the sense, for instance, is frightfully important. But in this case it was the feeling of the French words; my French wasn't frightfully good but I had a very good translation of Helen Rootham's which helped me in these very obscure but very beautiful poems.[10]

COOPER: You had them side by side, did you?

BRITTEN: Yes. In this volume there was the French on one side and the English on the other. It came from a volume of verse called *Les Illuminations* by Rimbaud.

COOPER: I'd like very much to hear something of this—have you got any record of it?

BRITTEN: Yes, there's a record I'm very pleased with; I think perhaps this section, 'Antique' and, yes, and then the previous section 'Phrase' which leads

[9] Arthur Rimbaud (1854–91), extraordinary French poet, deliquent schoolboy, and sexual revolutionary.

[10] Helen Rootham (d. 1938), English translator, notably of Serbian epic poetry, governess to Edith Sitwell (1887–1964) from 1903, with whom she lived from 1914 until her death. It was through Rootham's encouragement that Sitwell published her first volume of poetry, *The Mother* (1915).

into it, might interest you most. [Excerpt 4: 'Antique' and 'Phrase' from *Les Illuminations*]

COOPER: Were you conducting that?

BRITTEN: We—little Eugene Goossens [was] conducting.[11]

COOPER: You do conduct a lot of your own works?

BRITTEN: Yes. Actually I should have conducted that particular record, but I wasn't well and Eugene Goossens very kindly and very brilliantly took over at the last moment—and a very beautiful job he made of it.

COOPER: And of course that was Peter Pears singing.

BRITTEN: Yes.

COOPER: When did your musical association with Peter Pears actually start? Because now you've become so famous as a duo couple with your concerts all over the world that I wondered when it actually started.

BRITTEN: Our first concert we gave together I think was in thirty-eight, a concert at Balliol at Oxford, but it didn't really get going until the middle of the war. Since then we have given many, many concerts together, but not only that too, we've been associated in many artistic ventures together. We have very similar tastes in music. I mean I enjoy too the travelling and giving concerts.

COOPER: Now let's see, let's get this right: you went to America, when was that—that was in 1939?

BRITTEN: It was the beginning of 1939 and then I returned in the middle of the war—no, early 1942.

COOPER: Were you writing in America; were you writing any music?

BRITTEN: Yes, I wrote a great deal of music over there. I supposed my principal work there was the *Michelangelo Sonnets*, which since then we've given many, many times all over the place.

COOPER: Would you mind if we had some now, because I'd like to hear them. Which shall we have?

BRITTEN: Well the third one, and perhaps the sixth; they are the two that make the most immediate impression. [Excerpt 5: Sonnetto XXX and Sonetto XXXII from *Seven Sonnets of Michelangelo*]

COOPER: I suppose it would be fair to say, and not exaggerating Benjamin Britten, that the Aldeburgh Festival is already as famous as any festival in the world today. I mean, spare our blushes, but you obviously founded it, and I think that it's spoken of all over the world. How did you get the idea for having a festival in a small fishing village?

BRITTEN: Now let me think. The original idea, I believe I'm right in saying, came to us while we were driving back from Lucerne where we'd been

[11] Sir Eugene Goossens (1893–1962), English conductor, violinist, and composer. Son of the conductor Eugene Goossens (1867–1958), hence Britten's diminutive appellation.

performing one of my operas, and it was very nice and we enjoyed it very much, but it was a very long way to go to do a performance of one of these pieces. And so we said, oh well, why don't we do such a thing at home? Where shall we do it?, we thought. Well, at home is always the nicest place. How could we do a festival in Aldeburgh? There isn't an opera house, there's a very beautiful church, but there's no opera house, but there is the Jubilee Hall, but could we get an opera in there? It's tiny—it holds less than 300 people—but we'd try it. And it worked somehow; it took an awful lot of hard thinking, but we've been very lucky in the towns people; they've helped us, they've collaborated from the very first moment, and they work extremely hard, and in many ways the Festival would not be possible without their very close cooperation.

COOPER: But, forgive my asking and butting in, but how on earth do you—the enormous number of people that come down to Aldeburgh, I imagine there are about two hotels—I can think of two in Aldeburgh—but where do they all stay?

BRITTEN: Well, Aldeburgh you see has a very flourishing life of its own as a resort, and I don't know whether this is actually true, but one says that in the summer months and over holidays—school holidays—that Aldeburgh actually doubles its population, which means somehow or other it takes in up to two thousand people. There are two or three hotels, but there are lots of places where people can stay; people stay in the district around. A lot of people do come, it's perfectly true, and we're awfully happy, Peter Pears and I—because we really were largely responsible for starting it—that so many people like the kind of music that we like. It isn't by any means all my music, as some people think it is . . .

COOPER: Ah, that I know . . .

BRITTEN: . . . it ranges from the earliest to the very latest, the very youngest composers; each year we have a concert of the very young composers and performers. We do not only music of course; we have lectures—I mean, E. M. Forster, Edith Sitwell, Auden, people like that come regularly; we have art exhibitions in our church halls, in our Moot Hall; we have many different kinds of concerts. Perhaps you'd like to hear one of the records that we have of the Aldeburgh Festival, because it has a rather an important—it features a rather important side of the Festival—that is the singing of the local choirs. Every year we come together, a sort of mixed bag of choirs from all over the country, and have two choral concerts. This year we're doing the *St John Passion* of Bach, but *Saint Nicolas*—a cantata I wrote about ten years ago—has always been really closely associated with these concerts. This is just a little bit of the end of *Saint Nicolas*. [Excerpt 6: from *Saint Nicolas*]

COOPER: What was it like trying to put an opera into a village hall? I mean, what I'd like to know is did you write your various operas with Aldeburgh in mind? Or did Aldeburgh come first, or did the operas come first? How did it all happen?

BRITTEN: Well it actually, the idea of the small operas came first. In fact it was from a performance of the English Opera Group, which we founded in 1946 I think, that we thought of the idea of the Aldeburgh Festival.[12] That was really started because after the war it seemed that the chances of getting works performed written by young English—or any English—composers was very remote. Opera is such an expensive medium: the orchestra costs so much; the maintenance; the productions; the chorus. So we said, why not let's try to write an opera without chorus, without big scenery and without a big orchestra. So we tried. The Group really was—consisted of people like Joan Cross, Peter Pears, John Piper, Eric Crozier, most people who had been associated with my first opera at Sadler's Well, *Peter Grimes*. We wrote together with Ronald Duncan *The Rape of Lucretia*, then came *Albert Herring*, *The Beggar's Opera*, then I tried one for children, *Let's Make an Opera*.

COOPER: Oh that's been a tremendous success, hasn't it?

BRITTEN: That's been done in many places.

COOPER: Is it still being done now, is it?

BRITTEN: It's always being done somewhere or other in various languages, and I always collect very keenly all the photographs I can lay hands on of the various productions. It's nice to see that the—for instance, the Israelite version of a chimney—I mean they don't have chimneys in Israel, I believe; they sort of improvise them . . . It's very amusing.

COOPER: How lovely.

BRITTEN: And then finally the last opera I wrote was *The Turn of the Screw*, which was done a couple of years ago in Venice for the first time.

COOPER: When was it done in England? I saw it at the Scala here in London.

BRITTEN: It was done quite soon after Venice. The Scala was, I think, the second year. I mean, that was another sad miss; we had to go to Venice for our first performance. Actually I'll let you into a secret: we're going to build another theatre in Aldeburgh, specially for these operas; the Jubilee Hall really is a little small.

COOPER: How lovely. What will it seat?

BRITTEN: Well, not more than five hundred: that is the number of people which we can handle most easily in Aldeburgh.

[12] The Glyndebourne English Opera Company was founded in 1946 and became the English Opera Group a year later, following secession from Glyndebourne.

COOPER: Yes, but you'll have a bigger stage, better lighting, more room for the orchestra.

BRITTEN: Oh yes, it'll be a proper theatre.

COOPER: How wonderful. Well, when is the opening of that?

BRITTEN: Oh, we've got to collect the money first, and that's going to take quite a time.

COOPER: Well I hope listeners please note, don't you?

BRITTEN: Oh yes, I'm hoping everyone was listening with their cheque books in hand.[13]

COOPER: Going back to *The Turn of the Screw*, which was, in a way, one of the most spine-chilling operas probably that's ever been put on, because of the actual ghosts that come into the story. Have you got a little bit we could hear of that? The bit that I liked so much was when she writes the letter.

BRITTEN: Oh yes, saying that she can't cope with the situation any more—she writes to the guardian. Yes, here is a little bit of that, sung by the original governess, Jennifer Vyvyan.[14] [Excerpt 7: from Act II Scene 3, *The Turn of the Screw*]

COOPER: Would you say that this writing of operas for small groups had handicapped you; has it given you a taste which has made you feel that you don't like writing big operas?

BRITTEN: No, I wouldn't say that that is altogether true, although there's an element of truth in it. I have to confess that the degree of perfection one can achieve with a small group is lacking in the big operas, but there are so many things that one cannot say in the small form, and I shall continue as I have in the past ten years—I shall continue to write big operas. For instance, I've always got plans for the future. But the past has contained—I mean *Peter Grimes*, which was first done at Sadler's Wells, but has been done recently at Covent Garden several times; and then of course there was *Billy Budd*, that difficult piece because it's only men in the opera; and *Gloriana*, which I wrote for the coronation three years ago.

COOPER: Yes. Why did you suddenly branch out and write a ballet the other day? I say the other day because it's now, I mean, not news any more, but *The Prince of the Pagodas* was rather a bolt from the blue really for you, wasn't it?

BRITTEN: Well I've always been interested in ballet, although I have not known very much about it and had no actual direct contact with it before.

[13] The proposal was eventually abandoned, following a public campaign to raise funds. The Festival had to wait until 1967, with the opening of Snape Maltings, for a proper concert hall and theatre space.

[14] Jennifer Vyvyan (1925–74), English soprano, who apart from singing the first Governess also created the roles of Penelope Rich in *Gloriana* (1953), Tytania in *A Midsummer Night's Dream* (1960), and Mrs Julian in *Owen Wingrave* (1971).

Pieces of mine have been danced to, and also I was—in this particular case, what attracted me was that it was going to be a classical opera—a classical ballet, I mean—and that interests me far more than the psychological ballets. It was a nice story and so when John Cranko suggested I should do it I agreed readily, although I had no idea when I started it the labour it was going to be.[15] There are far more notes in a long ballet that there are in writing opera.

COOPER: Is that really true?

BRITTEN: I shouldn't like to count them.

COOPER: Well I'd like to finish the programme now, if we may, by hearing the waltz that finished up the whole ballet. Do you think we could have that?

BRITTEN: Yes, of course: here it is.

[Excerpt 8: from Act III Scene 2, *The Prince of the Pagodas*]

COOPER: Well Benjamin Britten, I'd like to thank you. I feel that we could do at least four talks on you because your output is so prodigious and your musical activities in every sphere are so enormous that I've only just touched on your life. But nonetheless I do thank you form my heart for letting me come and visit you.

BRITTEN: It's a great pleasure.

[15] John Cranko (1927–73), South African dancer and choreographer, who first collaborated with Britten on *Gloriana* (1953), for which he choreographed the ballet scenes. This was followed in 1956 by *The Prince of the Pagodas*, the scenario and choreography of which was devised by Cranko.

46 To the Music Lovers of Japan (1957)

It gives me great pleasure to send this New Year's greeting to the music-lovers of Japan. Although my acquaintance with Japan is very limited, the short time I have spent there remains very vividly in my mind. I was there in the early spring of 1956 for two weeks, and had the great pleasure of conducting a concert of my works with the NHK orchestra, and of giving with Mr Peter Pears (also for NHK) what in fact was our first recital for television anywhere in the world.[1] We were treated with great courtesy and friendship, and I was very impressed with the high standard of playing of the orchestra, and with the players' considerable understanding of my music. We greatly enjoyed these two concerts. In fact we were both (and I can include Mr Pears in this) astounded by the enthusiasm for and knowledge of Western music we met everywhere. One of the nicest examples of this was the excellent little group of Tokyo Madrigal Singers, under their intelligent conductor Kei [Kei-ichi] Kurosawa, which we heard at a party given for us. We even, after the serious part of the programme was over, took part light-heartedly in the singing ourselves.

But these were not our only musical experiences in Japan, because we had the tremendous joy of hearing a performance of some of the Imperial Court Music in the Imperial Palace. I think it is true to say that we expected this music would be utterly foreign and incomprehensible to us. Actually we [were] impressed immediately by the great beauty of the sound, especially of that wonderful instrument the *shō*, by the stately melodies, and the subtlety of the rhythms. I immediately set out to discover gramophone recordings of some of this wonderful music, and brought them home to England. This great impression has been deepened by repeated playings of them. Incidentally, our friend mentioned before, Mr Kurosawa, who was so kind to us during our visit, obtained a beautiful *shō* instrument, which I brought home with me. Although in no way a competent player, I derive great pleasure from making what seem to me beautiful sounds on it, and reminding myself of that memorable morning in the Imperial Palace.

Those two weeks were full of similarly exciting and novel experiences. I shall never forget the impact made on me by the Japanese theatre—the tremendous Kabuki, but above all the profound Nō plays. I count the last among the greatest theatrical experiences of my life. Of course it was strange to start with, the language and the especially curious kind of chanting used; but we were fortunate in having excellent literal translations to follow from, and

Source: Editor's transcript of recording (*GB-ALb*). Broadcast 1 Jan. 1958, NHK [Japan]. (Pre-recorded 3 Dec. 1957 at Bush House, London.)

[1] Transmitted on 9 Feb. 1956.

we soon became accustomed to the haunting sounds. The deep solemnity and *self*lessness of the acting, the perfect shaping of the drama (like a great Greek tragedy) coupled with the strength and universality of the stories are something which every Western artist can learn from.

Our short visit to Japan was not entirely confined to Tokyo. We took the train to Kyoto, being lucky to have a good view of Fuji, and also drove through the lovely country to Nara. In each of these towns we saw beautiful things which stay clearly in the memory: the stone garden; the Nijo castle (in the snow!); the Detached Villa; the Golden Pavilion; the particularly beautiful flute player on the lantern at Nara. We stayed in a Japanese inn, and found the service charming and efficient.

These few words, I hope, show a little why those fourteen days or so spent in Japan should be so precious to me. And I should like to take this opportunity to thank those Japanese who were so courteous and helpful to us, helping us to appreciate the beauties and subtleties of their great country. In particular the musicians, the orchestral players, the technicians and administration of JHK [NHK], those young composers whom we met and who are writing so enterprisingly in our Western idiom, the Imperial Court players, who showed us the intricacies of their instruments, as well as playing so beautifully on them; and of course I must not forget our sympathetic audiences; to all I wish a very happy New Year.

47 Dennis Brain 1921–1957 (1958)

Since the war, the horn playing of Dennis Brain has been one of the most familiar, certainly one of the happiest, features of British musical life. No season went by without his superlative performances as soloist in horn concertos. He was frequently to be seen at the first desk of one or other of the London orchestras, and no one will ever forget his inimitable tone and phrasing in the solo passages, from the small fragments in the works of the earlier masters (often devastatingly high—but so securely played), to the full dress melodies of more recent times (including Siegfried's horn call). Then there were his many appearances in chamber music either with a piano (Schumann's *Adagio and Allegro*, op. 70) or a string group (Mozart's Quintet, K. 407). His own excellent ensemble,[1] too, has delighted us with musicianly and beautifully rehearsed performances of music from Mozart to the present day, some of which was inspired by and written for Dennis.

The tragic car accident of 1st September leaves a musical gap which can never be filled.[2] It has robbed us of an artist with the unique combination of a superb technical command of his instrument, great musicianship, a lively and intelligent interest in music of all sorts, and a fine performing temperament, coupled with a charming personality. It has also robbed us of a man of rare generosity, simplicity and charm.

I first met Dennis in the early summer of 1942. I was writing incidental music for a series of radio commentaries on war-time England which were being broadcast weekly to America at the ungodly hour of 3 a.m.[3] The orchestra was that of the R.A.F., in which he was the first horn. I well remember being approached by him at one of the rehearsals, over, I think, some technical point in a solo passage. (Needless to say, having heard his playing in the first programme of the series I took every opportunity to write elaborate horn solos into each subsequent score!) We soon became friends, and it took him no time at all to persuade me to write a special work for him. This turned out to be the *Serenade* for tenor, horn and strings, the première of which he and Peter Pears gave in 1943. His help was invaluable in writing the work; but he was always most cautious in advising any alterations. Passages which seemed impossible even for his prodigious gifts were practised over and over again before any modifications were suggested, such was his respect for a composer's ideas. He

Source: *Tempo* 46 (Winter 1958), 55–6.

[1] Dennis Brain Chamber Orchestra.

[2] Brain was killed in a car accident on 31 Aug. 1957 following his participation in an all-Tchaikovsky programme in the Edinburgh Festival.

[3] Six programmes highlighting Anglo-American wartime cooperation, a collaboration between CBS, New York, and the BBC, under the series title 'An American in England'.

of course performed the work on many occasions, and for a period it seemed that no one else would ever be able to play it adequately. But, as usually happens when there is a work to play and a master who can play it, others slowly develop the means of playing it too, through his example. I must be grateful to Dennis for having challenged all other horn players in his playing of this piece. Some of my happiest musical experiences were conducting this work for him and Peter Pears—a succession of wonderful performances progressing from the youthful exuberance and brilliance of the early days to the maturity and deep understanding of the last few years.

Later, in 1954, I wrote another piece for Dennis, again with tenor, but this time with piano accompaniment, in memory of Noel Mewton-Wood.[4] Noel was a close friend of all of us, and had given many recitals with Dennis. His death was equally tragic and unexpected. (One is left aghast when one thinks of the loss sustained by English music in these two deaths and that of Kathleen Ferrier, all young artists at the beginning of dazzling careers, in the space of only four years). This time the work was a subdued *Canticle* (my third), the setting of a tragic poem of Edith Sitwell,[5] and from the start Dennis understood the remote, elegaic [*sic*] mood. I shall never forget his playing of the dark opening, the slithering chromatic scales, or the thunderous low notes.

He came many times to play for us at the Aldeburgh Festival, but last June he came primarily to conduct.[6] Here again he showed many of the same fine characteristics—musicianship, intelligence, enterprise, and hard work—and one felt that his conducting would soon possess the same ease and persuasion of his horn playing. However, what one remembers most clearly of that evening was not his conducting, but his playing in this same concert of the unfinished movement of Mozart's fragmentary horn Concerto in E.[7] The *tutti* started with its glorious richness. Delicate phrases followed with warm and intense counterpoint; brilliant passages for the violins, soothing oboe melodies. Then the solo entered—firm, heroic, and all seemed set for the best of all the wonderful Mozart horn concertos. And then suddenly in the middle of an intricate florid passage, superbly played, it stopped: silence. Dennis shrugged his shoulders and walked off the Jubilee Hall platform. That night, as always, he drove back home to London after the performance. Aldeburgh is not so far

[4] Noel Mewton-Wood (1922–53), Australian pianist, who gave the first performance of Britten's revised Piano Concerto (1946) and subsequent concerts in the Aldeburgh Festival. He killed himself following the death of his partner, Bill Fedriks.

[5] 'Still falls the rain – The raids, 1940' (*c.*1941).

[6] Telemann, Suite in F; Haydn, Horn Concerto No. 1 in D; Mozart, Symphony in B♭, K. 319; Stravinsky, Concerto in E♭ 'Dumbarton Oaks'; Racine Fricker, Concertante, Op. 13; Arnold, Sinfonietta, Op. 48.

[7] Fragment of a horn concerto in E, K.—/494*a* (?1783–7).

from London as Edinburgh, but far enough after a heavy day of rehearsals and performances, both conducting and playing. One protested, one always did, but off he went, laughing. That was the last time I ever heard him play, the last time I saw him. That Mozart fragment sticks in my mind as a symbol of Dennis's own life. But it is not so easy for us to shrug our shoulders.

48 Television and *The Turn of the Screw* (1959)

This is the first time in this country that an opera of mine has been specially produced on television, and I am extremely grateful to Associated-Rediffusion for its enterprise and courage in mounting THE TURN OF THE SCREW.[1] I am particularly happy that it should have been this opera that was chosen because it is one of my works most close to me, and also the one I feel most suitable for television.

Television can do an enormous amount to popularise opera in this country, especially if it avoids the spectacular Grand Opera so beloved by the eighteenth & nineteenth centuries and concentrates on the intimate and concise, which seems to me to belong particularly to the present day.

I cannot praise too highly the skill, taste and knowledge shown in adapting this difficult opera for television, especially when coupled with a respect for the score which did not allow one note to be cut.

Editor's title.

Source: Booklet produced by Associated-Rediffusion to accompany television broadcast of *The Turn of the Screw*, 1959.

[1] This extraordinary film, made live, was produced by Peter Morley, conducted by Charles Mackerras, and included in its cast a number of singers from the original production. Although the original print was subsequently destroyed, a copy of it was recovered and is now in the Britten–Pears Library.

49 Paul Beck 1895–1958 (1959)

This has been a sad year for us; Erwin Stein,[1] invaluable friend of the Festival, director of the English Opera Group, died in July; later in the year we lost Sir Arthur Jarratt,[2] also director of the E.O.G., and for many years a warm supporter of the Festival; and then in December came the sudden death of Paul Beck.[3]

There is an infinity of things great and small which every year must be done to keep the Festival running. These things happen behind the scenes, without even our small glare of publicity. Most people do not realise the size of such a job as keeping our keyboard instruments in tune and good order. We often have three or four pianos, large and small, usually more than one harpsichord, occasionally an eighteenth-century piano too, travelling to and from the [Aldeburgh Parish] Church, the Jubilee Hall, Framlingham, Blythburgh, each instrument with its own temperamental idiosyncracy. To see Paul Beck at work was a lesson to us all. Calm at the most tense moments, the few minutes between the last anxious rehearsal and the admittance of the audience, patiently waiting at the crack of dawn for the Church doors to be opened to prepare a harpsichord for the morning's performance or rehearsal, putting the instruments tenderly to bed after a Late Night, soothing and helping a nervous performer before and during a performance (I speak from personal experience)—all this was the sign of the true artist. Paul Beck since the first days of the first Festival had become the warm and trusted friend of us all. He will be most sadly missed.

Source: AFPB (1959), 83.

[1] Erwin Stein (1885–1958), Austrian conductor, music editor, academic, and critic. He was a pupil of Schoenberg and later worked for Universal Edition and Boosey & Hawkes, where he worked on the preparation for publication of Britten's scores. He and his family were close friends of Britten and Pears. See Essay 62 for a longer appreciation of Stein.

[2] Arthur Jarratt (1894–1958), businessman with keen interest in the arts, Director of EOG from early 1950s.

[3] Paul Beck (d. 1958), local piano tuner, whom Britten considered one of the best 'in the whole of England'. Imogen Holst, *Britten* (London: Faber & Faber, 1966), 49.

50 On Purcell's *Dido and Aeneas* (1959)

AMIS: *And now Purcell. No one has championed his music more than Benjamin Britten, and the first question I want to put to him is, what is it, Mr Britten, that you find so sympathetic about the music of Purcell?*

BRITTEN: That's a difficult question to answer briefly. He was open to many influences, he was a practical composer, he wrote for many different occasions, he was a Church composer, a theatre composer, wrote for the home—all that I find immensely sympathetic. Above all, I *love* his setting of words. I had never realized before I first met Purcell's music that words could be set with such ingenuity, with such colour.

AMIS: You've recently made a new version of his opera *Dido and Aeneas* that has been recorded for the BBC Transcription Service. I want to ask you *why* you felt it necessary to make a new version.[1]

BRITTEN: A work like *Dido* is not complete in itself. As we know, the continuo, the general bass, needs realizing: it's only a series of figures and the bass notes, therefore each generation particularly must find a new way of doing this. I'm not saying that what one does today supersedes what was done yesterday, but—except that today has a new point of view about Purcell.

AMIS: What about the sources? Where do you take your text from?

BRITTEN: There is no manuscript in Purcell's handwriting which exists. There are two copies, one as far as we know late eighteenth century, one early nineteenth century, which are sole sources. The earlier one is in Tenbury, in the library there.

AMIS: In Worcestershire?

BRITTEN: Yes. And the other one has had a curiously chequered career, and we discovered it fairly recently in Tokyo. There it is owned by a certain Mr Oki.[2] We had a photograph taken of it and he has sent it over to England. Neither of these manuscripts is really the infallible source. They are full of mistakes. They reflect the personality of the copyist, or whoever it was who commissioned the copy, and one has to guess a great deal.

Editor's title.

Source: Editor's transcript of recording (NSA T9340W). BBC Transcription Service: interview with John Amis for series *Talking about Music*. (Pre-recorded 13 Nov. 1959.) The programme celebrated 1959 as the 300th anniversary of Purcell's birth and the 200th anniversary of Handel's death.

[1] The new edition (1958–9) of Britten's 1951 realization was made in collaboration with Imogen Holst, who compared the Tenbury and Oki manuscripts. The cast for the September 1959 BBC recording included Claire Watson (Dido) and Peter Pears (Aeneas) with the Purcell Singers and the EOG Orchestra, conducted by Britten.

[2] Mr Kyuhei Oki, a Japanese collector.

AMIS: When you say mistakes, what kind of mistakes are you meaning? Sort of sharps instead of flats or something like that?

BRITTEN: Yes—bars left out, different wrong clefs, so many mistakes it is quite clearly that the manuscripts have not been used for performance—they can't have been. Therefore one has to do one's own editing.

AMIS: There are certain blanks in the score of *Dido.* What have you done about those?

BRITTEN: Well the controversial blank really isn't a blank, because each manuscript comes to the end of the second act with a full stop, draws a line and says 'end of the second act'. What gave us the clue—I say 'us' in this case because Imogen Holst[3] and I have been working closely together in this—was that in the libretto, which is in the College of Music—Royal College of Music—[there are] about eight lines not set by Purcell. Well that's quite possible that the libretto was printed earlier than the music was finished, but I felt—I've always felt, before I knew about the existence of this libretto—that this particular act, the second act, came to a very inconclusive end. Aeneas has been summoned away by the spirit, and instead of ending with a formal chorus as he does each other act, Purcell lets the music tail away. So when I found these other lines, I decided that I would like very much to see if I couldn't find some other music of Purcell which fitted these words. I hunted through. I found a really terrific chorus from one of the odes, which fitted the words perfectly well for a kind of chorus of exultation of the witches, and then I found a nice little dance which would end the act right in the key [in] which it started.[4]

AMIS: Perhaps we might hear that chorus, shan't we?

[Music excerpt: from Act II, *Dido and Aeneas* (real. Britten and Holst), 'A dance that shall make the spheres to wonder']

Well I think that goes very nicely.

BRITTEN: I personally think that it makes an excellent end to that act, but of course, this is all just waiting for the day of miracles when the real music that Purcell wrote to these words, which I firmly believe he did write, turns up again; but of course every day that passes makes the discovery of that music less likely.[5]

[3] Imogen Holst (1907–84), English music historian, educator, and conductor who worked as Britten's amanuensis from 1952 to 1964. She was co-director of the Aldeburgh Festival from 1956 to 1977.

[4] In the preface to the published vocal score, reference is made to these additions: 'The Trio for the Sorceress and the two witches, Act II, p. 46, is transposed from a trio in *The Indian Queen* (1960) [i.e. 1690]. The Chorus is transposed from the *Welcome Song* of 1687, and the Dance is taken from the overture to *Sir Anthony Love* (1690).'

[5] See preface to the Boosey & Hawkes published study score, Part V.

AMIS: Another thing I wanted to ask you—we're all interested in knowing what you're composing at the moment. Can we ask you what you're doing? One hears rumours of a new opera.

BRITTEN: I *am* writing a new opera at the moment. It's a formidable task; but a very lovely one, because I'm setting one of the loveliest of Shakespeare's plays, *A Midsummer Night's Dream*, to his own words. But it's a very big task and I'm rather nervous about it at the moment.

AMIS: Is this going to be another chamber opera, or—?

BRITTEN: It's a slightly large chamber.

AMIS: I see. What does that mean? What kind of orchestra?

BRITTEN: An orchestra of about twenty to twenty-five, and no chorus but a large cast, of course; I mean there are the fairies, there're the lovers, and it'll be in number, I should think, about fifty people.[6]

[6] i.e. fifty in cast and orchestra. Orchestra size with minimum string specification is twenty-seven. Amis concluded the programme with more music from Britten's realization of *Dido and Aeneas*, the dance following the above chorus at the end of Act II.

51 On Realizing the Continuo in Purcell's Songs (1959)

In practically every one of our concerts, given the length of three continents over the last twenty years, Peter Pears and I have included a group of Purcell's songs. Although they were not included for chauvinistic reasons, it has been nice to find that foreign audiences accept these English songs alongside those of their own great classic song-writers. It is pleasant to get cheers at the end of Purcell's 'Alleluia' in the home of Schubert and Wolf, requests for a repeat of 'Man is for the woman made' in the birthplace of Mozart, appreciative giggles at the end of 'There's not a swain of the Plain' in Fauré's home town, and an impressive silence as the last bars of 'Job's Curse' die away in Düsseldorf, where Schumann spent many years. And not only in foreign places; in England too—where, to our shame, the music of Purcell is still shockingly unknown. It is unknown because so much of it is unobtainable in print, and so much of what is available is in realizations which are frankly dull and out of date. Because all Purcell's solo songs, secular and sacred, as well as his many big scenas, have to be realized. We have these wonderful vocal parts, and fine strong basses, but nothing in between (even the figures for the harmony are often missing). If the tradition of improvisation from a figured bass were not lost, this would not be so serious, but to most people now, until a worked-out edition is available, these cold, unfilled-in lines mean nothing, and the incredible beauty and vitality, and infinite variety of these hundreds of songs go undiscovered. Therefore over these many years I have myself realized about twenty secular songs (mostly from *Orpheus Britannicus*), a few sacred songs, four of the big *Divine Hymns* (from the *Harmonia Sacra*) and half-a-dozen duets (some taken from the dramatic works reprinted separately by Purcell's widow in *Orpheus Britannicus*)—all with piano. I have also realized for other occasions the *Golden Sonata*, and continuo parts of the fine *Welcome Song* of 1687, and Purcell's masterpiece, *Dido and Aeneas*, for harpsichord. There is also a sequence of songs, a Suite from *Orpheus Britannicus*, where I realized the figured bass for strings.

Never have I attempted the ultimate realization of any of these songs. Since the accompaniments were originally intended to be improvised, they must be personal and immediate—and as we know only too well how ephemeral fashions are, how quickly tastes change, so each generation must want its own realizations. (I have myself in several cases changed my mind about my own efforts and after a few years rewritten them.) The most I have hoped for is to have

Source: Imogen Holst (ed.), *Henry Purcell 1659–1695: Essays on his Music* (London: OUP, 1959), 7–13.

drawn attention to some of these wonderful and useful songs by a lively enough version, and hope therefore that eventually other people will like these songs enough to arrange them themselves.

I have no theories as to how this should be done. But in the light of my experience here are a few deductions. It is an important rule of the game that one should stick to the actual notes of the bass (with allowable changing of the length of the notes—it seems in those days they were not too particular about this—and changing of the octave, such as could be done by different registrations on the harpsichord). And one must of course complete the harmonies in the way the figures indicate. If there are gaps in these (and there are many) a knowledge of the period and the composer's personal style should help. But just a filling in by these harmonies above the correct notes is not enough; one dimension is still lacking, the dimension of one's personal reaction to the song, which in former days would have been supplied by improvisation. This dimension comes from the *texture* of the accompaniment, the *way* the harmonies are filled in. If one is realizing for a piano it is important to be aware of the difference of sound from harpsichord and string bass, for which most of the songs would have been written. There must be compensation for the lack of sustaining power of the actual bass notes (repeated notes, octaves, trills, tremolandi for crescendi &c.), as well as an awareness of the difference between the plucked and hammered strings. Actually the sound that Purcell expected, this harpsichord sound, can give one ideas—dry clear arpeggios, grace-notes, octave doublings, sudden contrasts in dynamics or range, and that wonderful short staccato. However, the principal factors determining the texture are the form of the songs, the shapes of phrases in the voice part or the bass, and of course the mood of the words.

If the songs are simple verse songs, or songs not broken up into many sections, the accompaniment should reflect this by keeping to a consistent style. In 'I attempt from love's sickness to fly' I have supported the beautiful melody with simple continuous four-part harmony (with occasional doublings), with the top line occasionally moving in quavers suggested by the tune and the mood of the song. In 'Fairest Isle' I have used Purcell's own harmonies taken from his choral version (in *King Arthur*), with new keyboard spacing. In each successive verse of 'Man is for the woman made' I have invented new figuration to match the increasing dottiness of the words. In 'How blest are shepherds' and 'On the brow of Richmond Hill' the repetitions (I suggest, echoes) of each section of the tune have newly spaced harmonies to support it. The solo version of 'Turn then thine eyes' has rapid quaver triplets to introduce the coloratura of the voice part. The lively ♪♩ of 'will on thy cheek appear' is echoed on the piano. The elegant coquetry of 'Pious Celinda' suggested to me an ironic eighteenth-century phrase with a turn and grace note, which interrupts the amusing vocal line. 'Hark the echoing air' suggested imitations of trumpets and oboes (as did the 'Sound the Trumpet' duet) and the 'clapping of wings' suggested quick, snappy grace notes. In the songs with ostinato basses, which are many, I try to establish the ostinato clearly to begin with, and then colour each new image with new figuration—the 'snakes drop' in staccato thirds in 'Music for a while' after a clear four-octave start; in the 'Evening Hymn' the harmonies change very slowly and figuration is only gradually introduced.

In the form which Purcell perfected—the continuous movement made up of independent, short sections mysteriously linked by subtle contrasts of key, mood, and rhythm—the accompaniment must follow and emphasize these contrasts. Each miniature section of 'Sweeter than Roses' has its own figuration; the cool arpeggios of the 'roses'—in the short interlude, echoing the singer's first melting phrase—the growing intensity of 'warm' and the firm cadential 'kiss'; the 'trembling' is in oscillating sixths; high shivering chords 'freeze'; 'fire' has lively crackling chords; trumpets accompany the 'victorious love', and dizzy whirling quavers 'all, all, all is love'. This perhaps sounds naïve, but Purcell has himself suggested some such musical pictures in the voice and bass parts, and besides he has provided in these given parts a firm and secure musical structure which can safely hold together and make sense of one's wildest fantasies. This is only one of many similar cases. Perhaps the most beautiful and certainly one of the wildest, is 'Mad Bess'. Here to start, to finish, and to introduce many of the sections, I have used a scurrying semiquaver passage based on the first vocal phrase. Dramatically it can be said to suggest the movements of poor demented Bess.

In the *Divine Hymns* I have used the same kind of technique, but with a less exaggerated fantasy, since the moods are mostly less extreme. 'Lord, what is man' is in three fully worked out sections. The austere recitative which starts this fine Hymn I have accompanied quite barely: a turn for each of the long pedal notes—later a trill at the more animated 'Reveal ye glorious spirits'—chords at each change of harmony; and I echo the vocal run as 'joy' fades out into 'astonishment'. In the arioso 'Oh, for a quill' the little quaver passages in the piano part are all suggested by the voice or bass part, and by the intense though subdued mood of longing. The final 'Hallelujah' starts quietly—in figuration, largely octave doubling of the bass. I have added semiquaver figures as the momentum grows, and as the movement fades out into a soft ecstatic finish (which is the way we always do it) the right hand crosses and re-crosses the voice in flowing semiquavers.

The splendid opening tune of 'We sing to Him' suggests to me the singing of a thousand voices, so the accompaniment is in full ringing chords.

In 'Job's Curse' I have taken the liberty of repeating the last four bass bars as a little codetta after the voice has finished, in order to let the impact of this tremendous scena die away more gradually. It is however printed in small notes and can be omitted very easily. Similarly in 'I attempt from love's sickness to fly', that perfect opening song for a recital, I have preluded the song by a few bars; practical experience has shown us that this is necessary in order to accustom the audience to the style of the music, the sweet, subtle mood before the voice starts. The two little ariosi in 'The Blessed Virgin's Expostulation' are more contrapuntal—at 'me Judah's daughter', canonical, with the left hand gently filling in the harmonies.

One of Purcell's most elaborate dramatic Scenas is 'Saul and the Witch at Endor'. Misty slow-moving quavers at the start bind together the three voices, united in setting the gloomy scene. When they separate into their three individual characters I have used the simple device of different registers to add to the characterizations—the ghost of Samuel almost disappearing off the bottom of the piano.

'Celemene', the Dialogue for soprano and tenor from *Oroonoko* ('sung by the boy and the girl') could not be a greater contrast. The children prattle away about the puzzles of love, and I have followed the onomatopoeia of the voice parts: the heart-beats, the trembling, the touching. A five-finger exercise matches the innocence of 'When you wash yourself and play . . .' Again in 'I spy Celia' I have tried to follow every instruction in this young person's guide to love.

In the Suite from *Orpheus Britannicus* in which I arranged the figured basses for strings the problem was really the same as if realizing for piano, but with the big difference of thinking in terms of strings. At the start of 'Let sullen Discord smile' I added a viola part to the other strings because of the absence of a keyboard instrument. In the original the upper strings were dropped at the entry of the voice. I continue them in simple four-part harmony, adding *martellato* scale passages at 'let war devote this day to peace'. In 'Why should men quarrel' strings *pizzicato* fill out the harmony in between the spiky flute figuration and the cello solo. 'So when the glittering queen of Night' has the harmony filled out in the divided muted cellos and double bass. Against this funeral march-like background the voice and three solo strings stand out clearly like stars on a dark night. The introduction of 'Thou tun'st this world' is originally for two oboes and continuo. I have given the bass line to a bassoon and not completed the harmony. When the voice enters, the strings take over with simple detached chords, only occasionally flowing into figuration. At the end of this typically Purcellian song in a gay minor key, we repeat the second half of the introduction (as before on wind instruments alone). The splendid 'Sound Fame' has a rousing, but not Handelian, trumpet solo against one of Purcell's barest ostinatos. The latter I have given to a second string orchestra in octaves (at the end in four octaves). The first orchestra plays counterpoints and occasionally pizzicato block harmonies; finally joining the trumpet in diatonic semiquavers.

I know there are many other ways of realizing Purcell's figured basses—a highly distinguished series is now being brought out by my friends Michael Tippett and Walter Bergmann.[1] I hope there will be many more, and done with plenty of boldness of imagination, for what has kept so many of these wonderful treasures locked up in obscurity has been creative dullness or too much reverence. Purcell would have hated these two qualities above all; at least, that is the feeling one has after getting to know him through even these few works.

[1] Walter Bergmann (1902–88), British harpsichordist and music editor of German birth. He worked for Schott and taught at Morley College in the 1940s. In the 1950s Bergmann and Tippett were general editors of a series of Schott Purcell publications.

52 Back to Britain with Britten (1959)

REID: Please throw your mind back to 1930. You settled in London as a raw sixteen-year-old. Just where?

BRITTEN: I took a bed-sitter up under the roof in a boardinghouse at Prince's Square, Bayswater. I hired a small upright piano and took care not to play it after ten at night. I hadn't much money. As the youngest of four children I lived on a smallish allowance from my father. I was a 'scholar,' of course, but that didn't amount to much; it merely meant that my tuition fees were paid.

REID: I understand you weren't happy at the Royal College of Music. That true?

BRITTEN: Let's put it this way: I was rather a failure as a student. The trouble was, I had been studying with Bridge since I was a young boy. Bridge's approach was that of the highly professional international musician. The attitude of most of the R.C.M. students was amateurish and folksy. That made me feel highly intolerant.

REID: How did you get on with your two teachers—John Ireland and Arthur Benjamin?

BRITTEN: Well enough. But they didn't wield anything like as much influence on their students as the great Vaughan Williams. For my own part I was frankly suspicious of V.W. My struggle all the time was to develop a consciously controlled professional technique. It was a struggle away from everything Vaughan Williams seemed to stand for.

REID: But, like everybody else I suppose, you were swept off your feet by his Symphony No. 4?

BRITTEN: The Fourth Symphony impressed me greatly.[1] But an odd story went round the College after a rehearsal of it. Vaughan Williams was reported to have said of his own work, 'If that's modern music, all I can say is I don't like it.' This story, I must say, shocked me profoundly. In those days I was very violent in my opinions, very ready to have grievances.

REID: In a biographical essay he wrote about you several years ago, the Earl of Harewood said you won a travelling scholarship at the College and wanted to go to Vienna and study with Alban Berg but were stopped by the College 'authorities.' What's the background to this?

BRITTEN: I had won the Arthur Sullivan scholarship, worth £100 and enough to keep a youngster on the Continent for six months in those days. I decided to spend my £100 studying with Berg. I put in an application to the College administration, because the £100 had strings attached. I heard

Source: Interview with Charles Reid, *High Fidelity Magazine* (Dec. 1959), 72–6; 178–80.

[1] Composed 1931–4; Britten attended the Royal College from 1930 to 1933.

nothing more until one day my mother said she had been told by someone important at the College (she didn't say who it was, and I have never found out) that Berg was an 'unsuitable person.' The insinuation seemed to be that he was unsuitable on more than just musical grounds. I was furious. But there was nothing I could do. Berg died the following year.

REID: You were glad to see the end of your student days?

BRITTEN: I only started enjoying myself as a human being after I left college and got down to real work.

REID: Your first 'real work', I seem to recall, was writing documentary music for the G.P.O. Film Unit?

BRITTEN: *And* helping rig lights. *And* hold cameras. *And* cut films. *And* fix sound effects. All for £3 a week. The scores I wrote were for seven players at the outside. Exciting work. Exciting people to work with. W. H. Auden looked after the words side.

REID: By this time you had left your Bayswater attic?

BRITTEN: I was sharing a flat with my sister in West Hampstead.[2] It was a mews flat over a garage, the coldest in London, built on top of nothing, with nothing on either side of it. On the strength of my choral variations, *A Boy Was Born*, Ralph Hawkes the publisher gave me a contract.[3] I forget what he paid me. Something like £5 a week, I think. On his part it wasn't a hopelessly long shot, but he didn't start getting much of his money back for three or four years.

REID: But I always had the impression that after leaving college you prospered rather.

BRITTEN: Not really. A day came when the G.P.O. Film Unit no longer wanted me.[4] One had a struggle to get things performed.

REID: Which is why you decided to settle in America?

BRITTEN: Money was not really the issue. Frustration was more important. It was frustration that sent me to America. I felt there was a wall of laziness and apathy against new things.

REID: Did politics enter into it?

BRITTEN: Yes, politics too. I was under the influence of the Auden–Isherwood group and frightfully 'political', as all of us were in the Thirties. After Munich the morale of Europe seemed about as low as it could get. Things were becoming steadily more rotten.

[2] Beth Britten (1909–89).

[3] Ralph Hawkes (1898–1950), English publisher and visionary. The firm Boosey & Hawkes came about in 1930 as a result of an amalgamation between Boosey & Co. and Hawkes & Son.

[4] Britten's last score for the GPO Film Unit was *Mony a Pickle* (?1938). For the Realistic Film Unit he wrote music for *Advance Democracy*, his final film before *The Instruments of the Orchestra* (1945), which featured *The Young Person's Guide to the Orchestra*.

REID: And you were a pacifist.

BRITTEN: Yes, I was a pacifist. Not that I was running away from war when I went to America. At that time—the spring of 1939—there was no certainty that war was coming. But I wanted to have nothing to do with a military system that, to me, was part of Europe's decay. Mistakenly, as it turned out, I felt that Europe was finished. And it seemed to me that the New World was so much *newer*, so much readier to welcome new things.

REID: You travelled to America with Peter Pears?

BRITTEN: Peter was going to America on holiday and had fixed incidental singing dates there. He and I had been thrown together professionally a year or so before. I liked him enormously, admired his way of thinking, found him stimulating. So we made the voyage together, stopping off first in Canada for a few weeks' holiday in the Laurentian Mountains above Quebec. We rented a cabin there, very cheap. It was a combined walking and working holiday. I worked on *Les Illuminations* and the Violin Concerto. Then to Toronto, where I wrote incidental music and one commissioned piece (orchestral) for the CBC.[5] Next for a spell with Aaron Copland—I had met him in England and admired him a lot—at his holiday place in upstate New York.[6]

REID: It had been your intention to become an American citizen?

BRITTEN: True. But the war changed all that. The change wasn't an intellectual one primarily. I don't think I ever consciously reasoned it out. Certainly I underwent a lot of personal tension. Practically all of 1940 I was ill. Outwardly the ailment was infected tonsils. But the real cause was my mental perplexities. It was a frantically difficult position. Gradually I realized that, for better or worse, I was a European.

REID: Did you get any work done during your streptococcal phase?

BRITTEN: *Paul Bunyan* and the *Sinfonia da Requiem* date from that time.

REID: Tell me about *Bunyan*. As it isn't in print, I'm vague about it.

BRITTEN: Paul Bunyan as you know is the mythical giant of American folklore. Some of my music was good—I wouldn't say very good. When the piece was produced by the Opera Department of Columbia University, Auden and myself weren't at all popular. In fact, *Bunyan* caused quite a scandal, mainly because of Auden's words. Auden thought fit to utter many

[5] *Young Apollo* (1939).

[6] Britten met Aaron Copland (1900–90) at the 1938 ISCM Festival in London, at which Copland's *El Salón México* was performed. Britten was greatly impressed by the work and invited Copland to visit him at Snape, during which time he played through his new schools' opera, *The Second Hurricane*, the influences of which emerged three years later in *Paul Bunyan*. Copland returned the compliment in 1939 by inviting Britten to his place in Woodstock, Catskills Mountains.

home truths about America. It was as if an American living in England had written a derogatory piece about John Bull.

REID: And the *Sinfonia da Requiem*?

BRITTEN: That's an odd story. While I was in America, the Japanese government approached various composers (Strauss for Germany, Milhaud for France, me for Britain) and asked us to write pieces in commemoration of the 2,600th anniversary of the foundation of the Mikado's dynasty. The invitation came to me through the British Council. I cabled back to London accepting, subject to my not being expected to write anything jingoistic. On this point I got the necessary assurance. The *Sinfonia* as I had originally conceived it was in memory of my mother, but in scale and type it was well suited to a festival. Through the British Council I cabled to the Japanese a description of the work, with title and subtitles [*Lacrymosa*, *Dies Irae*, and *Requiem Aeternam*], all of which struck me as compatible with a creed that involves ancestor worship.

REID: Did it strike the Japs that way?

BRITTEN: The Japanese people in London made no difficulty. They accepted the outline at once. I completed the score and sent it off to Tokyo. Then all hell broke loose. I was summoned to the Japanese Consulate in New York and had an absolutely furious letter from somebody in Tokyo. The letter said, among other things, that it was an insult to Japan to submit a work of Christian character. I replied formally, by letter, that, as I *was* a Christian, that was only to have been expected.

REID: It was through the *Sinfonia*, was it not, that you met Serge Koussevitzky?

BRITTEN: Koussevitzky must have heard about Barbirolli's performance of it. He did two performances of the *Sinfonia* himself in Boston before taking it on tour. One of them I attended. Wonderful conductor. He took infinite pains. He told me how impressed he was by the dramatic qualities of my score. Then he said, 'Why don't you write an opera?' I told him I was so busy writing incidental music and shorter works that I simply couldn't afford to take the time off. I saw him next about a week later. He said, 'Well, I've got some money for you [$1,000 from the Koussevitzky Music Foundation]. Will you write an opera now?' I said 'Of course'. *Peter Grimes* was the result.

REID: By that time you were homeward-bound?

BRITTEN: I had decided in August 1941 that I must get home at all costs. Peter and I stayed for six months with our trunks packed awaiting passage, always ready to leave at twenty-four hours' notice. I hadn't much money. I did all kinds of odd jobs, including proof correcting. We came back on a Swedish ship, New York to Belfast, originally in convoy, but the funnel caught fire and for a while we steamed alone. The voyage lasted a month and was frightening at times. But I had started composing again. On shipboard I wrote the *Hymn to Saint Cecilia*, *A Ceremony of Carols*, and several things I didn't finally use.[7] Scares apart, that month at sea was one of the most enjoyable of my life.

[7] A scenario of *Peter Grimes* was also undertaken during this voyage.

53 People Today: Benjamin Britten (1960)

HAREWOOD: I think I've probably caught you at about as busy a time of year as you can get, haven't I?

BRITTEN: Well, it certainly is with the preparation of the Festival and with the opera rehearsals in full swing and of course many other things to cope with as well, but it's a time of year one—let's face it—enjoys very much indeed.[1]

HAREWOOD: And you've been preparing for it, what—for really most of the year, one way and another, thinking about it and then gradually working out—?

BRITTEN: One really prepares each Festival almost before the previous one is finished, I find. In fact one of the most pleasant things to do, I think, while you're preparing one Festival, is to think what you'd like to do for the next year.

HAREWOOD: It's really one of the marks of Aldeburgh, in fact, this feeling that it's been prepared a long time in advance, that the whole programme's been worked out, things that you've been wanting to do, pining to do for a number of months and then working at finding the performers . . .

BRITTEN: Yes, it is—it's a very pleasant way of making music, especially as we have found that there are enough people who like the kind of things that we like to come and make the Festival worthwhile without a great deal of advertising and of trying to make the Festival known.

HAREWOOD: How do you start on the programme? Do you start by looking for the composers you want to do, or do you always find you have a queue of works in your mind—things you want to do that other people aren't doing?

BRITTEN: I think the shape of the Festival—that is, the works you want to perform in the Festival—is very much dictated by the town itself, the buildings, the size of those buildings, and the quality of those buildings. For instance there's this very beautiful church and the churches in the district that can take a certain number of performers, not too many. Then there is the Jubilee Hall which as you know is a tiny little theatre, holding an audience of not more than 320 or [3]30; [a] very small orchestra, although we've enlarged it this year with a bigger orchestral pit—it will take an orchestra of about forty—but the nature of these buildings dictates the fact that we cannot do big-scale works. Again, the chorus, which is a local amateur

Source: Editor's transcript of recording (NSA T9341R). Broadcast 23 June 1960, BBC Home Service, 10.15 p.m.: Britten in discussion with the Earl of Harewood for the series *People Today*. (Pre-recorded 29 May 1960, at The Red House, Aldeburgh.)

[1] Britten was rehearsing for the premiere of *A Midsummer Night's Dream* (1960).

chorus, can only perform at weekends, therefore the choral concerts can only be at weekends. What I'm getting at is that the nature of the town and the people working for the Festival dictates very much the shape of the Festival.

Now in the works which are of that size are many works that one has been wanting to do for many years. One is always saying, when one hears or reads of a new work by Schütz or Monteverdi that one has never heard before, 'Oh, it'd be lovely to do that'. Or modern works—when Stravinsky writes a new piece which would suit us very well one remembers those works and so they begin to line up ready for the next programmes.

HAREWOOD: One of the criticisms I've sometimes heard of Aldeburgh is that after the first year or so that you put too little—or you allowed too little of your own music to come in. It's certainly a criticism I've heard from some people.

BRITTEN: Well I feel very strongly about this point. It is not a festival for propagating one's own works. Obviously—as I am a kind of—a composer who likes writing for occasions, it is fun for me to write new operas, new works to fit into the Festival; but essentially I don't feel—and I hope people are gradually all beginning to feel that with me—that this is not a festival like Bayreuth, which is obviously designed for Wagner's own works. This is *not* the case at Aldeburgh. We are only too happy to do works of all composers of any age or any generation, of any kind, that fits into our plans.[2]

HAREWOOD: What about Aldeburgh as a background? You weren't born at Aldeburgh, after all.

BRITTEN: No. I was born very near Aldeburgh. It's what, only twenty-eight miles, I think, Aldeburgh; Lowestoft is north of Aldeburgh.

HAREWOOD: You've lived about half your life here, or near here.

BRITTEN: In this district, yes, since 19—I think 37 it was when I moved south from Lowestoft.[3]

HAREWOOD: And that was the sort of thing you *wanted* to do?

BRITTEN: Yes. I've always felt I wanted to live by the sea. I've tried living away from the sea but something has gone slightly wrong, I always felt. I have needed that particular kind of atmosphere that the house on the edge of the sea provides.

HAREWOOD: Some people have thought that you've made it into a sort of sanctuary for yourself, and that's not an unreasonable thing for a composer

[2] See Paul Kildea, *Selling Britten*, (Oxford: OUP, 2002) ch. 5, for a breakdown of Britten premieres at Aldeburgh, 1948–76.

[3] Britten acquired the Old Mill, Snape, in August 1937, and moved in, after renovations, in April 1938. Although he had not lived in Lowestoft since 1930, it was the death of his mother on 31 January 1937 that caused him to sever domestic links with Lowestoft.

to do—to want to make his own home in a place where he's away from—if you like, from the things that worry him, in contact with the things that stimulate him. You find Aldeburgh's the perfect atmosphere for working?

BRITTEN: Yes; I would—I agree with that. It's the sized town that I like very much. It's not big enough to be a metropolitan in feeling, and it's got enough people around to, for instance, to help us run a festival like this. I don't like living in London. I have tried. I've lived on and off in London for quite a few years, but I don't feel happy there. Essentially I like living in small communities. One can be absolutely quiet. For one thing one needs, as a creative artist, to have a lot of time to oneself. On the other hand there are the times when one has to have a little—well, recreation, and it's nice to be able to play tennis with one's friends and to meet them or go to a film or something like that.

HAREWOOD: What sort of timetable do you set yourself, or do you find evolves when you're working at Aldeburgh?

BRITTEN: I like working to an exact timetable. I—I often thank my stars that I had a rather conventional upbringing, that I went to a rather strict school where one was made to work and I can, without much difficulty, sit down at 8.30 or 9 o'clock in the morning and work straight through the morning until lunchtime without too much difficulty. I don't say I always enjoy the work at that time, but it isn't a great struggle to do so each day. I find actually the day divides up quite naturally into, say, three or four periods: the morning, as I've said, when I work until lunchtime, and then in the afternoon I do letters or—rather more important, actually, is that I go for a walk, where I plan out what I'm going to write in the next period at my desk. I then come back after tea, up to my studio here and work, say, through to dinner time, about 8 o'clock. After dinner I usually find I'm too sleepy, too exhausted with working, to do much more than to read a little bit and then go to bed rather early.

HAREWOOD: That makes it sound a very solitary existence. That's not the only sort of thing you do here—you mentioned the community, the agreeable removal from your work by your friends, by people you want to talk to and see.

BRITTEN: Oh yes—when I say I work, for instance, until lunchtime, there's always the moment before lunch when a short discussion on the next year's Festival can take place, and then of course I must confess I like playing tennis or in the summer swimming, and that I always find time for somehow.

HAREWOOD: You said just now that you had what you described as a conventional upbringing with a certain emphasis on working when you were told to at school and generally being used to a discipline of work. When did you actually start on what one might describe as a disciplined musical life? I'm sure you started to make music when you were very small, when you were a small child.

BRITTEN: Yes, I actually started playing the piano, as one would expect, at a very early age. I started writing—music, I was going to say, but hesitated before, because it was really not much more than dots and dashes on a bit of paper; but that I did start at a curiously early age, about—when I was about 5, I think, the story is. But it was much more the *look* of the thing on the paper which fascinated me.

HAREWOOD: You already wanted to write it down?

BRITTEN: Yes. In fact I was more interested in writing it down than even what it sounded like, but very soon, when I—for instance I got my mother to try and play these curious things I'd written down—I realized that one has to connect the notes with the sound, and that started, I suppose—I had a very good piano teacher,[4] a local one—when I was about 8—and then I started to write in a little more orderly fashion songs and counterpoint exercises, harmony exercises, and that went on all the time I was at my private school. I used to disconcert the other children by writing music in the dormitory and all that kind of thing; but my serious composition lessons started when I was about 12, I think it was, when I had the very good fortune to meet Frank Bridge, who was the friend of my viola teacher (I learnt the viola at an early age), and he took a great interest in me and every holiday I used to go and stay with him, either in his house in Sussex where he lived, or occasionally in London where he also had a house; and he taught me an enormous amount.[5] He taught me other things to think about and gave me a broader horizon generally. I'm most grateful for him for having taught me to take infinite trouble over getting every note quite right. He used to perform the most terrible operations on the music I would rather confidently show him. He would play every passage slowly on the piano and say, 'Now listen to this—is this what you meant?' And of course I would start by defending it, but then one would realize as one—as he went on playing this passage over and over again—that one hadn't really thought enough about it. And he really taught me to take as much trouble as I possibly could over every passage, over every progression, over every line and I'm most grateful to him for that.

HAREWOOD: Did he start you off on your love of poetry?

BRITTEN: No, that I think was already, even then, when I was a boy, fairly strong with me. I've always—I had always read poetry. I find it, in a way, easier to read than prose; but the person, I think, who developed my love was the poet, Auden, whom I met, I think, in [my] late teens. We collaborated over

[4] Ethel Astle (1876–1952).

[5] His viola teacher was Audrey Alston (1883–1966).

music and verse for a film,[6] and he had an enormous influence on me for quite a considerable period. He showed me many things. I remember, for instance, he it was who introduced me to the works of Rimbaud,[7] who was only a name to me then; and many people, he taught me to—showed me the different periods in verse. I remember he showed me Chaucer for the first time. I'd always imagined that was a kind of foreign language, but as he read it, which was very well, I understood almost immediately what it meant, and I find now that it isn't so difficult to read—one must just have confidence and read ahead and then the meaning comes very strongly, very easily.

HAREWOOD: In fact it was influenced by Auden that you decided to go to America a year or so before the war.

BRITTEN: Yes. I was very much influenced by Auden, not only in poetry but in life too; and politics, of course, came very strongly into our lives in the late '30s. He went to America, I think it was late '38, early '39, and I went soon after.[8] I think it wouldn't be too much oversimplifying the situation to say that many of us young people at that time felt that Europe was more or less finished. There was this great Nazi Fascist cloud about to break at any moment and one felt that Europe didn't—nor did it have the will to—resist that. I went to America and felt that I would make my future there. It took me a long time to realize that that would not be so, and perhaps it's interesting to say that that realization came partly through illness. I was very ill for a year or so in the early days of the war in America. When the illness cleared, I knew quite definitely that my home did not lie there, that whatever the situation was, that I was a European, and so I came back. It was, I think, the early days of '42—yes, it was—I'd tried very hard to get a boat in '41 but, as you might imagine, the boats weren't running very frequently, or easily, in those days, and it took six months to find a passage. I remember the uncomfortable situation of being packed, having all one's clothes and belongings packed ready to sail at an hour's notice, for more than six months.

HAREWOOD: And from then the American influence on your life has really been very small. It wasn't very large on your composition even in those two years in America, was it?

BRITTEN: No, I wouldn't say it has. I've—I have very good American friends, but my actual contact with America since then has been rather limited. I feel enormously sympathetic to Europe at this moment, and in my travels which

[6] *Night Mail* (1936) is probably what Britten is referring to, although there were two previous, less famous collaborations: *Coal Face* (1935) and the abandoned *Negroes* (1935; made as *God's Chillun* in 1937).

[7] Whom he set in *Les Illuminations* (1939).

[8] Auden left Britain in January 1939, Britten in May of that year.

must—necessarily [be] rather limited—I would much prefer to go east rather than west.

HAREWOOD: Can we get back to the actual business of composition? I remember you once saying something very interesting about the actual nature of inspiration—that there were two sorts of inspiration. One is somebody who had a particular stimulus from which everything he wrote depended, and then on the other side, in opposition, so to speak, were composers who wrote all the time as a matter of course.

BRITTEN: Yes, I think that is—I still agree, still feel that is so. Of course, I belong very much, as I described earlier in our talk, because of my routine of working, to the person—the kind of composer who writes as a matter of course. Now that is very much against what the public seems to think is the nature of artistic creation. The feeling is that the creator, the artist, has a moment of sudden inspiration, dashes to the paper or the canvas or the typewriter, and in the *height* of inspiration, writes down, paints this wonderful picture that is in his mind. In my experience that isn't the way that I want to work. I mean I hastily say that I don't think that—that mine is the only way of working, but composers have to find their own form of work which suits their own talent best; but if I could say it like this: the composer is really only writing down the result of many hours' thinking, many years of experience. The actual writing on the paper is *not* the moment of inspiration. That comes much earlier in his life—he may not even be aware of it. The work is planned, and then when the plan of the work is fixed—is finished—the actual notes are decided on.

HAREWOOD: You said once to me, when I asked you how—I don't know—a movement, or another act of an opera, or something of that sort—how it was going—you said, 'Oh, I think I know exactly how it's going. It's now only a question of finding the right notes.' You meant that the plan was there in your mind and that your problem was to find exactly how to express it in pure music.

BRITTEN: Yes; and how one defines those notes really is this matter of technique, of fitting—filling these—this plan that one has evolved—with the notes that complete the design.

HAREWOOD: Can you give any example of this sort of situation in your own works—perhaps from *Peter Grimes* or something like that?

BRITTEN: Yes, I think one could. I don't know if you remember in the end of the first act, there's a storm and in the pub the tempers are getting strained and Auntie suggests that they should sing a song.[9] Well, if one thinks of it dramatically, songs don't—aren't—in such a situation in a pub, organized by

[9] 'Old Joe has gone fishing'.

a conductor beating time—they're taken up very much one after another. Someone thinks of a tune and the others follow on. Well that in musical, technical terms is a round, where one voice sings a tune and then goes on to another but while he goes on to the second one the next character comes on and sings the first strain. Well *there* is a case where one decided that a round was the most suitable dramatic form, and so one had to write a round. Well, that is a matter of intellectual exercise as one writes a short phrase and then one has to write another phrase to fit that, and what makes one a good or bad composer is to make these phrases sound natural and not contrived.

HAREWOOD: In fact your problem there one was of finding the notes, as you said before, finding the notes to fit the situation and of then managing to make those notes provide the climax of a fairly substantial act of opera, act of music. Do you find that with songs, for instance, do you find that reading poetry, when you are perhaps either reading for your own pleasure or even reading to look for the poetry that might provide a song cycle or material for music, do you find suddenly that it hits you just like that—that you know immediately that is the piece you want to set, and you want to set it in a particular way?

BRITTEN: It *can* work like that, or another rather interesting aspect of the same thing can be rather the other way round. Quite often I find that I am in the mood for writing a song about a certain kind of subject or in a certain kind of mood, and even I have in my experience—had the experience of having even the suggestion of a tune which would like to have words attached to it. I then look through volumes until I find such a thing, but nearly always, and I suppose this is where the subconscious comes in, it's poems I've known, and I suspect that poem has been going on ringing in one's subconscious and has produced the tune but I haven't been aware of it.

HAREWOOD: I imagine another source of inspiration, or at any rate a factor in the inspiration in writing music, and that is knowing the sort of performers you're writing for. You've usually written with either a certain set of performers in mind, certain individuals with individual characteristics, or for a particular company, let's say, or body of instrumentalists, haven't you?

BRITTEN: Yes. I've always found that a most exciting and stimulating thing. It's partly, I think, that I've got so strongly the feeling that I want my music to be used, I—and therefore I like to provide music for my friends to use; and it's also that I get a great inspiration from the sound of their voices or the sound of the way they play their instruments; and I have—certainly, I think you're quite right, in the last fifteen, twenty years I've almost never written a piece of music that wasn't attached to some performer or group of performers. In this particular case of the opera we're working at now, the *Midsummer Night's Dream*, that was entirely planned for an occasion. I was actually going to write another opera for the Aldeburgh Festival this year, and then very much at the last moment, the opportunity to rebuild the little Jubilee Hall of Aldeburgh presented itself, and I realized that the opera I was going to write wasn't suitable for such an exciting specific occasion as this.[10] I thought I'd like to write an opera on a grander scale with perhaps a little less personal, peculiar background as this other piece. It was then—what—July, August last year? There was not time to get a libretto specially written, so one had to take a piece or think of a piece where the words already existed. Shakespeare was of course a wonderful and ready-to-hand example of that. I had incidentally thought a few years ago of doing this same piece as an opera, the *Midsummer Night's Dream*, so the task then was to divide it up into an operatic form, which we have done; and we planned the opera really entirely for this reopening of the Jubilee Hall which will happen in a week or so's time; and of course written for the friends who so often visit the Aldeburgh Festival, the singers and the players whom we like working with, the producer, the designer whom one feels happiest with,[11] because under these circumstances when the work was being done very much at the last moment, a year is not a great deal of time to prepare the libretto, write the music, and to rehearse and to have all the material made.

HAREWOOD: When you write music, whether it's to commission or for a particular occasion (after all the particular occasion is presumably not where you mean the music to end), do you ever think in terms of the public which is going to hear it?

BRITTEN: It's a very difficult question to answer simply and concisely. Obviously one does consider one's public. For instance one doesn't write an opera which lasts eight hours without an interval—that could be socially very inconvenient. That's an extreme case.

HAREWOOD: You have had temptations that way, I think.

BRITTEN: On the other hand you see, one doesn't write music that is calculated to please them. I don't write a tune and think 'Oh yes, my Aunt Mary's going to like that tune very much.' On the other hand I perhaps don't write a tune that would be so complicated that Aunt Mary won't know where one's going. For instance, I can say in writing for children, at no point does one write *down* to them, but one tries not to give them something outside

[10] Possibly already *Curlew River*, which he was discussing with William Plomer as early as 1957.

[11] Singers included Pears, Jennifer Vyvyan, Johanna Peters, April Cantelo, Owen Brannigan; John Cranko produced; John Piper designed.

their experience. For instance, one doesn't want to write a piece for children which is so long that their attention will wander. On the other hand I don't hesitate for one moment writing music which is new to them. That, in my experience, stimulates and excites them. The artistic compromise is too risky for a composer—serious composer—to undertake.

HAREWOOD: You've often written music for children and, if I may say so, with outstanding success. You wrote—in the first children's opera you wrote, of your two children's operas[12]—you wrote even a duet which you said was going to sound perfectly well if they sang it in canon as they were supposed to, or if they sang it together if they got wrong;[13] but you've also written occasionally music for amateurs, haven't you?

BRITTEN: Oh yes. I—I'm very keen on doing that, partly because I'm a rather keen amateur performer myself—for instance, on an instrument like the recorder, [and] there one tries to write music which, as you say, even if they get it wrong, doesn't sound too awful, where the actual polish of the performance isn't the ultimate aim.

HAREWOOD: Have you ever thought of writing what one calls a musical nowadays—a musical show?

BRITTEN: Yes, quite honestly I have recently considered that very seriously. I was asked to do—to write the music for a musical and have very reluctantly turned it down.[14] I don't say that I never will be able to do that, but I don't see at the moment a way of—if I can put it like this—jettisoning all one's actual technique. I don't want [to] by any means to talk disparagingly of musicals, but their aim seems to me very different from what I'm aiming at. They aim at a kind of directness, a kind of melodic simplicity, a kind of formal simplicity that I don't feel at the moment I can manage. The best musicals of many years have been those written by essentially simple people who can turn out a short melody which fits very neatly into the conventions of harmony at that moment and which is entirely dependent on that. Now one day I would love to be able to agree to write such a thing because I feel that it's an important part of the artistic life of our time; but I don't feel my public is quite—what my public—well, I say by that—what public I'm aiming at is quite of that kind. I think, to put it simply, that I'm aiming at the sort of—the serious popular or the popular serious, rather than the entirely commercial popular world.

You see, although I did perhaps paint a rather too rosy picture of one's life as a composer, as when we first started talking about how I could make myself go and work at my desk at specified hours, I must also add that one

[12] *The Little Sweep* (1949); *Noye's Fludde* (1958).

[13] Most likely the Shanty ('Pull the rope gently until he is free'), sung by all the children, with imitative, although not strictly canonic, parts.

[14] Not identified.

can only really write the kind of music that one's heart is in. I hope to be able to extend that to include a more popular or a more serious vein later, as I grow older, but at the moment I am very happy with the small public that seems to like the kind of music that I like and that I want to write. You know, in fact one can only write the kind of music that one loves.

54 A New Britten Opera (1960)

Last August it was decided that for this year's Aldeburgh Festival I should write a full-length opera for the opening of the reconstructed Jubilee Hall.

As this was a comparatively sudden decision there was no time to get a libretto written, so we took one that was ready to hand. I get a lot of letters from young people asking me how they should use their talents, and I always reply that they should try to fit them into their surroundings. This is what has happened with my new opera. It is an example of how local conditions can determine what you do.

I have always loved the 'Midsummer Night's Dream'. As I get older, I find that I increasingly prefer the work either of the very young or of the very old. I always feel the 'Midsummer Night's Dream' to be by a very young man, whatever Shakespeare's actual age when he wrote it.[1] Operatically, it is especially exciting because there are three quite separate groups—the Lovers, the Rustics, and the Fairies—which nevertheless interact. Thus in writing the opera I have used a different kind of texture and orchestral 'colour' for each section. For instance, the Fairies are accompanied by harps and percussion; though obviously with a tiny orchestra they can't be kept absolutely separate.

In writing opera, I have always found it very dangerous to start writing the music until the words are more or less fixed. One talks to a possible librettist, and decide together the shape of the subject and its treatment. In my case, when I worked with E. M. Forster or William Plomer,[2] for instance, we blocked the opera out in the way that an artist might block out a picture. With the 'Midsummer Night's Dream', the first task was to get it into manageable shape, which basically entailed simplifying and cutting an extremely complex story—one can only hope that one hasn't lost too much, but since the sung word takes so much longer than the spoken word, to have done the complete 'Midsummer Night's Dream' would have produced an opera as long as 'The Ring'.

Peter Pears (who sings Flute, the bellows-mender) and I had endless trouble with the references and the proportions of the play. We stuck faithfully to

Source: *Observer* (5 June 1960), 9, reprinted in *The Britten Companion* (ed. Christopher Palmer, London: Faber & Faber, 1984), 177–80.

[1] *A Midsummer Night's Dream* was probably written in 1595 or 1596, when Shakespeare was in his early thirties.

[2] William Plomer (1903–73), South African writer and librettist, who wrote for Britten four librettos: *Gloriana* (1953), *Curlew River* (1964), *The Burning Fiery Furnace* (1966), and *The Prodigal Son* (1968). They also planned together a children's opera, which was never written.

Shakespeare's words, actually adding only one line: 'Compelling thee to marry with Demetrius'.[3] We worked from many texts, but principally from facsimiles of the First Folio and the First Quarto.

I do not feel in the least guilty at having cut the play in half. The original Shakespeare will survive. Nor did I find it daunting to be tackling a masterpiece which already has a strong verbal music of its own. Its music and the music I have written for it are at two quite different levels. I haven't tried to put across any particular idea of the play that I could equally well express in words, but although one doesn't intend to make any special interpretation, one cannot avoid it.

The opera is more relaxed than 'The Turn of the Screw'; it has far more scenes, and is much less uniform. In form, it is more like 'Peter Grimes'. I have felt it to be a more difficult task to write than these, partly because the work in hand is always the hardest, partly because of the tremendous challenge of those Shakespearean words. Working at it, one was very conscious that one must not let through a single ill-considered phrase because it would be matched to such great poetry.

I actually started work on the opera in October, and finished it on, I think, Good Friday—seven months for everything, including the score. This is not up to the speed of Mozart or Verdi, but these days, when the line of musical language is broken, it is much rarer. It is the fastest of any big opera I have written, though I wrote 'Let's Make an Opera' in a fortnight.

Writing an opera is very different from writing individual songs: opera, of course, includes songs, but has many other musical forms and a whole dramatic shape as well. In my experience, the shape comes first. With the 'Midsummer Night's Dream', as with other operas, I first had a general musical conception of the whole work in my mind. I conceived the work without any one note being defined. I could have described the music, but not played a note.

It was a particularly bad winter for me, writing it. Normally I work perfectly regular hours, in the morning and again between four and eight. Around Aldeburgh, the weather seems always to be better in the morning; it clouds over about midday and I don't work then. I cannot work at night. In Suffolk the air is strong, and by nightfall I want to do nothing but sleep. This winter I became quite ill, but had to go on working. A lot of the third act was written when I was not at all well with flu. I didn't enjoy it. But I find that one's inclination, whether one wants to work or not, does not in the least affect the quality of the work done. Very often it is precisely after one has had what one feels

[3] The addition of this one line allowed Britten and Pears to make extensive cuts but retain narrative sense.

to have been a wonderful morning, that one needs to watch out—perhaps one's critical faculties may have been asleep.

I haven't tried to give the opera an Elizabethan flavour. It is no more Elizabethan than Shakespeare's play was Athenian. Perhaps one or two points may seem strange. The Fairies, for instance, are very different from the innocent nothings that often appear in productions of Shakespeare. I have always been struck by a kind of sharpness in Shakespeare's fairies; besides, they have some odd poetry to speak—the part about 'you spotted snakes with double tongue' for instance. The Fairies are, after all, the guards to Titania [*sic*]: so they have, in places, martial music.[4] Like the actual world, incidentally, the spirit world contains bad as well as good.

Puck is a quite different character from anyone else in the play. He seems to me to be absolutely amoral and yet innocent. In this production he is being played by the fifteen-year-old son of Leonide Massine: he doesn't sing, but only speaks and tumbles about.[5] I got the idea of doing Puck like this in Stockholm, where I saw some Swedish child acrobats with extraordinary agility and powers of mimicry, and suddenly realised we could do Puck that way.

The opera, since it was written for a hall which holds only 316 people, is small-scale. The forces one uses must necessarily be small, which has great advantages: one can work in a more detailed way with them and get a greater degree of discipline. The singers do not have to sing with such uniform volume, so that the voice can be used throughout its full range of colour. Besides, on a small scale, we can choose singers who either can act or who are prepared to learn to do so. Some opera-goers seem to prefer singers who cannot act: there is a curious inverted snobbery current in this country which even prefers operatic acting to be as bad as possible. They do not want opera to be serious at all. They like singers who merely come down to the footlights and yell.

For my part, I want singers who can act. Mozart, Gluck and Verdi wanted the same thing. There is one singer in this production who has never been on a stage before in his life;[6] but his strong concert personality fits naturally on to the operatic stage and his acting is developing very well. How many singers know how to move? I think it's essential for every potential opera singer to have a course of movement in an opera school. I must say one hoped, after the war, that audiences would revolt at seeing opera performed with bad acting, bad scenery and in a foreign language.

[4] Britten had chosen a different, archaic spelling from that used in modern editions—Tytania.

[5] Leonide Massine II, son of Leonide Massine (1896–1979), American choreographer of Russian birth.

[6] Alfred Deller (1912–79), English countertenor, created the role of Oberon, having never performed in opera before this.

We are taking the 'Midsummer Night's Dream' to Holland immediately after the Aldeburgh Festival. If it is any good it will get many different interpretations in many different places and all with translations. I have even heard 'Peter Grimes' in Serbo-Croat. But the new opera was really written as part of the Aldeburgh Festival, for the reopening of the Jubilee Hall. Ultimately, it is to me the local things that matter most.

55 *A Midsummer Night's Dream* (1960)

BBC: Mr Britten, this work is called an opera based on the work of Shakespeare. Have you in fact set Shakespeare's lines to music?

BRITTEN: Yes, Shakespeare's text is the basis of the whole work. I think we've included half a line which is not written by Shakespeare, but otherwise it is only his words which we've used.[1]

BBC: What were your feelings about the shaping of Shakespeare's thoughts to a medium he didn't intend them for?

BRITTEN: Well, that doesn't worry me so much, because Shakespeare can look after himself and however well or badly or much I cut the work, the text—thank goodness—remains. But my main feeling in setting this work was enormous love and reverence and respect for the text. I feel that everyone ought to set Shakespeare to music in order just to get to know the incredible beauty and intensity of these words.

BBC: What made you want to write an opera, then, based on *A Midsummer Night's Dream* particularly?

BRITTEN: Well, I wanted to set a play of Shakespeare's for several reasons. One was that it had to be done in rather a hurry, and there wasn't time to get a libretto specially written, and so one had to take work—words which already existed. The *Midsummer Night's Dream*—oh, for several reasons—seemed to be most suitable; partly because it has such amazingly beautiful poetry already intended for singing. A lot of the fairies' words were intended to be songs. It is a very good operatic story—it has very clear situations and it has, what fascinated me particularly, these three different levels of creatures in it. It has the royal humans, Theseus, Hyppolyta, and the lovers; it has the rustics, these lovable peasants—rustics—who behave so beautifully and charmingly throughout; and then of course these curious fairy creatures, Tytania and Oberon and the—Puck and the others.

BBC: I believe you worked on the score in Venice. Is there—indeed subtly or any otherwise—is there any Venetian or Italian influence on it?

BRITTEN: I wish I could say there were, but I—what I can say is that I went to start the work in Venice because it's a place that I love very dearly and find work easy there, partly because it's a long way away from the telephone—

Editor's title.

Source: Editor's transcript of recording (*GB-ALb*). Most likely transmitted in connection with the first broadcast of Britten's *A Midsummer Night's Dream*, 24 June 1960, BBC Midland Home Service and Home Service.

[1] See Essay 54, n. 3.

certainly the English telephone—and there's something curiously restful and yet stimulating in that beautiful city.

BBC: How does it compare with your other major works—say *Peter Grimes*, *Rape of Lucretia*, *Albert Herring*?

BRITTEN: Well, I hope it's different because the subject matter and words are so very different from all those. It is smaller in size than *Peter Grimes*, being written for a smaller cast and a smaller orchestra. On the other hand it's bigger than *Lucretia*, which was written for an orchestra of twelve [thirteen] and a cast of only eight.

BBC: Does it in any way reflect, like so much else that you have written, your East Anglian birth and background?

BRITTEN: Well I don't know; except of course indirectly that I am an East Anglian and of course I think like one; but I can't say that there's much influence of the sea, which of course has played such a large part in many of my works—although I think that the beautiful woods that we get round this part of the world certainly inspired me now or *colours* the music.

BBC: And the people?

BRITTEN: Well, yes, I can say the rustics, perhaps, resemble some of my very good friends in this part of the world.

BBC: What do you think of it now it's finished?

BRITTEN: Oh I shouldn't like to say. I have moments when I'm almost pleased and of course moments when one is extremely depressed and worried.

BBC: I know it's a rather mawkish question to ask you: do you think it's the best thing you've written?

BRITTEN: Well, I think most parents are fondest of their youngest children; I think at the moment this is my youngest child and therefore I have a particular connection with it.

BBC: Getting away from music for a moment, what's it going to be like as a spectacle?

BRITTEN: Well, it's produced by John Cranko, it's designed by John Piper, and I think one knows—our listeners know enough of their work to know that it will look very splendid and suitable for this rather beautiful little stage that we've now built in the Jubilee Hall theatre in Aldeburgh.

BBC: At last you've got the money now to do it, haven't you?

BRITTEN: Yes, we've rebuilt the theatre and it's—we're all very happy with the form it's taken.

BBC: It's something you've wanted for many years.

BRITTEN: Yes. It holds a few more people and of course has a very well-equipped stage now.

BBC: It's more than 130 years now since Mendelssohn wrote music for *A*

Midsummer Night's Dream—colourful music, *very* well known. Will yours be in contrast to it or what will it be?

BRITTEN: It'll be in contrast to it in the same way that I myself am in contrast to Mendelssohn. I mean I live these numbers of years later in quite different circumstances; and of course the main thing is that Shakespeare is so great and so universal that he has many different sides and we can all find new aspects of it. Mine, I'm sure, is quite different from Mendelssohn's, although I happen to love his music very much.

BBC: So much of your work is fairly easily remembered, isn't it? *Let's Make an Opera* comes to mind; will this be music that'll be fairly easily remembered by audiences?

BRITTEN: Well that I simply don't know. It seems to me that it should be, but on the other hand sometimes music which is even simple turns out to be difficult to remember. That is a thing which time will only tell.

BBC: You don't think then, sort of speaking off-hand, that it has the kind of tunes that people will be able to sing after they've heard it a couple of times?

BRITTEN: I shouldn't think so, although I hope some of them will try!

BBC: One last question. You're conducting some of the first performances yourself, and I believe it's been said that composers rarely make good conductors. Apparently you don't agree?

BRITTEN: Oh that's a difficult one to answer. Oh—I like conducting my works. Whether I'm good or not remains to be seen, I think, after the first performance; but I've certainly had a lot of experience.

But I don't agree that composers aren't good conductors. After all, there's been through the last hundred years some very remarkable composer-conductors—I mean Berlioz, for instance, was a remarkable one. No, I think composers can be very good, and if they are it's inclined to help their music, I think, composers as performers. A performer is better if he's a composer and a composer is better if he's a performer.

56 Brighton Philharmonic Society (1960)

I send my warmest wishes to the Brighton Philharmonic Society for the 1960–61 season.[1] Nowadays, when the decentralization of the Arts in this country is becoming more and more important, when people must be encouraged to want their own 'live' concerts and theatres as opposed to 'canned' ones or ones in the few big centres, the work of such societies as the Brighton Philharmonic is increasingly vital. My great hope is that the Brighton audiences will flock in big numbers to appreciate this enterprising series of programmes.

Source: Autograph draft, 24 June 1960, (*GB-ALb*). Introduction to 1960–1 Brighton Philharmonic Society prospectus.

[1] Britten was President of the Society.

57 Discussion on *Billy Budd* (1960)

CROZIER: We began discussing the idea of writing an opera together some months before we found *Billy Budd*; I think it was in August 1948 that we had a first meeting and simply talked very enthusiastically, but very vaguely, about *an* opera that we might one day write. And a month or two later Morgan, you and I had a further meeting to discuss this idea of collaboration, but still we had no subject. And then I think you had a letter from Ben.

FORSTER: Then I had—he and I had discussed some subject; it was a comedy opera I think—wasn't it?—which was very nice but I didn't see what I could do about it.

CROZIER: You in fact weren't very keen on the idea of comedy.

FORSTER: Well I didn't think I could manage it—that was all.

CROZIER: Well, I remember one thing that you said to me which was that you didn't really approve of the idea of a comedy because if it were to be modern it would have to be satirical, and if it were to be an opera about the past it would inevitably be nostalgic, and you weren't very much interested in either of these fields.

FORSTER: Yes. I remember anyhow that died out and then I got a letter from Ben—unfortunately I have destroyed it, as I destroy so much—quite a short one suggesting this Melville thing *Billy Budd*, and I wrote back and said yes; it suited me at once and I was absolutely delighted to get this tiny note.

CROZIER: Yes. This must have been about the end of 1948 I think because I remember distinctly getting a telephone call from Ben in January 1949 asking me if I could come over to Aldeburgh as soon as possible because he had you staying with him and there was some great scheme in the wind. He didn't tell me what it was, but I got up very, very early next morning and set off for Aldeburgh and got there while you were both having breakfast. And as soon as breakfast was over you put me in a room by myself with a copy of *Billy Budd*, which I had never seen before, and left me alone 'til lunchtime to study it.

FORSTER: And then did you catch on to . . . were you delighted at once? I forget so much.

Source: Editor's transcript of recording (NSA 1CDR0011307). Broadcast 12 Nov. 1960, BBC Third Programme, 9.30 p.m.: discussion by Britten, E. M. Forster, and Eric Crozier. (Forster and Crozier pre-recorded on 4 Nov. 1960, Britten and Crozier pre-recorded on 9 Nov.) A BBC transcript of this discussion is available on microfilm (BBCWAC, CRO–COM, T103). This was the time of the opera's revision from four acts into two, the version that was subsequently broadcast by the BBC and which introduced the opera into mainstream repertory.

CROZIER: Well, I felt some doubt about the practicalities, the difficulties that it offered: an opera with an all-male cast; the setting being confined to a ship; the normal objections that one would feel at first reading of *Billy Budd*. On the other hand I did feel, I had sensed the excitement that you and Ben had in reading this story; I knew that you wanted me to like it, and I read it very, very carefully because I wanted to try and see what it was in it that had fired you both so much. And then at lunch that day we started talking and spent the whole of the rest of that day, I remember, discussing and discussing this very exciting story.

A very interesting point I think is that it was your broadcast talk on Crabbe which was reprinted in *The Listener* in I think 1942 or 1943 that first drew Ben to the idea of writing *Peter Grimes*.[1]

Well, here is Ben, let's ask him about it. Ben, we've been talking about the early days of *Billy Budd*, and I've just been reminding Morgan that it was an article that he wrote on George Crabbe in *The Listener*—it was reprinted in *The Listener*—that really set you off on *Peter Grimes*.

BRITTEN: Yes I read that article and immediately bought the complete works of Crabbe and got very excited by the section of 'The Borough' that you wrote about Morgan in your vivid style.

CROZIER: This is when you were out in California?

BRITTEN: Yes and it was very soon after that I came back to England and started work on it with Montagu Slater who wrote the libretto.

CROZIER: Did you happen to remember whether you were consciously reminded of *Billy Budd* by anything that Morgan had written?

BRITTEN: I have often asked myself whether it was the passage in the *Aspects of the Novel*, Morgan, whether that it was that reminded me of this extraordinary short story of Melville.[2] I can't remember exactly. I have a feeling that somewhere on tour in England, just after the war, I bought the little reprint of *Billy Budd* and that excited me very much, and I think I wrote to you almost immediately and you replied very warmly. But I cannot remember exactly; stupidly one forgets these things so easily.

CROZIER: I'd like to ask Morgan if he'd read us that passage from *Aspects of the Novel*; the particular chapter is the one dealing with prophecy in the novel, in which he treats Melville and discusses *Moby Dick* and *Billy Budd*. Morgan I wonder if you'd do that for us?

FORSTER: Yes I'd willingly read it. Which bit do I read Eric?

CROZIER: I think that bit: '*Billy Budd* is a remote, unearthly episode . . .'.

FORSTER: Yes, well here's the passage.

[1] 1941. [2] First published by Edward Arnold, 1927.

> *Billy Budd* is a remote unearthly episode, but it is a song not without words, and should be read both for its own beauty and as an introduction to more difficult works. Evil is labelled and personified instead of slipping over the ocean and round the world as it does in *Moby Dick*, and Melville's mind can be observed more easily. What one notices in him is that his apprehensions are free from personal worry, so that we become bigger, not smaller, after sharing them. He has not got that tiresome little receptacle, a conscience, which is often such a nuisance in serious writers, and so contracts their effects.
>
> Melville—after the initial roughness of his realism—reaches straight back into the universal, to a blackness and sadness so transcending our own that they are undistinguishable from glory. He says: 'In certain moods, no man can weigh this world without throwing in something, somehow like Original Sin, to strike the uneven balance.' He threw it in, that undefinable something, the balance righted itself, and he gave us harmony and temporary salvation.[3]

That's the passage you meant isn't it?

CROZIER: Yes. It seems to me the kind of pregnant description of a subject that would attract a composer by the fact that it describes a quality of extension from the story—that you start with real characters, with human characters, which are then extended on to other planes of significance—something that is obviously stimulating when it comes to thinking of writing music.

FORSTER: I just don't know anything about that of course. You think it is the kind of thing that would appeal to a person who saw the universe through music?

CROZIER: Ben, do you think that's true?

BRITTEN: Yes, I'm slightly out of my depth here honestly, because when I start writing these operas I always start from the characters themselves and the conflicts between the characters. What you've been talking about, Morgan and Eric, I hope comes in accidentally. If I'm any good as a composer it will—the music will—show a greater depth than perhaps I'm intending. I feel that very strongly with some of the creative artists I admire the most; I feel that with Mozart, for instance, that he is writing about Figaro and his relationship with Susanna and the Countess, and is not always quite clear of the tremendous moral significance that these pieces are going to have for us. They arrive because, with Mozart, his music is so wonderful, is always catching fire, and produces these effects, that my own guess [is] he would be surprised if we talked about [them].

CROZIER: I'd awfully like to press you a bit further on this because it seems to me that in your choice of subjects you are always guided by a strong emotional content in the conflict of the particular story that you choose.

[3] Penguin edn. (1990), 129–30.

This is the thing that you really catch fire from when you first read a book or a poem. Is that so?

BRITTEN: Yes.

CROZIER: I mean you're not really interested in human conflict simply in finite terms, social terms as it were; you're interested in human conflict because you respond very deeply to people's feelings.

BRITTEN: Yes. I think if one looks back over the operas that I have written up to date one does find a kind of pattern running through them, but I must admit that I haven't been very conscious of that pattern. But I think you are quite right: there are certain conflicts which do worry me a great deal, and I want to say things about them in musical terms.

CROZIER: I'd like to give an illustration of this. *Peter Grimes* could have been treated in a play or in an opera in a vein of, as it were, social realism; it could have been simply a story of a particular place, a particular injustice that was committed upon a fisherman who got at loggerheads with the rest of the community. Now this is much too narrow a definition for what you've done in *Peter Grimes*; you have really made of Grimes himself a figure who is any one of us at any time.

BRITTEN: I'm very glad that you feel that, Eric. Certainly I felt in the particular case of Grimes that he was more that just an ordinary fisherman who got across his own little bit of society. But he got across not only because he—well, had a bad temper and behaved badly—but also because he had ideas that they couldn't follow.

CROZIER: Yes. Now, it would be true to say, wouldn't it, that in this particular case of Melville's story of *Billy Budd*, he's not concerned only with one ship at one moment in time; he's concerned with what I called earlier the quality of extension that in a sense that ship is an image of the world. It is a world, which reflects the stresses and problems and concerns of our own world, and floats on the sea of time and of infinity.

BRITTEN: It certainly seems like that when I read that story. Whether Melville was as aware of that as we are, I don't know. But there of course, Morgan, you put it in the *Aspects of the Novel* so clearly.

CROZIER: Which of Melville's three characters was it who really attracted and fascinated you when you first read this story? Was it Billy, or Claggart, or was it Vere, the more complex character of Vere?

BRITTEN: It's difficult to answer now after so many years, but Billy always attracted me, of course—the radiant, young figure. I felt there was going to be quite an opportunity for writing nice dark music for Claggart; but I think I must admit that Vere, who has what seems to me the main moral problem of the whole work, round whom the drama was going to centre . . .

CROZIER: What do you feel, Morgan?

FORSTER: I tend to think Billy the central figure. He names the opera, and I think I consider the things from his point of view. And incidentally, this question of goodness, and of making goodness interesting, is one that does hold me very much, because I think if only writers were able enough—Dostoevsky was able enough—that you could make goodness very interesting; and I was very anxious to do that over Billy as far as I could, helped to no small extent by Melville. But I quite see the position of Vere as—it's very easy to place him in the centre of the opera, because he has much more apprehension than poor Billy, who's often muddling about in an instinctive way. Vere responds much more to what's going on. He really understands it. When he gets the facts, he understands everything, and Billy is always a little bewildered. Billy's not complete intelligence, though he is complete goodness.

CROZIER: Isn't it true to say, Morgan, that it's much more easy for a novelist to make goodness interesting than for a dramatist?

FORSTER: I don't think so. If you are a dramatist you can alter the scene—put on a light or turn it out . . .

CROZIER: No, the really good characters surely—Cordelia in *Lear* for instance—always tend to become either insipid or slightly irritating.

FORSTER: Yes, but perhaps not as bad as the good characters in Dickens.

CROZIER: No, that's true.

FORSTER: No, I think you see the stage can help the dramatist there. Certainly when one reads about Cordelia she is on the tiresome side—but I think the dramatist can . . . on the stage that can be rectified.

CROZIER: I'm just wondering whether a stage character doesn't exist by virtue of contradictions in itself—the fact that variety of moods, variety of responses to situations—and the good character is hampered from the beginning because the response always has to be good.

BRITTEN: Perhaps I can help a little here in this argument—dramatist versus novelist. Music has one great advantage I think in that it is an artificial medium; in the opera people sing all the time, and on board ship of course one only sings when one is singing shanties; one talks the rest of the time. But since one is in this artificial medium of music one can break into an aria which can be a statement about goodness or evil, and not seem to break the medium.

FORSTER: Do you think the novelist can get out of that? I don't know . . .

CROZIER: I think the novelist can show so much more variety—there's so much more possibility of simply describing, without directly showing the reactions of the good character; but if you simply have to show the man or the woman in action, there is nothing that that particular good person can do but *be* good. And this leads to a danger which is that it tends to make one over-villainize the villain as it were.

FORSTER: Yes. I was thinking that little different point of view is—after all when the composer wants to show you a good character he can give you good music.

BRITTEN: I presume by that Morgan you mean not 'good' music, because after all one always tries to write music which is good, but you mean music which has good character, which depicts goodness itself. That I think is true; but music is an inexplicit art, and what one person thinks is good doesn't necessarily seem music of goodness to someone else. The same with evil. One can think of lots of examples of that, for instance you yourself, Morgan, have said to me in the past that you have felt the Mozart G minor Symphony to be elegance personified, whereas I feel that it is one of the most tragic and tense pieces which has ever been written.

CROZIER: I think it would be worthwhile describing how when we got down to it we actually worked, because collaboration on a venture of this kind is, well, fairly unusual, and here where there was a composer and two librettists, it was particularly unusual, I think. What in fact we did was to live in the same house for not quite a month I think in the first instance. You Ben were then working along at the other end of the corridor in your study scoring the *Spring Symphony*, while we were getting on with the early stages of the opera. And what in fact we did was to settle down each morning after breakfast to discuss a particular episode in our proposed libretto in very considerable detail. We talked about it in all aspects—if there were technical points concerned with the routine of a sailing ship or anything like that which we didn't know about we looked it up—and then after perhaps three-quarters of an hour discussion we would decide that one of us should write that particular scene in draft version, sometimes that *both* of us should write a draft.

FORSTER: Yes I remember both of us writing.

CROZIER: This happened quite often didn't it? And then we would settle down and for half an hour sketch a draft of the scene we had been discussing; and then [we would] compare it, and very often amalgamate our two versions to arrive at a final version.

FORSTER: Yes, I remember that.

CROZIER: And then halfway through the morning I remember you used to come along and have morning coffee with us, Ben, and you were always very impatient to see what we had done that morning. You used to read through it and then we'd discuss it for ten minutes or so, and then off you'd go back to the *Spring Symphony* while we got on with the opera.

BRITTEN: Yes I remember very well. But this makes me sound a little as if I have a sort of two-track mind which isn't true. But I would like only just to explain that, because when I was scoring the *Spring Symphony*, as with any other work, it is really only an automatic job; when I sketch a work the instrumentation is always very clearly marked—I work it out very carefully as I go along, in the first sketches—and I remember very clearly that all my interests and emotions at that point were focused on *Billy Budd*.

CROZIER: And you didn't find *Billy* a distraction at all—in fact it was a stimulus.

BRITTEN: No, it was a stimulus.

CROZIER: Had you in fact, Morgan, ever tried this method of collaboration before that time?

FORSTER: I don't think I had ever collaborated with anyone. And if you read the history of collaboration—I think books have been written about it—it seems a lamentable theme. But in our case it was nothing but pleasure.

CROZIER: Oh it certainly was. Yes we had no disagreements at all that I remember . . .

FORSTER: None.

CROZIER: . . . and the work seemed to divide itself naturally enough. I tended to deal with the more technical aspects—we had a great deal of reading up to do to inform ourselves about the conditions of life on sailing ships and in the navy at the time of the Spithead and the Nore mutinies—and I remember your writing off for a great batch of books from the London Library to prime us with that information, and I see that we left gaps here in our first-draft libretto—certain things where we weren't quite certain what was wanted, we simply left to be decided later.[4]

FORSTER: You did the technical things and I think to a large extent the dialogues.

CROZIER: Yes.

FORSTER: When there was a big slab of narrative I was more apt to do it.

CROZIER: Yes.

FORSTER: I think that on the whole was the division.

CROZIER: Ah, work in this way on the first draft of the libretto was based on a kind of skeleton synopsis that we had got out previously; we had set out in very, very brief, dull little paragraphs how the story was to be told—the actual articulation of the tale as it were. So we had our foundations laid. What we did in writing this first-draft libretto was to build on those foundations and to erect what is quite a pleasant form of fabric I think. But looking back on it I see now that what we were really writing was a play.

FORSTER: Ah were we? Yes . . .

[4] There were naval mutinies at Spithead and Nore (the 'Great Mutiny') in 1797 where British sailors ran up royal flags with the union and cross removed.

CROZIER: Well, the script that I have here in front of me could perfectly well be acted as a play, and there was a good deal of unnecessary material—not unnecessary from the point of view [of] a play—it could perfectly well be acted and spoken as dialogue . . .

FORSTER: But from the libretto point of view.

CROZIER: . . . but from the libretto that was irrelevant, perhaps a little too verbose, perhaps not direct enough—and then later on when we had our second spell of work, six months after writing the first-draft libretto, when we settled to write the revised version . . .

FORSTER: We became better librettists.

CROZIER: . . . well, then we had you, Ben, with us all the time, watching what we were doing, saying 'there are too many words there. You must reduce these lines', or 'Here is an idea that I would like you to expand in a more lyrical form . . .'.

FORSTER: 'Make it flower . . .'.

BRITTEN: Yes I think what you mean by that, Morgan, 'Make it flower', is that there are times in opera—in all operas—when the words dominate for information's sake, and then there are moments when the music dominates, which one usually calls an aria or a set piece, and as you were working together, you and Eric, one saw moments where there was a chance for the music to flower.

FORSTER: Yes, I'm very glad it did. No, I don't think, although I've got this deep devotion to music, I know nothing at all about its technical requirements. I wrote in, as far as I remember you see, a great deal of emotion; I knew that music was somehow or other to be attached to my words, and whether this somehow got into the words and put them into the right order I don't know. In writing my part of the libretto and in the collaboration I felt quite differently to what I've felt about writing other things—completely different. I was on a kind of voyage.

CROZIER: I remember that after our initial discussions about the idea of writing *Billy Budd* that you got in a state of excitement and impatience to get on with it; you were so much on fire with the whole idea that you wanted to be up and doing. And it was at that point that you actually wrote the very opening speech of the opera, the prologue for Vere . . .

FORSTER: Was it? Yes.

CROZIER: . . . which you sent to me . . .

FORSTER: I would start before the time . . .

CROZIER: . . . and which wasn't altered at all, which Ben set exactly as you first wrote it, and which has such a musical feeling to it: 'I am an old man who has experienced much. I have been a man of action and fought for my King and country at sea. I have also read books and studied and pondered and tried to fathom eternal truth.' And here immediately you showed your grasp, I think, of what was wanted.

BRITTEN: Yes I can remember very well, Morgan, when you gave that passage to me how very excited I was by it; it was going to be quite clearly magnificent to set to music. You had obviously become by then a very good librettist.

FORSTER: I'm very glad if I did . . . I remember starting it quite easily. But in my writing I don't think I ever have tried very hard; I mean things come to me in little rushes. The agonies of composition are unknown to me.

BRITTEN: Oh dear Morgan, I wish I could say the same.

CROZIER: One of the things of course that we were ignorant of and had to learn about was about the actual mechanics of the sailing ship which was after all our setting for this opera. And I remember at our very, very first discussion on the first day that I myself read *Billy Budd*, we sat down at tea and drew up three little sheets on a notepad. One was a list of all the characters that Melville mentioned in his book, in order for us to try and see what the probable cast of the opera would be; the second one was a list of the crucial scenes in the telling of Melville's story, to show us what the architecture of our proposed opera might become; and the third was a naive drawing, a side view, of a sailing ship which I think Ben must have drawn . . .[5]

BRITTEN: Well, if it was a naive drawing I'm sure it was I who drew it.

CROZIER: And you, Morgan, very carefully and meticulously had written in against each bit of it the places where the action had to happen. There was a little squiggle saying 'quarter-deck', one saying 'captain's cabin', 'lower-deck' . . .

FORSTER: Did I? Did I?

CROZIER: . . . and this was simply to help us find our way about and know in which parts of the ship action would be going on. And then later of course we became much more professional and you and I set off . . .

FORSTER: We went down to Portsmouth.

CROZIER: We went to Portsmouth together and went over the *Victory*, which was a remarkable experience.[6]

FORSTER: Yes, the *Victory* was very useful for the scene below decks wasn't it?

CROZIER: And to see the incredible darkness and confinement in which those sailors lived. It was something to me quite extraordinary; I shall never forget seeing the surgeon's cabin, which was the size of a small wardrobe, and where presumably all the major operations and amputations had to be carried out. And we also went to the National Maritime Museum at Greenwich.

[5] Reproduced in Mervyn Cooke and Philip Reed, *Billy Budd* (Cambridge: CUP, 1993), 47.

[6] HMS *Victory*, Nelson's warship, was launched in 1765 and commissioned in 1778. It is moored at Portsmouth.

FORSTER: We did indeed, yes.

CROZIER: I remember I went to the Science Museum to look at their models of ships. In fact we did our homework pretty thoroughly and were fairly well up in the technique of sailing ships and the kind of life that was lived aboard. I think we did do all that we could to—and our intention throughout was to be as faithful to Melville as possible. We did steep ourselves in this story; we had very great respect for it as a work and we tried to follow it or we tried to translate it very faithfully to a new form as an opera. But when we came to make our second draft—that was in August 1949—of the libretto, you, Ben, wanted a bigger climax for the end of the first act; and it was there that for the first time we added a scene that was not directly taken from or hinted at by Melville, and we did a big finale for the end of the first act with Vere addressing the whole ship's company.

It's interesting that in the revision that's now been made of the opera for this broadcast performance that this is one of the scenes—well in fact it's the main scene—that has been omitted.

BRITTEN: Actually I've worried about this scene for many years, and it was the fact of this broadcast performance which impelled me to—well maybe suggest omitting this scene. Originally as far as I can remember we had planned it all in two acts and for some reason which I cannot remember now we decided at a later date to make it into four acts, and that meant of course that the first act had to have a finale. We put this rather public oration scene in, and I think, Morgan and Eric, we agree that it was rather against our will; we didn't feel very convinced about this scene.

CROZIER: No, I think it was a—well not a stop-gap exactly, but it was something that we *imposed* on our original idea.

BRITTEN: And I'd always wanted to go back to the two-act form, and this gave one the chance of rethinking that scene, and when we met recently we decided to do away with the reappearance of the quarter-deck and Vere, and make an intimate scene among the sailors we were interested in, discussing Vere, which led very naturally to the next scene which is Vere in his cabin.

FORSTER: That is very interesting. So the present broadcast version approximates more closely to the original Melville.

CROZIER: Yes. Yes.

FORSTER: That's very interesting, that.

CROZIER: This is the distinction I think between doing a work for the theatre and doing it, say, for a broadcast. We were thinking of the big finale in terms of the opera house, where it was to be given in four acts. But now, without the big finale at the end of the first act, acts one and two succeed each other and the work falls into two parts instead of four.

FORSTER: I'm very glad it should. I'm never very happy about the four acts in the great opera house.

CROZIER: When we discussed doing an opera together, very distinctly you said that you wanted it to be a large-scale opera that could be done in any opera house, and not a chamber opera; this was something that you felt quite strongly at that time.[7] And I'm glad you did insist in this way.

BRITTEN: Yes the situation was rather like this at the time: because of the operatic situation in England in 1945, Eric, we'd started the English Opera Group and we'd been together working on three or four chamber operas before the idea of you, Morgan, coming and writing an opera with us; and I know you did feel very strongly that you wanted to write a big opera because that seemed to you to be the way that opera should be. I mean, I personally feel that you can have two different kinds of opera; you can have the big—the grand—and the small, just as you can have a symphony and a string quartet.

FORSTER: I don't think I had any idea what would be made of the music; the music is I think on the whole rather solemn and somber, and I've sometimes wondered—this is only a theoretical idea—to what extent the fact that the libretto was mostly written in prose and not in poetry may have influenced the music. That's an idea that has occurred to me, but not to you I think Eric, has it? It's a particular idea that has interested me. A prose libretto is rather unusual and it had to be in prose because I can't write poetry, though you can. So we had to plump out the prose, and I've often wandered whether this prose style has influenced the music.

BRITTEN: Of course, Morgan, the prose style did influence the music. One is always influenced by the words one is setting; but I must say that your and Eric's prose is not ordinary prose. On all the occasions when I wanted it to be heightened, your prose came up to this height, and I was at no point worried by the fact that I was dealing with a prose libretto and not a poetic one.

FORSTER: Yes—we attempted to heighten it, certainly.

CROZIER: Well, an example of that, I think, is the beginning of Claggart's aria—'O handsomeness, O beauty, O goodness'. One can't say this is poetry, but again it isn't prose—it's more than prose, isn't it?

FORSTER: No. You mean the . . .

CROZIER: Well in fact the whole of this passage: 'O handsomeness, O beauty, O goodness, would that I had never encountered you. That is my torment. Would that I lived in my own world always and in the depravity to which I was born.' This is attaining the grandeur of poetry, really, isn't it?

[7] Britten's three previous operas had each been written for chamber forces—*The Rape of Lucretia* (1946), *Albert Herring* (1947), *The Little Sweep* (1949)—as had his realization of *The Beggar's Opera* (1948).

FORSTER: Yes, we were raising it there.

CROZIER: An example of what I called earlier heightened prose, I think.

FORSTER: In Claggart's—that particular monologue of Claggart—I was thinking a bit of the one in Verdi's *Otello*, of the Iago monologue.[8]

FORSTER: Yes—the Credo, yes. Did that occur to you at all Ben?

BRITTEN: Yes I can see a parallel here because it is perhaps—Claggart's monologue is perhaps the one case in *Billy Budd* where the character gets, as it were, outside himself and sings about himself, which brings us perhaps to the symbolism or the second meaning behind the action in the work. Do you feel, Morgan, for instance that in writing the piece that the meaning behind the action was a part of your intention, or did it come in casually?

FORSTER: I had the general feeling of salvation of course, but I don't think we put in anything in that region which Melville did not give us. We imagined ourselves anyhow to be following his symbolism.

CROZIER: There has been a curious divergence of opinion among critics about this really, hasn't there—about what in fact Melville was trying to say in *Billy Budd*? One critic—I have a note here which says in his opinion Melville set out to justify the ways of God to man. Another thinks that the book was Melville's final protest against the nature of things and against fate. Another one still interprets the book as the triumph of innocence and the recognition of the necessity of evil in the world. Well I think I can see the final protest against the nature of things and against fate, and I think I can see the last one about the triumph of innocence; I'm not sure that I understand what the critic meant who thought it was justifying the ways of God to man.

FORSTER: No I think that much too smug an account of it.

BRITTEN: Isn't this surely what always happens with a parable? The people argue indefinitely about what the allegory is. In fact, everyone is right and everyone's wrong.

CROZIER: But this in a way goes back to something that we had enormously long discussions about, I remember, without ever getting anywhere conclusive, and that was this whole question of Melville saying in the book that the devil slips his visiting card into every cargo of human goodness, or some such words—that there is nothing perfect, no human perfection that doesn't have its flaw.

[8] Act 2 scene 2. Iago sings: 'I believe in a cruel God | who has created in His image | and whom, in hate, I name. | From some vile seed | or base atom I am born. | I am evil because I am a man; | and I feel the primeval slime in me. | Yes! This is my testimony!' Claggart's monologue continues: 'There I found peace of a sort, there I established an order such as reigns in Hell. But alas, alas! the light shines in the darkness, and the darkness comprehends it and suffers. O beauty, o handsomeness, goodness! would that I had never seen you! Having seen you, what choice remains to me? None, none! I am doomed to annihilate you, I am vowed to your destruction.'

FORSTER: Yes.

CROZIER: Now, as against that he gives us in Claggart, apparently, the man of pure evil, the man who is evil without flaw, and I remember that the three of us discussed at great length whether this is possible. If goodness must essentially be flawed, whether in fact it is possible to have evil which hasn't got its corresponding flaw.

FORSTER: Well, perhaps—you mean whether God's visiting card had been slipped into Claggart?

CROZIER: Yes. There's no sign of it in Melville.

FORSTER: Well, certainly Claggart is not happy in his evil. Whether that's owing to the presence of the visiting card I don't know.

CROZIER: I don't think you ever brought that up before. I don't remember your saying—

FORSTER: No. I think . . .

CROZIER: It's an interesting point.

FORSTER: . . . you evoked it, and I think it would have been difficult to treat it musically; but certainly he does not enjoy his evil to the extent to which I think Iago enjoys his.

CROZIER: Melville did seem to envisage him really, didn't he, as a kind of fallen Lucifer; I don't remember if he actually describes him as that but there is this sense of a man almost of greatness, a man of great capacity, who has fallen into evil, and who is profoundly distressed and melancholy.

FORSTER: I hardly recognize the presence of good in him; various things of course of Claggart indicated by Melville—indicated [it] also about Billy—that each of them might have had aristocratic blood in them—a thought which rather depresses me and [one] which I don't think we made any use of.

CROZIER: Well Billy was a foundling, found in a basket on a good old man's doorstep, wasn't he? I can't remember how it was described that he had aristocratic blood, but there was definitely a hint that he was a bi-blow.[9]

FORSTER: There's a hint in Melville of it and I think also a hint of it in Claggart; but there is a different sort of visiting card.

CROZIER: I seem to remember something about your saying at one point how odiously, in fact, Vere was made to behave by Melville in this trial. We surely humanized him and made him much more aware of the human values that were involved, and not simply sticking by a book of rules and saying 'Thus it must be because it's laid down'.

FORSTER: Yes. We felt that Melville was disgracing Vere. I suppose *he* would feel we had disgraced *him*.

[9] i.e. bastard.

BRITTEN: I think several things about this. One, I think there's a difference of the time that we were writing and the time that Melville was writing. One sees things a little bit more liberally now. Also, I feel that we after all were making a new work of this. We were adapting into a different medium, with all that means. I think one is free to make changes—as, after all, in *Peter Grimes* I'm quite sure Crabbe would not have approved at all of what we did with the character of Peter Grimes. Also, for my own particular point of view of the way that Melville made Vere behave in the trial would not have been sympathetic or encouraging to me to write music.[10]

CROZIER: Yes. I think in all your operas, really, that you have—whether you intended to or not—expressed the dilemmas and the unhappiness that people of today go through, and I think this is certainly true in Vere. He is a man who is torn between duty and expediency, as very often we are in our own lives. Would you say that it's true to make this statement about your operas?

BRITTEN: I think that it was the quality of conflict in Vere's mind, as we said earlier, which attracted me to this particular subject. The fact that he realized later he could have saved Billy and yet circumstances forced him to sacrifice him.

CROZIER: Yes. It is in this sense, I think, that Vere becomes perhaps the most dramatic character. Claggart has to do what he is—he's evil and he acts evilly; Billy is good and destroys Claggart by being good, and is himself destroyed by the law; but Vere is the man of feeling who has a choice of action and who finally has to stick by a code but knows that he was wrong to do so, or feels that in the final resort he must have been wrong to do so.

FORSTER: Yes, I think he's the only character that is truly tragic. The others are doing their jobs, following their destinies, to put it that way.

CROZIER: Yes. So this gives some meaning, I think, to those critics who at the time that the opera was first performed thought that Vere was the main character rather than Billy.

FORSTER: Yes. It's one of those discussion subjects, of course, which never interest me that much, and I think that one certainly could argue that Vere was the main character; though simply talking out of my instincts I put Billy. Now I think of the play and before I think of anything else I think of Billy.

[10] In the trial scene in Melville, when one of the officers protests that Budd intended neither mutiny or homicide, Vere responds: 'Surely not, my good man. And before a court less arbitrary and more merciful than a martial one, that plea would largely extenuate. At the Last Assizes it shall acquit. But how here? . . . Budd's intent or non-intent is nothing to the purpose . . .' (Melville, *Billy Budd Foretopman* (London: John Lehmann, 1946), 97–8).

58 On Writing English Opera (1960)

Since *Peter Grimes*, more than fifteen years ago, I have written ten works for the operatic stage—that is, including two intended primarily for children, an arrangement of *The Beggars'* [*sic*] *Opera* and a realization of *Dido and Aeneas*. I am often asked why, living in England where there are only two permanent opera houses, I have spent so much of my creative time in writing operas. Here, at random, are some of the answers I give.

I have become more and more interested in human beings, in their foibles and characteristics, and in the drama which can result from their interplay. I have also strong points of view to which I find opera can give expression. I have always been interested in the setting of words (some of my earliest efforts in composition were songs) and Purcell has shown me how wonderfully dramatic the sung English language can be. My interest in the human voice has grown, especially in the relation of sound to sense and colour; for me, this interest applies to the English voice in particular, singing our subtle and beautifully inflected language. Also, I believe passionately in the intelligibility of the words—opera being a fusion of music, acting, painting and poetry, of which the last-named demands to be understood. Because I do not speak Italian, it was not until I heard Mozart and Verdi operas sung in English that I realized to the full their fabulous subtlety, wit and dramatic aptitude. I always encourage my works to be sung, abroad, in the vernacular, even pieces like the *Spring Symphony* and the *Nocturne*, which contain some of the greatest English poetry. Of course, something is lost, but not a great deal when you substitute the gibberish which can result from singers using languages they do not understand and cannot pronounce.

I am also often asked why, among my operas, so many have been written for small forces. It stands to reason that I, being English, want my operas to be done here in England; and when I and a group of friends started the English Opera Group, the forces had to be small, for our primary idea was to tour new English opera in England. If the last fifteen years have shown that this idea does not work in this operatically naive country, the case is by no means the same abroad. The Group itself has appeared all over Europe, and *The Rape of Lucretia* and *Albert Herring* themselves have each in turn far surpassed *Peter Grimes* in number of performances and productions. The Komische Oper in East Berlin did more performances in one year (1959–60) of *Albert Herring* than Covent Garden has done of *Peter Grimes* since it reopened in 1947. And I have just sent a congratulatory telegram to an *ad hoc* company formed in Frankfurt to tour

Source: *Opera* 12 (Jan. 1961), 7–8. This was part of a symposium on 'Modern Opera'.

Albert Herring in West Germany, on its last and sixty-first performance in three months. Criticism of my writing for small operatic forces will hardly touch me on practical grounds. And from the aesthetic point of view, I find small-scale operas satisfying. There is a subtlety, and intimacy about chamber music which is usually lacking in grander forms, and many great stories are more suitable for chamber opera. I hasten to add that I also love the broad sweep and bold colours of grand opera and will, if the chance is there, continue to write such works.

But there is another reason, more important than all these statistics. Many of the greatest works of art, including the west pediment at Olympia, the plays of Shakespeare, and the church cantatas of Bach, have grown from a desire of the artist to serve or be in contact with his public—have been made or written for a specific public, for a specific purpose. While not expecting every artist to feel the same, I get great inspiration from writing for a sympathetic audience, and, on occasion, from stimulating the public's taste in the direction I think it should go. So, having created a Festival, with its own small opera house, in the part of the world where I live, I intend to continue to write for the people who come there. And in my own small experience I have learned that if one concentrates on the local, the particular, if one writes for particular singers, instrumentalists, local occasions, the works can have an actuality, a realistic quality, which may make the result useful to the outside world.

59 Britten and Pears in Canada (1961)

GARVIE: Mr Britten, we've seen you rushing from studio to studio to conduct in Vancouver these last few days, and you seem to spend a great deal of time performing with Peter Pears around the world, conducting your own works, recording them, and yet you seem to write more than most contemporary composers.[1] How do you arrange your time to compose?

BRITTEN: I try to keep a certain period of each year clear to write, but you know I don't write very much; I mean compared with Schubert or Mozart or the great ones I write awfully little.

PEARS: But here you are, 48, and you've reached Op. 62 or something; Mozart had reached Köchel 600 or something and he had been dead for fifteen years hadn't he?

BRITTEN: Yes I know. Don't make me feel smaller than I feel already.

GARVIE: Well I think it's true though that the modern composers do write more slowly or write less. Is this something to do with the climate of the time? Is it the actual business of writing out is now much more arduous?

BRITTEN: That I think is quite true. I think today, I mean to write a symphony means an orchestra very much bigger than ever Mozart or Schubert contemplated. I mean I think someone once said that there are more notes in one Wagner opera than there are words in the whole of Shakespeare; I mean whether that's true I simply don't know, I've never counted, but I think that is an indication of the complication of modern music. But I think there is another side to the question which I deplore and that is that I think so many modern composers take themselves too seriously. They *will* write great works all the time. I think greatness happens accidentally—that sometimes one can write a little tiny piece for children or for brass band or something like that, and it may quite easily turn out to be much more important for posterity—if one can worry about posterity—than anyone's symphonies in B flat minor. I think Schoenberg himself said that you can't save the world with every Adagio.

GARVIE: Peter Pears, can I ask you something? You've been so identified now with singing Mr Britten's works, do you actually get in on the act of composition to try out passages to see how they are singable?

Editor's title.

Source: Editor's transcript of CBC recording (NSA NP8122R). Broadcast 21 Nov. 1961, CBC Vancouver: interview with Peter Garvie for the series *Music Diary*; rereleased BBC Transcription Service, 24 Sept. 1962, in the series *Talking About Music* No. 36.

[1] Britten and Pears were in Canada for a series of recitals and a televised recording of the *Nocturne*.

PEARS: I don't know that I do really very much. I think that in fact Benjamin Britten writes for the voice . . .

BRITTEN: Jolly badly . . .

PEARS: No, on the contrary—I wouldn't put it like that. No, he writes . . .

BRITTEN: . . . difficult music . . .

PEARS: . . . not easily, but always rewardingly. I mean you have to work at it; it doesn't come in one practice.

GARVIE: I've often read a reaction to your music, Mr Britten, which suggests that as you have written many more vocal works I think than instrumental, if one counted up and particularly counting in operas as well as song cycles and so on, that you have been more successful in your vocal music. Do you feel any reluctance about these, the sort of standard shape of the symphony, the standard orchestral works.

BRITTEN: Yes I think I do. I know that my inclination is to start from the vocal point of view—that has been for many years now. But on the other hand when a performer like Slava Rostropovich comes along, who excites me—I've found that I wrote a cello sonata for him with a great deal of ease, and a great deal of pleasure. I don't know whether it's a good piece or not—that's not for me to say. But I haven't got any conscious restriction about writing instrumental music. I think quite honestly that it is a time of change in music now, whether one likes to admit it or not. The old tradition has split, and I think we all—all composers—need some kind of guide. In England we have this wonderful lyric tradition of poetry and I get the same kind of security from English poetry that continental composers—the Austrians, the Germans that are perhaps threatened with this Wagner cloud more than I am—that they get from the twelve-tone system; I mean whether this is true I simply don't know, but I get a kind of security in working with words. But on the other hand I would also like to say that I am by no means going to stop writing instrumental music. In fact I am now planning a cello concerto for this wonderful Russian cellist, as well as of course other vocal works.[2]

GARVIE: As a pianist yourself, have you ever thought about writing a large-scale piece for solo piano?

BRITTEN: I don't feel inclined. I *like* the piano very much as a background instrument, but I don't feel inclined to treat it as a melodic instrument. I find that it's limited in colour. I don't really *like* the sound of the modern piano.

[2] Eventually composed as the Symphony for Cello and Orchestra (1963), and first performed in Moscow in Mar. 1964 by Mstislav Rostropovich (b. 1927), the Russian cellist, pianist, and conductor. Britten also wrote his Cello Sonata (1961), and his three suites, Op. 72 (1964), Op. 80 (1967), and Op. 87 (1971), half of the intended six suites, for Rostropovich.

Garvie: I find when I hear Mr Britten's music played—particularly on a first hearing—that there may be some things that I don't entirely figure out, but it does in that sense communicate. What can be done about this gap between the more advanced composer and the audience?

Pears: It's terribly difficult to judge, you know, isn't it? You see in the old days, for singers in any case, more or less any music which a professional sang was available and perfectly possible in theory for an amateur to sing. But the music—the vocal music, or the vast majority of it which has been written in the last, well since the war—twenty years—and of course a lot that was written before that—is of such frantic difficulty that only about one or two professionals in a country like England can perform it at all adequately. I mean Benjamin Britten and I have done together some of the early Webern songs for instance, some of the really comparatively simple Webern songs, and he has worked hard at it at the piano, and I have worked hard at it on the voice. And he, I think I can say, has generally played the right notes, but I, I know very well—we've performed them in public at least four times, if not more—I know that in each performance I have sung a different set of notes; I have not sung the right notes, although I have spent hours and hours practising them.[3] And you see, nobody notices, virtually. The avant-garde boys come up to one with tears in their eyes saying: 'We've never heard this Webern sung like this'. Indeed they probably haven't, but I mean that's not the point; they think it's absolutely marvellous. And if they don't know the difference between the right and the wrong, well now who does? And the amateur can never get within a thousand miles of this stuff.

Britten: I have a feeling that a lot of the young composers are *not* satisfied now with this almost entirely critical reaction and not public reaction. I think a composer—a very gifted one like Hans Henze in Germany has swung right away from the strict serial technique because he has *felt* a need of stronger communication.[4] From the other point of view, if one does receive a bit of music sent to one through the post, which happens very frequently, and it's written in the old tonal system, one's heart sinks because it's nearly always dreary. There's no doubt that the best composers are writing in the avant-garde manner—which is sad, but I don't know what the answer is. But on the other hand I would rather music were bad and used, than bad and not used. I think that one should write as clearly and as simply as possible to communicate the thoughts one has, but one should be perfectly prepared that at any moment those thoughts—those ideas—one has may not be acceptable.

[3] *Vier Lieder*, Op. 12 (1915–17).

[4] Hans Werner Henze (b. 1926), German composer and conductor.

GARVIE: Communication is important to you?

BRITTEN: I think communication is for me entirely important. It seems to me that there's no point having great thoughts if you keep them to yourself. You can, it's fine, but then don't expect anyone to get excited about it.

GARVIE: What about the composing process Mr Britten? How does the seed of a work come to you?

BRITTEN: Well I can only quote T. S. Eliot now. Someone asked him how were the *Four Quartets* getting on, and he said that they were practically finished; but he hadn't written a word—I mean the words came later. The actual thematic material is a very, very late stage, and that it's almost dangerous if you do get thematic ideas in an early stage, in my experience.

GARVIE: Do you sort of tend to get the feel of a whole work then before any of it is written down?

BRITTEN: You get the sense of the whole work and you then plan it, and you sit down and write it and it takes charge and it all goes to pieces in my experience.

GARVIE: You do find that the piece itself takes charge and insists on heading in its own direction?

BRITTEN: Yes, you try and control it and sometimes you succeed but not always—I mean I think as E. M. Forster writes very wisely in the *Aspects of the Novel*, I mean the work has to take over. One doesn't like it taking over because it does things quite often you don't like. But there is no doubt that there is in my experience an inner compulsion that one does one's best to control.

GARVIE: Well, thank you very much Mr Britten and Mr Pears.

60 Speech on Receiving Honorary Degree at Hull University (1962)

My Lord and Chancellor, Mr Vice-Chancellor, Ladies and Gentlemen,

I am really very touched by the great honour which the University of Hull pays me today, and also for the charming and flattering words in which this honour has just been expressed. I am a creative artist, and therefore suffer frequently from depressions and lack of confidence (most such creatures do), so I cannot help feeling that this honour is a little exaggerated—that I do not really deserve these great compliments; and yet it is these very compliments, and the appreciation behind them, which can lift one out of these depressions, and give one confidence to go on. I am really happy therefore to be able to say thank you in public to you all. Your Vice-Chancellor may not believe me, because I bombarded him with protests when he told me that I should be expected to make a speech this morning. I admit that I hate speaking in public. It is not really a matter of natural shyness, but because I do not easily think in words, because words are not my medium. This may surprise some people, but I suppose it is the way one's brain is made. I have always found reading music easier than reading books. Even at school I can remember clearly the vocal and energetic surprise with which the other small boys caught me reading orchestral scores in bed. I also have a very real dread of becoming one of those artists who *talk*. I believe so strongly that it is dangerous for artists to *talk*—in public, that is; in private one really cannot stop them!—the artist's job is to *do*, not to talk about what he does. *That* is the job of other people (critics, for instance, but I'm not always so sure about this). I am all for listening to music, looking at pictures, reading novels—rather than talking about them. It is natural for composers to have strong opinions about music, and very narrow ones. They have to be selective. The whole business of giving a musical shape to one's ideas is so complicated, that when one is in difficulties the influences that can 'rescue' one, so to speak, are so precious and important that they are inclined to obscure everything else. I can give an example from my own experience. When I was very young, my music was inclined to be hectic, to rely on exciting crescendos and diminuendos, on great climaxes—in one word, to rely on 'gestures'. At this time I was absorbed in the music of Beethoven. But for myself I felt the danger of this technique, so I turned away from that great pillar of music, turned to another—to Mozart, the most controlled of composers, who can express the most turbulent feelings in the most unruffled way. But why should anybody be interested in this but me? Of course I have said silly things—and these were

Editor's title. *Source*: *The London Magazine* 3 (Oct. 1963), 89–91.

eagerly taken up in some quarters. This sort of thing, provocative and rather scandalous, always is taken up, because it makes news. Why, only the other day I was asked to make a television appearance to talk about Beethoven—not, mark you, about Bach, Purcell or Mozart whom I love, but about Beethoven, since—as they said—'my appreciation of him is somewhat less than complete', and this, not the other, would be news. And one particular composer I can think of, one of the greatest artistic figures of our time, has said some very misleading things, things which must have bewildered many young composers, many musical people.[1] His judgements of other men's music often seem to me arrogant and ignorant, and they are always changing. But to him I am sure they are all-important: they certainly help him to solve some problem or other—but how I wish he would keep quiet about them. And to turn to literature, just think of what Eliot has said about Milton, what Yeats said about Wilfred Owen, and what Professor Robert Graves has said about practically everyone.[2]

But, to change my tune completely, perhaps in another way it is right that I should be talking now, however inadequately. Because artists are not only artists, they are men, members of society, and must take their place in society—indeed insist on doing so. Artists cannot work in a vacuum—they need society, and society needs them—and I need not emphasize this to you; artists occasionally forget this, or refuse to admit it, and as a result art has got itself into a bit of a jam today. The craze for originality, one result of the nineteenth century cult of personality, has driven many artists into using a language to which very few hold the key, and that is a pity. To use a language which can be understood is an advantage, not a disadvantage. Now, I don't for a moment think that *what* you say will immediately be liked or welcomed, but language should not be an additional difficulty. Composers should always try to keep in touch: write for people, compose for particular performers or groups (even if they are young or inexperienced), write for special occasions (even if they seem trivial)—do other jobs which take them out of their study—play the piano, conduct, organize Festivals—even do jobs *outside* their art, if they wish. This has often happened in the arts. There was, for instance, a great poet who was a Member of Parliament for Hull in the seventeenth century,[3] and don't forget

[1] Stravinsky, whom Britten often referred to as the 'greatest living composer' or subtle variants of this. In Britten's draft, this sentence is rather more revealing: 'Stravinsky, one of the greatest artistic figures of our time, has said some very silly things, and unless one is careful they are liable to prejudice one against his great music' (*GB-ALb* 1–02053796). See Essay 30 for some of Stravinsky's 'misleading' thoughts.

[2] Robert Graves (1895–1985), outspoken English poet, writer, and critic. Britten set his poem 'Lift Boy' in 1932, one of his Two Part-Songs.

[3] Andrew Marvell (1621–78), English poet, elected MP for Hull in 1659. Britten did not set any of his poetry, although he did set one piece by his friend, John Milton ('The Morning Star' in the *Spring Symphony*), whose release from prison Marvell effected.

that in classical Athens everyone was expected to take part in public life. So my advice to young artists (I wouldn't dare to advise older ones) is not to be frightened of outside contacts. Do not forget that the *Matthew Passion* and *A Midsummer Night's Dream*[4] were both written for special occasions, and that Rubens was his country's ambassador. We should try to be obliging if we are asked to speak in public, but keep off our own personal likes and dislikes.

Now, ladies and gentlemen, I have given excellent reasons as to why I should not be speaking here, and so I think I had better stop. But please let me end with a heartfelt thank you for the honour you have paid me today, for the great honour which Hull University has conferred not only on me personally, but on the great art of music, of which I have the honour to be a humble servant.

[4] i.e. Shakespeare's play, not Britten's opera.

61 Freedom of Borough of Aldeburgh (1962)

Your Worship, ladies and gentlemen—

It may seem an odd way of saying 'thank you' for the great honour paid to me this evening, if I start by saying that I'm afraid I rather distrust honours. In the arts, at least—it is so often the wrong person who gets them, or for the wrong reason. It is the dull, the respectable, the one who kow-tows, who sucks up, the members of that favourite name today—the Establishment. You know what I mean (conveniently forgetting for the moment honoured names like Sir Peter Paul Rubens, Lord Tennyson, Chevalier Gluck)—think of Schubert, unwanted; Mozart, a pauper's grave; Van Gogh mad like Blake; Wilfred Owen killed at the age of 25—how far honours were from these great names and hundreds like them. The trouble really is that the people who hand out honours usually know so little about the artists. They take a famous name, and that's that. Why is it then that I am unexpectedly proud and touched this evening? After all, I shall not be able to write H.F.A.B.A. (Honorary Freeman of the Ancient Borough of Aldeburgh) after my name; and I am very clearly made to understand that I cannot (as the result of being a free man) park my car on the wrong side of the High Street without lights, and I gather I must continue to pay 24 shillings in the pound! No, I am proud because this honour comes from people who know me—many of whom have known me for quite a long time too, because, although I didn't have the luck to be born here in Aldeburgh, I have in fact lived all my life within 30 miles of it.[1] As I understand it, this honour is not given because of a reputation, because of a chance acquaintance, it is—dare I say it?—because you really do know me, and accept me as one of yourselves, as a useful part of the Borough—and this is, I think, the highest possible compliment for an artist. I believe, you see, that an artist should be part of his community, should work for it, with it, and be used by it. Over the last 100 years this has become rarer and rarer, and the artist and community have both suffered as a result.

The artist has suffered in many cases, because, without an audience, or with only a specialised one—without, therefore, a direct contact with his public—his work tends to become 'Ivory tower', 'hole in the corner', without focus. This has made a great deal of modern work obscure and impractical—only useable by highly skilled performers, and only understandable by the most erudite. Don't please think that I am against all new and strange ideas—far from it (new ideas have a way of seeming odd and surprising when heard for

Source: Draft (typescript), n.d., (*GB-ALb* 1–02053797). Speech was given on 22 Oct. 1962.

[1] Discounting his time at the Royal College of Music in London and as a young professional in the capital, and then his years in America.

the first time). But I am against experiment for experiment's sake; originality at all costs. It's necessary to say this because there are audiences who are not discriminating about it: they think that everything new is good, that if it is shocking it must be important. There is all the difference in the world between Picasso, the great humble artist, or Henry Moore—and tachist daubers; between Stravinsky—and electronic experimenters.

On the other hand, the Public has also suffered from this divorce. It has stopped using the serious artist for occasional or commissioned work, as hundreds of monstrous public monuments, acres of hideous stained-glass windows, nasty cheap music in the theatre or cinema, bare [*sic*] witness. None of this would have been necessary if the public and the artist could have got together—with an open mind on both sides.

It is this gulf between the public and the serious artist which has helped to encourage a deep-seated philistinism about the arts, which there is—I hate to admit it—in so many English people. It was not always so. In the glorious 16th Century, for instance, it was considered an essential part of good social behaviour to be able to sing a part in a complicated madrigal; and in the waiting rooms of the 17th Century there were not glossy periodicals, but a lute to be strummed on to while away the time. It is difficult to see that being popular in the 20th Century,! but we are making progress; we are getting back to thinking of the arts as important again, not something just silly, or suspect, or even wicked. And here I think I can blow Aldeburgh's own small trumpet. It is a considerable achievement, in this small Borough in England, that we run year after year, a first-class Festival of the Arts, and we make a huge success of it. And when I say 'we' I mean 'we'. This Festival couldn't be the work of just one, two or three people, or a board or a council—it must be the corporate effort of a whole town.!! And, if I may say so, what a nice town it is! Festival visitors are always charmed by it, by its old buildings, though like me they are nervous about how its new developments will look in 50 years time. But Everyone is charmed by its lovely position between sea and river, and the beach with the fishing boats and Life-boat, the fine hotels, the golf course, wonderful river for sailing, the birds, the countryside, our magnificent churches, and of course the shops too:! I have a very choosy friend from abroad who regularly re-stocks her wardrobe here, and buys most of her Christmas presents too, I believe.[2] All these excellent qualities are the result of the hard work, the imagination and friendship of everyone in the town.

If you have chosen to honour me as a symbol I am deeply grateful, but I can't help feeling that it is all of us, all of you who deserve it. So, in the name of all of us, all of you, I want to say a heart-felt 'thank you' for this touching, very special, and very treasured honour, which I have received this evening.

[2] Probably Princess Margaret of Hesse.

62 Erwin Stein: *Form and Performance* (1962)

Erwin Stein's name was known to a comparatively small circle of people.[1] He himself was the last person to complain about this since his was a retiring nature and he believed (and how rightly!) that some of the most important work is done without the glare of publicity. There were occasions, however, such as that of a particularly execrable performance of one of his favourite works, when he would regret that he had not the chance to conduct more often; forgetting his natural modesty, he would say he 'could have shown them how!' And after reading this book one can easily believe that he was right, for it shows a rare gift for detailed analysis, and at the same time a warmth and understanding of the music which, in my experience, is unique.

He was not inexperienced as a conductor. Between 1910 and 1919 he conducted at many German opera houses and was responsible for the preparation of many different kinds of works, from the lightest to the most serious. Later he prepared and conducted the famous series of performances of *Pierrot Lunaire* with Erika Wagner, first in Vienna and then touring across Europe to London.[2] In the 'twenties he trained a chorus in Vienna and conducted Beethoven's ninth symphony. After he came to England, he only gave one public performance, that of *Pierrot lunaire*, at the Æolian Hall in 1943. Instead of conducting he listened, and so came to write this book. He listened to all kinds of musical performances with that devastating yet good-humoured criticism which was so characteristic: 'It was bad, of course', he might say, 'but not *so* bad.'

He could talk in fascinating detail of his early, and certainly his most important, listening experiences—those performances of operas and concerts conducted by Mahler in Vienna. He went to them with his friends Schoenberg, Zemlinsky, Webern, and Berg, and they would sit together for most of the night discussing what they had heard. It is from Mahler that Erwin learned most of the art of performance—the moulding of a work's form, a taut yet flexible rhythm, the balance of tone, sensitive phrasing, and intensity.

Although he was an admirer of Mahler's he never actually studied with him. He was however for some time a pupil of that great teacher Schoenberg. Erwin himself gave up writing music many years before he died (I never saw any of

Source: Foreword to Erwin Stein, *Form and Performance* (London: Faber & Faber, 1962), 7–8.

[1] He had died in 1958, before publication of his book.

[2] Erika Wagner, German theatre and film actress, who in 1921 took over from Marie Gutheil-Schoder for a number of performances of *Pierrot lunaire* (1912) when the latter found that she could not prepare the *Sprechstimme* in time. Wagner's association with the role continued through her participation in the Pierrot Lunaire Ensemble of Vienna, which was formed to tour the piece, giving the British premiere of it in 1930 in a BBC contemporary music concert.

his compositions, and often wondered whether his critical faculty was not used too harshly on himself), but he was able to pass on much of the invaluable experience of his lessons with Schoenberg to young composers—whether they were his pupils or those with whom he dealt while acting as editor to two important publishing firms in Vienna and London.[3]

Erwin's reaction to the new music one played him was never very quick. He needed time to assimilate it—the over-excited and inaccurate bangings to which he was subjected passed gently over him until he had had time to study the actual notes. And that to me is one of the most important things in this book—his insistence on the composer's actual notes, and on what lies behind them.

Those of his readers who are also performers may despair at the complicated task of following and carrying out such detailed advice; but they should not forget that after the intellect has finished work, the instinct must take over. In performance the analysis should be forgotten and the pieces played as if they were at that moment being composed. Although most of Erwin's work was done, as it were, behind the stage, he had the strongest understanding of those *on* it. He believed profoundly that one of the most important jobs in life was the communication of great musical truths, the truths he helps to reveal with such care and affection in this book.

[3] Universal Edition and Boosey & Hawkes.

63 A Tribute to Wilfred Owen (?1963)

I am delighted to read that Birkenhead Institute is paying a tribute to its old pupil, Wilfred Owen. I have read with interest of his days at the Institute, and feel sure that he owed a great deal to its sympathetic encouragement.

I would only like to add that Owen is to me by far our greatest war poet, and one of the most original and touching poets of this century.

Source: T. J. Walsh (comp.), *A Tribute to Wilfred Owen* (Birkenhead Institute, n.d.), 26.

64 Imogen Holst: *An ABC of Music* (1963)

A young friend of mine has been playing the guitar for several years now.[1] He has a real aptitude for it: a feeling for the sound of the instrument, a considerable gift for technique, and patience to work hard. But he cannot read music and knows nothing of how music is made, and, what is more, he simply refuses to learn. 'Too dull and too much trouble', he says, 'and anyhow not worth it'. It is true, of course, that a lot of his time is spent in playing dance music, when sight-reading is perhaps not so essential, but he has a considerable interest in straight music, and the lute parts of Dowland have a real fascination for him. When this book is published I want to send him a copy, because he will see that learning to read music, and learning its grammar, need not be dull or too much trouble. He will also discover when he can sight-read that it is really 'worth it'. Maybe you *can* pick up tunes and approximate block harmonies without being able to read, but I challenge anyone with that (rather over-rated) gift of playing or singing 'by ear' to pick up easily and quickly a Dowland accompaniment *exactly* as he wrote it (and the 'exactly' matters), or the Stravinsky dance-rhythms, or the inner part of a complicated madrigal or part-song—as most of us with experience of amateur choral singing can testify.

No, it won't be only to this guitar boy that I shall send copies of this book, but to many of my friends who sing or play the recorder in amateur groups, and who spend frequent and distressing moments 'getting lost'.

Luckily most state and many private schools are now teaching rudiments of music as a matter of course. I strongly recommend teachers to use this book. Miss Holst has an unrivalled knowledge of teaching; she knows how to keep the interest of the pupil—by being serious, and yet not turgid; by being brief, but not telegrammic; and by illuminating her text with intelligent parallels from her wide knowledge of art and life.

Source: Foreword to Imogen Holst, *An ABC Of Music* (London: OUP, 1963), pp. iii–iv.

[1] Not identified.

65 British Composers in Interview: Benjamin Britten (1963)

SCHAFER: Born by the sea, you have returned to it to live and work in the natural environment of a fishing village. Is the physical presence of the sea an incentive for your work?

BRITTEN: Yes, a very central one. To what extent its presence is a stimulus I cannot say, but I love the sea and certain works of mine communicate this affection. About three years ago I moved from my house absolutely on the edge of the sea to my present home half a mile inland.[1] But I miss the old place; I often go walking by the sea and these walks are a stimulus to the extent that they help me sort out my ideas.

SCHAFER: Do you have special feelings about large cities—London, for example?

BRITTEN: I hate them! When I come up for a day to London to do the usual boring things, I rush about and in the end get terribly behind and utterly exhausted. Probably I don't appreciate London. I realize that on a spring or an autumn day it can be ravishing, but as I don't live there I don't often have a chance to appreciate that.

SCHAFER: Do you hate all cities?

BRITTEN: I adore Venice, but it's unique. I used to like Amsterdam and I enjoy my occasional visits to Copenhagen.

SCHAFER: Are your memories of your student days at the Royal College happy ones?

BRITTEN: They don't seem happy in retrospect. I feel I didn't learn very much at the Royal College. I think I can say that at the Royal College not nearly enough account was taken of the exceptionally gifted musician. When you are immensely full of energy and ideas you don't want to waste your time being taken through elementary exercises in dictation. Frank Bridge was my prime mentor and I gained most from him—that was earlier of course. I might also say that while I was a student at the Royal College only one of my compositions was performed there.[2] I had to go outside to get my music played, but I daresay things have changed in the last twenty-eight years.

Source: Murray Schafer, *British Composers in Interview* (London: Faber & Faber, 1963), 113–24.

[1] In 1957 the painter Mary Potter 'swapped' her home, The Red House, for Britten's residence on Crag Path, giving the composer and Peter Pears more privacy.

[2] This was his Phantasy in F minor (1932), which won the Cobbett Prize and was performed by fellow students of the College. His *Sinfonietta* (1932) received numerous rehearsals by students at the College, but the actual first performance was in a Macnaghten–Lemare concert in January 1933.

SCHAFER: Originally you had hoped to be allowed to study with Alban Berg. Yet your music is quite different from his. What was it that intrigued you about this composer?

BRITTEN: I don't know how much of Berg's music I really knew at that time, perhaps not much. I heard the first performance of the violin concerto in Barcelona in '36 and I had earlier heard the *Lyric Suite*. I think it was Frank Bridge's suggestion that I leave England and experience a different musical climate. I did in fact eventually go to Vienna on a scholarship but I never got to Berg. I had suggested to the R.C.M. authorities that I'd like to study with Berg, but later I discovered that it had been hinted to my parents that he was in some way 'immoral', and they thought studying with him would do me harm.

SCHAFER: In what ways was your early friendship with W. H. Auden beneficial to you? Did Auden stimulate your interest in poetry?

BRITTEN: Yes, altogether. Auden was a powerful, revolutionary person. He was very much anti-bourgeois and that appealed. He also had some lively, slightly dotty ideas about music. He played the piano reasonably well, and was a great one for singing unlikely words to Anglican chants. In the 'thirties I spent a lot of time with Auden's friends, Isherwood, MacNeice and others.[3]

SCHAFER: Did he introduce you to only modern poets?

BRITTEN: Not at all. Auden got us to take Donne seriously.[4] One didn't get much of him at school, or at least we didn't appreciate him properly there. He also introduced me to Rimbaud.

SCHAFER: It is, perhaps, strange that the only libretto Auden produced for you was that of the youthful *Paul Bunyan*. Yet you have gone on to write operas and Auden has gone on to produce libretti for others. Were no other projects contemplated?

BRITTEN: Yes, other things were contemplated. Auden produced the libretto for a Christmas oratorio but it turned out too big and literary to set. There was one chorus (about Caesar) with stanzas eight lines long. Auden thought of it as a fugue with each entry occupying a stanza, but that was out of the question. He did write the fine text of the *Hymn to Saint Cecilia* for me and, of course, I set other poems of his.[5] I think *Our Hunting Fathers* was our

[3] Christopher Isherwood (1904–86), English writer, who first collaborated with Britten in 1936 on *The Ascent of F6*, which received its first performance in February 1937. He declined Britten's suggestion that he write the libretto to *Peter Grimes*. Louis MacNeice (1907–63), English poet and writer. Britten set his 'Cradle Song (Sleep, my darling, sleep)' in 1942 and collaborated with him on the radio drama *The Dark Tower* in 1945.

[4] Britten set the poet ten years after meeting Auden, in his *The Holy Sonnets of John Donne*.

[5] Apart from *Our Hunting Fathers* (1936), *Hymn to St Cecilia* (1942), and *Paul Bunyan* (1941), Britten set these Auden texts: *Chorale after an Old French Carol* and *A Shepherd's Carol*—both set in 1944 and taken from Auden's *Christmas Oratorio*; six miscellaneous songs (1937–41), later

most successful collaboration. Since 1942 we have not been together very often and I couldn't ask anyone to prepare a libretto for me without being in on it myself from the start.

SCHAFER: You like to help shape the libretto yourself?

BRITTEN: I have to. I get lots of libretti in the post but I have never accepted one. A few of the ideas are attractive enough, but I have to be in on it from the beginning.

SCHAFER: Can you account for the fact that there are so few contemporary composers who have worked in the medium of opera with continued success?

BRITTEN: Virtually all good composers have a dramatic approach. A stage work has to make an immediate impact. Perhaps the whole symphonic trend of the nineteenth century which became expressive at the expense of form distorted the operatic approach and vision.

SCHAFER: In writing opera you must see the action before you so as to adjust the tempo of the music to it. Do you have special ways of creating this physical atmosphere in your mind?

BRITTEN: Being present at productions of many operas gives one a sense of proportion in these things. One begins to know exactly what kind of music and how much of it will transport an actor from A to B on the stage—not the exact number of footsteps, but the general dramatic shapes. I don't have to physically create the production for myself when I work, although on one or two occasions I have had to give some serious thought to it, like the kids' game with the ball in *Albert Herring*.[6]

SCHAFER: An inexperienced person looks at a libretto and is struck by its flat, often abrupt, manner of expression; but an operatic composer realizes at once the full musical and dramatic potentialities of directness. What other qualities do you desire in a libretto?

BRITTEN: Unfortunately, I seldom go to the theatre, but reading some of the new plays I am struck by the similarities they have with libretti. One might say they read flatly too. What I require is memorable and thrilling phrases. I think the Pub Scene in *Grimes* was successful partly for this reason; on the other hand, there were other parts which gave me more trouble, such as Ellen's passages at the opening of the second act.[7]

SCHAFER: You came on the idea for *Grimes* yourself.

published in the volume *Fish in the Unruffled Lakes*; the four cabaret songs (1937–9); *Ballad of Heroes* (1939) (text by Auden and Randall Swingler); *On This Island* (1937); and 'Out on the lawn' in the *Spring Symphony* (1948).

[6] Act 1 scene 2, 'Bounce me high | Bounce me low | Bounce me up to Jericho!'

[7] This is the scene in which Ellen sits with the young boy apprentice, John, rather than going in to church, and sings 'Glitter of waves | And glitter of sunlight . . .'.

BRITTEN: Peter Pears and I were in California in 1941 waiting for a ship to return home. We read about the Crabbe poem in the *Listener*. We got a second-hand copy of Crabbe's poetry and read it. It moved us deeply. Perhaps it was partly a home-sick reaction—war and our eagerness to return home; one was aware of a sharp tug at one's heart right from the first. Peter Pears started working on it with me, sketching out bits here and there, so that when we did, in fact, get home in 1942, it was all ready to go to Montagu Slater with clear ideas on how it was to run.

SCHAFER: The Grimes of your opera is rather different from the Grimes of Crabbe's poem.

BRITTEN: A central feeling for us was that of the individual against the crowd, with ironic overtones for our own situation. As conscientious objectors we were out of it. We couldn't say we suffered physically, but naturally we experienced tremendous tension. I think it was partly this feeling which led us to make Grimes a character of vision and conflict, the tortured idealist he is, rather than the villain he was in Crabbe.

SCHAFER: At one time your political sympathies were quite clear. There was no mistaking your position during the Spanish Civil War. Are your political persuasions unchanged today or would you describe yourself as a-political as far as practical politics go?

BRITTEN: Politicians are so ghastly, aren't they? After all, the job of politics is to organize the world and resolve its tensions. What we really need is more international technicians, artists, doctors. Political institutions ought to have shown signs of withering away by now. My social feelings are the same as they have always been. I disbelieve profoundly in power and violence.

SCHAFER: No ideology has a monopoly on violence.

BRITTEN: Certainly. The side of communism which is violent is abhorrent to me. But when one travels to Iron Curtain countries as I have had occasion to do, one is conscious simply of human beings—how plucky and spirited those people are in Poland and Yugoslavia. That is what interests me.

SCHAFER: You are a pacifist. In an absorbing article on your music Hans Keller[8] has written: 'What distinguishes Britten's musical personality is the violent repressive counter-force against his sadism; by dint of character, musical history and environment, he has become a *musical pacifist* too.'[9] How does Keller's observation strike you?

[8] Hans Keller (1919–85), Austrian musician, writer, and intellectual, who had a strong interest in Britten's music.

[9] Original footnote: cf. Keller's article in *Benjamin Britten: A Commentary on his Works by a Group of Specialists*, edited by Donald Mitchell and Hans Keller (London: Rockliff, 1952).

BRITTEN: It is difficult, if not impossible, to comment objectively on what is written about oneself. But I admire Keller's intelligence and courage enormously, and certainly about *others* he is very perceptive!

SCHAFER: It has often been said, perhaps uncharitably, that the British are a nation of musical amateurs. As a dedicated professional you have, nevertheless, written many works for the enjoyment and participation of amateurs: the *Saint Nicolas* cantata, *The Little Sweep*, and *Noye's Fludde*, to name only a few. You certainly don't seem to scorn the status of the amateur or child musician.

BRITTEN: Oh never! I want to write for people. I passionately believe in professionalism and I think the professional must know his business thoroughly, but this shouldn't prevent him from writing for amateurs. Just the reverse. After all, they have always been an important force in the shaping of our musical tradition. Even on the Continent, at least until a few years ago, it was the amateurs who performed and loved the songs and string quartets of the great composers. There is something very fresh and unstrained in the quality of the music produced by amateurs. What annoys me more is the ineptitude of some professionals who don't know their stuff. I have no patience with that.

SCHAFER: We have mentioned your interest in Alban Berg. One of the points of difference between his music and yours is your different concept of orchestration. There is nothing of the heavy, lush effect with you.

BRITTEN: Berg and Schoenberg share common ground in the respect of the complexity of their musical thought. The multiplication of parts in their music is often staggering. But I am at precisely the other end of music. Music for me is clarification; I try to clarify, to refine, to sensitize. Stravinsky once said that one must work perpetually at one's technique. But what is technique? Schoenberg's technique is often a tremendous elaboration. My technique is to tear all the waste away; to achieve perfect clarity of expression, that is my aim.

SCHAFER: Are you satisfied with the constitution of the symphony orchestra as it stands today, or would you alter it in any way to render it a more perfect instrument for your expression?

BRITTEN: Of course with such a wonderful and sensitive instrument as the modern symphony orchestra to hand, one wants to write for it. But my inclination is not to use *all* of it all the time. I like to use contrasting sections; and there are many occasions when far smaller units—forms of chamber orchestra—seem nearer to one's ideas. Stravinsky in *L'Histoire du Soldat* and Schoenberg in *Pierrot lunaire* have successfully paved the way.[10] I often use

[10] *L'Histoire du soldat* (1918) is scored for clarinet, bassoon, cornet à pistons, trombone, violin, double bass, percussion; *Pierrot lunaire* (1912) is scored for speaking voice, piano, flute/piccolo, clarinet/bass clarinet, violin/viola, and cello.

small groups to accompany my operas—and not only for economic reasons either.

SCHAFER: Do you have any favourite instruments? I notice, for example, that you employ the whip more frequently than most composers, though often as a delicate *pianissimo* tap.

BRITTEN: I don't think I have any favourite instruments, although I expect I have favourite sounds and, therefore, probably seem to have a bias towards certain instruments in order to make these sounds. I wasn't aware of any predilection for the whip—any more than for the alto flute or saxophone or piano.

SCHAFER: A composer who has influenced you orchestrally, but also in terms of melody-shaping and generically, is Mahler. Would you discuss your indebtedness to this composer?

BRITTEN: I was tremendously moved when I first heard Mahler and I am still moved and impressed by his work—especially by his wonderful ear for sound but also by his great sense of form. My experience of conducting the fourth symphony at Aldeburgh showed me what a master of form he is, particularly in the first movement of that great work.[11]

SCHAFER: But your sympathy does not extend to Beethoven and Brahms.

BRITTEN: I'm not blind about them. Once I adored them. Between the ages of thirteen and sixteen I knew every note of Beethoven and Brahms. I remember receiving the full score of *Fidelio* for my fourteenth birthday. It was a red letter day in my life. But I think in a sense I never forgave them for having led me astray in my own particular musical thinking and natural inclinations. Only yesterday I was listening to the *Coriolanus Overture* by Beethoven. What a marvellous beginning, and how well the development in sequence is carried out! But what galled me was the crudity of the sound; the orchestral sounds seem often so haphazard. I certainly don't dislike all Beethoven but sometimes I feel I have lost the point of what he's up to. I heard recently the piano sonata, op. 111. The sound of the variations was so grotesque I just couldn't see what they were all about.

SCHAFER: Many of your works show a more than casual interest in the twelve-note method and yet you have never abandoned tonality to give yourself up to serialism unreservedly. You must sense certain limitations or deficiencies in the serial method.

BRITTEN: It has simply never attracted me as a method, although I respect many composers who have worked in it, and love some of their works. It is beyond me to say why, except that I cannot feel that tonality is outworn, and find many serial 'rules' arbitrary. 'Socially' I am seriously disturbed by its

[11] Aldeburgh Festival, 1961.

limitations. I can see it taking no part in the music-lover's music-making. Its methods make writing *gratefully* for voices or instruments an impossibility, which inhibits amateurs and children. I find it worrying that our contemporary young composers are not able to write things for the young or amateurs to play and sing. But I have always been interested in different organizations and I am prepared to experiment with organizing my music on different lines, although that is no virtue in itself. No system guarantees quality.

SCHAFER: Do you find the cerebral aspects of serialism disturbing?

BRITTEN: It really depends on how the music is approached. One can make a big thing of approaching it intellectually, but I don't think it is the best way. For example, my *Nocturne* opens with a long vocal melisma descending, and it closes with its inversion ascending, but I would consider it no great virtue consciously to know that. All that is important is that the composer should make his music sound inevitable and right; the system in unimportant.

SCHAFER: As the editor of Purcell's music do you think there are any aspects of Purcell's achievement which have not been fully appreciated?

BRITTEN: Purcell is not fully appreciated in this country. *Dido and Aeneas* is unquestionably a masterpiece, but it is not a box-office success and therefore it is only rarely performed. It's the same old business of the inveterate philistinism of this country. They want us to perform Purcell in Sweden.

SCHAFER: Are there any aspects of Purcell's achievement which have interested you in particular?

BRITTEN: Purcell is a great master at handling the English language in song, and I learned much from him. I recall a critic once asking me from whom I had learned to set English poetry to music. I told him Purcell; he was amazed. I suppose he expected me to say folk music and Vaughan Williams.

SCHAFER: Writing in 1952 Peter Pears referred to your *First Canticle* as your finest vocal piece to date.[12] Would you have agreed with him at that time?

BRITTEN: Yes, I think so. The *First Canticle* was a new invention in a sense although it was certainly modelled on the Purcell *Divine Hymns*; but few people knew their Purcell well enough to realize that.

SCHAFER: And today?

BRITTEN: About three years ago I set some fragments by Hölderlin for voice and piano.[13] They have not been published yet but Peter Pears and I have performed them a number of times. They are short—just fragments—perhaps ten minutes in all, but I believe they are probably my best vocal works so far.

[12] Canticle I 'My Beloved is Mine' (1947). The text is by Francis Quarles based on the 'Song of Solomon'. Pears made this observation in the Mitchell–Keller volume (1952).

[13] *Sechs Hölderlin-Fragmente* (1958). The songs were not published until 1963.

SCHAFER: Some people would say *Grimes*.

BRITTEN: Some people seem to want another *Grimes*, and still another! But they are mistaken if they expect me to give it to them. I have different challenges before me and I respond to them.

SCHAFER: Vocal works make up the large body of your compositions. Does vocal music present the fewest problems to you?

BRITTEN: No fewer problems, just different problems. Composition is never easy.

SCHAFER: You have written songs on texts in several languages: English, French, Italian, Latin and German. Is there any language you have a particular sympathy for?

BRITTEN: I enjoyed setting them all. The *Rimbaud* and the *Michelangelo* cycles were necessary for me in order to shed the bad influences of the Royal College.[14] With both the French and the Italian I was perhaps responding to Nietzsche's call to 'mediterraneanize music'. The Italian songs have predominantly sunny lines. I am sure Purcell felt the same way in his own day about this, for surely he was influenced by French and Italian music too. As for the technical question of setting a foreign language, I am not a linguist and there are one or two small errors I believe in the setting of *Les Illuminations* (the French have never complained—the English are the only people who are annoyed by details of this kind), but I pride myself that I have a feeling for languages, even if I don't speak them very well.

SCHAFER: What kind of literature interests you to read for relaxation?

BRITTEN: I read a great deal of poetry of all sorts, ancient and modern. Of the moderns I enjoy especially the work of those poets who are my friends: Plomer, Auden, and, of course, E. M. Forster though he writes only prose. I am very fond of Dickens and I try to read at least one of his novels a year.

SCHAFER: In giving you the following quotation from Puccini I am only concerned in discovering to what extent your own creating may be 'feverish' in the way this master's was: 'I am afraid that *Turandot* will never be finished. It is impossible to work like this. When fever abates, it ends by disappearing, and without fever there is no creation; because emotional art is a kind of malady, an exceptional state of mind, over-excitation of every fibre and every atom of one's being, and so on, ad aeternam.'

BRITTEN: Of course everyone gets excited about work in hand. Often I get exceedingly impatient if prevented from completing a work. If I have to leave Aldeburgh and an incompleted work, I am often ill because I fret so

[14] *Les Illuminations* (1939) and *Seven Sonnets of Michelangelo* (1940). Britten is presumably here referring to what he considered to be the parochial, inward-looking Royal College of Music.

much. My state of mind is reflected in my body. But 'fevered' in what sense exactly?

SCHAFER: Let me give you another example. Auden once said he wrote one of his finest poems just after he had had a tooth out. Creation and acute tension or pain—is that clearer?

BRITTEN: I wrote my *John Donne Sonnets* in a week while in bed with a high fever, a delayed reaction from an inoculation. The inoculation had been in order to go on a tour of concentration camps with Yehudi Menuhin in 1945.[15] We gave two or three short recitals a day—they couldn't take more. It was in many ways a terrifying experience. The theme of the *Donne Sonnets* is death, as you know. I think the connexion between personal experience and my feelings about the poetry was a strong one. It certainly characterized the music.

SCHAFER: One gathers that while most of your composition is done at home, much conceptual work is done away from home, on trains, or in hotel rooms while on concert tours. Are there any conditions which seem especially conducive to this kind of work?

BRITTEN: I like train-rides and car-rides. They help one to work things out in one's mind; but I rarely write music while touring. I have on one or two occasions—once in Venice—but that is not my usual practice.[16] Usually I have the music complete in my mind before putting pencil to paper. That doesn't mean that every note has been composed, perhaps not one has, but I have worked out questions of form, texture, character, and so forth, in a very precise way so that I know exactly what effects I want and how I am going to achieve them. I only write while I am at home in Aldeburgh. I believe strongly in a routine. Generally I have breakfast at eight o'clock and am at work before nine, working through until a quarter past one. Then I have a break with a walk before returning to work from five until eight again.

SCHAFER: No midnight inspirations?

BRITTEN: The night is for sleeping. I go to bed early and I get up early. When I am in a rush and have to get something off to copyists, I may work into the small hours but that is on scoring, not composition.

SCHAFER: Do you revise a great deal?

BRITTEN: Yes, during the composition of a work. I revise until it is sent off to be copied, but rarely after that. Usually I write for specific performances and specific dates, so there is a deadline to work to. I have revised one or two

[15] Britten and Yehudi Menuhin (1916–99), American-born violinist and conductor, visited German concentration camps in July and August 1945, giving two or three recitals per day for ten days. Belsen was one of the camps visited.

[16] This was for *A Midsummer Night's Dream*.

works later: I wrote a new movement to my piano concerto and made some changes in *Lucretia*, partly to do with the libretto.[17]

SCHAFER: An incidental question: do you have perfect pitch?

BRITTEN: I used to have it, but it seems to have sunk slightly. It's now about a semitone flat and I hear the overture to *Meistersinger* in 'my' C sharp major instead of C major.

SCHAFER: Is perfect pitch of negligible value to a composer?

BRITTEN: It's undoubtedly of some value, but it's certainly not necessary, for many composers did not have it. It's probably of greater importance to singers, especially if they must sing serial music.

SCHAFER: Are you content with the way in which the younger composers of this country are developing?

BRITTEN: Composers must always write for people. Young composers ought to write for young people. There are signs that one or two young composers are working with children and that is encouraging.

SCHAFER: But what about the infatuation with Webern and his followers?

BRITTEN: I think there is a snobbery of enormous pretentions [*sic*] connected with the most recent trends in music. People in this country who thought Schoenberg was mad until recently have suddenly swung the other way and they think it's all wonderful. Neither estimation is honest. A lot of contemporary music is terribly difficult to perform and that is bound always to stand against it. Peter Pears and I have performed some of Webern's songs. We die a thousand deaths trying to get them exactly right and it is still nearly impossible.

SCHAFER: Is the snobbery of recent trends in music your only criticism of our musical climate?

BRITTEN: I have few complaints personally. I am touched deeply by the response given me. If I did not communicate I would consider I had failed. Perhaps people in this country don't warm to things quite the way they do on the Continent but that is not so depressing as the basic philistinism which exists in this country. It is not a matter of appreciating Schoenberg; it is a deep prejudice to any kind of music. It is possible to encounter people in this country who don't know anything about music and are proud of it. I remember at a tennis party at Lowestoft once, about the time I was leaving school, I was asked what career I intended to choose. I told them I intended to be a composer. They were amazed! 'Yes, but what else?' Attitudes of that kind die hard, but oh, how one wishes the basic philistinism of this country would wither away. Perhaps it will!

[17] Revisions to the Concerto were effected in 1946, and to *Lucretia* in 1947.

66 The Artist—to the People (1963)

In the packed concert halls of Moscow and Leningrad flutter the national flags of Great Britain and the Soviet Union. The Festival of British Musical Art is in progress.[1]

The outstanding composer Benjamin Britten, who heads the group of English musicians, said in conversation with Pravda's correspondent:

I must admit that right up to my departure for the Soviet Union I was beset with doubts whether our musical art, which has developed in national traditions different from those of Russia, would be understandable and acceptable to Soviet audiences. I am glad that my anxieties were dissolved at the very first concert. Soviet audiences are unusually musical—this I knew beforehand—but are also remarkable for the enviable breadth of their musical appreciation. They are a wonderful public.

PRAVDA: What do you think, Mr Britten, about the role of the composer, and the artist in general, in present day society?

BRITTEN: I think that one of the fundamental dangers in creative artistic work in our day lies in the tendency of a certain section of composers and other artists towards a departure from themes prompted by real life, towards abstract experimentation in their workshops. Instead of serving as a creative laboratory for the artistic interpretation of reality, the workshop of a different type of artist is turned into the well known 'ivory tower' in which he seals himself tightly off from the real world.

In general I think that 'art for art's sake' cannot exist. One of the principal social obligations of the artist consists of the moulding, education and development of the artistic taste of the people. Nor do I accept the division of audiences into the 'elite' and all the others. The works of Mozart, Bach and Shakespeare are understandable both to the former and the latter. Obviously the main point is not who the artist chooses to address himself to in his work, but what he has to say to people.

PRAVDA: What, in your opinion, is the main result of the Festival of British Musical Art in the Soviet Union?

BRITTEN: England knows and likes many musicians from the Soviet Union. I can say that Soviet musical art has become an inseparable part of our cultural

Source: *Pravda* (18 Mar. 1963). English trans. (*GB-ALb* 1-9501178). Translator unknown.

[1] Britten's involvement in the Festival of British Musical Art was through five concerts held between 8 Mar. and 17 Mar. 1963. These included two recitals with Pears of *Winter Words* (1953) and a selection of songs by Schubert and Purcell; a recital featuring *Sechs Hölderlin-Fragmente* (1958), again with Pears; a performance of his Sonata in C (1961) with Rostropovich; and an orchestral concert, conducted by Norman Del Mar, featuring the *Sea Interludes* from *Peter Grimes* (1945).

life. The warm welcome given to us in the Soviet Union permits one to hope that now our musicians too have friends in your country. There are no barriers between the art of our peoples. I think that there is in this a happy promise of mutual understanding and friendship.[2]

[2] Martin Cooper responded to this interview in a *Daily Telegraph* article (30 Mar. 1963), 11, entitled 'For People—or "the People"':

> The actual circumstances of the interview with Benjamin Britten published in *Pravda* on March 18 made it appear in quite different lights in the two countries concerned.
>
> In Britain it seemed to be a gesture of solidarity with the musicians of a country which had just welcomed a group of British musicians and had shown interest and enthusiasm for much of the music performed, and always for the performers.
>
> Mr. Britten, it may well have seemed, had every right to express his distrust of 'ivory tower' composers, to emphasise the fact that he himself did not compose for a clique, and to state his belief in 'the artist's social duty—to form, educate and develop [the] people's artistic taste.'
>
> But it may be doubted whether he realised the important implications, for Russian readers, of the difference between 'people' and 'the people'; and whether this implication, quite clear in the Russian text, was made clear to him before it was published.
>
> 'Art for the people'—not 'for people'—is a slogan that appears in Russian concert-halls in any case; but during the British musicians' visit it took on a heightened significance as a result of Mr. Khruschev's violent attack not only on contemporary Western art (that was to be expected, perhaps) but on any art that cannot be interpreted as active support for the Communist cause, any 'peaceful coexistence in the ideological sphere.'
>
> It may be doubted whether any Englishman who is not a daily reader of *Pravda*—as I was during the time of the British musicians' visit—can imagine the hysterical violence and absolute unbendingness of these speeches of Mr. Khruschev's, or the importance attached to them.
>
> When the interview with Britten was published Shostakovich had already appeared in *Pravda* with a grateful and respectful message of thanks to Mr. Khruschev on behalf of Soviet composers. It was inevitable, therefore, that when Mr. Britten at the end of his interview declared that 'between the arts of our two peoples there are no barriers,' readers of *Pravda* would understand that he was in fact subscribing to the full Communist doctrine of art as an instrument of ideological propaganda.
>
> English readers might feel sure of his real intent—to express his solidarity with Russian musicians, as human beings and artists, and his belief in art as a means of human communication. What he presumably did not know (though I find such ignorance culpable in an intelligent man in his responsible position) was that Russians allow of no distinction either between the artist's private personality and his public, official capacity as an accredited Communist propagandist, or between humanity as a whole (regardless of race, class, and so on) which interests the Western artist, and 'the people' who are the official concern of the Soviet artist and tie him all too often to the search for an aesthetic Lowest Common Multiple rather than Highest Common Factor, as Soviet music shows.
>
> The Russians should understand—and we should make it perfectly clear—that whatever may be the aesthetic divergences among British musicians, whether they are traditionalists, dodecaphonists or practitioners of electronic or 'concrete' music, they are united in rejecting the view of the artist's role as being one of a propagandist for any political or sociological creed whatever.
>
> In the free world the artist speaks to people, to human beings as such, and he is free to say what he likes as he likes. That much of to-day's art is experimental only reflects the

spiritual crisis through which the whole world (including the Communist countries, of course) is passing. That much of this art is trivial does not distinguish it from the art of other periods which we remember now by a few great names but which were, in fact, often dominated by now forgotten nonentities.

The tragedy of the Soviet artist lies in the fact that only in the most exceptional cases can he operate freely, with his own individual face unmasked; and, far worse, that in the vast majority of cases the mask has grown to the face—that after two generations of 24 hours' conditioning a day from childhood onward he is no longer aware of having grown up in the straitjacket of Communist ideology.

The first duty of artists in the West is to force an awareness and resentment of this strait-jacket on Russian artists, since no prisoner will escape if he is unaware of being chained.

How quickly and deeply the varying waves of ideological indoctrination can affect the artist's attitude to his work struck me at the Bolshoi and Kirov Opera Houses. For almost 10 years now the 'cult of personality' [Kruschev's phrase, first used in 1956] has, as we know, been employed as the official explanation of all that was wrong during the Stalinist era; and since Soviet propagandists make no distinction between politics and aesthetics—which are merely regarded as two facets of the same struggle—'personality' has presumably been at a discount in educational establishments, including artistic academies.

At least this seems to be a not altogether fantastic explanation of the fact that, although I heard several excellent singers in a number of good performances, not one struck me as projecting a role with the whole force of his or her personality. The performances were safe and correct and left the listener—or at least me—tantalised by the feeling of unused potentialities.

The most noticeable instance was that of Shtolokhov, who is the best Boris at the Kirov Theatre in Leningrad and certainly has a magnificent voice and a fine stage presence. To say that his performance gave the impression of conscious inhibition would be an exaggeration. It was rather as though his personality were muted by some instinctive avoidance of complete self-expression, an instinctive cautiousness that made him first and foremost a good colleague unwilling to 'hog' the stage (as any Boris should) or to assert freely the claims of the character that he was impersonating.

Even among the top ranking Russian artists who have been received so rapturously in the West, it would be difficult to mention more than one, or at most two, whose performances are not merely technically magnificent but great individual interpretations. Rostropovich certainly and, within the limits of a somehow maimed personality, Richter, but neither Oistrakh nor any of the singers.

Those who saw Vishnevskaya's Aida at Covent Garden may have had the same impression as I of a 'muted' personality escaping full dramatic expression by a mixture of ham acting and careful vocalisation.

67 On *Pravda*, Art and Criticism (1963)

One of the most disturbing features of this time is that so many people seem to prefer to read about art rather than to experience it. Hence the great popularity of the arts pages, the magazine sections of the Sunday papers, the almost 'best seller' success of conversations with famous composers, & if I remember correctly not so long ago a book on Hardy's poems was published when the poems themselves were out of print. Perhaps it is easier to read about things than to do them, or is it that having read the critics one knows what to feel without bothering to think? These oversimplified feelings are prompted by a recent reading of some lectures given on literature by a well-known poet & professor, which put forth points of view so narrowly personal that from the general reader's point of view I would have thought them quite useless; and by a recent interview given by myself for a foreign newspaper, in which I was quite misreported, and which made nonsense for people who know me or my work.

Artists of course are the last people who should talk or write about art, especially their own. I probably expressed my-self badly on this occasion, or the changes were made for reasons of space or other editorial demands. But the fact that this interview has been widely reported in this country (by people who should have known better) prompted me to accept the invitation of the Observer to try & correct some of the impressions.

One impression I apparently gave was that I thought that art should be made for everyone, & that I feared that there was a tendency today for the serious composer to shut himself up in his Ivory Tower & to experiment—'sealing himself off totally from the real world.' While most people would admit the presence & danger of this 'tendency', I should like to make it quite clear that I believe that the opposite aim is quite impossible. Taking it literally, art cannot be for everyone, even supposing there were no tone-deaf or colour-blind people in the world. All arts, aural, visual or tactile, depend on having a language for communication, & I think everyone really agrees (pace the Non-Art theorists) that art is a communication. Otherwise artists would not bother to make art, they would just think about it. Now language depends on associations—the meaning of words, the shape of objects, the pattern of a minor chord—& unless you are familiar with that language the art must be largely

Editor's title.

Source: Autograph draft, n.d. (*GB-ALb* 1–02053901). This is a reconstruction of Britten's draft article intended for the *Observer*, written in response to his *Pravda* interview and subsequent furore. The article was never published, although some of the themes were included in his Aspen speech one year later (Essay 72).

lost on you. I admit we can learn some languages, & I admit one has been as a Western European deeply stirred by the vitality & actual sound of Indian, Balinese or Japanese music. But in Japan, among all the artistic experience one had, it was only in the No plays where one was provided with a translation, & could follow stories which often transcended the barriers of race, culture & religion, that it was possible to have a profound emotion. Unless these associations are part of one's life, I do not think that an art can transmit its message.

Again, the environment should be suitable. The performing arts are created for particular people in particular circumstances, and these circumstances must be preserved if the art is to continue to make its full effect. A piece of Indian music may take several hours, the best part of a hot tropical night, to wind its way to its leisurely close. How can we appreciate it, brought up as we are to the compressed drama of Die Schöne Müllerin—in not much more than 60 minutes? And the Matthew Passion written for a small group [of] young singers (half of them boys) in a smallish Gothic Church—how can we recapture its original edgy resonance across the spaces of the damp (acoustically) Festival Hall with a large chorus, mature & expressive soloists (half of them women)—to say nothing of the pitch having crept up nearly a tone, and with a paying audience rather than a worshipping congregation?

I do not deny that there is much in the greatest of art that can transcend circumstance, & we would be silly, just because our conditions are different, to give up trying to perform the masterpieces of other ages. But, the communication cannot be complete. So I do not see how we could please everyone, all kinds & conditions of man, even if we wanted to. But should we want to? Have we, as artists, a social duty? I think we have, or to put it differently, I think we all fundamentally have a wish to take our part in society. I really cannot believe that even the oddest of composers seriously wishes to be ignored or neglected. After all a score is only a plan for a work, & until it is realised in sound it cannot be said to exist. Speaking purely personally, I have got so much richness out of art, especially music, that I have a real desire to help others do the same. Besides I like to encourage the love & practice of the arts among the young, because it develops their sensitivity, their imagination, their personalities, their 'neuroses' ('differentness') even—qualities which I value above all in people. Therefore I like to encourage & help the young when they come to play or sing to me, or when they bring me the music they have written. And therefore I like to write music for the young, & I think the young appreciate the compliment of having things written especially & seriously, for them (but, woe betide us if our music is not serious or well-made—the young see through us very quickly!) I wish all young serious composers would write for the young, & for the amateurs of all ages, and for the general public on special occasions (Occasional Music) too. They would learn enormously from it, learn not to condescend, but to condense & simplify their language.

But what about this language problem? It is obvious that the language of most lively and serious composers to-day is beyond the comprehension of any but the most sophisticated audiences, beyond the skill of any but the most technically-advanced performers. There is no point in writing an Occasional piece for a social occasion that no one in the audience can follow, or a complicated atonal piece for the local Choral Society, or a serial fanfare for a band of buglers (which being limited by the natural harmonic scale can only play 1/2 dozen notes). Is sticking to a preconceived idea of language so important? Is the latest trend sacrosanct—is it a passport to future fame, & anyhow is it so important to aim at the future? No, language is a means to an end—a means of saying what one wants to say, and should be as simple & direct as one can make it—marvellous, of course, for the specialist to analyse & observe, but unobtrusive to the general public. Of course, however simple the language, it is no use pretending that appreciation will necessarily follow. New ideas have a way of seeming bewildering & shocking. Again—new ideas often need startling new developments in language to express them. But it must be this, not the other way round—the new ideas must lead to the new language, otherwise artificiality & self-consciousness occurs. This also applies to notation, the spelling & punctuation of the language, the servant of the servant. Often, looking at so-called 'avant garde' scores, it seems as if the notation has acquired some mystic value of its own. As a performer I resent wasting my time unravelling a notation which should be helping rather than hindering me, & which has no earthly effect aurally, except to produce inaccuracy & tensions. These, if wanted, should be calculated musically, not by accident.

Although it is impossible to please everyone all the time, I hope I have made the point that, as a composer, I wish to play my part in social life & to try to communicate my ideas in this way[.] I am heartily against the Ivory Tower which has become a very real danger. But I suppose we are all two-sided, & I have to admit that there are moments when I crave for such a building. There are moments when I want to say something subtle & intimate, which will possibly be only understood by people who feel about things the way I do. This is when one wants to write a string quartet, or for an odd collection of instruments, or to write songs or song-cycles. And sometimes, by accident, this kind of work can slowly amass quite a public. The Winterreise is not for a great auditorium; but for those who like intimate song recitals there is no work which is more loved that this highly personal, introspective, & devastatingly pessimistic, document. And we can think of many examples (the Mozart G minor quintet for example[1]), & they include most of ones most treasured

[1] String Quintet in G minor, K. 516 (1787).

possessions. There is no doubt that finally one treasures the private rather than the public work of art. But both are necessary, both for the public & the composer, and the greatest figures have produced both, and the public work of these great figures can be good & of more than just temporary use, because of their 'gift'.

Which brings me to 'gift', that mysterious quality, which so far has never been explained, which makes a sequence of notes, of chords & rhythms & even of colours, seem inevitable & memorable. In the particular interview I am referring to, & it is a question one is always being faced with, I was asked my opinion of serial techniques. My reply can only be that the system itself is not interesting (in fact no system by itself can be interesting) but what is written in the system—the 'gift', the personality which shines through any system. I love personalities which have expressed themselves in many, many different systems—even in the 12-tone system, that I myself have so far found no need to use. I find it has jettisoned too many devices that I wish to retains: key centres, melodic & rhythmic patterns, for instance. Without these I find it impossible to vary the tensions of my music. In a way the relation to a key centre can be said to be equivalent to the amount of distortion of a subject in a painting. Fond as I am of much abstract painting, I cannot get involved with them as with 'subject' paintings. I enjoy them only as patterns or decoration. But this is not to say that other composers need the devices that I do, but my guess is that a lack of these devices may have helped to cause the well-known gap between contemporary music & the general public—because of a sense of bewilderment or boredom caused by lack of perceptible design.

As I said at the start, one reason for the false impressions given by these reports, is certainly one's inadequacy of expression in words. A composer's job is to create, not to comment; and this is not a theory, but a conviction & an inclination. I hate talking about my own music, or my own musical inclination, & avoid it whenever I can. But having broken the rule here, I reserve the right to change any of my opinions whenever I want to. These opinions included liking or disliking any of the great figures of the past (a purely personal matter, derived from temporary needs, which must seem irritating & bewildering to other people). They include a reluctance to treat contemporary subjects in opera—preferring the parable technique. They include a dislike of listening to songs, operas & so on in a language I can't understand, & a dislike of singers who don't sing their words clearly or perhaps more important, don't use their words, but equally of singers who forget that music has line and tune as well as words. They include . . but one could continue indefinitely.

Anyhow, the 'opinions' of creative artists are really rather valueless—even to the artists themselves. However strongly held, opinions should anyhow be discarded entirely while actually one is working. Works should be planned to the minutest detail, but once the writing has started everything must give way to the 'still, small voice' which is the heaven-sent guide to the next note, the sign of gift or personality, or whatever one wishes to call it, & which is after all the only thing in art which really matters.[2]

[2] The following is a redrafting of the opening pages in Pears's writing (and style):

Let me make it clear to start with: it is not the business of the creative artist to write about his work, and his aims should not need clarifying. Discussion is the job for the critic and the art-historian, after the work is written and preferably after the creator is dead and past caring.

But it is understandable I suppose that people should be curious about us composers, and that a foreign public should want to be introduced to us in print before our works are played. It is rude, too, always to refuse to talk to well-intentioned journalists. Reporters however can be guilty of distortion and inaccuracy, either from willfulness, incoherence of the examinee, exigencies of space, or indeed from editorial pressure. This has recently been my experience, and as my distorted remarks have been widely repeated in print here by people who might have been expected to know me better than to believe them, I have therefore accepted the Observer's invitation to correct them.

I was reported as saying that Art must be made for the people—for everyone—& that I regretted the tendency of the serious Western composers to shut himself up in his Ivory Tower—'sealing himself off tightly from the real world.' While most people—including myself—would admit the existence and danger of such a tendency, I am quite clear that the alternative presented—'a composer must write for the people'—is inadmissible. For everyone? the tone-deaf, the anti-musical, the 12 noter, the anti-12-noter, the Political, the non-Political, the Jazz-man, the Pop-man, the Trad-girl? Everyone? No, not EVERYONE—but of course ANYONE—who has ears to hear & cares to listen, and understands the language. For Art communicates through its language which must be mastered before the communication is intelligible. And beyond the intelligibility, indissolubly bound up with the stuff of the language, are the associations within it, and to my mind of infinite value. True, a great art-form or work of art can communicate powerfully past all barriers of language, race, culture & religion. The Japanese Noh-drama gave me such an overwhelming experience, so in a different degree did Indian & Balinese music, though the language was wholly (in case of Noh) or largely (with the others) strange, and associations non-existent.

pleasure of his company for I
have to pick a bone with him!

[Warder Laughs]

Ward. so have I, but it is getting
late and I must be off to
my cabin, good night!

Captain. Good night!

Exeunt

ACT V scene I

Scene in Percival's House Study

[Percival sitting at his desk, and
Edourd knocking at Door]

Percivale. Come in

[Enter Edourd]

Edourd; Percivale, I have something sad to tell you, you are
wanted at the hall tomorrow at

9.

3' clock in the afternoon for the
trial, I am very sorry for you
because I know how you must
feel, as it is not your fault, and also
because I am not able to be there
as I have to go to Calais today
and cannot return untill the day
after tomorrow; I have written to the
judge to say that I can pay
all things if it is possible to
get you out of a hole; he answered,
saying that if I did not keep
quiet I should have to
go to court too, on account of
contempt of court. The judge
is a strict revolutionist and
a very hot tempered man, I
think that there is no hope for [illegible]

1. The young writer: a speech from the six-act play *The Precious Documents*, written by Britten with his school friend John Pounder, probably in the early 1920s.

Queen's Hall

Sole Lessees: Messrs. Chappell and Co., Ltd.

SPECIAL CONCERT

Wednesday 18 March 1936 at 8 p.m.

Dmitri Shostakovitch

(Born 1906)

The Lady Macbeth

OF MTSENSK

(Katerina Ismailova)

First Concert performance in England

An Opera in Four Acts

Libretto according to N. Leskov by A. Preis and D. Shostakovitch

English Translation by M. D. Calvocoressi

ODA SLOBODSKAYA	DOROTHY STANTON
ENID CRUICKSHANK	PARRY JONES
HUGHES MACKLIN	TUDOR DAVIES
ROBERT CHIGNELL	HAROLD WILLIAMS
TOM KINNIBURGH	SAMUEL WORTHINGTON

MARTIN BODDEY, PETER PEARS, EMLYN BEBB

STANLEY RILEY, VICTOR HARDING, SAMUEL DYSON

(Coach Arnold Perry)

THE B.B.C. CHORUS

Chorus Master: Leslie Woodgate

The B.B.C. Symphony Orchestra

Leader: Arthur Catterall Organist: Berkeley Mason

CONDUCTOR: Albert Coates

There will be an interval of fifteen minutes between Acts II and III

In accordance with the requirements of the London County Council:

I. The public may leave at the end of the performance or exhibition by all exit doors, and such doors must at that time be open.

II. All gangways, corridors, staircases and external passageways intended for exit shall be kept entirely free from obstruction, whether permanent or temporary.

III. Persons shall not be permitted to stand or sit in any of the gangways intersecting the seating or to sit in any of the other gangways. If standing be permitted in the gangways at the sides and rear of the seating, it shall be limited to the numbers indicated in the notices exhibited in those positions.

3

2. The programme for the first concert performance in England of Shostakovich's *Lady Macbeth of Mtsensk*, 18 March 1936 (see Essay 1). Peter Pears, then a member of the BBC Singers and unknown to Britten, sang the role of Second Foreman.

3. Britten photographed during the writing of *Billy Budd* with E. M. Forster, Robin Long ('the Nipper'), and Billy Burrell, an Aldeburgh fisherman and friend of Britten's (see Essay 57). The photograph, taken in Burrell's boat off Aldeburgh beach in 1949, was included in a *Picture Post* feature on the making of the opera.

169

Britten Sees Small-Scale Opera as More Contemporary

From Our Special Correspondent

Musical exports may not, perhaps, contribute very substantially to our balance of payments, but they more than make up for it in goodwill. Recently back from an immensely successful tour of Russia with the English Opera Group, Mr. Benjamin Britten talked enthusiastically of the reception there.

"What struck us most of all about the audiences was their extraordinary receptivity; they listen incredibly quietly, and are tremendously responsive theatrically." I asked Mr. Britten just how much he thought Russian audiences were able to make of the three chamber operas, which of course were given in English—especially the comedy of *Albert Herring*. "Well, *Albert Herring* was really very successful. You know, there's a link between the English and the Russian sense of humour. When it's given in German, it's apt to become mere knockabout comedy; the German don't seem able to mix serious characters and comic situations. But, like us, the Russians—as you can see in Chekhov—are capable of doing this; they appreciated that the characters in *Albert Herring* are serious, as of course they are, although the situations in which they appear are funny."

Which of these three very different operas, I wondered, made the strongest impression? "On the whole *The Turn of the Screw*, so far as the public was concerned." I quoted to Mr. Britten a review from the Leningrad *Pravda* which said that "this phantasmagoria does not appeal to one because it is based on a pathological idea of communication of the children . . . with the nether world . . . a trifling subject". Mr. Britten smiled. "This is the only unfavourable criticism we received that I know of. Of course, *The Screw* is not the kind of work they are used to—its subject would be considered ideologically unsound—and for about the first quarter of each performance the audiences seemed a bit mystified. But once they grasped what it was aiming to do the reaction was very warm, very warm indeed."

Did the Christian theme of *The Rape of Lucretia* also create ideological difficulties? "Well, again it was very favourably received, and the audiences did listen most attentively to the end of the opera, the part concerned with its Christian significance." The theatrical side of the productions was also much praised: "I think they found our stage techniques rather sophisticated—at the Bolshoi, they're use to big, spectacular, 'ice-revue' style stagings but nothing as subtle as ours, especially as regards lighting." Did Mr. Britten think that the appreciation they met was, in part, specifically because they came from England or the west? "I think this made little difference, if any; some of the English music we played on a previous tour they liked—the *Planets*, and an Elgar work—and some they didn't. They're naturally a very musical people. And I do admire their system of musical training, spotting talented children at a very early stage and sending them to specially geared schools."

Bearing out the sincerity of the praise accorded to the English Opera Group is the fact that it is now being imitated in Russia. Mme. Furtzeva, the Minister of Culture, had a long talk with Mr. Britten, asking him questions about the staging of chamber operas and the problems of touring (already there are two new groups in the Leningrad area planning to give chamber operas), and she talked of the particular suitability of the form for Russian needs—there is a tremendous appetite for culture in outlying parts of the country ("there's nothing Rostropovich enjoys as much as travelling miles to play to an audience of peasants who've never heard a cello before") and obviously it would be impractical to take full-scale opera on tour.

Mr. Britten was asked in Russia if he had ever contemplated an opera on cosmonauts. "I did in fact start on one, for children, about 10 years ago, with William Plomer—who'd written a superb first scene; we occasionally look back at it and I may finish it some time. It had a character with the magnificent name of Madge Plato. Of course, it's difficult to return to a work after so long; and things have changed in the meantime as regards space travel."

A space opera is not, of course, the most important project for a new work. 1965 is to be a Sabbatical year for Mr. Britten—surely not a year of rest from composition, I asked. "Oh no, most certainly not. It's that Peter Pears and I aren't doing concerts in the usual way, except regular engagements, of course, like the Aldeburgh and Long Melford festivals, and Peter's Matthew Passions in Holland. We're going to have six weeks in India, at the beginning of the year, and a trip to Russia in August (we're driving down to the Black Sea with Rostropovich and his wife); these will be almost entirely holiday."

One part of Mr. Britten's activities unlikely to be much curtailed next year is his work on behalf of the English Opera Group, which is very close to his heart. "We must certainly keep on developing the group; it has a vitally important job to do."

How does Mr. Britten see its main tasks? To provide opera where it is needed, and to help train opera singers. "The provinces are starved of opera: even Oxford, where the group recently performed for a week, has only some five weeks of opera in the whole year. At first our houses were thin; then, later in the week, word got around, and they began to fill up. You see, opera-going is a habit, and, as things are, people outside London just don't have the chance to acquire it.

"Yes, we'd like to give seasons in London, too—our new production of *The Rape of Lucretia* hasn't been seen here yet—but it's difficult to get a theatre. We hope the group will appear at various festivals, but it would be better still if they could give longer seasons." Mr. Britten emphasized that one of its main functions is to help young singers leaving the music colleges to get the stage experience they need and at present cannot get. "There's marvellous talent available. Several of our young singers, new to the stage, came on wonderfully during the Russian tour. But the long seasons we need cost so much."

I asked Mr. Britten if, with his great enthusiasm for the group, he was intending to increase its repertory himself. "Yes, certainly; I want to write a comic opera for them. But first I'm going to do another, like *Curlew River*, for church performance. William Plomer and I are meeting soon to talk about it—we've got two or three possible ideas in mind. No, it won't be connected with Japanese Noh plays, but it'll have the same medieval framework. It'll be for the same instruments as *Curlew River*, probably using the same kinds of technique—but something much less sombre, an altogether gayer affair, with more opportunities for brilliance."

Does the fact that he is writing music-drama for non-theatrical presentation suggest that Mr. Britten has less interest in opera as a theatrical form? "No, certainly not." And does his keenness on chamber opera suggest a lack of faith in the future of opera on a Covent Garden scale? "Again, no. Because I write for the cello it doesn't mean I think the violin is finished. I've written three large-scale operas and I'd like to do another. But it takes so long; all those notes!" Mr. Britten wondered if perhaps the small forms are not a more natural expression for today: "I was talking about this with Khachaturian recently, and we both felt that there's something specifically contemporary about small-scale opera."

Curlew River, it has been said, represents a marked departure in style, with its use of canon and echo effects, and improvisation; were these to be taken as suggestive of future paths or were they specific for the subject and its treatment? Mr. Britten made it very clear that he is a composer, not a critic or analyst. "I can't say; the technique really stems from the actual work you're writing. I know *Curlew River* had to take the special shape it did; and writing it has certainly broadened my technique. No, I'm too naive a person to say what its style may or may not portend."

Had Mr. Britten any plans for instrumental works? or did he feel it was true (as it is sometimes said) that he is really happiest with voices, and with words to set? "For a time I did feel this, but not now. It's more true that I get excited and stimulated by something in particular—it could be words, or performers, or occasions. I'm now doing a solo cello sonata for Rostropovich, which will make four instrumental works in quite a short time. And I'd like to write for other players, like Gervase de Peyer or Osian Ellis, and I'll get around to it in time—Rostropovich got his works by bullying me!"

Did the Cello Symphony, the largest of the works for Rostropovich, have any kind of programmatic content, as its shape might be taken to suggest? Again I was reminded that it was a composer, not a critic, who was answering. "Not that I'm aware of. It has a musical programme, of course; it must have. So does every piece of music. If I may cite another, infinitely greater work to set alongside it, Mozart's G minor string quintet, you can see that there's a kind of similarity between the two works' musical programmes." Had Mr. Britten any plans for a ballet, I wondered? "No, not really; perhaps, if a subject or a choreographer comes along." Or at least an orchestral suite from *The Prince of the Pagodas*, which is languishing unheard? "I've tried, several times, and I can't do it. The problems aren't solved. But perhaps I'll try again."

On the future of British music Mr. Britten was optimistic and encouraging—"the best generation we've had for hundreds of years". He named a few of the younger composers whose talent impresses him—Malcolm Williamson, Nicholas Maw, Peter Maxwell Davies ("immensely gifted"), Richard Rodney Bennett ("I'm looking forward to his new opera, which he has very kindly dedicated to me"). "What is so good is that they are all obeying their own musical impulses, not just following what their foreign contemporaries are doing."

Mr. Britten emphasized how essential it is for young composers to write with performance in mind, to think in terms of living sound (a point he elaborated in his recent Aspen Award lecture). "All art is a communication; I'm quite, quite sure that composers always want to communicate their ideas, whether it's to a tiny audience of seven connoisseurs, or to one of seven million." Mr. Britten received the first Aspen Award for "Service to the Humanities"; and it is his burning sincerity about the vital human purpose of his art that so forcibly impresses one on meeting the man.

4. The diligent interviewee: Britten's corrections to the proof copy of a 1964 interview in *The Times*.

5. Britten with members of the Armenian Composers' Union at Dilidjan, Armenia, August 1965 (see Essay 80). Edvard Mirzoyan, head of the Union, is holding the ancient amphora presented to Britten by the townspeople.

6. The reluctant public speaker: Britten delivers his speech after receiving the Freedom of the Borough of Aldeburgh at the Moot Hall, Aldeburgh, 22 October 1962 (see Essay 61).

68 Address to Kesgrave Heath School, Ipswich (1963)

Boys and girls, my Lord, ladies and gentlemen:

I have just seen a little of your new school. I went round some of the classes in the infants' school and it is a wonderful, wonderful new building that you have there, and I congratulate you all on the achievement of these new, reconstructed buildings.

However, there are some of you, I expect, you who remember the old school as it was, who find it a little uneasy in your new buildings.

I always think that moving house, moving school, is a little like getting a new suit of clothes. You've got to get used to it. They're very smart and—but they don't always quite *fit* properly and sometimes one's mother may be quite right when she throws away that old pair of trousers that one was so fond of, because it did get a little small, and I think the old buildings as they were got a little bit too small for you.

And so now you've got these splendid new buildings and I think your architect has done very well, and I'm sure you're going to be very happy in your new suit of clothes—I mean your new buildings.

It is very good, I think, that we should have nice places to work in. Now I'm not going to be a silly old man and say how dreadful life was when we were young and how we used to work in dark, black cellars and were beaten every day of our lives, because it simply isn't true; but we didn't have such beautiful buildings as you have here. We didn't have lovely airy rooms—at least, *I* didn't.

We didn't have wonderful views—well actually I think a wonderful view can be a bit of a distraction. At the moment, in my studio where I work in Aldeburgh (not so far from here) there's a blackbird making its nest just outside the window and I'm very interested to know whether she's sitting on her eggs when I should be working; so I think there are snags in beautiful views.

But anyhow this is a digression. I would like to say how very honoured I am today to be asked to come and open this new—new school, can I call it?—for you.

Now why did you ask *me* instead of really important people like MPs or colonels or bishops?

I'd like to think perhaps that some of you—well I know some of you have

Editor's title.

Source: Editor's transcript of private recording (*GB-ALb* 3–02053798). Speech given at the opening of new buildings of Kesgrave Heath School on 15 May 1963.

sung some of my music, because I've just heard a splendid performance, and a graphically illustrated performance, of *The Little Sweep.* Also some of you—I don't think any of you *here* today—but this school took a very big part in my *Noye's Fludde*, which may be a legend to some of you who actually didn't sing in it yourselves.

Now *Noye's Fludde* was performed by many, many children in Orford Church two or three years ago, including some boys and girls from Kesgrave. Why I mention *Noye's Fludde* was this, because I am very proud of the fact that *Noye's Fludde* was performed by Suffolk boys and girls.

About two weeks ago I was in Hamburg, a great city in Germany with a great opera house, and they were performing an opera called *Noah's Flood.*[1] The same words but not the same music. The music was by perhaps the most famous composer living today, called Stravinsky.

Stravinsky is a great man. He's a great composer and he's very old—two very important characteristics in a composer; they should be old if possible. Now his music was frightfully difficult—much more difficult than *The Little Sweep* which is in 5-in-a-bar—much more difficult, and it needed the greatest singers and the greatest players in the world to perform it.

I wasn't jealous of Stravinsky; not at all. I was much happier with my performance in Orford church two years ago, sung by Kesgrave boys and girls, than of Stravinsky in Hamburg Opera House by famous singers with long names ending in '-ovitch' and '-ousky' than I was—I was much more proud of my performers two years ago. Now *why*?

I think it's awfully important that at school one should learn lots of different kinds of things. We can't all be wonderful carpenters, we can't all be specialist electricians and doctors. We can't all be wonderful mechanics. I say that rather particularly because I'm a very bad mechanic. I've been told lots of time what happens in a car, but when I press something I can never remember what it is.

All the same, it's a very good thing to have learnt about mechanics. Why? Because the most complete people—the most useful people in society—the people who are going to make the most—to help their friends the most in society—are the ones who know about most things. That is why I think it is so right that you should learn lots of different kinds of things: how to draw. I've just seen earlier in the infants' school wonderful elephants, wonderful—I saw a hedgehog, I've seen some little mice—it's very good, even if we don't remember later what they all are, these things—it's very good to *know* about them.

And that is why, when I was asked to come today, to declare your school open, I said I would—because in Kesgrave they do the kind of things that I think should be done.

[1] *The Flood* (1961–2), a musical play.

Now one—before I shut up—just one little tiny thing. You've all been singing very well today. You've been playing marvellously over there on your new instruments that I want to explore in a moment. When you leave school and there's no one to chase you to practise the recorder, don't forget about it altogether. Go on playing, go on singing. Doesn't matter what kind of music—it can be old or new or sad or gay—but go on trying. Don't let other people get away with it all the time. You try too, and perhaps in twenty years' time, when this school is too small for all the thousands more Kesgravians that there *will* be, when someone else—because I shall be dead—is asked to come and open it, maybe we'll have a performance by you sitting here, twenty years in time—twenty years ago—when you are performing yourselves and—who knows—even have written the music yourselves. That's the best thing—go on—go on performing, go on drawing, go on looking at hedgehogs.

Now I think I must now formally declare the new extension of Heath School and Kesgrave Infants' School—I now declare it open.

69 An Interview (1963)

So many composers are given to making statements about their music, often to such an extent that their pronouncements tend to overshadow the music itself. Benjamin Britten is emphatically not one of these; indeed, so seldom has he ventured into print on the subject of his own work that I feared to talk to him might be a difficult and hesitant affair. I was wrong. The slender, youthful, alert, surely not almost fifty-year-old man with the shy, friendly smile was not only affable, direct and unassuming, but answered all my questions, some of which must have struck him as tediously obvious, with patience and even an eager helpfulness. I began the conversation rather blunderingly by trying to isolate what I felt to be Britten's unique quality, something of night, sleep and silence that permeates much of his music. One hears it not only in, for instance, the Keats sonnet in the Serenade for tenor, horn and strings, *but in so many passages in* Gloriana, The Little Sweep, *through to* A Midsummer Night's Dream. *It is somehow bound up with Britten's almost Mahlerian emotional use of the apparently simple. But what I found myself saying was: 'There is, in some of your earlier music in particular, a very personal blend of what I can only call some quality of innocence with a very sensuous sound. This is badly expressed, does it convey anything to you?'*

BRITTEN: I wouldn't have thought my sound *sensuous*, although I love the clear and the resonant. This, I suppose I've learned from Mozart, Schubert, Tchaikovsky, Debussy, Stravinsky and others.

OSBORNE: You must be tired of hearing about the Mahler influence in your music. One knows of your admiration for Mahler; indeed, I remember an ear-opening performance of his Fourth Symphony you once conducted. But in what music of yours do you yourself hear any traces of Mahler? The Bridge Variations, I suppose. What else?

BRITTEN: It's very difficult to discover influences in one's own work. Emotionally, Mahler can be rather remote from me, but I love and admire his 'ear' for sound. That can be spotted in my writing for orchestra. I think I appreciate his sense of form: perhaps this is apparent from the Requiem and the Spring Symphony. And I certainly love his vocal melody, as no doubt you can tell from many of my songs and folk-song arrangements.

OSBORNE: You are in no way a consciously national composer, and this to me is a good thing. What in your music is English seems both incidental to and deeply and unconsciously integral to your own personality. I think of you as continuing a tradition that comes through Mozart, by-passing Beethoven but including Schubert, re-emerging in Mahler.

Source: 'Interview with Charles Osborne', *The London Magazine* 3 (Oct. 1963), 91–6.

BRITTEN: I'm not aware of being in a particular tradition. In fact, I feel a curiously local composer with strong roots in the English language and folk-song, but the tradition of Dunstable, Wilby [*sic*], Dowland, Purcell and so on has been too broken in the last two hundred years for one to be said to belong to it.

OSBORNE: What living composers do you most admire?

BRITTEN: Stravinsky, Shostakovich, Copland, Tippett. And among the not so long dead, Poulenc, Bartok, Bridge, Holst.

OSBORNE: I think of you as primarily an opera composer, and—

BRITTEN: Well, I don't know that I do. Certainly I respond very deeply to words, but not necessarily only opera. At the moment, I think the finest thing I've written is my work for 'cello and orchestra which hasn't yet been performed.[1]

OSBORNE: This is the piece you wrote for Rostropovich, whose first performance had to be postponed because of his illness?

BRITTEN: Yes.

OSBORNE: Regarding your operas, I wonder which of your libretti you think most successful? I'm inclined to think *Turn of the Screw* the *least* successful. Did you have a hand in shaping Myfanwy Piper's treatment of the story?

BRITTEN: Yes, I *always* have the greatest say in shaping my operas, and could claim the credit, if that's the word, for their form. But credit for the details of the writing obviously I cannot claim, although I do criticize and demand here too.

OSBORNE: *Gloriana* I think is a most unjustly neglected piece, a beautiful lyric experience and [b]y no means simply the *pièce d'occasion* it tended to be written off as.

BRITTEN: There'll be a concert performance of *Gloriana* in November which I look forward to, since I have, in spite of all, an affection for the work and happy memories of its first performances, which were magnificent.

OSBORNE: In company with most people, I think the *War Requiem* a masterpiece. The warmth and extent of its acclaim are somehow also moving and heartening. Is it true, however, that it was less well received in Vienna? If so, have you any idea why? I assume it's not the well-known Viennese distrust of the new, because surely your musical language doesn't present many problems?

BRITTEN: I have heard tell of a bad notice in Vienna, but I don't keep track of these things. It doesn't surprise me, as Vienna has alway been *traditional* in its tastes and the *War Requiem* is certainly not in the *traditionally* 'avant-garde'

[1] Symphony for Cello and Orchestra (1963).

language. But new works can be misunderstood not only for how they say something, but for *what* they say.

OSBORNE: Yes, indeed. Incidentally, one of our younger poets—a great admirer of your music—recently said to me that he was somewhat disturbed by a 'sweetness' in the *War Requiem*. I *think* I see what he means, though I don't in fact share his feeling. He said that, for this reason, he preferred—rather irrelevantly, I thought—your *Midsummer Night's Dream*.

BRITTEN: I don't, of course, understand what your friend is referring to, though I can't see any great defect in sweetness as long as it's not weakness. I can't imagine, though, how the *War Requiem* could be considered sweeter than *A Midsummer Night's Dream*.

OSBORNE: Leading on from this, the problem of communication. It's said, and not necessarily as a criticism, that your language, as opposed to your musical thought, is fairly conventional in a world geared to cope with Boulez, Cage, Stockhausen, Barraqué, and so on. Now, you obviously don't deliberately simplify your music in order to reach a wider audience in the way in which, say, a Soviet composer might. But does the question have any relevance to you at all? In other words, do you distinguish between writing for yourself, and writing for a particular audience?

BRITTEN: I really can't judge whether my language is conventional or not. Certainly I use key-centres, melodic and rhythmic patterns still. But I don't see any virtue—or the reverse—in chucking these over, if many other composers do. I certainly can't imagine making my language more obscure on purpose. When I write for a 'wider' audience, I obviously don't want to write very subtle things, and the language is, as a result, simpler.

OSBORNE: I believe you usually write with specific performers and performances in mind, like Mozart. Do you find this practice—writing to commission—at all restrictive?

BRITTEN: As I get older I find working to a commission more and more irksome, and now, usually, I only accept one when it coincides with some already existing plan of my own.

OSBORNE: What are your feelings about *musique concrète*, electronic music? Their validity?

BRITTEN: Not being much of a scientist, I'm not very interested in electronic music—although I admit it can be damnably effective as background noises—mostly because music is, to me, an art for performance, for live people to play in front of a live audience—be it two or two thousand. Gramophone, radio and TV are for me like a photograph of a painting, simply a very convenient reminder. My reactions to the film, even, are quite different from my reactions to the other arts. More immediate, perhaps, but less profound.

OSBORNE: Amongst your more recent songs, I'm most intrigued by the

Hölderlin settings which I heard you and Peter Pears perform a year or two ago. Do you plan any further settings of German, or do you feel it's musically too well-worked over a language?

BRITTEN: I have no immediate plans to set more German poetry, but I certainly have no theories about it being over-worked musically. I might easily set more Hölderlin one day, or Rilke, or George.

OSBORNE: Do you go for long periods without composing?

BRITTEN: I go for quite long periods, the odd month or so—usually when I'm giving concerts—without actually writing. But I'm always planning.

OSBORNE: In writing a large work, do you find it difficult to sustain the initial inspiration or impulse? You appear not to. There's very little Brahmsian deadwood, I'd say none at all, in such major works as the Spring Symphony, *War Requiem* and so on, in which the act of creation seems completely spontaneous. But you must encounter problems of this kind. Have you ever, for instance, had to abandon any large-scale work once you had embarked upon it?

BRITTEN: I seldom abandon big works now, because I don't start them until the details are pretty well complete in my head. But I don't say it never happens when, for instance, what is on paper doesn't seem so magical as what was in my head.

OSBORNE: You mentioned earlier your response to words. I wonder which writers most stimulate you? You were a close friend of W. H. Auden in the thirties. Was he very musical then? What put me in mind of this was a recent re-reading of Frank Howes's foolish reference to Auden in his Grove article on you.[2] Did Auden's verse spark your musical imagination strongly?

BRITTEN: I've always read a great deal, especially poetry, of all styles and periods. I don't know what Frank Howes said in Grove, but I was certainly greatly influenced by Auden *personally*, but never musically.[3]

OSBORNE: You and he collaborated on an opera, *Paul Bunyan*, which was performed in the United States in 1941. Would you resuscitate it, so to speak, nowadays?

BRITTEN: I should consider it an honour if Auden wanted to collaborate with me again, but I don't know how it would work now. *Paul Bunyan* would need too much working on to make it acceptable generally, and I don't know that either he or I would have the interest to do this.[4]

[2] Original footnote: 'Auden's skirmishes on the frontiers of unintelligibility, which spoils the songs.'

[3] See Paul Kildea, 'Britten, Auden and "Otherness" ' in Mervyn Cooke (ed.), *The Cambridge Companion to Britten* (Cambridge: CUP, 1999), 36–53.

[4] *Paul Bunyan* (1941) was eventually resuscitated and revised by Britten following the successful performance of extracts in the 1974 Aldeburgh Festival—one year after Auden's death. The new version was broadcast in full on 1 Feb. 1976 and staged in the 1976 Festival.

OSBORNE: Have you ever, in view of Arthur Benjamin's *Tale of Two Cities*—to say nothing of *Oliver!* and *Pickwick*—thought of writing a Dickens opera? I could well imagine a Britten *Christmas Carol*, for instance.

BRITTEN: I am a great reader and lover of Dickens, but although many of the scenes I could think of operatically, I would find the overall shape almost impossible to cope with. One, however, I have thought about seriously.[5]

OSBORNE: Would you say this was a good period for a composer to work in?

BRITTEN: Well, this period has some obvious disadvantages for a composer, considerable problems in communication with the general public and difficulty in obtaining patronage for ambitious enterprises, and I can imagine easier periods to work in, but I imagine that they had considerable disadvantages too, unless one was incredibly lucky.

OSBORNE: I wonder what you think of the music of Webern and its gradual emergence since the composer's death?

BRITTEN: I'm not particularly attracted by Webern's music, though he was clearly a master and a very brave man. To my taste his was too limited a nature artistically on which to found a school.

OSBORNE: Do you listen to much music other than your own?

BRITTEN: Alas, I haven't time to go to many concerts, or to listen to records. But I read many scores, old and new. At the moment, Haydn is one of my favourites, a rich and often strange figure. And Mendelssohn and Sibelius, wholly different but equally neglected. And many new scores, especially of the young.

OSBORNE: Have you ever retrieved, or do you think worth retrieving, any of the music you wrote for the Auden–Isherwood and other stage and radio plays of the thirties, and for films?

BRITTEN: Practically without exception—no.

OSBORNE: Hearing you in recital with Peter Pears, one knows you're a pianist as distinct from a composer who plays the piano. You *both* uncover new areas of feeling in songs one thought one knew completely—in *Die Winterreise*, for instance. I wonder if anything in the timbre or technical ability or musicianship of Pears has had any appreciable influence on your vocal writing?

BRITTEN: I've learned a great deal from many artists I've written for and worked with, singers particularly (Joan Cross, Ferrier, Fischer-Dieskau,[6] Vishnevskaya[7]), some instrumentalists (Dennis Brain, Rostropovich, and

[5] Possibly *A Christmas Carol*.

[6] Dietrich Fischer-Dieskau (b. 1925), German baritone who sang the premiere of Britten's *War Requiem* (1962) and the *Songs and Proverbs of William Blake* (1965).

[7] Galina Vishnevskaya (b. 1926), Russian soprano for whom Britten wrote the soprano part in his *War Requiem*, although she was prevented from singing in the premiere by Soviet authorities. Heather Harper stepped in, although Vishnevskaya did subsequently perform and record

many young English instrumentalists like Julian Bream[8] and Ossian [*sic*] Ellis[9]), but obviously most from Peter Pears, with whom I have worked longest and most intimately.

Osborne: I believe you're at work on a new opera?

BRITTEN: Yes, with William Plomer as librettist, and for church performance. I don't want to say much about it now, as we're just beginning to work on it.[10]

We ended by talking again of the War Requiem. *I had written in* The London Magazine, *after its first performance in Coventry Cathedral last year: 'The quality of Britten's musical intellect is matched by the quality of his feeling, and in this work the immediacy and strength of the musical experience are overwhelming. This prolonged cry of desperate compassion consolidates Benjamin Britten's position as one of the few great living composers.' Britten himself still has strong feelings about the work. 'Some of my right-wing friends loathed it,' he told me. '"Though the music is superb, of course," they'd say. But that's neither here nor there to me. The message is what counts.'*

But the music is *the message, as its composer knows full well, and those who begin by loving the sound are in dire peril of having to admit the sense.*

the work. She is married to the cellist Rostropovich, with whom she gave the first performance of Britten's *The Poet's Echo* (1965), a work dedicated to them both.

[8] Julian Bream (b. 1933), English guitarist and lutenist, for whom Britten composed his *Nocturnal after John Dowland* (1963).

[9] Osian Ellis (b. 1928), Welsh harpist, for whom Britten wrote his Suite for Harp (1969). Ellis frequently accompanied Pears, especially after the heart operation that in 1973 put an end to Britten's performing career.

[10] *Curlew River* (1964).

70 Britten Looking Back (1963)

As a child I heard little music outside my own home. There were the local choral society concerts and the very occasional chamber concert, but the main event was the Norwich Triennial Festival. There in 1924, when I was 10, I heard Frank Bridge conduct his suite 'The Sea,' and was knocked sideways.[1]

It turned out that my viola teacher, Audrey Alston, was an old friend of Bridge's. He always stayed with her, and when the success of 'The Sea' brought him to Norwich again in 1927 with a specially written work called 'Enter Spring,' I was taken to meet him.

We got on splendidly, and I spent the next morning with him going over some of my music (I'd been writing music since I was about five).[2] From that moment I used to go regularly to him, staying with him in Eastbourne or in London, in the holidays from my prep school.

Even though I was barely in my teens, this was immensely serious and professional study; and the lessons were mammoth. I remember one that started at half past ten, and at tea-time Mrs. Bridge came in and said, 'Really, you must give the boy a break.' Often I used to end these marathons in tears; not that he was beastly to me, but the concentrated strain was too much for me. I was perhaps too young to take in so much at the time, but I found later that a good deal of it had stuck firmly.

This strictness was the product of nothing but professionalism. Bridge insisted on the absolutely clear relationship of what was in my mind to what was on the paper. I used to get sent to the other side of the room; Bridge would play what I'd written and demand if it was what I'd really meant.

I continued to write a vast amount under his guidance—orchestral music, string quartets, piano music and many songs, of which the only one to survive publicly is 'The Birds'.[3] I had a terrible struggle with this before finding what has been called 'the right ending in the wrong key.'[4] Bridge made me go on and on at it, worrying out what hadn't come right, until I spotted that the cycle of changing keys for each verse needed such an ending.

I badly needed his kind of strictness; it was just the right treatment for me. His loathing of all sloppiness and amateurishness set me standards to aim for

Source: *Sunday Telegraph* (17 Nov. 1963), 9. Also published as 'Early influences: a tribute to Frank Bridge (1879–1941)' in *Composer* 19 (Spring 1966), 2–3. Britten adapted this article for a talk broadcast 9 Jan. 1966, BBC Music Programme, 11 a.m., in a programme dedicated to Frank Bridge as part of the series *Music Magazine* (NSA M692WR).

[1] *The Sea* was written in 1910–11.

[2] See Essay 21, in which Britten lists some of this music.

[3] Much more of Britten's juvenilia has appeared in print since his death.

[4] The song finishes on a dominant seventh over a pedal of E, the tonality of the first verse.

that I've never forgotten. He taught me to think and feel through the instruments I was writing for: he was most naturally an instrumental composer, and as a superb viola player he thought instrumentally.

For instance, by the time I was 13 or 14, I was beginning to get more adventurous. Before then, what I'd been writing had been sort of early 19th century in style; and then I heard Holst's 'Planets' and Ravel's string quartet and was excited by them.[5] I started writing in a much freer harmonic idiom, and at one point came up with a series of major sevenths on the violin. Bridge was against this, saying that the instrument didn't vibrate properly with this interval: it should be divided between two instruments. He fought against anything anti-instrumental, which is why his own music is grateful to play.

I also learned about bitonality from Bridge (one of his favourite later devices was to harmonise with two common chords simultaneously)—more than from Holst, whose music I didn't know well then, though later I was bowled over by the première of 'Hammersmith' in a concert that, incidentally, included the first London hearing of 'Belshazzar's Feast'. This was in Bridge's company. We also went to hear Stravinsky's Symphony of Psalms, and when everyone around was appalled and saying how sad about Stravinsky, Bridge was insisting that it was a masterpiece.

I studied Bridge's own music avidly, of course. It was at this time that he was consolidating his later style, highly intense and chromatic, although never actually atonal. Also at this time, after his considerable early popularity, the public and critics were turning against him, and I became his staunchest defender.

I still feel there is much of his music worth defending: the early music (many songs, pieces for string or full orchestra, also all the chamber music) has more than an easy superficial charm; among the later works the dramatic piano sonata is outstanding, and the magnificent piano trio (which made a deep impression at the Aldeburgh Festival this year), the third quartet and the orchestral piece 'Enter Spring' I mentioned before—I remember it as a riot of melodic and harmonic richness, although it is 30 years since I heard it or saw a score.[6]

The holiday teaching continued right through my schooldays (at my public school my musical education was practically nonexistent, though I continued with the viola) until I left in 1930 to go to the Royal College of Music. At about 18 or 19, perhaps naturally, I began to rebel. When Bridge played questionable chords across the room at me and asked if that was what I meant, I would retort, 'Yes it is.' He'd grunt back, 'Well it oughtn't to be.'

There were sharp conflicts as I came to resist his influence over me. Also,

[5] Holst's *The Planets*, Op. 32 was composed in 1914–16; Ravel's String Quartet in F dates from 1902–3.

[6] Piano Sonata (1921–4); Piano Trio No. 2 (1929); String Quartet No. 3 (1925–6; rev. 1927).

his approach was largely German, 18th and 19th century at that—and by then I'd discovered Purcell and the English madrigalists.

This meant that after a time the situation between us wasn't so easy over vocal writing. I didn't altogether like his approach to it, and he, brought up on a Hugo Wolf tradition, never liked mine. But he was very sweet about 'Our Hunting Fathers', which caused a lot of fuss at the 1936 Norwich Festival. He didn't really like it, but he defended it. Later he gave me a long talking to about the scoring, which he thought didn't work (he liked the approach to the individual instruments). He was severe on the last movement as being too edgy, and in the end I did change it.

He also got me to change the opening of 'Let the florid music praise,' the first song in my Auden cycle, 'On This Island.' Originally it began with a downward glissando on the piano. Bridge hated that, and said I was trying to make a side-drum or something non-tonal out of the instrument: on the piano, the gesture ought to be a musical one. So I rewrote it as the present downward D major arpeggio.

I was 24 by then, and still listening to him. His influence had gone on throughout my time at the College, where I was officially studying with John Ireland. Bridge intervened angrily when I couldn't get a performance of two choral psalms I'd written (I heard practically nothing of the reams of music I was writing then). He said I ought to hear them because without aural experience it was difficult to link notes and sounds. Vaughan Williams claimed that the singers weren't good enough, to which Bridge retorted that it was up to the R.C.M. to have a chorus good enough and that he ought to use his influence.

He intervened, with no greater success, when the question arose of my going on to study with Berg. I'd finished at the College with a small travelling scholarship and wanted to go to Vienna. Bridge greatly admired Berg (he later, after Berg's death, introduced me to Schoenberg). But when the College was told, coolness arose. I think, but can't be sure, that the Director, Sir Hugh Allen, put a spoke in the wheel.[7] At any rate when I said at home during the holidays, 'I *am* going to study with Berg, aren't I?', the answer was a firm, 'No dear.' Pressed, my mother said, 'He's not a good influence,' which I suspected came from Allen.

There was at that time an almost moral prejudice against serial music—which makes one smile today! I think also that there was some confusion in my parents' minds—thinking that 'not a good influence' meant morally, not musically. They had been disturbed by traits of rebelliousness and unconventionality which I had shown in my later school days.

[7] Sir Hugh Allen (1869–1946), English organist, conductor, and lecturer. He was director of the Royal College of Music from 1918 to 1937, during which period (and for nine years beyond) he was professor of music at Oxford.

I had been, for instance, already a pacifist at school, and a lot of my feeling about the First World War, which people seem to see in my War Requiem, came from Bridge. He had written a piano sonata in memory of a friend killed in France;[8] and though he didn't encourage me to take a stand for the sake of a stand, he did make me argue and argue and argue. His own pacifism was not aggressive, but typically gentle.

This perhaps suggests that it was not only in musical things that I learned much from Bridge. It was, of course, the first time I had seen how an artist lived. I heard conversations which centred round the arts; I heard the latest poems discussed, and the latest trends in painting and sculpture. Bridge was not intellectually over-sophisticated, perhaps, although well-read and full of curiosity, but he had a circle of highly cultured friends, many of whom were artists and musicians, but most of them distinguished amateurs.

He also drove me around the South of England (though to my hypercritical juvenile standards he was never a good driver) and opened my eyes to the beauty of the Downs with their tucked-away little villages, and to the magnificence of English ecclesiastical architecture. I can also remember a gay trip to Paris with him and Mrs. Bridge.[9] Opportunity for travel had never much come my way—I was the fourth child who had had to be expensively educated—so it can be imagined what I owe to Bridge's guidance at this particularly impressionable time of life. I repaid him a little by helping him with his tennis, which was wild and unconventional; I considered mine rather good and stylish.

But Bridge never wanted to influence me too strongly too young; and yet he knew he had to present something very firm for this stiff, naïve little boy to react about. He had no other pupils, and it was a very touching relationship across the 34 years separating us. In everything he did for me, there were perhaps above all two cardinal principles. One was that you should try to find yourself and be true to what you found. The other—obviously connected with it—was his scrupulous attention to good technique, the business of saying clearly what was in one's mind.

He gave me a sense of technical ambition. People sometimes seem to think that, with a number of works now lying behind, one must be bursting with confidence. It is not so at all. I haven't yet achieved the simplicity I should like in my music, and I am enormously aware that I haven't yet come up to the technical standards Bridge set me.

[8] Ernest Farrar. See Essay 23.

[9] This was in October 1937, when Britten, Bridge and his wife, and Marjorie Fass (a close friend of the Bridges) visited Paris to see an exhibition of modern art.

71 Francis Poulenc 1899–1963 (1964)

To the average Englishman, Francis Poulenc's music may have appeared that of the typical French composer: witty, daring, sentimental, naughty. In fact Francis was very easily depressed, shockable, unsure, and liable to panic. No one who saw it will ever forget his agony in a boat on Thorpeness Meare, and it was really his horror of the sea which finally stopped him from coming back to Aldeburgh in 1958 to play in *Tirésias*.[1] He was always re-writing his music and he burnt his only String Quartet. Which is not to say that he had not a strong personality. He was not ashamed to admire and to borrow—Mozart, Chabrier, Stravinsky, Mussorgsky—but the result was very definitely Poulenc. He proudly called himself Latin, yet admitted that instinct was his guide. He put a high value on Sincerity: he was himself too innocent to be insincere. The two sides of his art (as represented by the *Stabat Mater*[2] and *Les Mamelles*) were supposed to be very clearly and consciously juxtaposed; on the contrary it was one of his most adorable qualities that he was incapable of being anything but himself—a delightful friend and a lovable musician.

Source: AFPB (1964), 23. Written by Britten and Pears.

[1] Poulenc's opera *Les Mamelles de Tirésias* (1944).

[2] *Stabat Mater* (1950).

72 On Receiving the First Aspen Award (1964)

Ladies and Gentlemen, when last May your Chairman and your President told me they wished to travel the 5000 miles from Aspen to Aldeburgh to have a talk with me, they hinted that it had something to do with and Aspen Award for Services to the Humanities—an award of very considerable importance and size.[1] I imagined that they felt I might advise them on a suitable recipient, and I began to consider what I should say. Who would be suitable for such an honour? What kind of person? Doctor? Priest? A social worker? A politician? Well, . . .! An artist? Yes, possibly (that, I imagined, could be the reason that Mr. Anderson and Professor Eurich thought I might be the person to help them). So I ran through the names of the great figures working in the Arts among us today. It was a fascinating problem; rather like one's school-time game of ideal cricket elevens, or slightly more recently, ideal casts for operas—but I certainly won't tell which of our great poets, painters, or composers came to the top of my list.

Mr. Anderson and Professor Eurich paid their visit to my home in Aldeburgh. It was a charming and courteous visit, but it was also a knock-out. It had not occurred to me, frankly, that it was I who was to be the recipient of this magnificent award, and I was stunned. I am afraid my friends must have felt I was a tongue-tied host. But I simply could not imagine why *I* had been chosen for this very great honour. I read again the simple and moving citation.[2] The key-word seemed to be 'humanities'. I went to the dictionary to look up its meaning, I found *Humanity*: 'the quality of being human' (well, that applied to me all right). But I found that the plural had a special meaning: 'Learning or literature concerned with human culture, as grammar, rhetoric, poetry and especially the ancient Latin and Greek Classics'. (Here I really had no claims since I cannot properly spell even in my own language, and when I set Latin I have terrible trouble over the quantities—besides you can all hear how far removed I am from rhetoric.) *Humanitarian* was an entry close beside these, and I supposed I might have some claim here, but I was daunted by the definition:

Source: *On Receiving the First Aspen Award* (London: Faber & Faber, 1964). Speech given in Aspen, Colorado, on 31 July 1964.

[1] The Aspen Institute for Humanistic Studies was formed in 1950 by Walter Paepcke (1896–1960). Paepcke considered the natural beauty of Aspen ideal for reflection on the political and cultural values of society. The Aspen Music Festival (1950) grew out of this philosophy, as did the Aspen Award (1964). Other recipients of the Award include Martha Graham and Edmund Wilson.

[2] The citation reads: 'To Benjamin Britten, who, as a brilliant composer, performer, and interpreter through music of human feelings, moods, and thoughts, has truly inspired man to understand, clarify and appreciate more fully his own nature, purpose and destiny.'

'One who goes to excess in his human principles (in 1855 often contemptuous or hostile)'. I read on, quickly. *Humanist*: 'One versed in Humanities', and I was back where I started. But perhaps after all the clue was in the word 'human', and I began to feel that I might have a small claim.

II

I certainly write music for human beings—directly and deliberately. I consider their voices, the range, the power, the subtlety, and the colour potentialities of them. I consider the instruments they play—their most expressive and suitable individual sonorities, and where I may be said to have invented an instrument (such as the Slung Mugs of *Noye's Fludde*) I have borne in mind the pleasure the young performers will have in playing it. I also take note of the *human* circumstances of music, of its environment and conventions; for instance, I try to write dramatically effective music for the theatre—I certainly don't think opera is better for not being effective on the stage (some people think that effectiveness *must* be superficial). And then the best music to listen to in a great Gothic church is the polyphony which was written for it, and was calculated for its resonance: this was my approach in the *War Requiem*—I calculated it for a big, reverberant acoustic and that is where it sounds best.[3] I believe, you see, in *occasional music*, although I admit there are some occasions which can intimidate one—I do not envy Purcell writing his *Ode to Celebrate King James's Return to London from Newmarket*.[4] On the other hand almost every piece I have ever written has been composed with a certain occasion in mind, and usually for definite performers, and certainly always *human* ones.

III

You may ask perhaps: how far can a composer go in thus considering the demands of people, of humanity? At many times in history the artist has made a conscious effort to speak with the voice of the people.[5] Beethoven certainly tried, in works as different as the *Battle of Vittoria* and the Ninth Symphony, to utter the sentiments of a whole community.[6] From the beginning of Christianity there have been musicians who have wanted and tried to be the servants of the church, and to express the devotion and convictions of Christians, as such. Recently, we have had the example of Shostakovich, who

[3] The *War Requiem* was written for the new Coventry Cathedral, where it was first performed in 1962.

[4] *The summer's absence unconcerned we bear* ('A Welcome Song for his Majesty at his return from New Market October the 21—1682'). The King concerned was Charles II, not his Catholic brother, James II.

[5] The use here of 'people' and 'the people' interchangeably was perhaps Britten's way of discounting Martin Cooper's attack on his politics or political naivity in the footnote to Essay 66.

[6] *Wellingtons Sieg oder Die Schlacht bei Vittoria* ('Battle Symphony'), Op. 91 (1813).

set out in his 'Leningrad' Symphony to present a monument to his fellow citizens, an explicit expression for them of their own endurance and heroism.[7] At a very different level, one finds composers such as Johann Strauss and George Gershwin aiming at providing people—the people—with the best dance music and songs which they were capable of making. And I can find nothing wrong with the objectives—declared or implicit—of these men; nothing wrong with offering to my fellow-men music which may inspire them or comfort them, which may touch them or entertain them, even educate them—directly and with intention. On the contrary, it is the composer's duty, as a member of society, to speak to or for his fellow human beings.

When I am asked to compose a work for an occasion, great or small, I want to know in some detail the conditions of the place where it will be performed, the size and acoustics, what instruments or singers will be available and suitable, the kind of people who will hear it, and what language they will understand—and even sometimes the age of the listeners and performers. For it is futile to offer children music by which they are bored, or which makes them feel inadequate or frustrated, which may set them against music forever; and it is insulting to address anyone in a language which they do not understand. The text of my *War Requiem* was perfectly in place in Coventry Cathedral—the Owen poems in the vernacular, and the words of the Requiem Mass familiar to everyone—but it would have been pointless in Cairo or Peking.

During the act of composition one is continually referring back to the conditions of performance—as I have said, the acoustics and the forces available, the techniques of the instruments and the voices—such questions occupy one's attention continuously, and certainly affect the stuff of the music, and in my experience are not only a restriction, but a challenge, an inspiration. Music does not exist in a vacuum, it does not exist until it is performed, and performance imposes conditions. It is the easiest thing in the world to write a piece virtually or totally impossible to perform—but oddly enough that is not what I prefer to do; I prefer to study the conditions of performance and shape my music to them.

IV

Where does one stop, then, in answering people's demands? It seems that there is no clearly defined Halt sign on this road. The only brake which one can apply is that of one's own private and personal conscience; when that speaks clearly, one must halt; and it can speak for musical or non-musical reasons. In the last six months I have been several times asked to write a work

[7] Symphony No. 7 in C ('Leningrad'), Op. 60 (1941), was written following the German siege of Leningrad in 1941, and had great national and international success.

as a memorial to the late President Kennedy.[8] On each occasion I have refused—not because in any way I was out of sympathy with such an idea; on the contrary, I was horrified and deeply moved by the tragic death of a very remarkable man. But for me I do not feel the time is ripe; I cannot yet stand back and see it clear. I should have to wait very much longer to do anything like justice to this great theme. But had I in fact agreed to undertake a limited commission, my artistic conscience would certainly have told me in what direction I could go, and when I should have to stop.

There are many dangers which hedge round the unfortunate composer: pressure groups which demand true proletarian music, snobs who demand the latest *avant-garde* tricks; critics who are already trying to document today for tomorrow, to be the first to find the correct pigeon-hole definition. These people are dangerous—not because they are necessarily of any importance in themselves, but because they may make the composer, above all the young composer, self-conscious, and instead of writing his own music, music which springs naturally from his gift and personality, he may be frightened into writing pretentious nonsense or deliberate obscurity. He may find himself writing more and more for machines, in conditions dictated by machines, and not by humanity: or of course he may end by creating grandiose clap-trap when his real talent is for dance tunes or children's piano pieces. Finding one's place in society as a composer is not a straightforward job. It is not helped by the attitude towards the composer in some societies. My own, for instance, semi-Socialist Britain, and Conservative Britain before it, has for years treated the musician as a curiosity to be barely tolerated. At a tennis party in my youth I was asked what I was going to do when I grew up—what job I was aiming at. 'I am going to be a composer', I said. 'Yes, but what else?' was the answer. The average Briton thought, and still thinks, of the Arts as suspect and expensive luxuries. The Manchester councillor who boasted he had never been to a concert and didn't intend to go, is no very rare bird in England. By Act of Parliament, each local authority in England is empowered to spend a sixpenny rate on the Arts. In fact it seems that few of them spend more than one twentieth of this—a sign of no very great enthusiasm! Until such a condition is changed, musicians will continue to feel 'out of step' in our semi-Welfare State.

But if we in England have to face a considerable indifference, in other countries conditions can have other, equally awkward effects. In totalitarian regimes, we know that great official pressure is used to bring the artist into line and make him conform to the State's ideology. In the richer capitalist countries,

[8] Kennedy had been shot the previous year, news of which filtered through the audience at London's Festival Hall during a special performance of *Gloriana* to mark Britten's fiftieth birthday, on 22 Nov.

money and snobbishness combine to demand the latest, newest manifestations, which I am told go by the name in this country of 'Foundation Music'.

V

The *ideal* conditions for an artist or musician will never be found outside the *ideal* society, and when shall we see that? But I think I can tell you some of the things which any artist demands from any society. He demands that his art shall be accepted as an essential part of human activity, and human expression; and that he shall be accepted as a genuine practitioner of that art and consequently of value to the community; reasonably, he demands from society a secure living and a pension when he has worked long enough; this is a basis for society to offer a musician, a modest basis. In actual fact there are very few musicians in my country who will get a pension after forty years' work in an orchestra or in an opera house. This must be changed; we must at least be treated as civil servants. Once we have a material status, we can accept the responsibility of answering society's demands on us. And society should and will demand from us the utmost of our skill and gift in the full range of music-making. (Here we come back to 'occasional' music.) There should be special music made and played for all sorts of occasions: football matches, receptions, elections (why not?) and even presentations of awards! I would have been delighted to have been greeted with a special piece composed for today! It might have turned out to be another piece as good as the cantata Bach wrote for the Municipal Election at Mühlhausen, or the Galliard that Dowland wrote as a compliment to the Earl of Essex![9] Some of the greatest pieces of music in our possession were written for special occasions, grave or gay. But we shouldn't worry too much about the so-called 'permanent' value of our occasional music. A lot of it cannot make much sense after its first performance, and it is quite a good thing to please people, even if only for today. That is what we should aim at—pleasing people today as seriously as we can, and letting the future look after itself. Bach wrote his *St. Matthew Passion* for performance on one day of the year only—the day which in the Christian church was the culmination of the year, to which the year's worship was leading. It is one of the unhappiest results of the march of science and commerce that this unique work, at the turn of a

[9] Bach's cantata *Gott ist mein König*, BWV 71, was composed for the *Ratswechsel* ('change of council') in Mühlhausen in 1708. Dowland's *The Right Honourable Robert, Earl of Essex, his Galliard* was originally called 'Can she excuse', in its version as a secular song. The Dowland scholar Diana Poulton considers this poem to be by the Earl of Essex, hinting as it does at the troubled relationship between Essex and Elizabeth I, a subject Britten explored in his opera *Gloriana* (1953). Dowland changed its name in 1604, after the execution of Essex and Elizabeth's own death. 'Can she excuse' was originally published as the fifth song in Dowland's *The First Booke of Songes or Ayres* (1597), which included as the fourth 'If my complaints could passions move'—the basis of the variations in Britten's *Lachrymae* (1950).

switch, is at the mercy of any loud roomful of cocktail drinkers—to be listened to or switched off at will, without ceremony or occasion.

VI

The wording of your Institute's Constitution implies an effort to present the Arts as a counter-balance to Science in today's life. And though I am sure you do not imagine that there is not a lot of science, knowledge and skill in the art of making music (in the calculation of sound qualities and colours, the knowledge of the technique of instruments and voices, the balance of forms, the creation of moods, and in the development of ideas), I would like to think you are suggesting that what is important in the Arts is *not* the scientific part, the analysable part of music, but the something which emerges from it but transcends it, which cannot be analysed because it is not *in* it, but *of* it. It is the quality which cannot be acquired by simply the exercise of a technique or a system: it is something to do with personality, with gift, with spirit. I quite simply call it—magic: a quality which would appear to be by no means unacknowledged by scientists, and which I value more than any other part of music.

It is arguable that the richest and most productive eighteen months in our music history is the time when Beethoven had just died, when the other nineteenth-century giants, Wagner, Verdi and Brahms had not begun; I mean the period in which Franz Schubert wrote his *Winterreise*, the C major Symphony, his last three piano sonatas, the C major String Quintet, as well as a dozen other glorious pieces.[10] The very creation of these works in that space of time seems hardly credible; but the standard of inspiration, of magic, is miraculous and past all explanation. Though I have worked very hard at the *Winterreise* the last five years, every time I come back to it I am amazed not only by the extraordinary mastery of it—for Schubert knew exactly what he was doing (make no mistake about that), and he had thought profoundly about it—but by the renewal of the magic: each time, the mystery remains.

This magic comes only with the sounding of the music, with the turning of the written note into sound—and it only comes (or comes most intensely) when the listener is one with the composer, either as a performer himself, or as a listener in active sympathy. Simply to read a score in one's armchair is not enough for evoking this quality. Indeed, this magic can be said to consist of just the music which is *not* in the score. Sometimes one can be quite daunted when one opens the *Winterreise*—there seems to be nothing on the page. One must not exaggerate—the shape of the music in Schubert is clearly visible. What *cannot* be indicated on the printed page are the innumerable small variants of

[10] The C major symphony was composed in the period 1825–8. The other works mentioned were written between Feb. 1827 and Sept. 1828.

rhythm and phrasing which make up the performer's contribution. In the *Winterreise*, it was not possible for Schubert to indicate exactly the length of rests and pauses, or the colour of the singer's voice or the clarity or smoothness of consonants. This is the responsibility of each individual performer, and at each performance he will make modifications. The composer expects him to; he would be foolish if he did not. For a musical experience needs three human beings at least. It requires a composer, a performer, and a listener; and unless these three take part together there is no musical experience. The experience will be that much more intense and rewarding if the circumstances correspond to what the composer intended: if the *St. Matthew Passion* is to be performed on Good Friday in a church, to a congregation of Christians; if the *Winterreise* is to be performed in a room, or in a small hall of truly intimate character to a circle of friends; if *Don Giovanni* is played to an audience which understands the text and appreciates the musical allusions. The further one departs from these circumstances, the less true and more diluted is the experience likely to be.

One must face the fact today that the vast majority of musical performances take place as far away from the original as it is possible to imagine: I do not mean simply *Falstaff* being given in Tokyo, or the Mozart Requiem in Madras. I mean of course that such works *can* be audible in any corner of the globe, at any moment of the day or night, through a loudspeaker, without question of suitability or comprehensibility. Anyone, anywhere, at any time, can listen to the B minor Mass upon one condition only—that they possess a machine. No qualification is required of any sort—faith, virtue, education, experience, age. Music is now free for all. If I say the loudspeaker is the principal enemy of music, I don't mean that I am not grateful to it as a means of education or study, or as an evoker of memories. But it is not part of true musical *experience*. Regarded as such it is simply a substitute, and dangerous because deluding. Music demands more from a listener than simply the possession of a tape-machine or a transistor radio. It demands some preparation, some effort, a journey to a special place, saving up for a ticket, some homework on the programme perhaps, some clarification of the ears and sharpening of the instincts. It demands as much effort on the listener's part as the other two corners of the triangle, this holy triangle of composer, performer and listener.

VII

Ladies and Gentlemen, this award is the latest of the kindnesses for which I am indebted to your country. I first came to the United States twenty-five years ago, at the time when I was a discouraged young composer—muddled, fed-up and looking for work, longing to be used. I was most generously treated here, by old and new friends, and to all of these I can never be sufficiently grateful.

Their kindness was past description; I shall never forget it. But the thing I am *most* grateful to your country for is this: it was in California, in the unhappy summer of 1941, that, coming across a copy of the Poetical Works of George Crabbe in a Los Angeles bookshop, I first read his poem, *Peter Grimes*; and, at this same time, reading a most perceptive and revealing article about it by E. M. Forster, I suddenly realised where I belonged and what I lacked.[11] I had become without roots, and when I got back to England six months later I was ready to put them down. I have lived since then in the same small corner of East Anglia, near where I was born. And I find as I get older that working becomes more and more difficult away from that home. Of course, I plot and plan my music when I am away on tour, and I get great stimulus and excitement from visiting other countries; with a congenial partner I like giving concerts, and in the last years we have travelled as far as Vancouver and Tokyo, Moscow and Java; I like making new friends, meeting new audiences, hearing new music. But I belong at home—there—in Aldeburgh. I have tried to bring music *to* it in the shape of our local Festival; and all the music I write comes *from* it. I believe in roots, in associations, in backgrounds, in personal relationships. I want my music to be of use to people, to please them, to 'enhance their lives' (to use Berenson's phrase[12]). I do not write for posterity—in any case, the outlook for that is somewhat uncertain. I write music, now, in Aldeburgh, for people living there, and further afield, indeed for anyone who cares to play it or listen to it. But my music now has its roots, in where I live and work. And I only came to realise that in California in 1941.

VIII

People have already asked me what I am going to do with your money; I have even been told in the post and in the press exactly how I ought to dispose of it. I shall of course pay no attention to these suggestions, however well- or ill-intentioned. The last prize I was given went straight away to the Aldeburgh Festival, the musical project I have most at heart. It would not surprise me if a considerable part of the Aspen Award went in that direction; I have not really decided. But one thing I know I want to do; I should like to give an annual Aspen Prize for a British composition. The conditions would change each year; one year it might be for a work for young voices and a school orchestra, another year for the celebration of a national event or centenary, another time

[11] In his 1945 article 'Peter Grimes', and in subsequent interviews with Schafer and for the BBC at the time of the 1960 revision of *Billy Budd*, Britten was certain that it was Forster's article that brought Crabbe to his attention, and that his search for a volume of Crabbe's poetry was after he had read the *Listener* article.

[12] Bernard Berenson (1865–1959), distinguished American art critic and leading authority on the Italian Renaissance, who said that 'Art as art, not art for art, must be life enhancing'.

a work for an instrument whose repertory is small; but in any case for specific or general usefulness. And the Jury would be instructed to choose only that work which was a pleasure to perform and inspiriting to listen to. In this way I would try to express my interpretation of the intention behind the Aspen Institute, and to express my warmest thanks, my most humble thanks, for the honour which you have awarded me today.

73 Musician of the Year (1964)

WARRACK: Louis MacNeice once quoted you, in 1940, as saying, 'An artist ought either to live where he has live roots or no roots at all; in England today the artist feels essentially lonely, twisted in dying roots, always in opposition to a group.' Was this what was behind your going to America in 1939?

BRITTEN: That certainly describes my feelings at the time, but the phraseology sounds more like Louis than me! Or Wystan Auden—I was terrifically under Auden's influence at the time. He preached that one's roots should be in ideas and people, not places or environment.[1] Also, I was immensely depressed about Europe. I'd been vaguely political, as we all were. The Hitler pressure was mounting, and the governments seemed to be encouraging him or not standing up to him; Europe looked finished. So when Auden went off to America, in late 1938 I think, I followed as soon as I could, in the spring of 1939. Another thing was that it had been very hard to get started as a composer in England. My works had made a small impact, but there were never any number of performances. There had been some in New York and there were plans for more. I wanted to go there, to see if this meant there was a chance of getting going properly. I'd met Aaron Copland when he was in England. He'd been very nice to me and encouraged me to go to see the United States. I think I just had to abandon my roots for a while, to find out if I'd really got any at all, or to find out where they really were.

WARRACK: Apart from fears about Europe, did hope about America quickly get realized?

BRITTEN: We went to Canada first, Peter Pears and I; we went early in the spring of 1939 (I think we were in the first boat up the St. Lawrence that year after the ice had melted). But soon we came down to the United States and stayed with Aaron in New York State, where he'd taken a summer house for a couple of months. I did a lot of work at this time, going back to Canada for some jobs, but mostly staying around New York as well as with

Source: 'Benjamin Britten: Musician of the Year in Conversation with John Warrack', *Musical America* 84 (Dec. 1964), 21; 272–4.

[1] Two years later Britten returned to his 'dying' roots, where his opposition became more subtle than it had been pre-war. The short exchange between Balstrode and Peter in Act 1 scene 1 of *Peter Grimes* is Britten's coded refutation of Auden's ideas:

> *Balstrode*: Why not try the wider sea, With merchantman or privateer?
> *Peter*: I am native, rooted here.
> *Balstrode*: Rooted by what?
> *Peter*: By familiar fields, Marsh and sand, Ordinary streets, Prevailing wind.

friends on Long Island until the war. As to performances—yes, I did get in the swim quite quickly. I felt encouraged, I met lots of composers, everyone was very kind, there were quite a few commissions. In fact, in most ways I seemed quite well settled, and felt a great sense of relief, until the war came.

WARRACK: And then?

BRITTEN: Then there was a strong pull to the old country and one's old friends, even though it was felt in the first days of the 'phoney war' that nothing much was going to happen. It seemed the best idea was to stay put, as we were all instructed (unless one was of some 'military importance,' which, of course, we weren't) and to get on with one's work as best one could. Here again I was enormously influenced by Auden.

WARRACK: What was this about Auden in the thirties? Everyone, not only you, who's known him seems to have found him a whirlwind influence.

BRITTEN: I think it was really that he was such a large personality, a whirlwind one, if you like, and, of course, I was swept away by his poetry. He was incredibly intelligent, very, very vocal; he talked marvellously well, he was very engaging and sympathetic and deeply interested in people. He'd grown entirely away from Europe by the end of the thirties, and for several years seemed to have broken his ties with England.

WARRACK: Had you, too?

BRITTEN: Well, this was complicated. I went to the United States, I suppose to emigrate, but rather cautiously I had only taken a visitor's visa. To take out naturalization papers then, you had to go out and come back again. I planned to do this, and every time I tried it I somehow got ill and was prevented. Then, when the war started in earnest, and France fell, I became really tangled up. All my thoughts and interests were in Europe, and yet to return into the maelstrom seemed madness—my views on pacifism still held, so I couldn't do anything practical about the situation. At least in the States I could work, could be of some use to other people. I got extremely ill and was in and out of bed for a year. I couldn't solve the situation for myself intellectually—as Auden didn't fail to point out!

WARRACK: This must also have been about the time of your first opera, 'Paul Bunyan', with Auden. I dare say you're bored of being asked about a piece you've withdrawn, but what do you now feel about it? How did it affect later things, for instance?

BRITTEN: That was early in 1941 when I still hadn't really got over that illness. Paul Bunyan was a famous American folk subject, and I suppose it was cheeky for us two Britishers to tackle it. Some of the text was preaching, but it had some wonderful poetry, and it gave me the chance to try to write music in an absolutely simple manner, making an effort to be popular and writing straight tunes. Also, it was scored for a chamber orchestra, about 20 more than I use now—which was interesting and useful experience when I came back to chamber opera after 'Peter Grimes'. The music is not all good, but some is; perhaps we'll revive it one day.

I spent the summer of 1941 in California recuperating; and as I got better, I began to see things more clearly. By chance I'd read an article by E. M. Forster about the Suffolk poet Crabbe, and this set me planning a libretto on his character Peter Grimes. Then, by another chance, the delay in getting home enabled me to meet Koussevitzky, who liked the idea of the opera, and decided to commission it. He nearly cancelled it when he heard I was determined to go home to England. It was a fearful job to get a boat. We put our names down for a passage, and we had to wait on the east coast for six months, packed and ready to go at 24 hours' notice. I couldn't work at all—only some Purcell arrangements, some folksong bits. Then we got on the boat, and on the month's journey I couldn't stop the flow—the 'Hymn to St. Cecilia', the 'Ceremony of Carols', some settings of Beddoes that were not very good and which I withdrew,[2] and other little things.

WARRACK: All English verse settings, in fact, as you headed back to England. During the time in America the works seemed to have been either settings of foreign poetry—'Les Illuminations' and the Michelangelo sonnets—or concert works; and in all cases, it seems, an expansion on what had gone immediately before. Do you feel this to have been an effect of America?

BRITTEN: I think the effect of America was to broaden one, encourage one and to shake one. I was in danger of becoming parochial, and this worried me. One reason I didn't set English in America, though, was that I became discontented with the contemporary setting of English. It was necessary for me to get away from setting English for a time. I felt bolder with another language, or no language at all. So there was my first string quartet, which Mrs. Elizabeth Sprague Coolidge commissioned, the Sinfonia da Requiem, which the Japanese asked for and then rejected, the Violin Concerto for Antonio Brosa and two pieces for two pianos for Ethel Bartlett and Rae Robertson.[3]

[2] 'Wild with passion' and 'If thou wilt ease thine heart', each a setting of Thomas Lovell Beddoes, were published posthumously, in 1994.

[3] Mrs Elizabeth Sprague Coolidge (1864–1953), American patron of the arts who commissioned many works, including Britten's String Quartet No. 1 in D (1941), Stravinsky's *Apollon musagète* (1927–8), Copland's *Appalachian Spring* (1944), and Bridge's String Quartet No. 3 (1927). Bridge wrote a letter of introduction for Britten when he left for America. The *Sinfonia da Requiem* (1940) was rejected by the Japanese commissioning body because of its Christian theme. The Violin Concerto (1939) was first performed by the Spanish violinist Antonio Brosa with the New York Philharmonic Orchestra, conducted by John Barbirolli, on 28 Mar. 1940. The two pieces for two pianos are the *Introduction and Rondo alla Burlesca* (1940) and *Mazurka Elegiaca* (1941). Britten also wrote his *Scottish Ballad* (1941) for Ethel Bartlett and Rae Robertson, the talented two-piano team, whom he befriended in America and to whom he dedicated the work.

WARRACK: Is it right to feel that you're now coming into another patch of instrumental composition?

BRITTEN: This is really a question of opportunity. I've always had the advantage (or disadvantage, whichever it is) of needing occasions or performers to attract and inspire me—I mean inspire in the old sense; that is, the event or player blows enthusiasm into me. After Dennis Brain and Julian Bream, it's been Rostropovich. Nowadays I don't seem to lose confidence in writing vocal music, but I think I was getting a bit nervous about instrumental music. Rostropovich freed one of my inhibitions. He's such a gloriously uninhibited musician himself, with this enormous feeling of generosity you get from the best Russian players, coming to meet you all the way. I'd heard about him, and rather unwillingly listened on the wireless. I immediately realized this was a new way of playing the cello, in fact almost a new, vital way of playing music. I made arrangements to come to London and heard him again, and found him in the flesh even more than I'd expected. He took the bull by the horns and asked me to write a piece for him, which was my cello sonata written 'on condition he came to Aldeburgh!' Then came the cello symphony.

WARRACK: Yes, and I remember from the first performance of the symphony in Moscow last March how close the Russians seemed to feel you to be. Is this an old association?

BRITTEN: No, not at all: I first went to Russia in spring, 1963, but I've been back and have made some close friends—particularly Rostropovich and his wife Vishnevskaya, Sviatoslav Richter and his wife Nina Dorliak,[4] a singer too, and of course, Shostakovich.

WARRACK: How do you get on with Shostakovich?

BRITTEN: I am closer to him now, and he seems completely relaxed with us. There was a touching occasion this autumn. I met him in Moscow, and he insisted on Peter and me having lunch with him (I'd only been to his flat once before): there were two new pieces he wanted to play us. These turned out to be his Ninth and Tenth string quartets written during the last months. His hands are rather arthritic now, but his piano playing still has great conviction. The Ninth was characteristic, formally very interesting, quite up to what one might expect. But the Tenth was a real knockout—very strange, mostly very quiet, muted in feeling, and very simple and bald. I think it's a great new development for him. We were deeply impressed.

WARRACK: How did your own pieces with the English Opera Group go over? I mean, 'Herring' has so much local humor, and 'The Rape of Lucretia' might have been attacked for being 'decadent.'

[4] Nina Dorliak (1908–98), Soviet singer and teacher, who married the homosexual Richter in 1946.

BRITTEN: 'Albert Herring' was a terrific success, and they really did seem to follow it all and find it amusing; though it was 'Lucretia' that surprisingly had the greatest critical success.

WARRACK: 'Turn of the Screw'?

BRITTEN: Well, ideologically it did worry them, for being dark and pessimistic and so on; but musically it was the piece that seemed to appeal most—especially to the younger generation. Did you know that Shostakovich said publicly he liked it best of my operas? Of course, the Russians have this marvelous talent for the stage. They're wonderful actors, with a born instinct for theater, and this gives them a quick understanding of operas a little more difficult musically than they are used to. There's an immense amount of talent in Russia, but it may take a little while to break out. And there's a terrific need for music which can be used by this vast, ravenously hungry audience. I was pleased that Mme. Furtseva,[5] the Minister of Culture, was taken enough with the English Opera Group to want to form similar Russian groups for touring. Getting a large company around their gigantic country is a problem, and groups our size would suit them well. She felt that the audience's reaction she witnessed in Moscow showed that the country could take this kind of operatic style.

WARRACK: What about repertory? Do they have anything suitable?

BRITTEN: They'll take some of our pieces, in fact they want all my operas, but they must write operas themselves, of course. Khatchaturian was very taken with the idea, and said in a speech that he now felt opera had a future after all.[6]

WARRACK: Will you go there again?

BRITTEN: I hope so, because I enjoy giving concerts there (besides, I should like to see 'Midsummer Night's Dream' at the Bolshoi, and 'Peter Grimes' at the Kirov), and I enjoy getting to know the Russians more and more—they are such warm, friendly people. I feel also, that our two parts of Europe have been separated too long, and we can learn so much from each other. They have missed so many later developments of the technique of the art, and we have lost so much of the immediate contact between the audience and contemporary art that they have.

WARRACK: Will you write something for them?

[5] Ekaterina Furtseva (1910–74), Soviet politician, first woman appointed to the Praesidium (1956), and in 1960 appointed Minister of Culture. She strongly disapproved of decadent modern art and had a significant impact on Soviet culture in the period in which Britten developed his links with the composers and music of her country.

[6] Aram Khachaturian (1903–78), Armenian composer, who wrote ballets, orchestral works, some chamber and incidental music, and scores for nationalistic films, but no opera.

BRITTEN: I'd like to write an opera for Vishnevskaya, but I can't say what. There's the language problem, for one thing. She's the kind of artist I want to compose for—vocally very personal and accomplished, and a wonderfully gifted and subtle actress.

WARRACK: How about your sabbatical year? I gather you and Pears are taking 1965 off from performing. What are the plans?

BRITTEN: To write a lot of music! But first a holiday. We're going to India for six weeks in January and February, and in the late summer there's a very exciting plan to drive through Russia with the Rostropoviches. Then, apart from the Aldeburgh and Long Melford festivals, composing. I'm going to do a solo cello sonata for Rostropovich—nothing down yet, though. And there is to be a song-cycle for Fischer-Dieskau, in memory of his wife, for baritone and chamber group—English poetry, but it's not even chosen yet.[7] That'll be for Aldeburgh.

WARRACK: What about other opera subjects?

BRITTEN: I want to do another church parable kind of work, like 'Curlew River'. A Christian subject—or rather, Old Testament, if you count that![8] And one day, something on a modern subject: we've thought of doing it on the theme of a young innocent for whom things in the modern world always go wrong—a bit 'Dog Beneath the Skin' in idea. I'd like a scene in an airport (always waiting!) and I'd like to include a tennis party! But these are really no more than possible ideas for the future, like 'King Lear'. I'm still hoping to do that, but I'll need to be older and wiser. Certainly I'd like to come back to Shakespeare—John Gielgud wants me to do 'The Tempest'. As I found with 'A Midsummer Night's Dream', Shakespeare is wonderful to set, and there is in him an absolutely unparalleled series of librettos.[9]

WARRACK: I wish you'd do another comedy some time.

BRITTEN: Yes, I'd like to fit that in—if only there were more time! It's terribly difficult, this whole question of dividing one's time between playing and writing, public and private. I haven't solved it. If only we had the old, more flexible, even haphazard arrangements for concerts. I've got to decide now exactly how to map out my 1966, what engagements to accept. What I'd like would be to look a month ahead—to be able to say, 'Now, I've finished this piece, let's do some concerts.' I can't do that. All the same, I don't want to give up performing, playing and conducting. I treasure this contact with live audiences too much.

[7] Eventually the *Songs and Proverbs of William Blake* (1965), composed for baritone and piano.

[8] Eventually *The Burning Fiery Furnace* (1966).

[9] None of these ideas eventuated.

74 British Music in the World Today (1964)

AMIS: *Benjamin Britten returned to the studio and we started a conversation. I asked him if he agreed with Michael Tippett's statement that the two of them showed British composers once more belonging to the mainstream of music.*

BRITTEN: I'm never very conscious of belonging or not belonging. Obviously one doesn't belong to the main German-Viennese tradition, I don't think. On the other hand I'm immensely aware of belonging to the English tradition.

AMIS: Yes, but it seems that the music of the Twenties and Thirties seems so homespun. The music of Vaughan Williams is obviously alien to people in France and Germany and Italy, whereas your music and Michael's seems to have got something that speaks a common language.

BRITTEN: Yes that is true. I think one has been immensely encouraged—partly because one wants to make friends—by the reaction of countries as widely apart as Russian and America to one's tunes.

AMIS: I mean your music and Michael's is profoundly English, but at the same time seems to speak a language that they can understand.

BRITTEN: What I think is awfully interesting is that in *this* country my music is not considered very English. When one gets abroad—and I'm sure it's the same with Michael's music too—one is considered enormously English. They can see the flavour of the nationality much more strongly than people here.

AMIS: But isn't that, don't you think, because you don't use all the apparatus that the Vaughan Williamses and so have used—I mean mainly the folksong and the rather homespun quality?

BRITTEN: Yes, I think that is true. But I never think it matters awfully if one is fifty years behind or in front. I mean so often in architectural styles we've been long after the continental schools, but I mean our Gothic architecture stands up proudly as ever; it doesn't *seem* dated.

AMIS: Oh no, as long as it's done with conviction then it's surely ok.

BRITTEN: Personally I feel it very dangerous for young composers to think, 'Oh goodness, I'm ten years behind. I must catch up, I must see what the latest continental schools, American schools, are doing.' In America it's had an awfully bad effect, this sort of conscious effort of trying to catch up Europe all the time.

Source: Editor's transcript of recording (NSA NP8123W). BBC Transcription Service: interview with John Amis for the series *Talking About Music.* (Pre-recorded 19 Dec. 1964.) An edited version was broadcast on 8 Mar. 1993, BBC Radio 3, in the series *Composer Portrait.*

AMIS: I was talking the other day to Martin Cooper, and he said that the setting sin of critics is vanity, writing for each other.[1] Don't you think that applies, to a certain extent, to composers? They're not sufficiently sure of themselves to write utterly with conviction; they're always wondering 'Oh goodness, I wonder what so-and-so will say if I put in a common chord here', you know.

BRITTEN: That I think is one of the terrible dangers—although it's a great pleasure—of knowing too many composers. I think if one is living apart or doing a job which doesn't involve you with too many composers, then you get a kind of freedom. I mean the café life, I think, the comparing of aims and all that, although awful fun can be very dangerous. You start writing for other composers. And after all what we are doing is not writing for the composers but we're writing for the public.

AMIS: Yes but how many of the composers today really believe that, one wonders? I mean the music gets more and more difficult, and the number of people it could possibly be understood by seems to be getting smaller and smaller.

BRITTEN: Yes. I mean Stravinsky's remark—I think it was made five or six years ago—that anyone who has followed all the latest trends in composition must know what I'm at now. But of course we can't *all* follow the latest trends, and you can't expect an intelligent concert-goer, but not a professional one, to be aware of all the latest trends. I think—as my old King Charles's head—that the *techniques* have become so frightfully interesting to people, and not the actual thing they say. Every time one steps out of an aeroplane one is asked by the journalists, 'what do you think of this style or that style of serial technique or electronics?', and one's reaction is always the same: It's not the style that interests me, it's what the chaps say writing in the style. The language is important as long as it conveys what the man has to say to me. But the language itself is a means to an end and not the end itself.

AMIS: Do you listen to a lot of music?

BRITTEN: Not nearly as much as I should like to, partly because one does work really frightfully hard, and I'm now starting to listen more to gramophone records, which I haven't before but I find it a very good way of getting to know things. I mean I have certain blanks in my understanding of composers, which I'm afraid is well known; I shall certainly not mention any names . . .

AMIS: What a pity . . .

BRITTEN: . . . but there are one or two pieces that I have really listened to a lot, now, just to see if I can't break through a kind of resistance which I have.

[1] See Essay 66 and Martin's Cooper's controversial response.

AMIS: Some of the composing boys have been saying that they think the big orchestra has had its day. Do you think that's true?

BRITTEN: It's awfully difficult to say 'had its day', because when you have this wonderful repertory of music written *for* a big orchestra, obviously as long as people love Beethoven and Tchaikovsky and Wagner they will want to have and demand big symphony orchestras.

AMIS: Yes, but modern composers, with the possible exception of Shostakovich—I mean *you* don't write much for the big orchestra—Shostakovich I suppose is the great composer today, the only one writing regularly and often for the big orchestra—but I mean if they don't write for the big orchestra, and you just get these terrible commissioned works, you know, which get one or two performances, there's going to be so little repertoire that we're going to have a sort of museum orchestra.

BRITTEN: My own inclination is *not* to write for the great, full orchestra except on very special occasions, and even I find now that when I do use an orchestra—a full orchestra—in the Cello Symphony, for instance—is that I don't want to use the orchestra as it's normally constituted—that particular kind of sound that became the bread and butter of the nineteenth century. It isn't *my* bread and butter.

It's the same with opera, too. I feel that I do want to write the occasional big opera, but my inclination is really nearly always now to write for the small. I like that sound better; but of course it's terribly difficult to generalize because one simply doesn't know what ideas are round the corner.

You mentioned Shostakovich, but I still think by far his best music goes into his chamber music. When I was in Moscow he played Peter and me his two new string quartets—the ninth and the tenth, I think they were.[2] And I must say I was *shattered* by the tenth. I thought it was the most extra*ordinary* piece of music—completely new for him, im*mense*ly simple, im*mense*ly direct, but quite, quite surprising and new, and much more for instance than the last two or three symphonies which I don't feel an awful lot of sympathy with.

AMIS: It's the curious thing about Shostakovich, isn't it, that you can never rely on the next piece being anything like the same standard of quality as the last one.

BRITTEN: I think that is one of his *enormous* gifts. I think he can become—he *is*—the most wonderfully *use*ful composer to have around, because most of us, you know, unless our inspiration is working at its highest pitch, hesitate before starting a new work. He I think is relaxed and plunges ahead and—I don't think he'd pretend for a *mo*ment that every work he wrote was a masterpiece or even that it will continue to be used—but if you have a demand from the

[2] String Quartet No. 9 in E♭, Op. 117 (1964), and No. 10 in A♭, Op. 118 (1964).

public or orchestras or society to produce music, it's *mar*vellous to be able to do it as well as that, even if you're not perhaps always frightfully interested.

AMIS: But it's a terrifying business—it must be—these days, with the mass media and everything, that every work you write is scrutinized almost immediately by the whole world, whereas in the old days you perhaps wrote a symphony for a particular occasion and perhaps your chums were there and the person you wrote it for, and you didn't have this terrible, terrifying business of criticism; don't you find that paralysing?

BRITTEN: Now that is inclined—terribly inclined—to make one self-conscious. If one could only somehow say, 'All right, this is a work which is written for a special occasion', and then *burn* it. I feel that—I mean so many of one's pieces that were written, as I say, for special occasions, and one's not desperately proud of them but they were quite useful at the time, but now they're sort of turned out and, well, naturally they don't stand up to a great deal of wear.

AMIS: Do you ever practise the piano?

BRITTEN: No; not really. There are certain bits which I jolly well *have* to look at if I've got to play. But I wish I *did*, and it's not a recommendation. I think it's very, very dangerous to play as little as I do, and I find it catches me out seriously if I'm nervous.

AMIS: That's like Michael Tippett who always says about every work, 'Oh it's child's play, poppet.' And he thinks of course everything is terribly easy to play.

BRITTEN: Oh does he?

AMIS: Only your piano—your own piano parts lie wonderfully under your hands. I mean I always think it's rather like some of, for instance, Rachmaninov's music: if you look at the printed page you get a sort of idea how Rachmaninov played. And I think it's the same with your music.

BRITTEN: Yes, I think it's fairly in*evitable*, that. After all, I suppose one's other instrument in music also has a kind of instrumental imprint, which can't come from playing. Although I have always a kind of *technical* interest in the instrumental parts, and I like to work at—and I wrote this piece recently for Julian, I worked out every single chord, although I've never played the guitar in my life, but I had a little diagram of all the fingerings and all that, and I found it absolutely fascinating. And I find it so often that gives one sort of ideas for colour and for harmonies and the technical thing is very, very useful.

AMIS: I remember Julian Bream telling me that when you first gave him the music, he looked at it and said, 'Well, you know, I don't think this is possible, Ben, I really don't think it's going to come off.' And then you said, 'Well I wonder, have you thought about fingering it this way?' And Bream goes away quietly into a corner and says, 'Damn it, he's right!'

75 Tribute to Michael Tippett (1965)

My dear Michael,

Now it is *your* turn! A year ago I had one of these 'memorial' years and so I know what you are in for. I am sure you will be touched by the tributes, but I hope you won't be too embarrassed by all the 'evaluations'. You must not be made to feel—as I was—that you are already dead and that the musicologists are busy on the corpse! We both have a lot more notes to write yet!

Evaluations, comparisons—the whole apparatus; does it mean anything to you? It doesn't to me, much. Slaps or bouquets, they come too late to help, long after the work is over. What matters to us now is that people want to use our music. For that, as I see it, is our job—to be useful, and to the living. Criticism likes to separate, to dislodge, to imply rivalries, to provoke jealousies. But I don't think I am jealous—(yes, envious, possibly of the man who can do something much better than I can), and the colleagues whom I admire, I regard as friends on the side of the angels rather than as rivals. Do you remember the story of Haydn banging the table and rushing from the room when someone poked fun at *Don Giovanni* (I think it was)? He knew very well the problems of finding the right notes and balancing forms. Schumann, too, who later found such difficulty in getting the courage to write at all, was the tenderest of critics. What does it matter if some of the people he admired mean little to us? His first duty was to his contemporaries, not to us. No one could have expressed the agony of composition more sympathetically than yourself, Michael, when you wrote about me last year.[1] For you are a composer, living in the same environment, facing the same problems as myself. This is the natural soil for friendship, and friendship is stimulating and creative and unifying.

We have known each other now for more than twenty years; we have been very close often, at other times we have seemed to be moving in different directions. But whenever I see our names bracketed together (and they often are, I am glad to say) I am reminded of the spirit of courage and integrity, sympathy, gaiety and profound musical independence which is yours, and I am proud to call you my friend.

Your devoted
BEN

P.S. I wish your piano parts weren't so difficult!

Editor's title.

Source: Ian Kemp (ed.), *Michael Tippett: A Symposium on his 60th Birthday* (London: Faber & Faber, 1965), 29–30. Tippett turned 60 on 2 Jan.

[1] This was Tippett's fiftieth-birthday tribute to Britten, published in the *Observer* on 17 Nov. 1963, in which Tippett spoke of the 'prolonged struggle, even agony, which composition is for Britten'.

76 Tribute to Zoltán Kodály (1965)

There can be no composer of our century who has done more for the musical life of his country than Zoltán Kodály. He and Bartók, together and separately, may be said to have re-created Hungary's whole musical language. When he started to compose, the dominant influences in central Europe were Wagnerian and Viennese; Hungarian music was equated with mere gypsy music. But turning his back on Austria and looking to Paris, where he first met Debussy in 1907, he could free himself for Folk Song and National Expression. His first major international impact occurred with *Psalmus Hungaricus*, written in 1923, and first performed in England—who that was there will ever forget it?—in 1927. His later symphonic and orchestral works are firmly in the repertoire of every orchestra. In our concerts this Festival we are to hear his rather less well known chamber works, all written before the *Psalmus*, but wholly characteristic of the man. With these, we shall have audible witness to that other triumph of Kodály's later career, the creation of a tradition of children's choral singing which has already become something mythical.[1] 'Nobody', said Kodály, 'is too great to write for children; in fact, he should try to become great enough for it.' He started by creating a repertoire for children, and then revolutionised their education; and he based it on active music-making, and not on passive appreciation; thus he has created a new standard in sight-reading, as well as in vocal intonation and in rhythmic vitality, which listeners to the Budapest girls' choir called after him will recognise as being quite unique.

Like many other creators, he has been subjected from time to time to most venomous criticism, but his courage and integrity has triumphed. He is now, at eighty-two, the most honoured and loved man in Hungary, and we are proud and lucky to have him with us.

Source: AFPB (1965), 12–13. Written by Britten, Pears, and Imogen Holst. A German translation of this essay appeared, under Britten's signature alone, in Zoltán Kodály, *Mein Weg zur Musik* (Zurich: Verlag der Arche, 1966).

[1] The programme included his *Serenade*, Op. 12 (1919–20), for two violins and viola, his Duo, Op. 7 (1914), for violin and cello, some solo songs, and ten part-songs.

77 Tribute to Jean Sibelius (1965)

I must confess that, for many, many years, the works of the Finnish master meant little to me.[1] Then, by chance, hearing a performance of the 4th Symphony, I became interested; and since [then] I have taken every opportunity to study his scores and hear authoritative performances. I find his conception of sound extremely personal and original, and his musical thinking most stimulating. I pay sincere homage to him in his centenary year.

Editor's title.

Source: Timo Mäkinen (ed.), *Jean Sibelius* (Helsinki: Sibelius Centenary Committee, 1965), 26.

[1] See Essay 8 and Essay 78 for different responses at different times in Britten's life to Sibelius's music.

78 Sibelius (1965)

AALTONEN: Mr Britten, as a composer you are master of a variety of branches of music. Would you please tell us which one you prefer working in?

BRITTEN: I think the answer to that is a very short and simple one: I prefer working in them all. There's no kind of music that I don't want to write. The occasion, of course, demands which kind of music I write in, but it can be any kind from opera, to songs, to instrumental music, to symphonies to quartets; it just depends what I'm asked to do and what I want to do. But I have no blinkers on, if I can put it like that.

AALTONEN: You are often referred to as the national hero in the realm of music in Britain; that is exactly the title given to Jean Sibelius in Finland. What is your relationship to Sibelius's music?

BRITTEN: Well I hope I can fulfil a tenth of what Sibelius did for music in Finland. I think my own reactions to Sibelius are *personal* but perhaps interesting. When I was young I found Sibelius—the music of Sibelius—unsympathetic. I was interested much more in the Schoenberg–Berg–Webern school, and of course the overwhelming personality of Stravinsky. And then quite by accident, not so many years ago—perhaps ten, perhaps fewer—I heard some music of Sibelius without knowing what it was, and I was deeply interested and surprised and even bewildered by this music, which seemed to me to be so new and so personal that I was eager to find out what it was. I discovered it was the Sixth Symphony of Sibelius, which I think is a very, very fine one. After that moment I bought all the scores that I could possibly find of his music, and although I wouldn't pretend that I know or understand or even like everything he wrote, I find it a most sympathetic, interesting phenomenon in the musical world, and a most important figure. I think it only goes to show how *ludicrously* unimportant fashions in music are—that for instance in the Twenties there was *only* Sibelius in England, which was not true, and now there is *no* Sibelius, which is also not true; a great man like Sibelius can weather all storms of fashion.

AALTONEN: What is it in your opinion that makes Sibelius unique?

BRITTEN: Well, I think what makes Sibelius unique is what makes any great artist unique, which is his own personality. His music is unlike that of anyone—just as the music of Berg or Stravinsky is unlike anyone else.

AALTONEN: Did you have a chance to meet Mr Sibelius himself?

BRITTEN: Oh no, I didn't, unfortunately.

Editor's title.

Source: Editor's transcript of recording (*GB-ALb* 3–02053902). Broadcast 9 Oct. 1965, Radio Finland: interview by Ulla-Maija Aaltonen.

AALTONEN: This year there have been dozens of concerts to commemorate Jean Sibelius. Mr Britten, what do you think this kind of celebration can do as far as a composer's fame and popularity are concerned?

BRITTEN: Well, in my *private* opinion, I'm afraid always of celebrations because having too much or a great deal of one composer can sometimes do them a disservice. There are some composers who need to be rather rare—one can overplay them. Whether that will happen with Sibelius, I don't know. It may—on the contrary it could help him, by performing works which are not so often done and which could make him again more popular. But I think it is a danger.

AALTONEN: We know, Mr Britten, that you have been commissioned to compose a choral work for the United Nations' twentieth anniversary. Would you please give us a few details on this particular work.

BRITTEN: This work is a choral work which I wrote only a few months ago, and I call it—particularly carefully—a work for men, women, and children, and the words are all very appropriate for the aims of the United Nations, and they come from sources of, well, BC, starting from the great Indian Asoka, and right up to the great Russian Yevtushenko of today.[1] And these sentences exhort the public, the singers, to think a little bit more seriously about their methods of arguing—in other words to limit it to words and perhaps not venture into weapons quite so easily. This will be performed in England and in New York and in Paris—unfortunately not in Moscow as we'd hoped—and in one or two other capitals in Europe on October the 24th.[2]

AALTONEN: You have stated that it's important for you to know the audience in advance. Well then, you have three different audiences this time simultaneously; did this raise any special difficulties?

BRITTEN: No, because I knew they were all human beings.

AALTONEN: Well then, as Moscow is excluded it isn't such a great difference after all.

BRITTEN: I don't quite understand that question, I'm sorry.

AALTONEN: I mean, there would be extremes, in a way, these audiences, if you had Moscow and New York, for instance.

BRITTEN: No, because they are all people. I love the Russians as a nation very much, and there are many Americans to whom I am devoted. And, curiously enough, I find them all human beings.

AALTONEN: I have one more question and it is: we are living in an age of transistor radios and tape recorders and records; should I say *easy* music is heard

[1] *Voices for Today* (1965).

[2] In the event it was performed simultaneously in New York, Paris, and London.

all over the world. There is perhaps a possibility of a decline in the young people's musical education and taste. Do you think there are still enough children interested in other things than just the Beatles and the Rolling Stones?

BRITTEN: Well oddly enough I think in England the children are more interested in serious music than ever before. Education—our state schools are doing more and more to encourage children, and they find them excellent pupils. Of course there are always the moments when children want to dance and play around, and why shouldn't they? I don't think the Beatles by *any* means a wholly bad influence. I think they're charming creatures; I don't happen to like their music very much, but that's just me. But I think it's very natural that light music should exist; but if a person likes the Beatles, it doesn't by any means preclude their love of Beethoven.

AALTONEN: Thank you so much.

79 Dreams (?1965)

I have never been able to eat mushrooms—. One night I dreamed that I was standing on the top of a mountain with a friend. Together we watched the final atomic-bomb explosion, the explosion that was going to end the world as we know it. As we watched the great mushroom-like cloud approaching us, I turned to him & said, quite calmly, 'Now you see why I have never liked mushrooms'.

Editor's title.
Source: Autograph draft, n.d. (*GB-ALb* 1–02053799). Draft of contribution to proposed *Book of Dreams*, planned by the Imperial Cancer Research Fund, *c*.1965.

80 A Composer in Russia (1965)

On the way to the airport we found we were short of things to read, and a hurried search at a bookshop produced the Penguin edition of Pushkin's poems. With the verse in Russian and an English prose translation, this was the ideal supplement to our pre-breakfast struggles with irritatingly forgettable vocabulary and irregular verbs. And so, with Slava and Galya Rostropovich, we flew into Moscow for dinner and drove out to their *dacha* for the night.

Two days later the Armenian hospitality began in all its touching, overwhelming force. We were going merely on a holiday, with Slava as host and ruthless sentry against intrusion—what he called donning imaginary tunic and bearskin, 'a soldier of Buckingham'. Yet up from Yerevan[1] came an important official from the Composers' Union to look after us; and on the plane we were greeted on the loudspeaker by name, and we fastened our seat-belts to instructions in English first, before Russian and Armenian. At dinner in Yerevan that night we had our baptism of fire from Armenian alcoholic toasts.

Next day we were whisked off to the Composers' Colony at Dilidjan, about 100 km. over mountainous roads from Yerevan. Driving up towards the Caucasus through thick fog, we missed the bands of children waving flags and holding flowers for us (though some of them did appear later and said, 'Weelcome', once or twice).

There was a bungalow for us, with Slava and Galya in another, 20 yards along the lane; here we ate a succession of superb meals produced from rather primitive conditions in the cellar by the top Intourist chef, a charming character called Hachik who had cooked for Khruschev and Nehru.[2] And here we settled in for three weeks, 5,000 feet up in a circle of wooded mountains, reading, sunbathing, swimming and picking mushrooms.

A member of the Armenian Composers' Union can spend weeks in this colony with his wife and family for a very small cost. He can either live in one of the individual bungalows, as we did, or in one of the blocks of bed-sitting rooms. In the bungalow he will have a study with a piano, a living room, a bedroom and bath-room, simply but attractively furnished. He will eat in the big central building which also has a library, a room with gramophone and tape-machines, and also contains the administrative offices.

Source: *Sunday Telegraph* (24 Oct. 1965), 15.

[1] Capital of Armenia.

[2] Jawaharlal Nehru (1889–1964), Indian nationalist leader, first prime minister of independent India (1947–64). Nikita Khrushchev (1894–1971), Soviet politician, named First Secretary of the Soviet Union following Stalin's death in 1953. In 1957 he oversaw the Central Committee conference on writers and artists, which prescribed constrictions on artistic freedom. He was deposed by Brezhnev in 1964.

The composers work or meet together and discuss while their families walk, sit in the sun, swim in the big swimming pool, or play that curious 'free' badminton, without court or net, so beloved in northern European countries.

Performers and musicologists are not excluded, but must pay more. The whole enterprise, which also includes an efficient farm, is run and owned by the Composers' Union, with the help of the Armenian Ministry of Culture.

I wish something similar could happen in England, but I fear that composers are still not taken as seriously here as over there, nor have we English composers quite as much public spirit as our Russian colleagues. Would one happily face looking after one's foreign counterparts as Edic Mirzoyan looked after us—devoting almost every minute of every day for a month to our comfort and entertainment, as well as attending to endless duties as Chairman of the Armenian Union?[3]

I decided that setting some Pushkin might help my obstinately bad Russian. I got Slava and Galya to read the poems I chose from the English crib in my Penguin and painstakingly they set about teaching me to pronounce them properly. I worked out a transliteration of six of them, and began setting them to music.

I would write a song, then play it over and get Slava to correct the prosody. It is not perhaps a method I would recommend to composers setting foreign words: it is best to learn the language first. But it was nice to find that I seemed to have got the emphasis right, and have caught something of the mood of these vivid, haunting poems: if I haven't, Pushkin still remains intact!

The result we have called, in Russian 'Echo Poeta', literally 'Poet's Echo'.[4] It is really a dialogue between the poet and the unresponsiveness of the natural world he describes: in one of them, when the thunder sounds or a beast roars, an echo comes back, but the echo itself gets no answer—and this is the poet's nature too. The songs were being done by the Rostropoviches in Moscow a week or so ago.

No atmosphere could have been happier in which to do a holiday task; and the support Russian composers feel in this kind of backing is obviously immensely encouraging to them. The dangers of too much security are so small compared to those of worrying artists as much as we do. I can't believe an artist is often ruined by too much security, and without it one may frighten off potentially useful creators.

With the Russians, being a composer is no more precarious than being a doctor: there is a highly organised system of training, then a carefully worked out life for the artist according to the kind of talent he has developed. It seems

[3] Edvard Mirzoyan (b. 1921), Armenian composer, became head of Armenian Composers' Union in 1957.

[4] *The Poet's Echo* (1965).

that when a composer finally graduates to the Composers' Union, he receives, on application, a subsidy for each work he wishes to write; the size will depend on the nature of the work and the composer's reputation. Then there is a second fee when the work is finished if it is considered suitable for publishing.

Of course, if the work does not please, since the publishers are State-controlled, there is no alternative choice for the composer, no court of appeal, and the work gets shelved. But there does seem a genuine reluctance to turn works down (perhaps too much), and a genuine desire to overcome purely ideological prejudice. And of course unjustified failures are not exactly unknown in the West either.

The modern Russians accept culture as a basic part of national life, requiring proper conditions so that it can produce the greatest possible benefits. Thus everyone who is accepted as worthwhile becomes part of a system of cultural activity that extends over the whole of the enormous area of the Soviet Union.

The hunger for music and art which is felt in remote villages and settlements is something very moving to hear about, and it is very keenly fostered. Many of us have seen the simple peasant types crowding the Moscow and Leningrad museums. Both Slavas, Rostropovich and Richter, treasure their tours to small towns and villages all over the Union (as Rostropovich has already written in *The Sunday Telegraph*) and this seems common to all the great Soviet artists.

Slava Rostropovich told me that he, and artists of his rank, can decide where he wants to go to play, and Gosconcert, the State agency, has to arrange it;[5] he even gets more for playing outside the major cities, Moscow, Leningrad and Kiev. He gets all of his very considerable fee for playing even in the tiniest villages: they find what funds they can, and Gosconcert makes up the difference.

We heard a certain amount of the music of the Armenian composers, and were quite impressed by some of it. Mirzoyan has written a personal symphony for Strings and Timpani, Bobodjanyan some exciting piano pieces (he is a superb pianist himself).[6] And the two central movements of Arutunyan's Symphony are charming and full of character, though the outer movements are too rhetorical and sprawling for my taste.[7]

That is the weakness of many of the symphonies in Russia today: one gets the feeling that they are written to satisfy a demand only, and not from aesthetic conviction. It is difficult to write Tchaikovsky-like symphonies today, as Russian audiences (one is told) seem to demand; good big tunes, for one

[5] Infamous Soviet concert agency, which was also responsible for administrating the Central Committee's vetting of programmes and artists for tours abroad.

[6] Arno Harutyuni Babadjanian (1921–83), Armenian composer and pianist.

[7] Alexander Arutunyan (b. 1920), Armenian composer, made Artistic Director of Armenian Philharmonic Orchestra in 1954 and perhaps best known in the West for his trumpet concerto.

thing, are difficult to find. I tactfully suggested that a small by-law might be made restricting double-octave string writing for a few years. The point was taken, I think.

But one must underline the fact that the inspiration of the Revolution is, genuinely, still with them: so it is completely natural for them, not least for Shostakovich, to celebrate events that have affected all their lives. Our trouble is so often that we are too introspective and shut-off, and this really bothers the Russians about a lot of Western music; whereas they in the East have so much communicative urge that they, unless very gifted, tend to become rather hollow.

So the days passed, surrounded in kindness, with excursions to neighbouring places. One was up a tortuous road to a monument on top of a mountain where Pushkin had met a procession carrying a coffin, and discovered inside it the body of his friend the playwright Griboyedov, murdered by the Persians.[8]

The last four days of our visit, we were told, had to be spent in Yerevan. It emerged that they had arranged a complete five-day festival in our honour—an orchestral concert, two chamber concerts (including both of my string quartets, piano pieces, many songs and folk song arrangements), recitals (including my cello suite and sonata), a concert-reception for Peter Pears in which he spoke at length about musical life in England (with Slava as gallant 'Aldeburgh-Deutsch' interpreter), gramophone performances of the whole of 'Peter Grimes' and the 'War Requiem'.[9] Defying Slava, the Soldier of Buckingham, we did actually do half a concert ourselves. It was all a charming compliment, but very strenuous in the almost tropical heat of Yerevan.

And then it was back to the north, and marathon drives in Slava's new Mercedes around Novgorod, Pskov and so to Pushkin's home, where, with that extraordinary Russian timelessness that we never could get used to, we arrived a whole day late to find our host and hostess had stayed up all the previous night waiting quite calmly.

At Mikhailovskoye there is the family estate where he was born and lived and worked and, when exiled there, had to worship once a day in the little nearby church, when the famous bell struck one.[10] It is remote, but 200,000 people go there every year to pay their homage. The Russian love for Pushkin cannot be exaggerated, and it finds perfect expression in this miraculously beautiful group of wooden houses surrounded by forests of enormous trees, peaceful lakes and streams.

[8] Alexander Griboyedov (1795–1829), Russian playwright and diplomat, killed defending the Tehran embassy against Persian attack.

[9] 'Aldeburgh Deutsch', the somewhat corrupted German spoken by Britten, Pears, and Rostropovich.

[10] The bell of the village church that summoned Pushkin to daily worship when he was in exile.

PART IV

*

1966–1976

'My mind beats on'

INTRODUCTION AND CHRONOLOGY

Britten's final opera, *Death in Venice* (1973), opens with the fraught character of Aschenbach, a distinguished novelist, deliberating on his creative block: 'My mind beats on and no words come'. Having reached a point in life when the creative ideas that had supported Aschenbach no longer did so, art and intellect, long united in his work, break apart. Although comparisons have frequently been made between Aschenbach and Britten, on this one point they are opposites, for in this final period of Britten's life his intellect and his music overlap—not with the didactic urgency of his early years, but with a lucid introspection brought on by fame, withdrawal, and eventual sickness. He continued in his role as artistic conscience to a corrupted society, but in his music, not his words. *Owen Wingrave* (1970), *Children's Crusade* (1969) and (less obviously) *Who are these Children?* (1969), each picks up the mantle of the *War Requiem* to warn against the horrors and moral turpitude of war. The mantle is not simply this pacifist theme, either: ambiguity, one of Britten's favourite dramatic devices, is exchanged (on some levels) for clarity and certainty, as it had been in the *War Requiem*. Each of these pieces is recognizably Britten's, yet the layers of narrative and musical ambiguity so favoured by him in his dramatic works from 1945 onwards, are less important here than getting the message across. Even *Death in Venice* operates as a plea for tolerance and understanding of the creative mind, if not for the hidden sexuality that mind might harbour.

These pieces, and a handful in the first part of the decade, marked out the 1960s and early 1970s as a period of dark, intimate works—an exploration of the abyss, in Aschenbach's words ('But this is beauty, Phaedrus, | Discovered through the senses | And senses lead to passion, Phaedrus | And passion to the abyss').[1] In *Curlew River* (1964) and the *Songs and Proverbs of William Blake* (1965), Britten initiated a darker style that would dominate his compositional ideas for the remainder of his life. Even *The Golden Vanity* (1966), his 'vaudeville' written for the Vienna Boys' Choir, is morally unrelenting—a boy's own *Billy Budd*. Next to these, the gaiety of *A Birthday Hansel* (1975) seems contrived, almost out of place—of course befitting its role as birthday tribute to the Queen Mother. *Hankin Booby* (1966), rescued from its commissioned origins and placed into the *Suite on English Folk Tunes* (1974), reminds listeners that this work is no mere romp through Pastoral England, but is instead centred

[1] *Death in Venice*, Scene 16.

around a nightmare of almost Berliozian intensity and hallucinogenic power. If this is not enough, Britten's subtitle to this folk collection, 'A time there was'—Hardy's prayer for nescience, for the innocence of ignorance, amidst human hopelessness—is an indication of the dark mood prevailing.

His musical language changed, too—not simply in the mild notational indeterminacy of the Parables, which quickly made its way into other genres, but in the sparse textures now employed, and the smaller forces required to articulate these new musical arguments. And the frantic pace at which new works were produced slowed—perhaps in recognition of his busy recording schedule, perhaps because his focus was more and more on Aldeburgh, a commitment that resulted in the opening of the Snape Maltings Concert Hall in 1967.

Although, like Aschenbach, words came more slowly to Britten in this final period, when they did they were on remarkably personal themes: his playful, vibrant ideas about his old friend E. M. Forster (Essay 90); his honest and revealing interview with Donald Mitchell (Essay 91); his thoughts on Mozart's *Idomeneo* (Essay 94) and Percy Grainger (Essay 102). Yet it is difficult not to think that in the latter part of this period Britten, with his 'one skin less', was more than anyone aware that his time left was limited: he channelled almost all of his creative energies into what he would have considered his only real legacy, his music. Even today, the moral, ethical, and creative arguments put forward in *Death in Venice* seem audacious. Yet Britten protected himself and his latest child by talking or writing about anything but the new opera he was then composing. The mental energy required to articulate such private thoughts, and to keep them as philosophically complicated on stage as they were in the composer's mind, marks out this opera as the creative culmination of many of the themes that weave through the earlier stage works. Quite whether they are resolved or merely explored is less clear; ambiguity, Britten's creative friend, was once more a guiding force.

1966 Abdominal operation; recital tours with Pears in Austria and later in Soviet Union; revises *Gloriana* for new Sadler's Wells production; completes second Church Parable *The Burning Fiery Furnace*, Op. 77; composes *The Golden Vanity*, Op. 78, and, for the opening of Queen Elizabeth Hall, *Hankin Booby*, which later becomes a movement of the *Suite on English Folk Tunes*, Op. 90.

1967 With Imogen Holst, realizes new edition of Purcell's *The Fairy Queen*; composes *The Building of the House*, Op. 79, to inaugurate Snape Maltings Concert Hall in the presence of Queen Elizabeth II, at the beginning of the twentieth Aldeburgh Festival; tours with EOG to Montreal, and with Pears to New York and South America; records *Billy Budd*; composes Second Suite for Cello, Op. 80, for Rostropovich.

1968 Commences work on his BBC television commission, *Owen Wingrave*; composes *The Prodigal Son*, Op. 81; receives Sonning Prize; revises childhood songs as *Tit for Tat*; with Pears, records little-known repertory of Grainger, sparking renewed interest in him.

1969 Conducts *Peter Grimes* for BBC television; completes *Children's Crusade*, Op. 82; Snape Maltings Concert Hall burns down at the start of the twenty-second Aldeburgh Festival; composes Suite for Harp, Op. 83, and *Who are these Children?*, Op. 84.

1970 EOG tour and recital tour, with Pears, of Australia; conducts Mozart's *Idomeneo* for BBC television and then in the rebuilt concert hall as part of the Aldeburgh Festival; completes *Owen Wingrave*, Op. 85, which he conducts in television premiere.

1971 Composes Canticle IV 'Journey of the Magi', Op. 86, and Third Suite for Cello, Op. 87; records Bach's *St John Passion*, Elgar's *Dream of Gerontius*, and works by Mozart and Schubert; participates in another festival of British music in Soviet Union.

1972 Diagnosed with heart disease, although refuses operation until *Death in Venice* is completed; gives what turns out to be final performance as conductor (Schumann's *Scenes from Goethe's Faust* for Decca).

1973 Gives last public recitals with Pears in Germany (programme includes Schubert's *Winterreise*); completes *Death in Venice*, Op. 88, which is conducted by Steuart Bedford at its premiere in the twenty-sixth Aldeburgh Festival and in the later London season; undergoes heart surgery, which is only partly successful, leaving him unable to play piano, conduct, or compose without difficulty; sixtieth birthday is celebrated.

1974 Revises String Quartet in D (1931) and makes minor alterations to *Death in Venice* prior to its Decca recording; oversees performance of excerpts from *Paul Bunyan* (1941) in Festival; composes Canticle V 'The Death of Saint Narcissus', Op. 89, for Pears and his new recital partner, harpist Osian Ellis, and *Suite on English Folk Tunes*, Op. 90, 'A time there was . . .'.

1975 Revises *Paul Bunyan*; completes *Sacred and Profane*, Op. 91, and, at Queen Elizabeth's request, composes *A Birthday Hansel*, Op. 92, in celebration of the seventy-fifth birthday of the Queen Mother; attends productions of *Death in Venice* and *Peter Grimes* (with Jon Vickers as Grimes) at Covent Garden; composes *Phaedra*, Op. 93, for Janet Baker, and String Quartet No. 3, Op. 94, incorporating musical and extra-musical themes from *Death in Venice*.

1976 Creates new version of *Lachrymae*, Op. 48 (1950) with orchestral accompaniment; is made a Life Peer; arranges eight folksongs for voice and harp; composes *Welcome Ode*, Op. 95, and commences work on *Praise We Great Men* which remains incomplete at his death on 4 December.

81 Sir Arthur Bliss at 75 (1966)

My dear Arthur,

When one is very young, tales of one's elders' youthful exploits set one's sympathy strongly vibrating . . . 'so they know too what it is to be young and frustrated'. In my boyhood you, Arthur, twenty years older than myself, were the avant-gardist of *Rout* and *Conversations* and daring (possibly apocryphal) Parisian exploits.[1] You were almost a myth.

When one is very young no one is growing older, least of all oneself: time may pass, but we stand still. For me the zestful avant-gardist of *Madame Noy* still peeps out of the silvery halo of today.[2] Happy you, who can preserve youthful exuberance without youthful immaturity!

So today's young will perhaps find it difficult to equate The Master of the Queen's Musick with the avant garde of 1920.[3] If they are not blind they will make a note that Youth's the Season made for Joys—not for Responsibility.[4] At twenty-five or so the Plateau of Responsibility comes into sight, and once on it, we are there for good.

You, Arthur, have given us fifty years of active responsibility. Few of your juniors have not been helped directly or indirectly by your practical benevolence. British music, and music in general, has profited by your experience and wisdom—on the BBC, the British Council and the PRS, to name only a few. And we do not forget your compositions, which so many choral and orchestral societies, singers and chamber groups (often starved of playable new works) continue to enjoy.[5]

We, thousands of us, send you our warmest thanks for all this, and, since you are the youngest 75 imaginable, look forward confidently to many more years of tireless energy and sane guidance.

Yours ever,
Ben

Source: *Performing Right Society Bulletin* (Aug. 1966), 3.

1 *The Rout Trot* (1927) for piano and *Conversations* (1920) for chamber ensemble.

2 *Madam Noy* (1918) for soprano.

3 Bliss was Master of the Queen's Musick from 1953 up until his death in 1975.

4 An adaptation of a lyric from Act 1 of Gay's *The Beggar's Opera*, in which Macheath sings to the ladies: 'Youth's the season made for joys, | Love is then our duty; | She alone who that employs | Well deserves her beauty. | Let's be gay | While we may, | Beauty's a flower despised in decay.' Britten would have known it well from his 1948 realization of the work.

5 Two works by Bliss were given their premieres at Aldeburgh: his Cello Concerto, Op. 107 (1970), and *The world is charged with the grandeur of God*, Op. 136 (1969). Britten had set the Hopkins poem himself in 1938 in his radio cantata *The World of the Spirit*.

82 Benjamin Britten Talks to Edmund Tracey (1966)

TRACEY: It is a great honour and pleasure for us to have you back at the Wells after twenty-odd years. I wonder if you could throw your mind back to the occasion of 'Peter Grimes', your first opera for the Wells: when you started to write it, had you had any sense of musical tradition or direction or did you just trust your own instinct?

BRITTEN: The history of the first performance of 'Peter Grimes' at the Wells is really too well known for me to go into it now, but the actual background of the performances there is perhaps rather interesting. I did feel at that time that there was a great void in English opera. English operas had been written in the previous fifty years, but none of them meant much to me—and I had to find my own language. But I had a great piece of luck, and that was that I was able to go to rehearsals and performances of virtually the whole of the repertoire of the Wells at that time. I had friends who were singing in the Company and as I was planning 'Grimes' and actually writing it, I made use of the opportunity of getting to know the repertory extremely well. I learned a tremendous amount, particularly from 'The Magic Flute', 'Traviata', 'The Bartered Bride' and 'The Barber of Seville'.[1] I felt particularly sympathetic to these, but I also learned a lot from the ones to which I was not so sympathetic. But there was something else: at that time I was very much involved with institutions like, for instance, Morley College,[2] where Michael Tippett was Musical Director and we were both tremendously sympathetic to the music of Purcell, from whom I learned an enormous amount about the setting of the English language, about its rhythms, its sonorities. That gave me a greater sense of confidence and of not being quite so alone as I might have felt.

TRACEY: I notice that you mention 'The Magic Flute' and 'Traviata', and one of the questions I was going to ask you was this: were Mozart, Verdi and Berg particularly important to you as influences? What about 'Wozzeck' for instance?

BRITTEN: 'Wozzeck' had, for about ten years, played a great part in my life, not only, I may say musically, but also psychologically and emotionally.

Source: *Sadler's Wells Magazine* (Autumn 1966), 5–7.

[1] In addition to his roles in *La Bohème* and *La traviata*, Pears performed Almaviva (*The Barber of Seville*), Tamino (*The Magic Flute*), Vašek (*The Bartered Bride*), and Ferrando (*Così fan tutte*) for Sadler's Wells during 1943–4. Joan Cross was Fiordiligi in this production of *Così*.

[2] Morley College, founded in 1889, is an adult-education centre, and has boasted many significant music directors, including Gustav Holst, Michael Tippett, Peter Racine Fricker, and John Gardner.

Particularly as war approached us, of course, the figure of the lonely, miserable soldier trapped in the great machine of war was something I thought about and felt for deeply; in many ways I am aware now that I was strongly influenced by 'Wozzeck' when I wrote 'Grimes'. I am not at all ashamed of this: on the contrary I think I should have been very silly if I hadn't made use of this great master. The influence of Mozart and Verdi, of course, is more obvious. The wonderful stagecraft and wit and aptness of Mozart; Verdi's trust in melody and his sense of form—both these composers taught me a great deal. I was particularly influenced by the sectional division of the operas which Verdi used all his life—working on different dramatic layers rather than the one slope up and down that other composers have used.

TRACEY: Since you started to write operas, there could be said to be a real English school developing. Though there were isolated cases before—a few operas by Vaughan Williams and Holst and so on—there wasn't the same interest in writing opera that there is now, when almost all the young composers are looking for subjects and wanting to write for the opera house. Do you have a sense of personal achievement in having influenced this course of events, or do you think it would have happened anyway?

BRITTEN: I think it would have happened anyway with the operatic development that has taken place in this country: first the emergence of the two big repertory theatres at Covent Garden and Sadler's Wells, then the Welsh and Scottish National operas and our own English Opera Group. Where there is a genuine demand, nearly always that demand is fulfilled. But I think the fact that 'Grimes' was a success did spark this off perhaps sooner than it might otherwise have happened. However, I must emphasise that we all felt incredibly depressed by the break-up of Sadler's Wells, as we knew it, immediately after the war: suddenly there seemed to be no future for English opera at all. What one wasn't prepared for was the emergence of Covent Garden so soon: I was probably wrong not to realise that that would probably have given one a stage to work for, but it didn't seem at all likely or even possible at that time.

TRACEY: Are there purely aesthetic factors governing the graph of your operas? I mean, after 'Grimes', which was a full-scale chorus opera, you wrote two chamber operas, then after that there were two large-scale works, 'Billy Budd' and 'Gloriana', but since 'Gloriana' in 1953, with the exception of 'A Midsummer Night's Dream,' you haven't written large pieces and have tended to concentrate on smaller forms. I wonder whether this is an aesthetic principle with you, or is it governed by musical personalities and politics and the fact that you don't like living in London?

BRITTEN: I find it very difficult to answer that question, because when one is making something one doesn't really know what starts it off—whether it is one's own impulse, one's own imagination, or whether it can be the result of outside forces. I would think, in my own case, that the outside stimulus is extremely strong, particularly where operas are concerned. I think I would have been wrong to have written another big opera immediately after 'Peter Grimes', because there was no stage to put it on. Unlike most composers of today, it seems, I am greatly stimulated by the outside influence. The singer, the player, the place of the performance—all these give me ideas, and I don't think, if the result is good, that that is necessarily a bad thing. It would have been silly to go on writing big operas when there didn't seem to be a platform for them, and the series of little operas which I started with 'Lucretia' and 'Albert Herring' somehow seemed more suitable first for Glyndebourne and then for the English Opera Group. These pieces are making their way only slowly in this country—that is perhaps inevitable, since we have so little immediate operatic history and therefore we cling to what we know best—but in Germany, which is a country much more naturally responsive to opera, these little pieces have gone very well, and I think have contributed something to the operatic medium which I hope composers will use when they want to write something that fits that scale. The other thing, as you say very observantly about my environment, my life does tend, through the Aldeburgh Festival and other things, to have settled down in the country—in the provincial life rather than in the metropolitan. I like at the moment to write pieces which suit the buildings and the occasions down in Suffolk. That is how these small operas have continued, and the church pieces like 'Curlew River' and 'The Burning Fiery Furnace' have developed; although, of course, when occasion has demanded, I have been happy to go back to the bigger forms in 'Budd' and 'Gloriana'. Perhaps I could say a word here about the church operas, which come really from an inclination I have had, ever since I was a child, for what I might perhaps call the 'Gothic acoustic': where the note reverberates for some time after it is struck or sung, an acoustic which produces a string of notes together, its own form of harmony; and although this is not the only reason I started on these church operas, it was, I think, a very strong one. Another point: the development of technique in our instrumentalists, without a comparable development in conducting technique, has been relevant. I am obviously not going to name names, but so often you find a really first-class orchestra suffering under a not very gifted or very intelligent or technically developed conductor; and in these church operas I have given a great deal of responsibility to the player—even the responsibility of following the singers, which after a certain amount of experience they do brilliantly and easily—and this has led to a level of seriousness and creativity in the playing which you don't always get when there is a conductor leading. I know conductors are rather cross about this, and perhaps they have reason to be so, but I can assure them that you cannot, as far as I can see at the moment, have a full operatic outfit—chorus and soloists and full orchestra—without a conductor, so they must take heart!

TRACEY: Can we talk a bit about how you like to have your own team of singers and instrumentalists, with whom you work over and over again? Do you find this particularly stimulating, or does it imply that standards in general are not as high as you would wish them to be?

BRITTEN: I think the answer to that is a rather curious one. It is that I think music-making is a co-operative affair, and it is very nice to work with people with whom you are in sympathy. I enjoy rehearsals enormously when they are done with people I like—people who are good players and good singers. I get irritated if they are bored, or if they can't or won't do what one wants. And therefore one tends to have a group, which I hope is also enlarging all the time, of players and singers with whom I like to work and who, I fancy, like the circumstances under which we work. Again, if you know a singer, you know what he or she can do, and that is a stimulant. You also, perhaps, know what they can't do, and that in its way is a stimulant too—as limitations always are.

TRACEY: I am interested by the fact that, unlike Mozart and Verdi and Puccini, you don't seem to like to work over and over again with the same librettist. Do you find the libretto problem particularly difficult?

BRITTEN: You are right in saying that I haven't often used the same librettist, but that has usually been because the librettists have been writers with work of their own to do or because I didn't feel they would be sympathetic to the subject I was about to launch on. For instance, take the case of E. M. Forster: he now feels too old to tackle a big creative work. In the case of William Plomer, a writer with whom I have worked quite frequently in the last two years or so, and who of course did 'Gloriana' with me, he, being a distinguished writer, has a large number of other things to do as well, and cannot always make himself free to work with me; but whenever possible, I like to work with him because his gifts are very special. His writing is succinct and clear and beautifully lyrical; he has a way of putting words together so that they belong to each other absolutely. Another librettist whom I have just worked with for the first time is Colin Graham, on a little opera I have written for the Vienna Boys' Choir.[3] Here I needed a person

[3] Colin Graham (b. 1931), English director and designer, associated with the English Opera Group (1961–75), English National Opera (1967–75), and English Music Theatre (1975–80). In this time he directed first performances of the three Church Parables; *The Golden Vanity* (1966) written for the Vienna Boys' Choir to his own libretto; *Owen Wingrave* (1970) with Brian Large; and *Death in Venice* (1973).

with great knowledge of stage-craft and stage movements as well as a sensitive feeling for words—and Colin was ideal for this.

TRACEY: William Plomer says that you had thought of doing an opera on the subject of Elizabeth and Essex long before there was any question of an official commission for the Coronation. If you hadn't had to consider this official occasion, do you think you might have made it a more intimate work in scale?

BRITTEN: I think that is possible. I know that we consciously planned the work for the Coronation year to show off certain facets of English musical life such as the remarkable ballet and choral singing, and we also wanted to use a large number of singers. I don't think we were wrong in doing this, because if you want to give a just picture of the Elizabethan age you need to show the rich ceremonial aspects of life at that time. But I must confess that both Plomer and I were principally interested in the extraordinarily tense relationship of the two protagonists, and of course in the strong supporting characters like Cecil and Walter Raleigh.

TRACEY: How do you feel now that 'Gloriana' is going to be staged again after this long gap? I think it is the only one of your operas that hasn't been remounted since it was first done. I wonder if you feel a particular affection for it?

BRITTEN: I do feel a particular affection for it, and not only, I think, a sentimental one as a mother may feel about a slighted child. I feel that this work does say something which at that time I wanted to say very clearly, and I hope people will get from it what I want to give them. Whether it's a good piece or one of my best operas I am not objective enough to say; but looking at it again and looking at it with the members of the Sadler's Wells team in it, I am very pleased indeed that it is being done.

TRACEY: There is one aspect of it that I would like to talk to you about. I am personally fascinated by the fact that quite often at a climactic moment in your operas you abandon vocal melody and put your trust either in speech or in the orchestra. I am thinking of the last words of Balstrode to Grimes; of the series of triadic chords after Billy Budd's trial; of the long scene that the Queen has at the end of 'Gloriana'; of 'Peter Quint, you devil' in 'The Turn of the Screw'; and I wonder if there is any special dramatic design in this?

BRITTEN: There is not a very conscious one, certainly. But in each of the cases you mention I felt, after reflection, that the silence of the singing voice would be more effective than the voice continuing to sing. At the end of 'Grimes', the shock of the spoken word and the silence before the orchestra comes in to herald the beginning of a new day: that pattern is important, I think.[4] The end of 'Gloriana' gave William Plomer and me a great deal of trouble—we wanted to focus very much on the Queen in a different way from before and we wanted to do something quite fresh with the time element. In the case of 'Peter Quint, you devil', I think I probably wanted something that the little voice of a child singing, in its normal way couldn't give, and therefore the free shouting, although it lost the value of the controlled note, communicated a sense of absolute release—which was dramatically very important. So, you see, in every case there was a specific dramatic reason; but I wouldn't go so far as to enunciate a general principle in the matter.

TRACEY: Since the very few later works of Strauss and Puccini that hold the stage, there don't seem to be many operas that pull the audiences in; chiefly Berg and Stravinsky and yourself, in fact. Do you think that this betokens a decline in the art of opera in general?

BRITTEN: I think it may show a decline in the operatic public—I mean that the opera public is perhaps more old-fashioned than the concert public. It may show that the operatic composer is too inhibited, that the fashion which dictates that the composer cannot write in the way that the ordinary opera-singer can, or likes to, sing makes it impossible for him to produce the vehicle that the public likes. I think that the composer has also lost his public, except in very special cases like Stravinsky; but let's not forget that in Germany Henze still has a public for his operas, and I'm sure this is partly because he is less inhibited than most of his colleagues over there.

[4] The spoken dialogue at the end of *Peter Grimes* was originally much longer than the short, effective exchange of sentences.

Balstrode (*speaking*): I'll help you with your boat now.

Peter (*speaking*): Why?

Balstrode: You can put yourself out to sea, out of sight of this town, then sink your boat.

Peter: You mean?

Balstrode: Go down with the boat. It's the best thing you can do. The plug moves easily. You know what to do.

Peter: What do you want of me?

Balstrode: We'll launch you now. There is no need to go far. Sail out till you lose sight of the Moot Hall. Then you can't be seen from the shore, and you know what to do. She's a good boat & she's yours. You wouldn't want to leave her for another man to sail. Sail her out. Then say good bye to your boat, & good bye to the Boar, & say your prayers. Goodbye Peter.

Peter: This is too early.

Balstrode: No. The Searchers will be turning home soon. Better not meet them here. Once at sea & alone, you'll know what to do. You understand? Not till the Moot Hall is out of sight.

See Paul Banks (ed.), *The Making of Peter Grimes I: Facsimile of Benjamin Britten's composition draft* (Woodbridge: The Boydell Press, 1996), 117^{r}.

TRACEY: But in Germany, where I think you would agree there is a natural opera-going public and people go to the opera in the way that people in this country go to the theatre, a composer like Giselher Klebe, for instance, who is not perhaps outstandingly gifted, can write operas which are put on and very successfully received.[5] Is it that audiences there are more adventurous than here?

BRITTEN: I think audiences there are more trained. They have their series of operas, they nearly all subscribe to the series, and if there is a new opera staged, the inclination is not to waste their tickets but to go. I think that is a very good thing: people may go to the theatre for the wrong reason but they may stay for the right one. I only wish to goodness that we had something like that here. All of us—the public, critics, and composers themselves—spend far too much time worrying about whether a work is a shattering masterpiece. Let us not be so self-conscious. Maybe in thirty years' time very few works that are well known today will still be played, but does that matter so much? Surely out of the works that are written some good will come, even if it is not now; and these will lead on to people who are better than ourselves.

TRACEY: Quite. One must have a real living connection between the artist and his public; otherwise he is working in a vacuum.

BRITTEN: Yes, I feel that very strongly, and one has said it very loud and clear: why bother to write works down if you don't care whether people listen and respond to them or not? Why not just keep them in all their glory in your brain?

TRACEY: Are there any contemporary composers whose work particularly interests you?

BRITTEN: Oh yes, I am interested in a large number, and I only wish that one's life was a bit freer and one could get to hear them: Michael Tippett, of course, and Lennox Berkeley[6] and the many other English composers whom I am always interested to know about. Walton is writing a new opera for us next year, and I shall be fascinated to see what that is like.[7] And then the young ones, who I think are most enterprising and good. If Max Davies is getting on with his opera I shall be most excited about that.[8] Abroad, to me the most touching and important figure of Shostakovich always interests me with every new work; I don't say that I can always understand them, or that I always understand what he is after, but he has an interesting mind

[5] Giselher Klebe (b. 1925), German composer, who has written over ten operas.

[6] Lennox Berkeley (1903–89), English composer and friend of Britten's from the 1930s.

[7] William Walton (1902–83) wrote *The Bear* (1967) for Aldeburgh, where it was given its first performance in 1967.

[8] There is no extant correspondence between Maxwell Davies and Britten concerning a proposed opera, although Britten here is probably referring to his first opera, *Taverner* (1962–70).

and is a great, great figure. Henze in Germany, Aaron Copland in America—there are many others.[9]

TRACEY: Would you like to say at all what you think it is that audiences find so difficult in much modern music?

BRITTEN: I think it is the actual language: that is the thing that composers don't always, perhaps, realize—that music has got to have a clear connection, it has got to have overtones. That is why I myself cannot work without some kind of—to put it in its simplest way—tonal centre. I must have a form of scale—though I don't say it must be a scale that people know or like. I think that one of the things that an audience unconsciously feels is the tension that comes from having an established scale or mode—a recognisable centre which you can depart from and return to. The other thing, I think, that the public does find very difficult about a certain amount of music written today is the broken quality of it, the endless succession of isolated notes. Although the composer may feel passionately that the notes are connected, the ordinary public takes a very long time to follow those notes: and the result is that they are baffled and bored.

TRACEY: It's particularly difficult for them to remember the notes, isn't it?

BRITTEN: Virtually impossible. In one way, I think, the twelve-tone system could have got a larger public quicker: if it had, like the Indian Raga, announced its scale first, it might have imprinted it quicker on the mind of the public. I find it myself extremely difficult to work out the scales. I know Schoenberg says that he doesn't mind if people work them out or not, but that doesn't seem to be borne out by the way people write and talk about this sort of music; I think it would be a real advantage if you knew the order of the twelve notes because then you could follow it and the intellect could help the emotions to get going.

TRACEY: Do you want to say anything about future operatic plans other than the Vienna Boys' Choir piece?

BRITTEN: Well, I am certainly going to do another church opera quite soon, and the Vienna Boys' Choir piece is finished; and then I am planning another full-size opera, but I don't at the moment want to talk about it because people always hold you to what you innocently announce.[10] They are always saying 'Why isn't "King Lear" ready?'—it was a bad moment when I ever mentioned that I was going to do that!

TRACEY: Do you think that put a jinx on it?

BRITTEN: I'm sure it did!

[9] Hans Werner Henze had a close association with Britten and Aldeburgh, as did Aaron Copland.

[10] In the early 1960s Desmond Shawe-Taylor announced Britten's intention to write an opera based on Shakespeare's *King Lear*.

83 Tribute to Dmitry Shostakovitch (1966)

It must have been in 1936 or so, when I had not long since left the Royal College of Music, my mind greedy for every musical experience to come my way, that I went to the old Queen's Hall, London, to hear a concert performance of an opera by a new, young Russian composer, not many of whose works had reached England. In my experience a concert performance of an opera does not often succeed in giving much idea of its dramatic impact. But this one, of Lady MacBeth of Mtzensk (as it was then called) was a knock-out.[1] I imagine it was well done, enough anyhow to give me a sense of the violence, the irony, the tenderness, and the deep tragedy of the final Act. I was thrilled; I felt this music was new and personal, although stemming naturally from the great Russian past, and, in a wonderful way, relaxed and fluent. It used methods from all periods, and yet remained strikingly characteristic. I was furious with the attitude of the Intelligentsia [*sic*] sitting in the stalls, laughing and (I thought) sneering. The critics could not fit this music into any school: not that of the (then) all powerful Sibelius, nor Hindemith, nor Schönberg (gathering momentum among the young), nor Stravinsky (famous for his early masterpieces, but disapproved of for anything after 1920). In fact it could not be classified at all, and that, as we know, is always disturbing.

That performance of Katerina Ismailovna started a deep attachment to the works of Dmitry Shostakovitch. This close connection has never broken, and the faith in his wonderful gift has remained constant. What a pleasure, therefore, when many years later I met Dmitry Dmitriyevich, to find the man as lovable, as characteristic, as great and contemporary as his music. (This experience, like so many other happy ones, came through the good offices of our dear friend Slava Rostropovitch, who loves and honours Dmitry more even than I do—because he knows him better). And what a thrill to find that the great man admitted to receiving pleasure from my own works—so very different from his own, but conceived, many of them, in the same period, children of similar fathers, and with many of the same aims.

I have, in the last few days, been reading the scores of two of his finest Symphonies, the Fourth and the Fifth.[2] I am amazed that the same man could write them both—the Fourth so prolific with ideas, with a tumultuous

Editor's title

Source: Second draft [typed], n.d. (*GB-ALb* 1-02053817). Article appeared in a collection of essays on Shostakovich (Moscow: Sovetskii Kompozitor, 1967), 80–3.

[1] See Essay 1 and the brief footnote on Shostakovich's revisions and change in title.

[2] No. 4 in C minor, Op. 43 (1935–6), withdrawn during rehearsal and first performed in 1961; No. 5 in D minor ('A Soviet Artist's Practical Creative Reply to Just Criticism'), Op. 47 (1937).

exuberance, amounting at times to wildness, but with always a musical heart to sustain it, and never an empty or pointless gesture—the Fifth, so controlled, so classical, neat even, in spite of its energy. It is the musical heart which links these two works together.

But, much as I admire the Symphonies and the opera, to me Shostakovich speaks most closely and most personally in his chamber music. There is a time in every artist's life when he wishes to communicate intimate thoughts to a few friends—and I do not mean only his actual friends, but people unknown to him, who have souls sensitive to his (people from all over the world, whatever race or colour). And for this one doesn't need the man[3] of full chorus or orchestra and the big halls and theatre, but small groups of performers and small halls, sometimes only private rooms. I am thinking now of the Bach solo suites, our Elizabethan madrigals, the Haydn and Beethoven quartets, the Mozart Quintets, Schubert's songs, the Tschaikovsky Trio, the Quartets of Bartok and Debussy. And I also think of the Quartets of Shostakovitch (such as the wonderful Eighth, and the amazing new Ninth and Tenth), and the tragic Piano Trio.

The achievement of Shostakovitch is tremendous, and it is wonderful to realise that he is still a mere 60, with many years more to write in, and give joy, pleasure, hope and sympathy to countless people all over the world. I salute him on his Sixtieth Birthday, Dmitry Shostakovitch; great composer, great man, and I am proud to say, great friend.

[3] 'mass' in handwritten first draft.

84 Tribute to Zoltán Kodály (1967)

A great man has gone from us.[1] Not only a great musician but a great human being, and a very contemporary one. By that I do not mean necessarily a fashionable contemporary composer—Kodaly was beyond & above that. But he was a man who was able to make sense of contemporary life. He was there. He did not avoid problems. He remained and triumphed. And out of the problems he produced solutions which have changed our way of thinking. He made sense. He lived a long life, but to the end, kept his vitality, & his faculties. In Budapest when we saw him, late in the Autumn of last year, he was as lively as I have ever seen him. He talked animatedly about musical education, Ansermet's recent provocative essays on science & music,[2] the Winterreise, the reaction of the present day, urban, young to folksong. He was awareness itself about the problems of contemporary art. It is difficult to realise that he is no longer among us. But what a legacy he has left. Superb choral works, the Psalmus Hungaricus, stage works which still hold the stage, Hary Janos, & excellent chamber music, and, what I perhaps personally cherish the most—a volume of two hundred pages—folk-songs, collected by him & Bartok, arranged for childrens voices. They are of an originality, simplicity yet richness, which is startling. We can all learn from these, from their beauty of sound, freshness, their multum in parvo.[3] One is reminded of his famous words 'nobody is too great to write for children; in fact he should try to become great enough for it.' Not only did he leave these endless miniature masterpieces for children, but he worked for & re-planned their musical education—new methods of sight reading & vocal training, new curricula. One result of his educational efforts is that at this moment over 80 of the state schools in Hungary (& I do not mean the musical schools) have one hour's general music period every day. And with excellent young [young] men & women to teach the youngsters—I have seen some of them at work.

Many of us will never forget the happy days at the Aldeburgh Festival, 2 years ago, when he & his young wife were our guests, along with the Kodaly girls choir from Budapest, who sang many of his pieces. We tried to tell him

Editor's title

Source: Autograph draft of radio script (*GB-ALb* 1–02053827). Broadcast 7 Mar. 1967, BBC Central European (Hungarian) Service: tribute on the death of Kodály. (Recorded same day.) A final script does not survive, although an edited sound recording does (NSA LP30809/1LP0194968). Although there some changes in the later radio version, the original draft is published here since it is longer and more revealing.

[1] Zoltán Kodály (1882–1967), Hungarian composer and teacher, had died on 6 Mar.

[2] *Les fondements de la musique dans la conscience humaine* (2 vols.), published in 1961.

[3] *multum in parvo*: a great deal in a small compass.

by our words, presence & applause how much we owed to him, how much we loved him. He brushed all this gently aside, & got on with the business of rehearsals, concerts, meeting people, young & old, driving around, for him, a new countryside. In those few days Mr & Mrs Kodaly became welcome, familiar figures among us. Just as in a far greater way, his was a welcome, trusted familiar figure all over Hungary—at all times, war, & peace & under every régime. We send his young widow, all his pupils & colleagues, his innumerable Hungarian friends our deepest sympathy in their great loss.[4]

[4] Britten also prepared a statement for Reuters:

> I am deeply grieved to hear of the death of Zoltan Kodaly. When we were together in Budapest last October he seemed in splendid health and taking as large a part in the musical life of his country as ever. He was not only an important composer, but a great and brave social figure. His influence on musical education in Hungary, & happily spreading throughout the world, has been enormous—in fact he can be said to have invented a wonderful new system which has revolutionised our approach to this subject. We are proud to have been able to pay homage to him personally & publicly at the Aldeburgh Festival 2 years ago. I mourn a great composer, thinker, and a great human being.

85 An Interview with Benjamin Britten (1967)

The sixth group in a total of eight to participate in Expo's World Festival of Opera in Montreal was the English Opera Group. For those who had heard and seen Benjamin Britten's Peter Grimes, Billy Budd, *or* Albert Herring *at the Stratford Festival this summer, but were not familiar with his church operas, it was both a treat and a moving and memorable experience to see the productions of* Curlew River *and* The Burning Fiery Furnace *in Montreal under Mr Britten's direction.*

What has gone into the career of England's leading composer today? How does he work? Where does he get his ideas?

Mr Britten's first work in the operatic field was Paul Bunyan, *composed in 1941. His first grand opera was* Peter Grimes. *I asked him how and why he happened to compose it.*

BRITTEN: The story of how I came to write *Peter Grimes* was perhaps rather interesting. I was in California at the time and happened to pick up an old copy of *The Listener*, a very good English journal which reports radio talks; I found in it a talk by the English novelist E. M. Forster on the works of George Crabbe. There were quite a few quotations from the poem 'Peter Grimes' by Crabbe and I don't know whether it was homesickness or a sudden opening of my eyes to a new poetic style, or both, but I was amazed and thrilled by this poetry. I went into Los Angeles a few days later and, in an old second-hand shop, I found a copy of the works of Crabbe and devoured them avidly. The idea of writing an opera came almost immediately, although it would be the first full-length opera I'd ever written. I didn't start it until I got back to England, but meantime I had talked it over with Peter Pears, who was with me, and we had planned the action very thoroughly together. But it was a chance reading of that old copy of *The Listener* which sent me to the poem 'Peter Grimes' by Crabbe.

I told this story to Koussevitsky when he was performing a work of mine very soon after this chance finding and he asked me why I didn't start writing the opera. I said, quite frankly, that one must take a long time off to write an opera and one can't always afford to do it, but that I hoped one day to be able to. He then asked me whether if he found the money so that I could take the time off, I would write it. I said certainly I would . . . and that was how I began work on *Peter Grimes*.

MERCER: What do you feel are some of the highlights of that opera?

BRITTEN: I think the highlights are the shape of the work, the development of the character, the reaction of the people to Grimes, which I hope is a real

Source: Ruby Mercer, *Opera Canada* 8/4 (Dec. 1967), 12–15.

one and not an artificial or caricatured one, and the study of the characters that you get in a small village, maybe anywhere in the world, to someone who is a gifted eccentric—a person who doesn't fit. Particularly now, when people are inclined to be a little stereotyped, when the inclination is so much to mass communication and for people to think rather the same about things. I am interested in the people who don't think the same. So many of the great things of the world have come from the outsider, the lone dog, and that lone dog, or outsider, isn't always attractive. That is what I try to portray in *Peter Grimes*.

MERCER: What about your next opera, *The Rape of Lucretia*?

BRITTEN: I wrote that for The English Opera Group and because of the small number of people which had to be involved, the story was entirely different. There the inspiration came from a very fine play by the French writer, Beaudet [Obey], which suited the medium we were trying out at the time.

MERCER: Just how much has writing for particular voices influenced your writing of certain roles?

BRITTEN: I don't think I ever write an opera without knowing before I start who is going to sing the roles. That goes for all the other music I write too; I am most completely and hopelessly committed to the people I write for. For me, personally, it is necessary to know whether Rostropovitch or Dennis Brain or Julian Bream or any of the marvelous singers that I've had the honor to write for will be performing my music. I like to have their particular voices, their fingers, their harps, their lutes, in my mind when I write for them.

MERCER: It so happens that your *The Rape of Lucretia* was the first opera produced at The Stratford Festival, where opera has become an important part of the programming now, and where your *Albert Herring* was most successfully produced this past summer. Is there any special story connected with your composing that work?

BRITTEN: It was the second opera written for our Opera Group and we wished to have a good contrast to *The Rape of Lucretia*. It was produced at Glyndebourne and it was the most brilliant first production of any opera I've ever had. Frederick Ashton was the producer;[1] it was designed by one of our best English painters, John Piper; and fabulously well acted by Joan Cross, one of our greatest sopranos, as Lady Billows, and Peter Pears as Albert Herring with Mabel Ritchie, a very light coloratura soprano, as Miss Wordsworth—I could go on through the whole cast for there was not a single flaw in that cast, nor was there in the whole production.

[1] Frederick Ashton (1904–88), influential English dancer and choreographer, who later choreographed the games and dream sequence in *Death in Venice* (1973).

Mercer: How did you happen to choose Gay's *Beggar's Opera* for your next work?

Britten: It is part of our great national heritage, an extraordinary work, written as a kind of parody on the fashionable form of theatrical entertainment which was called opera. Most of the operas at that time were fairly dreary, but Gay came along and took those marvelous melodies, which were and actually are part of our lives, and fitted brilliant new words to them and wrote dazzling, sharp, bitter dialogue around them. Pepusch did the arrangements for Gay at the time but I think it's a piece that must be rearranged, because it has no arrangement of its own. All through the 19th century new arrangements were made and there was a famous one in the 1920's by Frederick Austin.[2] Then there was mine and Arthur Bliss has done one;[3] I think it's high time now for someone else to do a new one.

Mercer: In 1949 you wrote the work for children that you mentioned earlier, *Let's Make An Opera*. What about that and *The Little Sweep*?

Britten: Well I don't quite know from what angle to approach *The Little Sweep* because it is the opera of *Let's Make An Opera*. But I like writing for children and I like the sounds they make when they sing. So I wrote something in which children played a major part and I'm very glad that it sparked off, certainly in England, a new way of thinking about music for children. It is not only the custom there now, but it's considered the privilege of practically every composer that I know of in England to write operas for children. But as Kodaly said, 'none of us is too good to write for children—rather we must all strive to be good enough to write for children'.

Mercer: You began by composing the grand opera, *Peter Grimes*, and later gave us *Billy Budd*. But in the past few years you seem to have written more chamber operas. Is there any special reason for this?

Britten: No, I have alternated all my operatic composing life, as it were, between the two different forms. I should like to make it quite clear that because I have written some chamber operas does not mean that I think the grand opera style is finished. I wouldn't be so rash as to say that. But owing to the difficulties of getting operas put on the stage, some friends of mine and I evolved this style in order to make the work possible to perform. It was obviously cheaper to write and present chamber operas than to write and perform grand operas. So we started the British Opera Group [*sic*], a small chamber opera company. That was over 20 years ago now.

Mercer: Are you still active in that organization?

[2] Frederic Austin (1872–1952), English baritone and composer, who sang Peachum in his commercially successful version of *The Beggar's Opera* (1920).

[3] Bliss's version (1952–3) was composed for a film.

BRITTEN: No, I'm not artistic director as I was for very many years. I find my commitments elsewhere are too great and besides, I like to hand things over to rather younger people now. But I still take a very active interest; I write works for it and I'm a director of the Company.

MERCER: Generally speaking, the Company has performed more of your works than those of any other composer, I believe.

BRITTEN: Yes, I think it's very natural that I should have written more works for it since I was the most active operatic composer in England at the time we started it. But I'm glad to say that many of today's young composers are writing for this medium. Next year we hope to put on a new opera by Harrison Bertwhistle [*sic*] and one by a young composer called Gordon Cross[e] whom we have great faith in.[4]

MERCER: What is your concept of opera today?

BRITTEN: That's a very big question and I don't quite know how to answer it. I believe that opera is a most lively and immediate form of art and I think that the reaction to opera in many parts of the world bears me out in that. It isn't always easy to get audiences for opera in some of the smaller provincial towns, but in most of the big cities the interest seems to be enormous. I expect you feel that in Canada too.

MERCER: Yes, we do, particularly so in Canada. But in Italy, the original home of opera, it's on the decline in spite of the fact that many current composers are trying to find a new and successful formula for it. Germany, on the other hand, where your English Opera Group has performed a number of times, is evidently the most active country on the Continent, operatically speaking.

BRITTEN: Yes, I think it's true. Though I must say that in some of the northern countries the interest in opera is very great—also in Russia, where we went with the Opera Group recently. The interest there in what we produced has been so enormous that they have started two opera groups of the same kind themselves. They were particularly interested in this form because it is so much easier to tour than a great big opera company in that huge country of theirs.

MERCER: How do you account for the fact that your Group made such a big impact in Russia when you were singing in a language they did not understand—in English?

BRITTEN: Well, we made quite sure, first of all, that the program contained a very clear analysis of the events of the opera. Then I think that one of the things we have accomplished in our group is to make the acting side as

[4] Harrison Birtwistle (b. 1934), English composer, wrote his opera *Punch and Judy* (1966–7) for Aldeburgh; Gordon Crosse (b. 1937), English composer, wrote *The Grace of Todd*, Op. 20 (1967–8) for Aldeburgh.

important as the musical side. We try to make people look like they're supposed to look and behave as they are supposed to behave. For instance, *The Turn of the Screw*, which we gave in Leningrad and Moscow, and which is not, after all, a very easy story to understand, caught on in an amazing way. We didn't have an empty seat in the house for any of our performances there.

MERCER: Mr. Britten, you have been quoted as saying that 'opera is the most fascinating of all musical forms'. Do you still feel that way about it?

BRITTEN: Yes, but I wouldn't like to say it's fascinating to everyone—to me it is. I think it is the combination of the human being in his or her daily life and music which can point up the events of people's lives and their emotions in a most marvelous way. I think also that when you go to the theatre you don't want—at least I don't want—to see just a little touch of people's everyday lives. I want to see something heightened; I want to see something stylized. And that is why I believe the operatic form, like the poetic drama, is so much more illuminating than, for instance, just a straight drawing room comedy. I like the idea of the stylistic vision of people's lives.

MERCER: I read not too long ago that you had been tremendously impressed by the Noh plays in the Orient. How much have they influenced you?

BRITTEN: The Noh plays went straight to my heart just for the reasons I've been saying; they are the most stylized, crystalized form of art that I can think of and they have influenced me very directly. When I saw the play, *Sumidagawa*, the story of the mother looking for her lost child, I immediately felt that not only was it a wonderful story which had great importance for us in the West as Christians, but also that the actual form in which emotions were conveyed could be most useful and something we opera composers could surely learn from. So the first church opera that I wrote, which was in a style that I only recently evolved, was an Anglicization of this *Sumidagawa*, Sumida River, which we then called *Curlew River* and translated it, in every sense of the word, into East Anglian—the part of England where I live.

MERCER: Mr. Britten, do you have a set way of working when you're composing an opera?

BRITTEN: No, I wouldn't like to say there's a regular routine that I always stick to, but I can say that the idea for an opera always comes from me. Perhaps other people suggested subjects years before which have gone into my subconscious and come out again, but when I consciously decide to write a new opera, the idea comes from me. I then approach the librettist, discuss the idea with him, discuss the form and even discuss the links of the line sometimes. Then he goes away and writes it. After that, we discuss it again, but even through the writing period I find that I have new suggestions to make all the time—bits that have to be shortened—bits that have to be added—until the first performance. I find alterations go on being made even later than that—into first editions—until the work is published.

MERCER: How much depends on inspiration?

BRITTEN: When I hear that word I think of someone sitting at a table when suddenly an angel appears and gives him wonderful ideas and he writes for three days without stopping. That may happen, but mostly the true picture is of someone going to a desk, regularly at half past eight or nine in the morning, and sitting down and working. The inspiration is in us all the time. Otherwise, how could you explain Mozart, for instance, turning out one amazing work after another? He never waited for inspiration because his way of writing, his way of thinking, was always inspired.

MERCER: Looking ahead—do you plan to write another children's opera, and what are you working on now?

BRITTEN: I'm always writing new operas, new pieces, and there are nearly always children in my operas it seems, but at the present moment I'm doing another church opera to go with the other two, *Curlew River* and *The Burning Fiery Furnace*, to make a kind of trilogy.

MERCER: When do you expect to have that finished?

BRITTEN: For the Aldeburgh Festival next year.

86 Britten and Pears (1967)

Pears and I started working together I suppose because of similar musical interests, and being close friends because of convenience of environment: it was fun to sing and play together the music of all periods which we liked. But more fundamentally, I was attracted, even in those early days, by his voice, which seemed to me to emanate from a personality, and not, like many other voices, to be a manufactured affair, super-imposed. It has always been exciting to explore unknown music together; he is a fine musician and an excellent sight-reader. Added to this his flexible voice, with from the beginnings an excellent technique, enabled us to explore music from widely different styles: from the early lutenists (which in those early days, before the advent of Julian Bream, I used to play for him on the piano) and Purcell and Bach, through 19th century Lieder, and French and Russian songs, to the moderns and including operatic arias of all epochs and countries. Above all, perhaps, Pears has always possessed the all-important gift of being able to *phrase* music, of singing a series of notes in such a way that they make *sense*, musical sense. It is this gift, shared with all my favourite artist friends, from Dennis Brain to Rostropovitch, which has excited me to write music for him—which I've done with the utmost pleasure for thirty years.

Source: *Audio Record Review* (Dec. 1967), 16–17.

87 The Moral Responsibility of the Artist towards his Fellow Man (1968)

BRITTEN: I believe that the artist must be consciously a human being. He is part of society and he should not lock himself up in an ivory tower. I think he has a duty to play towards his—to his fellow creatures. It is not only a duty; I think it's a pleasure too. I want to have my music used. I would much rather—this seems perhaps a silly thing to say—but I would rather have my music used than write masterpieces which were not used.

COMER: Yes. Well don't you think that some of your work[s] are masterpieces?

BRITTEN: Oh that's not for me to say at all.

COMER: Why not? Why wouldn't you have the kind of confidence to think that you've done—?

BRITTEN: Because masterpieces—rather, the word 'masterpiece' has a kind of ring about it which suggests lots of dust on volumes in libraries.

COMER: Well what kind of attitude do you think society should have to the artist? You seem to have a very gregarious attitude towards society itself, and to give of yourself to society. Do you think society owes anything to you?

BRITTEN: Well, I hope society will keep me alive. I hope I shall be able to make enough money to live on, and live perhaps in a way which makes writing music possible, even easy. Not too easy, because we must all fight a little bit.

COMER: When you were a child you were a prodigy, weren't you? I mean you—you started to have ideas—I think you used to say 'I have an idea'—when you were, what, 5 years old?

BRITTEN: Well, I came from a very ordinary middle-class family, and I started writing music certainly when I was very small, when I was about 5 or 6; but I didn't have much musical education, and at my first school that I went to, my private school, where I went at the age of 8 to 14, there was no music at all.[1] That's not *quite* true. At the end of each term, on the last evening, we sang some songs.

COMER: That was nice.

BRITTEN: That was very nice—but that was the limit of our music.

COMER: Well how come when you were 9 you wrote an oratorio, and I believe you wrote an aria for God in C minor?

Editor's title.

Source: Editor's transcript of recording (*GB-ALb* 3–02053800). Broadcast 11 Apr. 1968, CBC: interview with Henry Comer.

[1] South Lodge Preparatory School, Lowestoft, where Britten was a student from 1923 until 1928, the last year of which he was Head Boy.

Britten: Yes, yes; I hoped it was a key He'd like. Well, I just looked—I found the way of writing music from reading other people's scores. I was, obviously, very keen on it, but I managed to do all the other things at school as well. Um . . . actually the staff at the school—the masters and the mistresses—they got a bit cross. They thought I was showing off, you know—they always do. And the boys themselves around me made no trouble at all. They thought it was rather amusing. I used to sit up in bed writing music, you know, and they took that for granted: 'Britten's at it again', you know.

Comer: Why would a man write opera? Because not very many people do write opera, do they?

Britten: No. I think we write opera because we are all human beings; we like studying human beings. Music expresses the emotions of a human being, and what more wonderful than to have a person on the stage singing, and to be able to accompany that person with musical noises? But in this simple, stylized form, which music also is, because after all it is—it's a made-up language; it doesn't *mean* anything, but it *can* convey to us the whole drama of human life in a very few notes if you are clever enough to find the right notes.

Comer: Is the voice a musical instrument, or is the musical instrument at its best as good as the voice?

Britten: I think that the—the acme of perfection in the art—in music art—is the human voice singing beautifully beautiful music, whether it be one's mother over one, trying to make one go to sleep when one is 2 years old and having a restless night, or—the Beatles, I don't know. Perhaps you'll convert me to that.

Comer: Well I think they're going towards a simplicity which I sense in everything you've said today. You're trying to be more simple, or to bring things down to a—some sort of clarity. It seems to me that the Beatles are trying to clarify something for the . . .

Britten: Yes, yes.

Comer: . . . for people today; for young people today, or for people like myself. I mean I don't think that I'm young any more, unfortunately, but if I were young I . . .

Britten: Younger than me? No, I think—I can't really say about the Beatles because I have a very busy life and I don't listen to gramophone records or go to concerts very often; but everything I read about the Beatles gives me pleasure. They have a wit and they have a directness—a freshness of approach which gives me a great pleasure, and I think they're also frightfully funny.

88 Britten on Aldeburgh and the Future (1968)

Rosenthal: Mr Britten, Marion Harewood suggests that the Aldeburgh Festival virtually came into being so that what was at that time the recently-formed English Opera Group might have somewhere to perform. Do you believe that opera must be an integral part of any music festival?

Britten: I suppose that the Aldeburgh Festival really came into being to bring music to East Anglia. But certainly a festival without opera is like bread without the jam—and had there been no English Opera Group in existence at the time of the first festival, I know we would have created a group to perform opera. I was writing operas at that time, and needed a platform for their performance.

Rosenthal: All the operas produced at Aldeburgh have been performed by the English Opera Group. Will this always be the case, or is it possible that a Festival Opera might be formed for certain works—as at the Holland Festival for example?

Britten: No, I think opera at Aldeburgh will always be based on the English Opera Group. But that is not to say that the Group is not expandable to a degree.

Rosenthal: What operas have you then in mind for production at Aldeburgh—or rather at the new concert hall-cum-opera house at Snape—that would require the Group to be enlarged in size?

Britten: Well, I would like to do *The Magic Flute*; perhaps *Fidelio*; and certainly some operas by Gluck, a truly great operatic composer—I am especially thinking of the second *Iphigénie* opera.

Rosenthal: Would these operas be performed in English or the original language?

Britten: In English of course; I hardly have to tell *you* that!

Rosenthal: How do you visualize those works being produced at Snape?

Britten: I imagine that a new open-stage technique of opera production might well be evolved. It's a very exciting prospect.

Rosenthal: Will there be the audiences for these, do you think?

Britten: Well, there were this year; and I'm sure the festival will always be a three-week one instead of the ten-day affair it was. This increase to three weeks means an increase in cost from between £16,000 and £17,000 to £34,000. But to return to audiences, ideally one would like to keep the audience a local one. As I said, that was the main reason for having a festival at Aldeburgh in the first place. By local, of course, I mean

Source: Interview with Harold Rosenthal, *Opera* 18 (Autumn 1968), 7–9.

Suffolk, and possibly extending to Cambridge and elsewhere in East Anglia.

Rosenthal: I was most struck at this year's festival by the number of young people in the audiences. This must have been most gratifying to you, for these people are surely the audiences of the future?

Britten: Yes, that is true. You know we have a scheme to enable about 50 young students, especially music students, to come to Aldeburgh and help in the festival in some way—either helping to copy parts, working on the stage, helping to paint scenery, etc.—and in return they get their board and lodgings, and can attend all performances. This scheme was instituted by the Duke of Hesse several years ago. It has certainly borne fruit; Gordon Crosse was one of our Hesse students.

Rosenthal: Is there not the danger that Aldeburgh might become too fashionable, like Glyndebourne; or do you think it is just that too far from London for this?

Britten: There is indeed this danger; and it's not only snob audiences from London we have to worry about; there is also the 'county'. We are always conscious of our audiences, however; one must remember that many of the local people who come to our performances are hearing works for the first time. Next year we hope to do Tchaikovsky's *Romeo and Juliet* with Galina Vishnevskaya singing. Why this piece, some people have already asked. But lots of people have never heard anything but the Fantasy-Overture.

Rosenthal: Let me turn to something more personal. What are your most vivid and lasting operatic memories of the last 20 Aldeburgh Festivals?

Britten: I think the 10th anniversary performance of *Albert Herring*, when Joan Cross, Peter Pears and others returned to their original roles; and then Janet Baker's first Dido.[1]

Rosenthal: And what of the future? How do you see Aldeburgh developing?

Britten: I suppose we'll have some more new buildings. We'd like to have the building next to the new concert hall at Snape. And then I suppose, as always happens, when we think we've got all that we want, some new need will become apparent, and we'll have to expand some more.

Rosenthal: And what about your own plans operatically?

Britten: Well, I'm completing my trilogy of church operas for next summer;[2] and then I hope to do something on a bigger scale once more.

[1] 1962 Festival. [2] *The Prodigal Son* (1968).

89 On Receiving the Sonning Prize (1968)

Ladies & Gentlemen, I suppose I shouldn't be pleased, honoured, flattered at receiving a prize.[1] As a composer I should be above success, honours & prizes. A composer should be entirely self-contained, communing alone with his muse, happy in his garret, in glorious self-sufficiency. But really, that is not the case, & having read alot about the lives of the great masters, I know it has never been so—they have never been fond of their garrets. What is more, I shouldn't believe a composer who said he was. Music, particularly of all the arts, must have an audience, an audience as well as performers. And what is more gratifying than when the audience & performers like your music? It is sad of course if no one likes what you do, &, apart from making your music better & clearer, there is not much you can do about it.

But when, as to-night, one has a fine performance of one's work, & at the end of it a handsome prize, well—one can't ask for much more![2]

Thank you (Mrs Sonning) for this wonderful prize—not only I, but many of the worthy causes that I have much at heart will benefit from it—thank you on the stage & in the pit for the lovely performance, & you in the audience for applauding it; thank you for welcoming me here to your beautiful city which I have known & loved for 20 years,[3] the city, the country & the people—thank you all from the bottom of my heart.

Editor's title.

Source: Autograph draft, n.d. (*GB-ALb* 1-02053801).

[1] The Léonie Sonning Music Prize was established by Léonie Sonning (1894–1970), wife of eminent Danish writer and editor Carl Johann Sonning, himself responsible for endowing a generous prize for contributions to European civilization. Stravinsky won the first prize in 1959.

[2] This was a performance of his First Suite for Cello (1964) on 25 May 1968.

[3] Copenhagen. Except for a few occasions, the prize has always been awarded at a concert in the city's Tivoli Gardens.

90 Some Notes on Forster and Music (1969)

There is no doubt that E. M. Forster is our most musical novelist. And I don't mean that he just likes music or likes going to concerts and operas, or plays the piano neatly and efficiently (all of which he does), but that he really understands music and uses music in his novels, and fairly frequently. The musical *locus classicus* is, of course, in *Howards End* (pp. 32–6) where a number of characters are presented in a tiny musical vignette—each of them reacting in a different way to a performance of Beethoven's Fifth Symphony.[1] Musically they range from Mrs. Munt, who wants to tap 'surreptitiously', via Fräulein Mosebach, who is reminded that it is 'echt Deutsch', Helen who sees pictures in it (goblins and elephants), and Margaret who just listens, to Tibby (poor Tibby!) who is up in the techniques of music and 'implored the company generally to look out for the transitional passage on the drum'. The whole remarkable passage shows a most sensitive reaction to music, and allows the novelist to make some perceptive observations on Beethoven—profound enough to help explain why his music has kept its hold on the public's affection all these years: '. . . the goblins were there. They could return. He had said so bravely, and that is why one can trust Beethoven when he says other things.' The passage also allows him to make some less valid observations on the acoustics of the lamented Queen's Hall, which make curious reading when one thinks of the acoustics and general concert atmosphere of the South Bank complex. The science of acoustics does not seem to have advanced much in the last half-century. Concerts in the Queen's Hall were a joy to hear; big and small music came winging to one with real resonance; the sounds were not dry or boxy.

In *A Room with a View* Lucy Honeychurch seems an inhibited, muddled little person until she is heard playing the piano by Mr. Beebe. Both her playing and her choice of music—especially the choice of Beethoven's opus 111 for 'one of those entertainments where the upper classes entertain the lower' (p. 41)—have previously surprised him, and now surprise us. But Forster knows his Beethoven sonatas (which I have heard him play with spirit), and he selects the music carefully. No wonder Mr. Beebe was 'disturbed'.

Forster certainly remembers his own piano-duet playing, and those painful collisions which skin the little fingers, in the music lessons which start the short story 'Co-ordination'. Again the pupils play Beethoven, and the dreadful ring of their names, Mildred and Ellen, Rose and Enid, Margaret and Jane, Dolores

Source: Oliver Stallybrass (ed.), *Aspects of E.M. Forster: Essays and Recollections written for his Ninetieth Birthday 1st January 1969* (London: Edward Arnold, 1969), 81–6.

[1] *Locus classicus*: the most cited or most authoritative study of a topic.

and Violet, echoes their dreadful thumping—it is hardly surprising that their teacher is at the end of her tether. Beethoven in heaven is concerned with the totting up of his performances, but still being deaf is deceived by his clerk about their quality. One wonders what the girls would have made of their celestial reward—a performance of his A minor quartet; what they actually hear is a brass band (more their cup of tea!).

Music is used superbly, not so much to colour a character as to push on the action, towards the end of *Where Angels Fear to Tread*. Here one may perhaps observe that the construction of Forster's novels often resembles that of the 'classical' opera (Mozart—Weber—Verdi) where recitatives (the deliberately un-lyrical passages by which the action is advanced) separate arias or ensembles (big, self-contained set pieces of high comedy or great emotional tension). As examples of the latter, think of the bathing episode in *A Room with a View*, the school Sunday dinner at which Ansell confronts Rickie in *The Longest Journey*, and, perhaps greatest of all, the trial in *A Passage to India*. The purpose of the big musical episode in *Where Angels Fear to Tread* is to dent deeper Philip Herriton's defences by confronting him with Gino at his gayest and most ingenuous. The scene, *Lucia di Lammermoor* at the Monteriano opera house, is long and gloriously funny: the fat lady of the railway journey 'who had never, never before . . .' turning up as the prima donna; Harriet trying to stop an Italian audience from talking, and trying to follow the plot; the triumph of the Mad Scene with the clothes-horse of flowers; and the cries of 'Let the divine creature continue'. But, as always with Forster (as with Mozart, too), under the comedy lies seriousness, passion, and warmth: the warmth of the Italians loving their tunes, being relaxed and gay together, and not being afraid of showing their feelings—not 'pretending', like Sawston.

Outside his novels and stories, Forster has written three important essays about music: 'The C Minor of That Life' (TC, 132–5),[2] 'Not Listening to Music' (TC, 136–9), and a broadcast talk, 'Revolution at Bayreuth' (*The Listener*, 4 November 1954, pp. 755–7). The Aldeburgh lecture 'George Crabbe and Peter Grimes' (TC, 178–92) only mentions music in passing; it is really about Crabbe's feelings, very involved ones, towards the town of Aldeburgh, and contains a long and detailed analysis of the poem. The Harvard lecture, 'The *Raison d'Etre* of Criticism in the Arts' (TC, 117–31), does not deal specifically with music, except once, again in connection with Beethoven.

The first of these essays, 'The C Minor of That Life', bravely tackles a technical problem which has baffled musicians ever since 'tempered tuning' came in. Is there actually a difference in character between keys other than highness

[2] *Two Cheers for Democracy* (London: Edward Arnold, 1951). Page numbers throughout this essay refer to editions published by Edward Arnold.

or lowness—for instance, is it just arbitrary that composers go pastoral in F, sensual in F sharp, stern and fateful in C minor, and so on? Without going too much into technical details, it is scientifically provable that, since tempered tuning has changed the intervals between the notes, the common chords of the different keys, and their scales, are slightly differently spaced, and so have slightly different characters. Apart from this physical aspect there is, of course, that of association, and this Forster does realise: because Beethoven has written some very memorable pieces in C minor, C minor has for us a special quality. The essay has some other acute observations, one inaccuracy (perhaps intentional?—there are no movements in C minor in the Razumovsky quartets), and a little jibe at Mozart.

'Revolution at Bayreuth' is Forster at his musical best. He writes wisely about Wagner, his music, our different attitudes to it (although I could quarrel with his calling his orchestration 'thick'), his qualities as a dramatist, and the interpretation of his extravagant stage directions. It is, of course, the attitude of the present 'Reich' at Bayreuth which started off the essay and justifies its title. I hope this most valuable piece of musical Forster will soon become more easily available.

'Not Listening to Music' is again amusing and acute, but in it there is the same curious tendency to mock at any intellectual approach on the part of the listener which we have noticed once or twice before. Thus in *Howards End* the novelist is determined to paint Tibby black, or dark grey—a determination which I do not think succeeds, since I can't help reacting sympathetically to the boy and want to know more about him—and one of the ways of doing this is to make him 'intellectual' about music, and therefore not 'feel' it; it is 'dangerous' to know a lot about it. In 'Not Listening to Music' we are told that no one can listen to a piece of music from beginning to end, consistently—unless one is a 'professional critic'. The alternatives to listening include watching the conductor, or the singer with her chin or chins, and noting the extreme ugliness of the audience (is this true?); and, of course, when one returns to the music, there are the pictorial images—the hunting scenes, Orpheus and the Furies (and Helen's elephants and goblins), in fact anything but the music itself. In 'The *Raison d'Etre* of Criticism' he refers to the Choral Symphony 'in A', when a reference book or catalogue would easily have put him right; his wistful 'Isn't it in A?' seems to suggest that this is a deliberate misnomer. No, for some reason Forster does not want to admit that knowing about music is a help: Tibby should not bother about such things as transitional passages. But surely no one pretends that to know this is all-important, any more than Helen's goblins are. Why does he take this attitude? It can be summed up in his attitude to Mozart, the Mozart who, 'in this respect [the use of a particular key for a particular mood], and indeed in others . . . did not go so far' as Beethoven:

the Mozart whom I have heard him call 'tinkling'.[3] Simply, Forster prefers music based on striking themes, dramatic happenings, and strong immediate moods, rather than on classical control and balance, beautiful melodies and perfection of detail; music which benefits from being listened to closely and from some knowledge of it. He prefers the Romantic to the Classical. And why shouldn't he?—he was brought up musically at the end of the nineteenth century. This is, of course, an overstatement, because, in spite of the pendulum swinging sharply away from Romanticism today, Forster *is* interested in new music—I have heard him react sympathetically to Stravinsky, to Michael Tippett, and also to some of my own pieces.

So when, in the late 1940s, having the deepest admiration for his writing, I suggested our doing an opera together, he agreed happily. At the start he was characteristically timid about it, worried by his lack of experience. But when Eric Crozier agreed to collaborate, with his considerable operatic background, he felt more confident—if we could find a mutually acceptable subject. We each suggested subjects, nearly settling on the Suffolk story *Margaret Catchpole*, but not quite. Who brought up the idea of *Billy Budd* no one can quite remember; it was probably telepathic and simultaneous. I think the writing of the libretto gave him great pleasure. Certainly the summer of 1950, when he stayed for a long time at Aldeburgh, when the sun seemed to shine continuously and we would go out for relaxation in a boat with a fisherman friend (curiously resembling the Billy we were writing about), was my own happiest operatic collaboration.[4] Naturally there were problems. He was worried that his writing in prose would inhibit my music; on the contrary, I found his terse, vivid sentences, with their strong rhythms, melodically inspiring. There was one passage which actually came out in blank verse (Claggart at the beginning of Act III); but when we did our revision after the first performances, condensing the work from four into two Acts, and removing Vere's sermon to the crew (neither of us was comfortable about this), Forster asked to be allowed to rewrite this passage in prose.[5] We had problems over the nautical terms and

[3] Forster's note: Lucy Honeychurch was found by Mr. Beebe on one occasion 'tinkling at a Mozart Sonata' (*A Room with a View*, 219).

[4] This friend was Billy Burrell (1925–99) whose photo appears on the CD cover of Britten's recording of *Billy Budd*. See Plate no. 3.

[5] Claggart's speech to Vere at the beginning of Act 3 of the 1951 version was as follows: 'With great regret do I disturb your honour. Duty compels me. Nothing but my duty Could bring me here to interrupt your state. . . . Your honour, I have served my Country long, My King and Country, and zealously I think Have I served you upon the *Indomitable* And striven in all ways to deserve your trust.' Forster also changed the beginning of Claggart's speech after the battle, which had originally been: 'With regret do I return to vex your honour. Duty compels me. Nothing but my duty could bring me back at such a time as this. Zeal for my country's welfare must excuse me.'

tactics, but Crozier did endless research over these, and a naval friend carefully checked everything. I am sure the rehearsals and problems of production interested him, and I know he had a great thrill when the perfect Billy Budd arrived from the U.S.A. (the casting of this part had been a great headache).[6] The pleasure which I derived from this collaboration I shall never forget: Morgan's deep perception, quick wit, tireless energy (though he was just recovering from an operation), and, in spite of his doubts ('I am not creative any longer') his consistent inspiration.

[6] Theodor Uppman (b. 1920), American baritone.

91 Mapreading (1969)

MITCHELL: Earlier this year you were heavily engaged in the television production of *Peter Grimes*. I know it was a great physical strain for you, because it must have been an enormous undertaking. But I think you were impressed and intrigued—were you not?—by all the possibilities of putting one of your major operas on television?

BRITTEN: It was a very great experience. It was, as you say, also rather alarming and tiring, simply because the handling of this enormous force of performers, and also of course fitting in with the wishes of the cameramen and the producers and directors, was something that I had never tried before. It was a much bigger enterprise than I had imagined I could ever try. But actually the people I was working with were so musical and understood the musical side of the work so well that my task was made much easier.

MITCHELL: Do you think, Ben, as a result of this experience with television—which took place, almost literally, on your own doorstep—that television opera has got a great future? That the possibilities for opera on television are really very considerable?

BRITTEN: I think the answer is a definite 'yes' for that, but I think there are one or two lessons that one must learn before really committing opera to television; and if I can be slightly technical for a moment I would like to say what they are, these lessons. One is that I am sure the opera must have a musical intensity on television: it must not get broken up into a vehicle for the cameras only. I have seen quite a few television versions of operas, and I think the danger can easily come that they are made, if I may say so, too reasonable, too realistic. And then one asks—I am sure the audience, the non-operatic audience, asks itself—why in the blazes people are singing and not speaking. You have got to keep this knife-edged balance between the photograph, the picture, which of course in a television medium must be rather realistic, it has that realistic impact on one, and also the musical excitement. And I think what I have learnt from the television [production] of *Peter Grimes* is that the drive forward of the music, the singing of the tunes, the elaboration of the ensembles, must never be forgotten. If you do, you get a kind of misfire, which is neither straight drama nor good opera. And that is the sort of thing that I've learnt and I'm trying to put into practice in this opera I'm now writing for television.

Source: Christopher Palmer (ed.), *The Britten Companion* (London: Faber & Faber, 1984), 87–96. This is Donald Mitchell's own transcript of his interview with Britten for the CBC in Feb. 1969.

MITCHELL: I wanted to ask you a question about that, whether in fact your experience with *Grimes* will be taken into account in this television opera that you are now just about to start writing?

BRITTEN: Yes. . . . Well, I've learnt—I mean, I'm deeply thankful that I did have that experience with *Grimes* before I actually put pen to paper in this new opera.

MITCHELL: Could you tell us briefly what the new television opera is to be? It's a short story by Henry James, isn't it?

BRITTEN: Yes. It's a very remarkable short story called 'Owen Wingrave'. It's like all Henry James's work: very reasoned, very intelligent, and full of very strong atmosphere. I've learnt, of course, a lot from doing *The Turn of the Screw*, and I'm also using the same librettist, Myfanwy Piper, for *Owen Wingrave* as I had for the *Turn of the Screw*. I won't tell you the story because people can always find the story in volume 9 of *The Collected Short Stories*. It's a very provocative story and a very strange one, but I think it's a very powerful one, and I hope it is a good choice for one's first television opera. It's not got a big chorus, in fact it's got scarcely a chorus at all. It's got a small number of characters, all of which I think is a good thing for the television medium. Although I think with careful handling large forces can be made to be successful.

MITCHELL: So this will be virtually a chamber opera?

BRITTEN: Yes. I shall use a slightly bigger orchestra than I used for *The Turn of the Screw*, because I need rather other effects, but it will not be a big orchestra. It will be an orchestra I think of slightly Mozart size, although not necessarily Mozart style.

MITCHELL: This will be a work, then, specifically designed for the television medium?

BRITTEN: Entirely designed.

MITCHELL: Have you got some special ideas in this respect?

BRITTEN: Oh yes. We're using the camera consciously throughout. I mean, it's quite an effort for me, but I'm being very careful to think throughout of the television medium and not of the stage. I've no doubt that one will, at a later date, be able to adapt it for the stage, but it will take a considerable amount of rewriting. But what is perhaps more interesting than my just talking about a work in the future is that one has learnt from this *Peter Grimes* experience so much that I've changed the libretto which was sketched before we started the television [production] of *Peter Grimes*. I've changed a great deal of it because of the lessons that I learnt in that. And it's all gone back to the operatic form of opera and away from the realistic form of opera. In fact I've been in the last days with Myfanwy Piper—we've been adding arias galore. Because I am convinced—and this comes from my recent television experience—that the audience needs the tunes, it needs the lyricism of the aria and the ensemble, rather than the realistic side of perpetual recitative. Which would prompt, as I suggested, the question 'Why in the blazes is he singing and not speaking?'

MITCHELL: Yes, so in a way what you're saying, Ben, is that the successful television opera is more likely to succeed in so far as specifically musical forms in a sense predominate, and the drift away from realism is pronounced?

BRITTEN: Yes, that's exactly what I feel about it. And I'm glad to say that John Culshaw, who is the producer of this opera, is in entire sympathy with my feelings about that.[1]

MITCHELL: I think this really is an extraordinarily interesting discovery or conclusion to have come to as a result of the *Grimes* filming.

BRITTEN: It's a very surprising one, quite honestly.

MITCHELL: It's a surprising one—I wouldn't have expected that. I'm sure that this is right in fact.

BRITTEN: Well, it's certainly right for *me*, and I'm sure that what one apologist for television opera said to me, I think entirely mistakenly, that the greatest praise that a television opera can have was that the viewer forgot it was opera—I'm sure that is the greatest mistake.[2] One should enjoy it *because* it's opera.

MITCHELL: Ben, how far have you a clear picture, compositionally speaking, of the work in your mind? I put this as a general question because it would very much interest me to know how this happens when you're approaching a new piece. Whether you come with your ideas already pretty fully formulated, or whether a lot happens once you get down to your desk.

BRITTEN: I never start a work without having a very clear conception of what that work is going to be. When I say conception, I don't mean necessarily tunes or specific rhythms or harmonies—or old-fashioned things like that!—but I mean the actual shape of the music—the kind of music it's going to be rather than the actual notes, they come very much later. But notes at this stage, which is about two or three weeks away from the first note to be put on paper—the notes are beginning to come already. Not necessarily the beginning, but little schemes throughout the work. I am beginning to plan it all from a textural point of view throughout. But there

[1] John Culshaw (1924–80), English record producer and writer, who produced the famous Decca recordings of Wagner's *Ring*, and who, following on from his equally brilliant recording of *Peter Grimes*, which explored the new stereophonic technology to great effect, was closely associated with Britten's recordings for Decca. He was head of music, BBC TV (1967–75), during which time he commissioned and produced *Owen Wingrave*.

[2] Not identified.

is always this element of chance, of improvisation, which happens once the work gets under way. I think E. M. Forster describes that very well in *Aspects of the Novel*, when he says that one must always be prepared as a creative artist to let the characters take charge. And I can quite often go to the paper perfectly clear that what I'm going to do, and to find that it doesn't work out quite like that. And I think one has got to have faith in one's subconscious, that it's going to direct one rightly. Quite often, you see, when you put a thing down on paper it lacks a certain quality which it may have in your imagination, which is not quite so precise as the actual instructions for the performers. Then you have to be prepared to adjust, and that particularly in opera when, as E. M. Forster says, the characters take over, where the characters do exist in a very big way. It's very difficult to remember precisely something which one wrote such a long time ago, but I know that the first drafts for *The Turn of the Screw* were in what one called then the normal three-act form, and even I think the libretto was written in that shape. And I realized there was something wrong. It was partly what was wrong I think because we had omitted some of James's own episodes, and put others together, and he planned that story, as one slowly found out, so very carefully that if you miss one rung in the ladder you miss your footstep, and something goes wrong. I then discovered that what we were really planning was something in a certain number of scenes which must follow very closely. And I was then looking for an idea which could be varied through these scenes which then would turn out to be a series of variations. Because really the story could be rather fancifully described as a theme with variations. Incidentally there are many close similarities between the two stories, 'Owen Wingrave' and 'The Turn of the Screw'.

MITCHELL: So in some ways the new piece will be a companion piece?

BRITTEN: Yes, I think it will be. In the number of characters it's comparable, in the intensity of it, and in the short scenes and the interludes, although I don't think I shall do it in the same variation form.

MITCHELL: Ben, I know dreams, sleep, night have clearly meant a great deal to you as a creator. 'Night and Silence, these are two of the things I cherish most': that's a phrase of yours I've always remembered.[3]

[3] This is a paraphrase of Puck's speech in Act 2, Scene 2 of *A Midsummer Night's Dream*, when he stumbles across the sleeping Lysander:

Through the forest have I gone.
But Athenian found I none,
On whose eyes I might approve
This flower's force in stirring love.
Night and silence.—Who is here?
Weeds of Athens he doth wear:

BRITTEN: Silence of course, these days, becomes a rarer and rarer presence, particularly in this house where we're sitting now, where the aeroplanes land with unfailing regularity close to the house. But night and dreams—I have had a strange fascination by that world since a very early age. In fact I can remember, rather precociously, when I was at my private school, saying to myself, the last thing before I went to sleep, or naming to myself, an algebraic problem which I had to solve the next day. Someone told me—I don't remember whom—that if you do that it gives a chance for your subconscious to work when your conscious mind is happily asleep. Whether that was a successful method I don't remember well enough, except I was fairly successful in mathematics when I was young. But I do treasure that moment and that's why I think I get so disturbed and distressed if I don't sleep, I find that I wake up in the morning unprepared for my next day's work.

MITCHELL: Of course, in a work like *A Midsummer Night's Dream*, for example, one does there—poetically—experience the healing power of sleep, because after the dream-world of the wood, and the imposed sleep of the spells, everything does come right in the end; and this is an image perhaps of what you've just been saying about the therapeutic effect of a good night's sleep. At the same time it is true—isn't it?—that night does also have a more disturbing aspect for you?

BRITTEN: Yes. It can release many things which one thinks had better not be released; and one can have dreams which one cannot remember even, I find, in the morning, which do colour your next day very darkly. And it's always very puzzling to me that I can't remember something which has had such a big emotional effect on the next day, on the next days even. Similarly, of course, it can have a very blessed affect on your next day. My recent dream about meeting Schubert in Vienna blessed the following days in a way that I seldom remember in my life before.

MITCHELL: I think you must in fact be the only composer known to me who

This is he, my master said,
Despised the Athenian maid;
And here the maiden, sleeping sound,
On the dank and dirty ground.
Pretty soul! she durst not lie
Near this lack-love, this kill-courtesy.
Churl, upon thy eyes I throw
All the power this charm doth owe.
When thou wakest, let love forbid
Sleep his seat on thy eyelid:
So awake when I am gone;
For I must now to Oberon.

has written a whole work virtually devoted to sleep and dreams—the *Nocturne*, the orchestral song-cycle.[4]

BRITTEN: Yes. Well, the *Serenade* gets near to it.[5]

MITCHELL: Yes, the *Serenade* leads into the later song-cycle—doesn't it?—with Keats's 'Sleep' sonnet. This foreshadows really the world to which the *Nocturne* is devoted in its entirety. Although that piece—I think it is true, isn't it?—does deal too with the disturbing aspects of sleep . . .

BRITTEN: Very much so, yes.

MITCHELL: . . . nightmare, for instance. It's not by any means all happy dreams.

BRITTEN: No. The Wordsworth I think is a very nightmarish poem—the dream about the French Revolution.[6] And of course the *Nocturnal* which I wrote for Julian Bream also has some very, to me, disturbing images in it, linked, of course, inspired by this—the Dowland song, which of course itself has very strange undertones in it. Dowland was a person who perhaps even consciously realized the importance of dreams.[7]

MITCHELL: Ben, you've often said to me that you've never had any desire or ambition to teach. Do you still feel that way, even though we might possibly live in a time when some teaching from you might be thought to be extremely valuable?

BRITTEN: Yes, I don't exactly know why I'm so shy about teaching. I know that when young people come to me with their works it gives me great pleasure to go through them—these works—with the young composers. I think I'm frightened of imposing my own solutions on their problems. Although I do believe strongly that even the personality of the teacher can be absorbed without much detriment to the scholar. Because if the personality of the scholar is strong enough it can absorb it easily, and perhaps get richer from it. But I have seen so many cases in my life where the tricks, the mannerisms of the teacher have been picked up by the scholar. And sometimes when the teacher has not been a professional composer they have been really unhealthy influences, I feel. They've been a secondhand version of the tricks of other composers and it produces so often a stilted quality in the music of these young chaps that has sometimes been almost impossible to eradicate. I think that the great composer, the great writer, painter, will survive almost any kind of treatment. But the great composers can look after themselves. It's the minor composers, the people who can make our lives so

[4] *Nocturne* (1958), one of several 'night pieces' from this period, an anthology of poems describing the different states of sleep and night.

[5] *Serenade*, Op. 31, for tenor, horn and strings (1943).

[6] 'But that night, When on my bed I lay' from *Residence in France and French Revolution.*

[7] Dowland's song 'Come, heavy sleep' is the basis of the *Nocturnal.*

much richer in small ways, that I want to preserve and to help. Also, I do think that at this moment of acute change in music that I perhaps am *not* the right person to guide young composers. My methods, which are entirely personal to me, are founded on a time when the language was not so broken as it is now. I think this is a moment of lack of confidence which I shall outgrow, but at the moment I feel that the young composer would not be interested in my criticisms.[8] Because virtually really all a teacher can do to help a student is to say 'Is this what you mean? And if not, let's try and find out what it is.' In other works, to shine a brighter light on the music than the scholar really has . . . is yet in possession of; and to make him see his work more clearly in order to get it, the real re-creation of what is in his mind. My methods, I feel, of doing that would be a little unacceptable to some of the young composers; and that I think is why at the moment—apart of course from the major one of lack of time—but I think that's one of the major reasons why I haven't taught.

MITCHELL: You do feel, do you, that this is a time of acute change in music? I think you're quite right to feel that, but . . .

BRITTEN: Yes, I do. And I don't always follow the new directions, and nor do I always approve of them, but that is only purely personal to me. I mean, that there should be new directions is obvious. Any new thought, in whatever language it's couched, has got to have this new element. But I sometimes feel that the seeking after a new language has become more important than saying what you mean. I mean, I always believe that language is a means and not an end.

MITCHELL: Of course language is a means of communicating; and I would have thought that you would regard yourself, as an artist, as a communicator.

BRITTEN: Entirely. I mean, why bother to write your music down, if you don't want to communicate it?

MITCHELL: Exactly. But I would have thought that the acute change to which you refer was bound up with the total abolition of the idea of comprehensible language on the one hand and of the idea of communicating on the other.

BRITTEN: Yes.

MITCHELL: This does seem in fact really to represent the immense gulf that has opened up in the arts in our time.

BRITTEN: I think one mustn't exaggerate that. I think it's only the very vocal few who make these extreme remarks . . .

[8] This was the period in which Britten's music was considered unfashionable in the universities and conservatoriums.

MITCHELL: . . . or who take up extreme positions?

BRITTEN: Yes, because in my experience, and I do see really a great deal of young composers' work, this only belongs to the very, very few. And I can name many young composers—I mean, of those already reaching maturity and those who have not yet reached maturity—who are passionately interested in telling us what they want to say. I think that one of the bores of the enormous newspaper coverage, and radio and television coverage, of opinions, is that the very vocal ones become very well known. And I think quite often they are not the best. But I do find in a young composer like John Tavener, for instance, who is writing very hard and very interestingly in this country at the moment, he is profoundly interested in telling us what he means.[9] And I think he and many of his generation are swinging far, far away now from what I call the academic avant-garde, who have rejected the past. He and many others like him *adore* the past and *build* on the past. After all, language is a matter of experience. When we're talking together now, we're using symbols which have been used by the past. If we rejected the past we should be just making funny noises.

MITCHELL: Ben, you were talking about some composers—some, only—young composers, who reject the past. Well, of course, certainly this has never happened in your case. To a composer standing at the point of his life where you do today, you have a great inheritance, not only in your own music but also with regard to the past. I would like to ask you how it feels standing in that situation? And are you conscious of this wonderfully exciting but also great *burden* of tradition behind you?

BRITTEN: I'm *supported* by it, Donald. I couldn't be alone. I couldn't work alone. I can only work really because of the tradition that I am conscious of behind me. And not only the consciousness of the *musical* tradition, but the tradition of painting, and architecture, and countryside around me, people around me. This may be giving myself away—if so, I can't help it. I feel as close to Dowland, let's say—because we mentioned him earlier in our talk, a few hundred yards back—I feel as close to him as I do to my youngest contemporary. I was reading a play of Euripides in bed this morning—*Ion*—which I had read before, but I hadn't reread for some time. And really, the first chorus of that—written, what, nearly three thousand years ago?—seemed to me as if it was being written about a crowd visiting the Maltings, looking around and making comments: 'What's this?'; 'Where do we go here?' I feel that there's no difference except the difference of environment, between Euripides and ourselves today. And we all have that feeling reading

[9] John Tavener (b. 1944), English composer, whose *Three Surrealist Songs* (1968) was performed at Aldeburgh in the 1969 Festival.

the Bible, reading any old sagas from Iceland or India. I cannot understand why one should *want* to reject the past. After all, we sit in this room surrounded by pictures and an amphora from Armenia, a very beautiful thing, which is five thousand years old. I'm given *strength* by that tradition. I know it changes—of course traditions change. But the human being remains curiously the same.

MITCHELL: It would be true then that you feel this sense of tradition as an aid and as an assistance in your own work. Could we just turn for one minute to one particular example: I was thinking we might choose possibly the *War Requiem*. Did you feel there when approaching this after all very big creative task, great precedents and examples of the Mass—for example, the settings of the Mass for the Dead—behind you in that work?

BRITTEN: I'd like to answer that question, Donald, in a rather roundabout way, by an example. Not long ago there was a young composer who had a first performance of an opera not far from here.[10] And at the same time there were other operas being performed in the neighbourhood. I know it was probably because of the tightness of time, and the absorption in his own job, but it seemed to me very strange that he didn't want to go and see how Mozart solved *his* problems. If he were setting out, from here to Newmarket, to drive, naturally he would use maps to find out how to get there. Why, if he used maps to get to Newmarket, didn't he use maps which show how to write an opera? I know he was trying to say something different, just as we are probably driving a different car to Newmarket from the mapmaker's, but after all, there are many similarities between all works presenting dramatic ideas to audiences, and I would think, even though he may have rejected it—just as one can find a new way of going to Newmarket—that it's useful to know how someone else has gone there. And actually, as far as we can know, achieved getting there. And I think that I would be a fool if I didn't take notice of how Mozart, Verdi, Dvořák—whoever you like to name—had written their Masses. I mean, many people have pointed out the similarities between the Verdi *Requiem* and bits of my own *War Requiem*, and they may be there. If I have not absorbed that, that's too bad. But that's because I'm not a good enough composer, it's not because I'm wrong.

[10] Harrison Birtwistle (b. 1934), whose *Punch and Judy* was composed for the Aldeburgh Festival and premiered at Snape in 1968.

92 No Ivory Tower (1969)

How and why is an opera written? First, as to the 'why,' the composer must love opera and have a real feeling for the form. I wouldn't like to say it's fascinating to everyone; to me it is. I think it is the combination of the human being, in his or her daily life, with music that can point up the events in people's lives, and their emotions, in a most marvelous way. I think also that when you go to the theater you don't want—at least I don't want—to see just a little touch of people's everyday lives. I want to see something heightened; I want to see something stylized. And that is why I believe the operatic form, like the poetic drama, is so much more illuminating than, for instance, just a straight drawing-room comedy. I like the idea of the stylistic vision of people's lives.

Now, as to the 'how,' the first thing that happens is the idea for the opera. Something strikes you that you would like to use, a particular story for an opera. The next step is to look for someone who together with you can work out the libretto. That can take a long time; in fact it usually does. With the writer you plan the shape of each act—the numbers, the solos, the choruses—and the writer will say, how many lines do you think that will be? You make a rough guess, and he goes off to write his first draft.

He then brings it back, and you tear it to pieces together. The actual operation of writing a libretto can take weeks or months. When you get to a sufficiently advanced stage, you start to write the music. I write quickly once I get down to it, but quite often I'm interrupted: I travel a lot, playing the piano and conducting. On the average a chamber opera may take me plus or minus a year to compose.

What happens after the actual music is started, as E. M. Forster says in his *Aspects of the Novel*, is that the work itself takes charge. As you set the words, fresh demands on the librettist will come, and you will say I'm sorry, but this line is too long, this line is too short—I need more, I need less—and so you work throughout the composition. It is in a sense a master–servant relationship, but both master and servant have to be experts at their job, and I don't wish to suggest for a moment that it is an unrewarding or undignified task for a writer to be a librettist. In fact, arguably the greatest novelist of our time, Forster, has written a libretto for me, *Billy Budd*.

Paul Bunyan, my first opera, was written in collaboration with W. H. Auden, another very notable literary figure. There are some good things in it, but as it

Source: *Opera News* 33/23 (Apr. 1969), 8–11. This article is a compilation of interviews given by Britten to *Opera News,* Martin Bronstein for CBC, Ruby Mercer for CBC, and *Opera Canada* magazine.

stands now I wouldn't want it performed without revision. The element of the preacher is what makes Auden very valuable. Some of the ideas in *Paul Bunyan* were perhaps critical of America, in the sense of asking Americans to look critically at certain aspects of themselves and their heritage. This wasn't received too kindly, in view of the fact that the U.S.A. was on the verge of war at that time (1941) and nationalistic feelings were high everywhere.

When music is composed to a text, the two are of course very close, but I wouldn't say the music is dictated by the words. You see, the idea really comes originally from the composer, probably in discussion with the librettist. It is true, however, that the precise form, the precise words—the inspiration of a given dramatic moment—will come from the librettist. That is why it's highly important to have a good writer. The composer needs the best collaboration he can get, because he is the one who is finally all-important and all-responsible. His music, if it is good enough, might transcend a bad libretto, but the greatest writer in the world will not transcend bad music.

Possibly I prefer writing operas to other forms of music, but I would never dream of giving up all other kinds of music for opera—and I have written a great deal else, and plan to continue to do so. One's mind is filled with subjects; if a need or opportunity should arise, one has only to switch on to the subject. Almost any situation *could* be made into an opera. I do hope, as I'm sometimes told, that my operas *are* all different, each with a style appropriate to itself, but I hope that comes from absorption with each subject while it is at hand. Many people at Expo 67 in Montreal were surprised at how different the church operas were, *Curlew River* and *The Burning Fiery Furnace*. But of course they are, because they are different works! Look at the Bach suites for solo cello: the form may seem rather uniform, but the suites are all different.

Opera composition is not only a matter of experience. Quite a few gifted composers have had considerable success in the theater but still didn't possess whatever the special quality is that's required. It has to do with dramatic imagination, with being able to make your musical imagination work along dramatic lines and serve dramatic ends. You can't write pretty music unattached to a dramatic situation—well, you can, but it doesn't work. Unfortunately, we don't always know what a composer's dramatic imagination was during a given passage: Mozart surely wouldn't have written the long instrumental introduction to 'Martern aller Arten' (in *Die Entführung aus dem Serail*) without a perfectly good reason, but today we have to guess at what it was. Nor is all dramatic music necessarily operatic, or conceived for the stage. Bach and Heinrich Schütz had a remarkable sense for expressive, dramatic recitative, for building dramatic situations in music. I only wish they had lived in a time when writing for the stage was the thing to do.

What makes an opera work? There are no computers that can tell what makes a tune really live. Sir Charles Villiers Stanford and others have written endless theories on how music should be written.[1] There is still no recipe for making music memorable, but we mustn't worry too much: it will happen if it possibly can. We should encourage people to try. If the result is useful now, fine; if it lives on, so much the better.

I have always, all through my life, been inspired by either individuals or special occasions. While the English Opera Group was being formed, naturally I felt that my main job was to provide a repertory for them, so I wrote *The Rape of Lucretia*, *Albert Herring* and so on. Now, since people like Julian Bream, the guitarist, and Mstislav Rostropovich, the fabulous Russian cellist, have come into my life, I have written works for them. And all the time, of course, for Peter Pears I have written one song cycle after another. It's always, I think, the individual or the occasion. The individual in the sense that I've usually known, while writing an opera, who the singers would be. The occasion in the sense that the *War Requiem* was written for Coventry Cathedral's opening. That attracts me. I am the furthest removed from an ivory-tower composer that you can think of.

Before 1945, when the English Opera Group started, there wasn't much tradition or literature of chamber opera, except for certain hints in that direction. There's a remarkable piece by an English composer I greatly admire, Gustav Holst—*Savitri*, built on an Oriental subject, an Indian story—that could be called a precursor of the chamber opera.[2] For that matter, Purcell's *Dido and Aeneas* has elements of 'chamber-ness' about it. On the whole, however, our English composers, like everyone else, were interested mainly in grand operas. And I certainly would not say that grand opera is losing its viability even now, just because there has been a rise of interest in chamber opera. Still, the nineteenth century was its heyday, and many English composers tried it. Some were successful, though the music wasn't very good. The Cambridge Circus opera house, for example, was built for Arthur Sullivan's *Ivanhoe*, which had an endless run, 155 performances.[3] Before that, the eighteenth-century English audience liked Italian opera, and English opera didn't do so well then—except *The Beggar's Opera*, written as a parody of that 'irrational' form.

People express curiosity about the fact that my most recent pieces for the English Opera Group have been a trilogy of short operas for church performance. Actually, this has been a quite natural development. Many English towns lack any auditorium as suitable as their church. There was great activity in restoring churches during the nineteenth century, and the church is the

[1] For example, *Musical Composition: a Short Treatise for Students* (1911).

[2] *Sāvitri*, Op. 25 (1908) is scored for two flutes, cor anglais, two string quartets plus double bass, three solo voices, and women's choir.

[3] *Ivanhoe* (1890), a grand opera in five acts.

basic building in every town and village. The west end of a church is usually suitable for performances. These buildings were the center of local life—rather than the town hall, used for committees and assizes. What we are doing has not been done much since the Reformation: religious drama with music used to be common before then, and little plays were used during the Mass, but this was driven out during the Reformation.

So the availability of churches has opened new possibilities for the English Opera Group on tour. We can now perform in localities where otherwise we could not, and the needs of the production are relatively modest. We don't have to take much with us, in the external sense. The basic lighting is about all that has to be controlled, and there one aims for daylight if possible and, if not, to approximate it as closely as possible. I've learned an enormous amount from the Oriental theater, especially the No drama of Japan.

The existence of the English Opera Group for twenty-odd years has stirred considerable interest in chamber opera. I'm very glad to say that many young English composers, and some not so young, are writing works that they send to us. Foreign ones, too. Poulenc was immensely interested in what we were doing and suggested we should give the first English performances of *Les Mamelles de Tirésias*, which we did at our Aldeburgh Festival, because he was so enchanted by *The Turn of the Screw*. Two years ago we paid a long visit to Russia, and as a result of that visit I believe there are two chamber opera groups being formed, one based in Moscow and the other in Leningrad. I think that was the highest sort of compliment one could possibly have. I have continued to write for the English Opera Group, of course; *The Prodigal Son*, sequel to the two church dramas we presented in Montreal, was introduced at Aldeburgh last summer. The extent to which this genre has succeeded can be judged by the fact that so many other composers are working in it now, on their own or on commission from us—Gordon Crosse, Harrison Birtwistle, Malcolm Williamson, for instance.[4]

The Aldeburgh Festival was an outgrowth of our English Opera Group, not the other way round. The group was started at a time when virtually no stage was open to an English composer: Covent Garden hadn't reopened after the war, and Sadler's Wells wasn't in a position to give us an opportunity. I wanted to go on writing operas—the Koussevitzky Foundation had commissioned *Peter Grimes*—but though this accounts for my interest at first, the company wasn't conceived by any means just to give myself an opportunity. I had in mind the plight of the composer in general, and the plight of English singers—

[4] Malcolm Williamson (1931–2003), Australian composer, pianist, and conductor, who had a number of his works performed or premiered at Aldeburgh from 1956 onwards. His opera *English Eccentrics* was first presented by the English Opera Group in the 1964 Festival. In 1975 he succeeded Bliss as Master of the Queen's Musick.

those who were not primarily opera singers but who had an operatic gift and wanted stage experience.

That's why we can't function year-round: the singers all have other work to do. The festival was thought up to bring some opera to that part of England, and to provide a home stage for the English Opera Group. Outside of the first favorable reaction, from special festival audiences, we've always had quite a struggle on our provincial tours, right up to [the] season before last, when we 'arrived,' so to speak, at Sadler's Wells. But we shall have to make our companies travel. What kind of operas is the English Opera Group equipped to do? I don't like to specify only chamber operas, but the distinction from grand opera must nevertheless be made; our most ambitious production has been *A Midsummer Night's Dream*, which was 'writ large' but with our company specifically in mind.

I'm often asked about the problems of being both a composer and an impresario. The whole of one's life requires managing—you know, deciding between this or that activity, and then how to go about it. Luckily, I'm surrounded by efficient and willing helpers, who make it possible for me to function in directorial work without having to write letters, to work out rehearsal schedules and so on.

Once the opera has been written and goes into production, how much interest do I take? Well, in cases where the English Opera Group is concerned, I do take a great deal of interest. But I'm afraid in many other productions, including the recent new one of *Peter Grimes* at the Metropolitan, I haven't been able to take an interest—except of course approving wholeheartedly the ideas that Tyrone Guthrie had about directing it—simply because if I did there would not be time for writing any more operas.[5] Once the child is born, it has to stand on its own feet.

[5] Tyrone Guthrie (1900–71), whose first opera staging had been of *Peter Grimes* at Covent Garden in 1947, with stylized designs by Tanya Moiseiwitsch. She later recalled the Met production of Grimes: 'Then another great contrast was *Peter Grimes* at the Met with miles and miles and miles of fishnet and vast windy seascapes, very unrealistically aimed for. We did it first at Covent Garden, when a real fog came in on the first night and practically obliterated the singers—it went down their throats—it wasn't very popular, but it did give them a *marvellous* effect from our point of view, but not to be repeated. And then twenty years later, we were asked to it at the Met where it all fitted on to various astonishing hydraulically arranged trucks and wagons. . . . *Peter Grimes* was practically all black and white and grey with here and there very modest colour introduction.' Britten was reputably one of those with whom the Covent Garden production was not popular. Alfred Rossi (comp.), *Astonish Us in the Morning: Tyrone Guthrie Remembered* (London: Hutchinson, 1977), 55.

93 Snape Maltings Fire (1969)

BRITTEN: Well, it looks pretty devastating—but it's difficult at this moment to say exactly what is sound. It looks as if the walls—the brick—these marvellous brick walls, you know, which have contributed so much to the—the beauty of the sound—it looks as if they are going to be all right.[1]

BBC: What were your feelings when you saw the devastation?

BRITTEN: I'm not a poet. I can't describe those feelings. It was—of course it's been a terrible shock and I'm afraid it's going to be dreadful for so many of our audience—audiences that have come, you know, to hear and see things in the Maltings this next two or three weeks—that they can't go to any concerts or operas at the Maltings, especially as so many of them have contributed towards the cost of the rebuilding of the Maltings.

BBC: Well how much is it going to cost to rebuild?

BRITTEN: I don't know yet. It's—I should think it can't be far off its original cost, which was, you know, in the neighbourhood of £570,000—but that's the—engineers, Arups, are coming down this afternoon to see it, and I'm going to go back now and to walk all over it again with them so we can have some idea of the assessing of the damage.

BBC: You lost your piano in this blaze. This must have been an extremely bitter blow.

BRITTEN: Oh it was a bitter blow, but there are so many things gone—I mean it looks as if one of those precious double basses is gone,[2] a harpsichord has gone, the costumes for some of the operas, scenery—all the rostrums which Stephen Reiss has carefully designed and planned over the years, and this lovely seating, of course, which was one of the prides of Snape—that has gone too.

BBC: Almost immediately after you heard of the fire you started planning the new Snape Maltings. Was there ever any question of not continuing?

BRITTEN: Oh no, not in the slightest; no. There was a moment of shock where we thought, 'Oh, we'd better go away and forget about it for a week or so,' but as soon as one got over that, one realized that the first thing to do was to go on with the concert and the operas as far as was possible. But of course it seemed then very difficult to know how we *could* go on; but the vicar of

Editor's title.

Source: Editor's transcript of recording (*GB-ALb* 3–02053903). Broadcast 8 June 1969, BBC Radio 4.

[1] Snape Maltings Concert Hall was destroyed by fire on 7 June 1969, the first night of the 22nd Aldeburgh Festival, only two years after its inauguration.

[2] Adrian Beers's bass was destroyed, which greatly distressed Britten.

Blythburgh Church, where we are here now, he has offered his church for everything that we wanted to do there, and the Bishop of Ipswich and St Edmundsbury, he's been *most* encouraging, and it does look at this moment that *all* the concerts and even the operas—the *Idomeneo* of Mozart, which has been sold out now for months—will happen, and will happen probably in this beautiful church here. We *could not* be more fortunate.

BBC: What sort of reaction has there been from the public and from the people you know in the world of music?

BRITTEN: Well, it's been deeply touching. I mean not only has one had telephone calls galore and telegrams, but even one telegram from an unknown person offering money to help to rebuild the Maltings—it has of course made a big reputation these last two years, and people have gone—got to love it as we have ourselves.[3] It's become a part of our family that—it's got a curious—tenderness. I—it had, of course it *will* have—this affection that it has grown up over these last two years.

BBC: Will it be the same sort of building or will you make any alterations?

BRITTEN: Oh well, I think there are certain things we have learned we could do better, but basically, of course, it will have the same glorious roof and keep the same brick if it's intact; and I think we've learnt perhaps some things not to do, but we've learnt an enormous amount of what to do in that hall.

BBC: It's been regarded very widely as one of the best if not *the* best concert hall in the world. Will it be that again?

BRITTEN: Well, we shall make it as good as we possibly can. Whether it is that, of course—I haven't been to all the halls all over the world, but I must say to perform in that hall is one of the great joys. It's—has a welcoming—I keep on saying it in the present because I'm sure it will be—well in the future. It has the most wonderful welcoming feeling as you walk on to the stage.

BBC: And how long in the future will it be before we see you playing there again?

BRITTEN: Well we are *determined* to do it by next Festival.[4]

BBC: *Very* best of luck, sir.

BRITTEN: Thank you very much.

[3] Queen Elizabeth rang personally to express her condolences, and in Parliament, when the Secretary of State for Education and Science, Miss Jennie Lee, was asked about the fire, she responded: 'I share the sorrow which every music lover must have felt at the loss of this fine building and I offer my sympathy in particular to Mr. Britten and his colleagues' (*Hansard*, 19 June 1969).

[4] They did.

94 *Idomeneo* in Performance (1969)

AMIS: *First of all, here is Benjamin Britten to talk about* Idomeneo. *This interview was recorded at the end of May, before the disastrous fire destroyed the Maltings, which should have been the setting for this new version of Mozart's opera.*[1]

BRITTEN: Ah, this is not really a new version. It's a fresh version; perhaps there's a subtle distinction. We decided on doing *Idomeneo* for the Maltings because it is the kind of opera, the kind of big, classic piece which would suit the—the character of the building and the fact, of course, that there is no proscenium arch. We had certain ideas of other operas we could do, but we decided on *Idomeneo* partly because it's a work that I've loved for many years, and it's a work which, well, Peter Pears wanted to do the part and he felt that it would suit him, and generally, I felt that perhaps I could guide our listeners—our audience—through the very intricate problem of what movements to play when.

Of course, there being the two major versions that Mozart left us, therein is the only way that one could possibly call it a new version, in that one has made a slightly different selection from the numbers in the various versions from people who've done it recently in the past. It is quite close to the Sadler's Wells version, with the major change that we are getting Idamante sung by a soprano and not by a tenor—of course [the tenor version] was the way that Mozart rearranged it for the second performance in his own lifetime.

AMIS: I didn't realize—I'm very ignorant on these matters—I didn't realize that there were two versions by Mozart. There are quite a number of different actual numbers, are there?

BRITTEN: Oh yes. I'm not a historian, and I perhaps won't get my facts absolutely right, but when it was first performed, which was, I think, when he was about 25, it was done as a full-length *opera seria*, with enormously elaborate arias; but he was a passionate creature, and he could *not* control his electric dramatic feeling for this subject. The work got more and more elaborate as he wrote it. He had an excellent producer with whom he worked a lot. He had, of course, his marvellous Mannheim Orchestra to write for, and the result was that the recitatives got more and more elaborate, and the nearer they got to the performance, they realized that the work was getting too long, and so right, I think, until a day or so before this first performance,

Source: Editor's transcript of recording (NSA M1603W). Broadcast 13 June 1969, BBC Radio 3 (Third Programme), 9.25 p.m.: interval talk with John Amis during the broadcast of *Idomeneo*. (Pre-recorded 4 June 1969.)

[1] *Idomeneo*, K. 366 (1780).

they were cutting the arias to leave a series, quite often, of accompanied recitatives.

The work was a great success, but the fashion was changing, and the work was only produced once again, I think in Vienna, about seven or eight years later, and [in] a quasi-amateur performance.[2] The singers weren't nearly so good. They couldn't do the 'garglings' which he called the earlier, elaborate scales and arpeggios in the vocal writing, so he did quite a lot of rewriting of the actual arias, changed some of them, and changed the original writing for Idamante from a castrato soprano to a tenor. He rearranged the two or three ensembles that Idamante was in, but, quite clearly, rather in a hurry, because they were done rather casually, and obviously he'd lost a great deal by the change of register.

We have gone back to the original version for these ensembles, and we are choosing some of the earlier versions of the arias and some of the later; but of course, we are following very much his own plan of making the work less artificial. The subject so took hold of him, and he felt so strongly about it that one must, I think, let the drama have full place in this—in this wonderful work.

It is a really astounding piece, and every moment of it is red hot with excitement. I think it was Einstein that said, 'He may have written better music later, but grander and more original music he never wrote.'[3]

AMIS: William Glock said with a smile on his face the other day 'Ask Ben if it's going to be anything like the Richard Strauss version of *Idomeneo*.'[4]

BRITTEN: I didn't hear the Strauss version of *Idomeneo*—I should be fascinated to hear it.

AMIS: But you haven't done any reorchestrating?

BRITTEN: No.

AMIS: Just a little tidying.

BRITTEN: No, just, really, making our own versions. One's had, in cuts, to write the odd bar here and there to get the keys right, but very—the minimal amount.

[2] This was most likely a concert performance, at Prince Auersperg's palace in Vienna in 1786.

[3] Peter Pears's copy of Alfred Einstein's *Mozart: His Character, His Work* (1946) has the following sentences highlighted in pencil: 'Mozart was never more independent than in *Idomeneo*. He wrote this work in a burst of musical inspiration.'

[4] Strauss's version of the opera was, like Britten's, an attempt to make sense of Mozart's different versions, and was produced in Vienna in 1931, the 150th anniversary of the work's premiere.

95 Radcliffe Music Award (1969)

For music & the University of Sussex, to-day is an important day. The first term of the Music School is only a few weeks old, and a most important & worthwhile Competition has been organised to celebrate it. Judging by the distinguished staff & the lively music students the department is going to have an exciting life, & enrich the musical life of the county & country. Our indebtness to the RADCLIFFE TRUST, which has made this possible, cannot be measured.[1]

We, the jury, assembled to judge this competition organised over a long period with great seriousness & intelligence have had a fascinating time, reading the scores & listening to the fine playing of the Allegri Quartet.[2] Four important British composers have been invited to write works and have clearly taken their task very seriously. We have listened carefully & sympathetically to the rehearsals & performances these last two days, & have come to the following conclusion. In spite of, in one case, a brilliantly intelligent gift; in another, a passionate and dedicated career; in the third, a most exciting promise; and lastly a vivid and original personality, we do not feel that one work stands high above the others—a 'flawless masterpiece'; nor do we feel that any of them lags way behind—a 'ghastly flop'. We would therefore like to divide the prizes equally between the four competitors, & suggest playing one movement from each of the quartets which we have selected. We are disappointed maybe to have come to this 'middle of the road' conclusion; but hope that you all, like us, have had an interesting & enjoyable musical experience.

We all feel that this has been a most worthwhile occasion to have produced four such remarkable compositions—that is, real works of art, & not just 'competition entries'.

Source: Autograph draft, [1969] (*GB-ALb* 1–02053844). Speech given on the occasion of the 1969 Radcliffe Music Award, 1 Nov. 1969. Nominees were Sebastian Forbes (b. 1941), Robert Sherlaw Johnson (1932–2000), Elizabeth Maconchy (1907–94), and Peter Sculthorpe (b. 1929). The award was administered by the University of Sussex. A concert of featuring these prize-winning quartets was held at Wigmore Hall on 15 Jan. 1970.

[1] The Radcliffe Trust, now Dr Radcliffe Trust, was fonded in 1714 to support craft and music education.

[2] British string quartet formed in 1953 by Eli Goren, James Barton, Patrick Ireland, and William Pleeth. It re-formed in 1968 with Hugh Maguire as leader, David Roth, Ireland, and Bruno Schrecker. There were further personnel changes in 1977 and 1983.

TUSA: The second time in five years you're setting out to raise money; how do you feel about it?

BRITTEN: Very depressed quite frankly. Depressed because one depends—one has depended in the past *so* much on our near and dear good friends to give us money. We've virtually never had one *big* gift; I mean the Arts Council has been very generous, and one or two business firms—Decca, for instance—have been very generous, but the bulk of the money in our first big money-raising appeal came from our subscribers to the Festival and the artists who've helped us over and over again. But the thought of having to start again, literally within a month of having achieved the first lot, is very frightening.

TUSA: Are you finding that there is more and more of a clash between the time that you have to spend in fund-raising and administration and the time you spend in writing music?

BRITTEN: Well one's life without administration is a very, very full one. And up 'til now one's been able to do it—to combine the two activities fairly easily. There have been clashes, I must admit, but now, with this *big* planning operation coming, the battle is already lost, I would say. I mean, for instance, these last few days I have been up in London conducting the operas, I've done some records,[1] and I came down here today to write music quickly before I go off to America and of course . . .

TUSA: We're here . . .

BRITTEN: . . . well I was not going to put it like that. No, but I'm very happy that, of course, that you have come to help us and say—and let us say—put our point of view to you, but it does take up time and, as I say, one's life is a rather full one. I do plan my writing very carefully and I've now got really only a matter of months to complete this opera I'm writing for BBC Television. In fact the cast is already booked for the recording in November of next year, and if I do break the schedule I shall get into trouble, and that's what keeps one awake in the early hours of the morning.

TUSA: Does it, do you think, actually affect the quality of what you write?

BRITTEN: I don't think actually it does; of course it affects the *quantity* of what I write, and that is the worrying thing, because actually the way I work is

Source: Editor's transcript of television interview (*GB-ALb* 3–9500661). Broadcast 1 Jan. 1970, BBC 2, 8.30 p.m.: interview with John Tusa for the series *The Money Programme*.

[1] *Children's Crusade* (1968) and *The Golden Vanity* (1966) were both recorded in October 1969, prior to Britten's and Pears's American recital tour. Also in October Britten conducted *The Rape of Lucretia* at Sadler's Wells.

basically to plan ahead and then find the time to write it down; so if the time doesn't come to write it down I don't think it makes the quality of the work any worse, but of course sometimes hurry can compel you to leave things that you're perhaps not very happy about.

TUSA: If this pressure continues, can you almost imagine yourself having almost second thoughts about being so deeply involved in the Festival?

BRITTEN: No, that I cannot imagine.

TUSA: At the same time this is something of a radical departure as far as the Festival is concerned, isn't it?[2] Getting in outside people to help like this . . .

BRITTEN: Yes. I think it means really that, you know, when you drop a stone in a pond, the circles get larger and larger, and this is an inevitable growth. I don't think we could expect the Festival, with its three weeks now and the arrival of the Maltings, to go on exactly as it did when we started—with ten days and the Jubilee Hall, with a seating capacity of 350. Naturally we must expand, we must be flexible; we hope it won't change the style of it and the atmosphere of it, but in order to fill 850 seats, say, once a day for three weeks, takes a certain amount of more organization, inevitably.

TUSA: How important is the larger sum that you're trying to raise—the over £200,000?

BRITTEN: It's really a sort of 'delayed desperately important'. You see, I can tell you the story a little about that. We've always realized, since we knew how good Snape was, that it was going to develop. And many things have happened to make us feel that it must get bigger and use all those very nice surroundings, but not yet. We didn't want to do it quite yet; we wanted to absorb what we'd got and then, at a later date, develop and improve. The fire has made any changes, any developments, immediate; we can't for instance have an appeal now for virtually £100,000 and then in five years' time have a third appeal for a large sum. So we really determined that we must do it all in one go. And so many things that have been *vaguely* in the back of all our minds have now got to come to the front of our minds.

TUSA: So this is not just a sum of money which it would be quite pleasant to have?

BRITTEN: No, it's a sum of money which we would have *certainly* had to ask for in say five years' or ten years' time, but because it's got to happen now, well, we've got to make these ideas which were vague, absolutely concrete. A part, of course, of that is for the endowment. We must have something to take this worry—this perpetual worry of money—away from us. Because

[2] With the advent of the new concert hall, issues of staffing, sponsorship, and Festival infrastructure were all suddenly very different from pre-1967.

that is really what this is: we've had, always, to think of every single penny, and sometimes one wants to be a little more relaxed than that.

TUSA: Aren't you going to be tempted to undertake a concert tour with Peter Pears, specifically for fund-raising? I mean, this would solve a lot of problems financially, wouldn't it?

BRITTEN: Yes I think it would. I mean, in these concerts that we're going to America to give now, we shall make a lot of money, but unfortunately I simply can't give up all that time for going around. What we're trying to do is to give rather special gala concerts, either here or in America, in the slightly more distant future.

TUSA: So this will be more of a burden on your time?

BRITTEN: That's what one comes back to over and over again. Because after all, one's main job *is* to write music, and one also musn't sort of get ill by betraying one's real self.

TUSA: You've said that you're constantly being worried by the financial side of the Festival, and you wanted some of these headaches removed, but what does money mean to you personally?

BRITTEN: Money is a means of doing what one wants to do, I would have thought. But I mean, certainly, I don't *exaggerate* the value of money, I don't think, because I know perfectly well that a shortage of money in planning Festival programmes is a good thing. It makes you economize. It makes you make the programmes have a shape. I mean, for instance, if you knew that you had unlimited money, this is a terrible thing to say at this moment, but I think it's true. If you knew you could suddenly have fourteen trombones, you would probably start using them, and then if you knew you could have thirty oboes you would use them. But that would make, I think, a diffused programme. The fact is that we know, because our budget is short, that you have to use the instruments to their fullest capacity, and that does give, I think, a shape and flavour to the programmes, which is a valuable thing.

TUSA: How important is the American side of fund-raising going to be to the overall success of the appeal?

BRITTEN: It's very difficult to say that at this moment. We *hope* it's going to be very important indeed. In fact we've had some very warm reactions from American foundations, and we have become a charity institution, whatever you call it—a foundation—in America, and so it should work well, but I think one must face the fact that America is having considerable difficulties in financing its *own* arts, and we know all of us what terrible difficulties the Metropolitan Opera is having, and there are many orchestras, and naturally they think home things must come first. And so it may not be as easy, and when Peter Pears and I go this week to America, I think we'll be able to gauge that a little bit more than we know now.

97 Aaron Copland: Seventieth-Birthday Tribute (1970)

Over the last few years Copland has been a regular visitor to this country; his lively and versatile conducting of the London Symphony Orchestra has become remarkably popular. It is a lot to do with these concerts that his own music has become so much better known here. For many of us no other music quite expresses the individual character and atmosphere of North America—young, fresh and gay, with considerable friendliness and warmth—but which also faces up to the disturbing problems which rack that enormous continent today. Notwithstanding this considerable 'local' colour the music is expressed in sophisticated and 'international' techniques which we can all appreciate. Not many people on this side of the Atlantic realise, however, although they might guess it if they had heard or met him during his visit to the [Aldeburgh] Festival in 1960, what a strong and healthy influence Aaron has had on the American musical scene; how he has supported all kinds of new music, helped younger composers, fought for higher standards of performance, for more adequate subsidies, and has taken brave stands on moral issues outside the purely musical world. Those who wish to find out something of his sympathetic attitudes should read his wise, instructive and entertaining books.[1]

We are happy to salute a fascinating, important composer and a lovable human being on his seventieth birthday, and wish him many more. Not only the U.S. musical world but ours could not easily do without him.

Source: AFPB (1970), 30.

[1] *What to Listen for in Music* (New York: Whittlesey House, 1939; 1988); *Our New Music* (New York: Whittlesey House, 1941, rev. and enlarged 2/1968 as *The New Music 1900–1960*); *Music and Imagination* (Cambridge, Mass.: Harvard University Press, 1952).

98 James Blades: *Percussion Instruments and their History* (1970)

Everyone knows that James Blades is one of our great percussionists.[1] He plays all the various instruments with accuracy and an infectious sense of rhythm, and his timpani playing is noted for its impeccable intonation and beautiful tone. I have been a lucky composer because, under my direction, he has played in ten of my operas, and also in those two difficult percussive nuts to crack—the *Nocturne* and *Cello Symphony*.

Not so many know that Blades is a brilliant and resourceful craftsman, experimenting with skill and ingenuity in the making and assembling of many of the instruments he plays, and in the creation of new ones. Some of the instruments he has made for me—often from the slenderest hints—are described in Chapter 16.[2]

All his colleagues, and I am proud to consider myself as one, know what a generous friend Jimmy Blades is; how he will help an inexperienced player; how he will hurry to this or that school to advise the young in their percussion problems, or turn up at a recording session to give them confidence; and he will lend out his instruments, often at serious inconvenience to himself. We, who have toured abroad with him, have seen excited groups gathering around him after rehearsals and performances, commenting or questioning. Goodness knows what language he uses, but no matter, since he has a Slav-like ease of communication with everyone.

Now, on the publication of this great book, a large public will realise what a scholar Professor James Blades is. Of course many will have heard his enchanting lectures, or read his informative guides to Percussion Instruments, but now the vast range of his learning must come as a surprise.

Man, thousands of years ago, discovered that hitting something in a rhythmic way excited his friends or terrified his enemies, and through the successive years, in every part of the world, man has experimented with hitting something different in a new way. The results of these experiments are described and catalogued here, and are shown to us in exciting illustrations. For all its exhaustive information, James Blades' great tome is never exhausting, but is endlessly fascinating and entertaining.

Source: Foreword to James Blades, *Percussion Instruments and their History* (London: Faber & Faber, 1970), 27–8. Foreword dated January 1970.

[1] James Blades (1901–99), English percussionist and teacher, who collaborated often with Britten, notably with the English Chamber Orchestra.

[2] This is a detailed study of 20th-century orchestration, 'Composers' Use of Modern Percussion'.

99 Artist's Choice: Cecil Aronowitz (1970)

Cecil Aronowitz has been a regular and welcome visitor to the Festival for about twenty years.[1] His remarkable playing has been heard each year from the pit of the Jubilee Hall, as our viola soloist in operas such as *The Rape of Lucretia*, *Albert Herring* and *The Turn of the Screw*, not to mention *The Little Sweep*. His musicianly leading of the violas (and what a joy to work with!) has been indispensable ever since the E.C.O. became our resident orchestra. Perhaps his most spectacular appearances have been in the Church Parables in Orford Church, where he can be seen energetically leading and encouraging the other instrumentalists (and of course singing the plainchant in the processions). We are delighted that his is the Artist's Choice of the year, and that he will be partnered for most of the programme by his young wife Nicola.

Source: AFPB (1970), 60.

[1] Cecil Aronowitz (1916–78), English viola player, was closely associated with Britten and his music, beginning in the 1930s, when he was principal violist of the Boyd Neel Orchestra, through to his performances with the English Chamber Orchestra. He was director of string studies at the Britten–Pears School from 1977 until his death a year later. Aronowitz gave the first performance of the revised version of *Lachrymae* (1950, rev. 1970) and, in 1977, the UK premiere of Britten's arrangement of this work for solo viola and string orchestra (Op. 48a).

100 *Therapy in Music for Handicapped Children* (1971)

This is an intensely moving, as well as a very important book. It is the story of a distinguished American composer virtually stopping his 'abstract' composing, as it were, in mid-career and using his talents and energies to discover ways of helping by music mentally deprived children.[1] I imagine Paul Nordoff previously knew little of this tragic side of life, and it was a shattering experience for him to come into contact with it: a glance at the illustrations at the back of this book can give a hint of that. This quietly written account of his and Mr. Robbins' patient experiments, their journeys into the obscured world of these children, will not easily be forgotten.

I am not qualified to comment on the importance of the psychological cures that these two men have achieved, nor of the extension of diagnosis. But this I can say—the book is as well highly important for musicians, particularly composers. At this curious moment in musical history the validity of communication in art has itself been called in question, and it is wonderful to have a book where the concentration is entirely on just this, on communication pure and simple. Any and every form of musical style and technique is tried and used: scales, old and new, chords, rhythms, new kinds of instruments—I long to introduce my friend Rostropovich to the one-stringed 'cello, to find out what *he* could do with it. It is indeed salutary to have a description of a composer humbly and un-self-consciously indulging in every sort of freedom, and being guided solely by his success in communicating with, and concern for the well-being of, his young, sick listeners. I can recommend this book wholeheartedly not only to humanitarian readers, but to my musical colleagues as well. We can all learn from it.

Source: Foreword to Paul Nordoff and Clive Robbins, *Therapy in Music for Handicapped Children* (London: Victor Gollancz, 1971).

[1] Paul Nordoff (1909–77), American composer and music therapist. From 1959 he more or less established the practice of music therapy for handicapped children in America.

101 Anthony Gishford: *Grand Opera* (1972)

I was most interested to learn that my friend Anthony Gishford was producing a book on opera, in the context of the great Opera Houses of the world.[1] His knowledge of the subject is wide, for he has been a keen amateur of opera all his life, and for the last twenty years or so he has actively taken part in its administration, encouraging those who perform and create it.

I am interested in the book because for thirty years writing operas has been my main musical occupation. Many complain about this, those who do not like the medium, who distrust it ('impure!'), would rather I wrote more symphonies, quartets, concertos, song cycles and cello suites. Be that as it may, ever since those fruitless struggles with *Paul Bunyan* up to the immediate struggles with the problems of *Death in Venice* I have been fascinated by the most powerful medium of musical communication that I know.[2]

There have always been Cassandras.[3] Before *Peter Grimes* there was no future for an English opera. In spite of its favourable reception in 1945 those responsible for its production were all summarily removed from Sadlers Wells.[4] There was no money (there never is) for opera, so a group of friends and I tried to devise a cheaper form of it—no chorus, tiny cast, an orchestra of twelve. After a successful opening of *The Rape of Lucretia* at Glyndebourne and an encouraging visit abroad, a dismal tour of the English provinces followed—'casts must be international'—and so we were compelled to start our own opera group, and our own Aldeburgh Festival.

In Germany the destroyed opera houses were going to be rebuilt, and indeed in London at the last minute Boosey and Hawkes had rescued the Royal Opera House from being turned into a Dance Hall, but the outlook was uncertain and Covent Garden was hardly the place for small-scale opera. At

Source: Introduction to Anthony Gishford (ed.), *Grand Opera* (London: Weidenfeld & Nicolson, 1972), 11–12.

[1] Anthony Gishford (1908–75), a director at Boosey & Hawkes from 1947 to 1958, and at Faber Music from 1966. In 1963 he edited a *Festschrift* in honour of Britten's fiftieth birthday. He is the dedicatee of Britten's fourth volume of folksongs, Moore's *Irish Melodies* (1957).

[2] Britten was at this time composing *Death in Venice*, a process that became increasingly urgent once he was diagnosed with heart disease. The revival and revisions of *Paul Bunyan* in the final years of his life prompted a change in Britten's attitude towards his first opera.

[3] i.e. a prophet of disaster, usually disbelieved. In Greek mythology her predictions were invariably correct.

[4] Britten's dramatic language here is not quite accurate. The *Grimes* rehearsal process had certainly been fractious—at one point a deputation from the company came to see the production team to complain of the time and resources that were being spent on this 'cacophony'—possibly fuelled by resentment of Britten's and Pears's pacifism and homosexuality, but it was ultimately their choice to leave Sadler's Wells for a more positive artistic environment.

Aldeburgh we made do with the Jubilee Hall. The critical Cassandras had again raised their voices—if only another *Peter Grimes* rather than these chamber affairs—*The Times* damned *Albert Herring*. But thank goodness the old piece survived, since many a small struggling opera company has relied on it to keep going, and five years ago Budapest totted up its fiftieth performance.

But art never wants to stand still, even the art of opera was once new and strange: even if all the great popular favourites of today belong to the proscenium-arch theatres, it has to express itself in the framework of an ever changing society. So we tried operas for children and by children, audience participation, operas in churches (usually the best buildings in small towns and villages), and finally opera on the open stage (the Maltings). And so it goes on.

Opera is not dead. The book before you demonstrates this. The view across the centuries is magnificent, revealing much beauty and truth, tragic, everyday—even occasionally funny.

One learns much from the past, but one is living in the present. There are many daunting problems, but there is much that is encouraging: think, in Britain alone, of the success of Covent Garden, the astonishing rise of the Coliseum, the Scottish and Welsh operas and the possibility of a new company for the Midlands.[5] Among the many problems, the financial one daunts us the most, with costs rising everywhere, and experimental works scarcely getting a look in. Opera has always cost a lot of money. But since there are today no princelings to put their hands deep in their pockets and show that the Darmstadt opera is as good as the Kassel one, now all opera houses are in receipt of substantial subsidies from the state, the municipality, from private communities of opera lovers, from great and small charities, from radio and television and even (if we are very lucky) from business firms. Yet not all of these together can dam the rising tide of costs. The answer seems to be that composers, producers, organisers of operas (or 'music-theatre' as some people prefer it to be called) must be flexible, think of different ways of presenting them, ways that suit the all-purpose hall, the factory canteen, the school gym, the college campus, with good lighting, or no lighting, with elaborate costumes, or in every-day dress, full orchestra or piano and drums—they will all work as long as singers can act and actors can sing, the producer can

[5] English National Opera grew out of Sadler's Wells. Stephen Arlen, director from 1966 to 1972, initiated the move to the Coliseum and in 1974, while the Earl of Harewood was director, the company's name was changed. ENO North, based in Leeds, was founded in 1978. It became Opera North in 1981. Welsh National Opera, based in Cardiff, was founded in 1946 and maintains to this day a reputation for innovative productions and prescient use of young singers. Scottish Opera was founded in 1962 by Alexander Gibson (1926–95) and others. It gave early independent performances of Britten operas, notably *Albert Herring*.

produce, the conductor (if there is one) can conduct, and composers can find the right notes.

For the great repertoire of the last three hundred years the beautiful baroque houses so well described and lavishly illustrated in this book will always be needed. This is what most people still consider to be 'going to the opera', but it isn't the only way.

102 John Bird: *Percy Grainger* (1976)

To have met Percy Grainger even as an old man is a cherished memory. His warmth, his originality, his charm were unforgettable, and his genial energy had already become a myth. The masterly folk-song arrangements with their acutely beautiful feeling for sound were our first musical introduction, and later the preparation of a record of his music was an exciting and revealing experience.[1] Repeated performances strengthened our respect for his work, and our few meetings confirmed our affection and admiration for the man.

It was hardly to be expected that the depth beneath the dazzling surface could be without some turbulence. In John Bird's sympathetic and tactful biography he has beautifully balanced the brilliance and turbulence of this unbalanced genius—we are grateful to him.

Source: Prefatory note by Benjamin Britten and Peter Pears to John Bird, *Percy Grainger* (Elek Books, 1976), p. ix; new edn. (Oxford: Oxford University Press, 1999).

[1] Britten had first been struck by Grainger's folksong arrangements in the 1930s. The LP of Grainger's arrangements was released by Decca in 1969, one of the first important modern recordings of Grainger's works. Britten 'lovingly and reverently' dedicated his *Suite on English Folk Tunes* 'A time there was . . .' (1974) to the memory of Grainger.

103 Tribute to Paul Sacher (1976)

Our dear Paul—

We want to join in the chorus of congratulation to you in reaching so triumphantly your seventieth birthday. Though we have not seen you as often as we would like to have done in these last years, whether at Schönenberg or Aldeburgh, we have been very clearly aware of how you (and Maja for we cannot think of one of you without the other) continue in your splendid dual capacity as performer and patron.

How much do all musicians owe to your skill and your dedication and what have not composers owed to you for many many years now! You have been a model as a patron and performer and all of 'Music's Children' are grateful to you and proud of you.

Thank you, dear Paul and dear Maja, for being what you are and Many happy returns of the Day is the heartfelt wish of,

Your old friends
Ben & Peter

Editor's title.
Source: Contribution by Benjamin Britten and Peter Pears to *Dank an Paul Sacher* (Zurich: Atlantis Musikbuch-Verlag, 1976), 65. Letter dated 23 Feb. 1976, published in facsimile and in German translation. Paul Sacher (1906–99), Swiss conductor and inspired contemporary-music patron, who founded the Basle Chamber Orchestra in 1926, the Schola Cantorum Basiliensis in 1933, and whose commissioned works include Bartók's *Music for Strings, Percussion and Celesta* (1936). He conducted the first performance of Britten's *Cantata academica, carmen basiliense* in 1960. Britten's other tribute to him on his seventieth birthday was the miniature *Tema 'Sacher'*, composed for solo cello, at Rostropovich's suggestion, and intended as the basis of a series of eleven variations by composers including Berio, Boulez, Dutilleux, Ginastera, and Henze. The twelve pieces—ultimately independent of Britten's theme and each other—were published in *12 Hommages à Paul Sacher pour violoncelle* (Universal Edition, n.d.).

PART V

Introductory Notes

ON BRITTEN'S MUSIC

Five Walztes (Waltzes) (1923–5, rev. 1969) (1970)[1]

When I was a child and composing like mad, I believed that all the best music not only ended exactly at the bottom of the page, but also only appeared in 'collections'. So, filling up my shelves were volumes consisting of:

> 4 Scherzos, 4 Bourrees, 6 Themas, 24 Themes, 5 Suites, 3 Toccatas, 4 Etudes Symphoniques, 2 Fantasies, 3 Canons, 12 Piano Sonatas, etc., etc.

There was seldom just *a* Polka or *a* March!

In 1925 came 10 Walztes, including a Petite Valse—it seems sad that my French spelling was better than my English. Several of them were written before that, and since the composer was a very ordinary little boy, they are all pretty juvenile (here was no Mozart, I fear). But perhaps they may be useful for the young or inexperienced to practise; certainly my publisher and I hope so.

Tit for Tat (1928–31, rev. 1968) (1969)[2]

Five settings from boyhood of poems by Walter de la Mare, for voice and piano

When I was at school, I wrote a great many songs, and there were far more settings of de la Mare than of any of the other thirty poets that I set. Last year I dug out some, written between the ages of fourteen and seventeen, cleaned them very slightly, and here at this first performance, offer them in gratitude to the poet's son, the wise and encouraging chairman of my new publishers, whose father's poems have meant so much to me all through my life. I evidently copied some of the poems from inaccurate reprints in anthologies, so some of the texts reproduced below differ from the definitive edition.

[1] Preface to published score (London: Faber Music, 1970).

[2] AFPB (1969), 65–6.

Tit for Tat (1928–31, rev. 1968) (1969)[3]

Five settings from boyhood of poems by Walter de la Mare, for voice and piano

Between 1922 and 1930 when I was a schoolboy, I must have written well over fifty songs—most of them straight off without much forethought; others were written and rewritten many times in a determined if often unsuccessful effort to 'get them right'. The choice of poets was nothing if not catholic. There are more than thirty of them, ranging from the Bible to Kipling, from Shakespeare to an obscure magazine poet 'Chanticleer'; there were many settings of Shelley and Burns and Tennyson, of a poem by a schoolmaster friend, songs to texts by Hood, Longfellow, 'Anon', and several French poets, and one to the composer's own words ('one day when I went home, I sore a boat on the sands'). In some cases the songs were written so hurriedly that there was no time to write the words in, or even to note the name of the poem or poet. The poet whose name appears most frequently is Walter de la Mare, whose verse caught my fancy very early on. I possessed several of his volumes but a few poems were evidently copied from inaccurate reprints in anthologies. The differences between these and the authentic versions are noted in the reproduction of the texts that follow.

Most of the settings are, of course, very naive, but I have chosen those which seem to me to be as complete an expression as is possible from a composer in his early teens. Once or twice when the fumblings were too obvious, the experienced middle-aged composer has come to the aid of the beginner. Oddly enough, the inadequacies seemed to be more striking in the later songs—new musical styles had appeared on the composer's horizon too recently to be assimilated. One of the songs was written during the early months of my first year at College, when I was on the way to becoming a professional; perhaps this is cheating, but it seems to me that the style is on a par with the others. At any rate, although I hold no claims whatever for the songs' importance or originality, I do feel that the boy's vision has a simplicity and clarity which might have given a little pleasure to the great poet, with his unique insight into a child's mind. It has given me great pleasure to dig these old scraps out, to titivate them a little, in honour of the poet's son on his birthday, and in gratitude for his inspiration and encouragement as a publisher.

[3] Preface to published score (London: Faber Music, 1969).

String Quartet in D (1931) (1975)[4]

I studied at the RCM from 1930 to 1933 but my musical education was perhaps more outside the College than in it. Although my teacher for composition was John Ireland, I saw Frank Bridge almost daily and I showed him every 'major' work. One of my problems at that time was how to hear some of the things I was writing and in two cases, at least, outsiders came to my help. *A Boy Was Born*, for instance, was tried over by the BBC Singers. I wrote this quartet in 1931 and Mr Howard-Jones (Evelyn Howard-Jones, the pianist and friend of Delius) arranged for it to be played through by the Stratton Quartet. Another of my extra-mural activities was singing madrigals in a choir conducted by Arnold Foster, and madrigals became a great passion; the influence of them can perhaps be seen in this quartet. I remember well that when I showed the quartet to Frank Bridge he complained that the counterpoint in it was too vocal. Maybe, particularly over the first two movements, he was right, but John Ireland did not agree. (Ireland and Bridge were old friends and had great fights over my education.)

1 *Allegro maestoso*

The material for this movement is stated immediately: seven bars unison of jagged phrases starting with a falling octave. There is a gentle, more flowing second subject in the viola. (There is much solo writing in this quartet for the viola; Bridge was a wonderful viola player and I was studying the instrument myself, so the viola was a popular instrument.)

2 *Lento ed espressivo*

A soft, sighing minor tune with some of that 'vocal' writing. A murmuring semiquaver passage accompanies a stately second subject which leads to a lively climax. The viola (unmuted) plays the return of the first tune.

3 *Allegro giocoso*

A gay little 6/8 movement in rondo form. It was not always so little, because I have made a sizeable cut in this movement—the only alteration worth mentioning that I have allowed myself in this forty-four-year-old work.

[4] AFPB (1975), 21.

Simple Symphony, Op. 4 (1934) (1955)[5]

For string orchestra

Once upon a time there was a prep-school boy. He was called Britten mi., his initials were E.B., his age was nine, and his locker was number seventeen. He was quite an ordinary little boy; he took his snake-belt to bed with him; he loved cricket, only quite liked football (although he kicked a pretty 'corner'); he adored mathematics, got on all right with history, was scared by Latin Unseen; he behaved fairly well, only ragged the recognised amount, so that his contacts with the cane or the slipper were happily rare (although one nocturnal expedition to stalk ghosts left its marks behind); he worked his way up the school slowly and steadily, until at the age of thirteen he reached that pinnacle of importance and grandeur never to be quite equalled in later days: the head of the Sixth, head-prefect, and Victor Ludorum. But . . . there was one curious thing about this boy: he wrote music. His friends bore with it, his enemies kicked a bit but not for long (he was quite tough), the staff couldn't object if his work and games didn't suffer. He wrote lots of it, reams and reams of it. I don't really know when he had time to do it. In those days, long ago, prep-school boys didn't have much free time; the day started with early work at 7.30, and ended (if you were lucky not to do extra prep.) with prayers at 8.0—and the hours in between were fully organised. Still there were odd moments in bed, there were half holidays and Sundays too, and somehow these reams and reams got written. And they are still lying in an old cupboard to this day—string quartets (six of them); twelve piano sonatas; dozens of songs; sonatas for violin, sonatas for viola and 'cello too; suites, waltzes, rondos, fantasies, variations; a tone-poem *Chaos and Cosmos*; a tremendous symphony, for gigantic orchestra including eight horns and oboe d'amore (started on January 17 and finished February 28); an oratorio called *Samuel*: all the opus numbers from 1 to 100 were filled (and catalogued) by the time Britten mi. was fourteen.

Of course they aren't very good, these works; inspiration didn't always run very high, and the workmanship wasn't always academically sound, and although our composer looked up oboe d'amore in the orchestra books, he hadn't much of an idea what it sounded like; besides, for the sake of neatness, every piece had to end precisely at the bottom of the right-hand page, which doesn't always lead to a satisfactory conclusion. No, I'm afraid they aren't very great; but when Benjamin Britten, a proud young composer of twenty (who'd already had a work broadcast), came along and looked in this cupboard, he found some of them not too uninteresting; and so, rescoring them for strings, changing bits here and there, and making them more fit for general consumption, he turned them into a SIMPLE SYMPHONY, and here it is.

[5] Sleevenote to Decca recording, LW5163 [1955].

Holiday Diary, Op. 5 (1934) (n.d.)[6]

Suite for piano

These little pieces were written just ten years ago, and they are (subjective) impressions of a boy's seaside holiday, in pre-war days.

I Early morning bathe: There is, as might be expected, a somewhat characteristic opening, before the main, rhythmic & flowing, section begins.
II Sailing: descriptive of the varying moods that can occur in small-boat sailing.
III Fun-fair: a lively & care-free rondo, with several side-shows.
IV Night: a cool, starry, seascape—the day & it's [*sic*] excitements are nearly forgotten.

Our Hunting Fathers, Op. 8 (1936) (1936)[7]

Symphonic cycle for high voice and orchestra

Poems on animals in their relationship to humans—as pests, pets, and as a means of sport—have been chosen by W.H. Ander [Auden] as a basis for this work. To these he has added a prologue and an epilogue.

The scoring is for soprano solo and a normal concert orchestra (with the addition of a saxophone).

Prologue—[*Lento quasi recitativo*]. The words are set in a natural recitative fashion for the voice—supported by simple chords for the full orchestra. At 'O pride so hostile to our charity' the strings introduce a phrase which receives considerable prominence in each subsequent movement.

[A] Rats Away!—[*Allegro con fusco*] [*sic*] Loud fragmentary phrases for full orchestra, and eventually for the soloist, lead to an emphatic protest from the wood-wind. The soloist interrupts this with a rapid chant, against a very light background in the orchestra. When 'St. Kasi' is reached, quick quaver figures in the flutes and bassoons indicate a more subjective aspect of the pests. After a slight lull, the chant reappears in a more dignified form. But this time it is swamped gradually by the orchestra—the fragmentary phrases (from the beginning of the song) even creeping into the soloist's part. At the end the wood-wind protest dies away somewhat hopelessly.

[B] Messaline—[*Andante Lento*]. Alternating with some emotional string passages the soloist repeatedly laments 'Ay me, alas, heigh-ho!' Then she tells

[6] Autograph draft, n.d. (*GB-ALb* 1–02053849). Programme note for recital by Clifford Curzon, 1944. Reproduced in Mitchell and Reed, 348–9.

[7] Programme note for 34th Triennial Musical Festival, Norwich, 25 Sept. 1936 (*GB-ALb* 7–02053446), 15–16.

the sad story in a simple melodic line, which grows more and more passionate. A horn *glissando* is the climax, then a long series of heart-broken lamentations follows—started by the soloist and culminating with the saxophone. A few quiet chords for violas and 'cellos commit the soul to rest.

[C] Dance of Death (Hawking for the Partridge)—[*Prestissimo vivace*]. The soprano runs rapidly through the names of most of the birds concerned in this hunt, interspersing it often with the cry 'whurret!' The orchestra takes this to a climax. A sudden outburst from the trombones is the first indication that all is not as well as it might be. However with an effort the orchestra recovers, and the soloist launches into a hearty song—'Sith sickles and the shearing scythes!' At a climax the roll-call is again called, but once more the trombones interrupt. Something depressing appears to have happened, as the succeeding passage is of a wailing nature, with sad 'whurrets' for the clarinet, and dismal 3rds in the bassoons—perhaps a bird has been hurt. But after another bang the movement continues with additional energy, and a big climax follows with a much extended version of 'Sith Sickles' on the trumpet and wood-wind. 'Well flown, eager kite!' is sung exultantly by the soloist. At this everyone falls to dancing a merry folk measure, but the trombones interrupt again and with a string *glissando* the movement proceeds with more desperation than before—the soloist is left far behind. The trombones continue with their interruption and eventually overwhelm everyone. The percussion maintains an exhausted roll; vain efforts are made to restart the movement: but the death is sounded by the muted brass. A 'whurret!' from the top of the soloist to the bottom of the double-basses finishes the movement.

Epilogue and Funeral March—[*Andante molto lento*]. A ghost of the hunting song on the xylophone appears at intervals. The soloist sings the words in a simple recitation, with fragmentary support from the orchestra. When the words 'that human company' are reached the fragments gather into a broader theme for violins, which reaches a climax at the word 'anonymous'. The work finishes with a funeral march for the whole orchestra (brass and percussion muted, strings *col legno* and *pizzicato*) with fragments from other movements, and the ghost on the xylophone persisting to the end.

Soirées musicales, Op. 9 (1936) (n.d.)[8]

Suite of five movements from Rossini for orchestra

These five short movements based on themes of Rossini were originally written for use in films—at the instigation of M. Alberto Cavalcanti of G.P.O. Films—in the summer of 1935.

[8] Autograph draft, n.d. (*GB-ALb* 1–02053805).

Originally scored for a few wind & percussion instruments & wordless boys' chorus, they were arranged for orchestra in the summer of 1936.

I. March—(Theme from William Tell—ballet music)
II. Canzonetta
III. Tirolese
IV. Bolero.

All these are founded on songs from a late volume of Songs entitled 'Soirrées Musicales'.

V. Tarantelle. These themes are from a part-song entitled Charity.

The orchestration is straightforward & simple, & was especially designed to be suitable for performance by either small or large orchestra. The latter version is being used to-night.

Variations on a Theme of Frank Bridge, Op. 10 (1977) (n.d.)[9]

For string orchestra

Benjamin Britten
Born in Lowestoft, November 1913. Educated at Gresham's & at the R.C.M. (Ireland for comp. B. [Benjamin] for piano). Otherwise pupil of Frank Bridge from age of twelve onwards. Performances at I.S.C.M. Festival Florence 1934 (Oboe quartet)[;] Barcelona ISCM 1936 (Violin Suite)[;] Norwich 1936 Festival (Our Hunting Fathers)[;] Salzburg 1937 (see below). Spends time writing incidental music to films, stage plays, & radio plays, with occasional conducting & piano playing.

The present work was written in June & July 1937 especially for Boyd Neel & his orchestra to play at the Salzburg Festival of that year. It was written as a tribute to my master Frank Bridge, on a section of one of whose Idylls for String Quartet it is based.

A normal string orchestra with soloists is used.

After a short introduction the theme is presented by a solo quartet & repeated by the full orchestra.

Variation I — Adagio. Sustained chords in lower strings with occasional flowing phrases in the violin.
Var II — March—in dotted rhythm.
Var III — Romance. A tune on the violins with the theme in the bass.
Var IV — Aria Italiana. First Violins, con bravura, with strummed accompaniment.

[9] Autograph draft, n.d. (*GB-ALb* 1–02053838).

Var V	Bourrée classique. Heavy & marked. Violin Solo in the middle.
Var VI	Wiener Walz [*sic*]. A fast waltz with long 'up-beats'.
Var VII	Molto Perpetuo. Everyone in unison.
Var VIII	Funeral march. Marked bass with sustained upper parts.
Var IX	Chant. Violas 'Soli' in three parts.
Var X	Fugue & Finale. The Fugue is in four parts (I) Fast & light mostly in unison (II) with prominent bass (III) Heavily marked (IV) muted & 'pp' in 11 parts with Canto Fermo for 4 soloists. Finale—theme is stated in its entirety with short coda.

Mont Juic, Op. 12 (1937) (n.d.)[10]

Suite of Catalan Dances for orchestra by Lennox Berkeley and Benjamin Britten

In April 1936 the composers attended the I.S.C.M. Festival in Barcelona, Catalonia, Spain, at which they both had works performed. One of the items on the schedule of the Festival was a Folk Dance exhibition in the Exposition Grounds on Mont Juic a mountain near Barcelona. The composers were struck by the charm and vitality of many of the tunes used for the dancing and jotted down some of them. Back in England in the summer they decided to collaborate on a work based on these tunes. Mount Juic is the result. It will be noted that the tunes resemble the French and Italian rather than the Castilian, or what is usually expected of the Spanish. There are four straightforward movements.

I. Andante Maestoso. A pompous dance somewhat in the style of a classical 18th century Minuet.

II. Allegro Grazioso. A gay dance like a Gavotte.

III. Lament—Barcelona July 1936. (it will be remembered that there was a civil war in Spain three months after the Festival) This is a slow Sarabande-like dance, but in the middle comes a suggestion of a Sardana, the Catalan national dance, now forbidden in Fascist Spain.

IV. Allegro Molto. A riotous number in Waltz time.

Piano Concerto, Op. 13 (1938) (1938)[11]

This Pianoforte Concerto in D was written during the first half of this year and finished on the 27th July. It was conceived with the idea of exploiting various

[10] Draft (typescript), n.d. (*GB-ALb* 1–02053834).

[11] Programme note for BBC Prom concert, 18 Aug. 1938 (*GB-ALb* 7–02053448), 9–10.

important characteristics of the pianoforte, such as its enormous compass, its percussive quality, and its suitability for figuration; so that it is not by any means a Symphony with pianoforte, but rather a bravura Concerto with orchestral accompaniment. In the first and third movements the effect is that of a duel between the orchestra and the soloist. The four movements are simple and direct in form, but a brief description may be found helpful.

Allegro molto e con brio.—The pianoforte starts the first movement with an energetic leaping *motif* which sets the mood for its own side of the argument. This is the principal subject of the movement. The orchestra continues with a subsidiary phrase which reaches an angry climax in the alternation of two not very closely related chords—an idea which has, however, important significance throughout the work. After some discussion the orchestra introduces hesitatingly the second principal subject—a longer flowing tune on the woodwind. This the pianoforte mocks in brilliant fashion, and the orchestra tries to further its cause, with the tune (*ff largamente*) in the strings. The second section of the movement presents a grimmer aspect of this material. The first subject appears as an *ostinato* growling in the bass, with the orchestra menacing above it. For a moment the tension is relaxed, but a fierce dialogue between bass and pianoforte interrupts, which in its turn dies away in a series of chromatic runs leading directly to the third section (recapitulation). Here a species of compromise (both subjects appearing at the same time) is attempted and worked out at some length, but it is only after the *cadenza* that the pianoforte is finally tamed and plays the second subject softly and tenderly.

Allegretto, alla valse.—The second movement, again in D, is quiet throughout—as if overheard from the next room. The viola solo and clarinet suggest the first tune and the pianoforte adds the chordal *motif* from the first movement as *codetta*. After a slightly more defined repetition, the pianoforte starts a running theme, supported ***pp*** by waltz-rhythms in the whole orchestra. This grows louder and louder and eventually the first waltz tune returns energetically and *forte*, as if the door has been slightly opened. But it is soon shut again, and to the end of the movement the mood is that of the beginning. The chordal *motif* is used again and again rather ominously.

Recitative and Aria.—The first section of this movement is in the form of a dialogue between the pianoforte and the various solo instruments of the orchestra (in order, oboe, clarinet, bassoon, flute, horn). One by one they hint at a tune, and the pianoforte rather impertinently makes fun of them. Their mood passes from that of sorrow to indignation, and finally in a burst of wrath (the brass ***ff*** stating the chordal *motif* from the first two movements) the pianoforte is made to see reason, and when the 'cellos start a broad theme, the pianoforte merely accompanies and interrupts no longer. This theme (which has grown from the seeds sown in the recitatives) is continued with increasing warmth, and is finally stated very broadly by the whole orchestra. As a *coda* the pianoforte, now very subdued, continues the figuration used before as an accompaniment.

Allegro moderato—sempre alla marcia.—Suggestions of marching rhythms follow directly from the previous movement, and lead to a series of march tunes, played full of confidence by the pianoforte and then by the orchestra. A somewhat jingoistic dialogue between the brass and the piano is started, but this has not progressed far when a feeling of doubt creeps into the music, and the marching rhythm fades away inconclusively. The violas and 'cellos have a solemn chant which the pianoforte echoes; but this moment of reflection is soon over, and the marching rhythm begins again in earnest. The development is wholly occupied with this element, and the mood becomes more and more tense. Finally, after a series of crashes in the orchestra against a furious running passage in the pianoforte, the chant reappears in agitated form and the music dies away with mutterings from the orchestra. But bass drum and cymbals start the rhythm again. The pianoforte has a short, excited *cadenza*, and the orchestra shouts the march in all its swagger. The feeling of triumph is increased by a *Presto coda*, and the music rushes headlong to its confident finish.

Piano Concerto, Op. 13 (1938, rev. 1945)

(1971)[12]

I wrote this Concerto in the spring of 1938, when I was living in Snape, and it is dedicated to Lennox Berkeley, who was sharing the Old Mill (at the top of the hill) with me. I played it first at a Promenade Concert conducted by Henry Wood on August the 18th of that year, and subsequently once or twice again with him. I decided in 1945 to replace the earlier third movement (*Recitative and Aria*) by the present *Impromptu*. For this movement I used only material contemporary with the rest of the work (notably from incidental music to a B.B.C. play *King Arthur*), and some of the figuration from the earlier movement.

The above note was written for a concert in The Maltings on June 18th 1967, on which occasion Slava Richter played this Concerto for the first time. Since then he has made the work very much his own, playing it with unbelievable brilliance and warm sympathy. He has played it in many countries, giving an extraordinary performance at the Covent Garden Gala for the Maltings Fund last December, shortly after recording it for Decca.

The theme of the *Impromptu* was the subject of the Improvisations for orchestra by William Walton, which had its first European performance here at the last Festival.

[12] AFPB (1971), 44.

Ballad of Heroes, Op. 14 (1939) (1973)[13]

For tenor (or soprano) solo, chorus and orchestra

In 1936 my Suite for violin and piano was played at the ISCM Festival in Barcelona, and I went and played it there with Antonio Brosa. There were many things which impressed me about Barcelona (not least the singing of Vittoria's music by the boys in the Abbey of Monserrat), but very evident also was the tension which was all too soon to erupt in the Spanish Civil War—that ghastly event which Communists and Fascists were to treat as a cynical try-out for a greater conflict. I had already written a suite of dances on Spanish tunes with Lennox Berkeley (*Mont Juic*), and when I was asked to write a piece for a Festival of Music for the People, it seemed natural to choose a piece which could express my sympathy with the beleaguered Spanish Republic and honour a brave, unhappy people. Auden had gone off to Spain, and before leaving he wrote in the flyleaf of a score of mine the poem 'It's farewell to the drawing-room's civilised cry'. This I used in the *Ballad*, with some other verses which Randall Swingler wrote, I think for the occasion. The *Ballad* was first performed at the Queen's Hall on 5 April 1939, with Walter Widdop as soloist, conducted by Constant Lambert.

Violin Concerto, Op. 15 (1939) (1971)[14]

1 *Moderato con moto* 2 *Vivace* leading to 3 *Passacaglia: Andante Lento*

This Concerto was written during the summer months of 1939, whilst I was staying with friends on Long Island, New York. The Spanish violinist Antonio Brosa gave the first performance at Carnegie Hall, New York, on March 28th 1940, with the New York Philharmonic Orchestra under John Barbirolli.

The first movement starts with a tiny phrase for timpani, answered by the cymbal. This becomes the accompaniment for the first long tune on the violin solo, reappears many times during the movement, and finally accompanies a melodic cadenza descending slowly from the violin's highest notes, in double- and triple-stopping.

There is a pleading middle section in the acrobatic *Vivace*, after which the previous material appears softly and muted. There is a slow crescendo to a tutti which introduces a cadenza. This leads directly to the *Passacaglia*, of which the theme is announced by the trombones.

A gramophone record of this Concerto, made by Mark Lubotsky with the Moscow Symphony Orchestra, was sent to me by a mutual friend. This was the performance I had been waiting for. At our invitation Mr Lubotsky came to

[13] AFBP (1973), 56. [14] AFPB (1971), 70.

England last summer to record it at The Maltings, also playing the work at a Prom. We are delighted to welcome him back to Aldeburgh again to play it at the Festival.

Young Apollo, Op. 16 (1939) (n.d.)[15]

Fanfare for Pianoforte solo, String Quartet and String Orchestra:

This short piece was written for the Canadian Broadcasting Corporation and first performed there with the composer as soloist in August 1939, under the direction of Alexander Chuhaldin. It is founded on the last words of Keat's [*sic*] unfinished Hyperion:

'—and lo! from all his limbs
Celestial -------------------'

The end of one order of Gods has come. Saturn, Hyperion and the other ancient gods, who ruled the world by might and terror, have to make way to the new order, gods of light, youth, beauty and laughter. Apollo, called to be the new god of beauty by Mnemosyne, the old goddess of memory, foresees his destiny; and in one final convulsion throws off his mortal form. He stands before us—the new, dazzling Sun-god, quivering with radiant vitality.

Les Illuminations, Op. 18 (1939) (n.d.)[16]

For high voice and string orchestra

'Les Illuminations' is the title of a volume of poems in prose and verse by Arthur Rimbaud, that astonishing young genius who in the two years that constitute his literary career, produced some of the greatest poems in the French language. In 1871, he left his bourgeois home at Charleville to help in the Paris Commune, two years later, at the age of eighteen, he stopped writing altogether, and in 1879 went off to Abyssinia as a trader, only returning to France to die in 1891.

His short life as a poet was an erratic and turbulent one, generally near starvation and often homeless, and much of it was set in the most sordid surroundings, in Paris, London and Brussels; but throughout it, the boy's inspiration remained radiant and intense. The word 'Illuminations' suggests both the vision of a mystic and a brightly coloured picture, and Rimbaud's biographer, Enid Starkie, says that at this time Rimbaud did in some way identify himself with

[15] Draft (typescript), n.d. (*GB-ALb* 1–02053839).

[16] Draft (typescript), n.d. (*GB-ALb* 1–02053831). Note by Britten and Pears.

God, and imagined these poems to be directly inspired. Intensely original and in many places obscure, they are in fact visions of the world he lived in, violent and sordid, which was for Rimbaud at the same time so horrifying and so fascinating.

The composer has taken seven of these poems, six in prose and one in verse, and has made them into a cycle. As a recurrent motto he has chosen the arrogant cry from 'PARADE'—J'ai seul la clef de cette parade sauvage—I alone hold the key to this savage parade. It appears in the opening 'FANFARE' and in the 'INTERLUDE', thus serving to bind the work together, as well as to remind the listener of the visionary quality in Rimbaud's utterances.

LES ILLUMINATIONS received their first complete performance in London, January 1940 by Sophie Wyss with Boyd Neel conducting, and were performed almost immediately afterwards in Basle (Switzerland) with Paul Sacher conducting.

The first American performance was in May 1941 in the I.S.C.M. Festival with Peter Pears as soloist, the composer conducting.

1. FANFARE—with the first statement of the Motto.
2. VILLES—cities—'crystal and wooden chalets on rails',—their brilliance, hardness, gaiety, noise [—] 'savages dancing endlessly the Festival of Night'. 'What lovely hour will return to me that place whence comes my sleep and my smallest movements!'
3a. PHRASE—leading to
3b. ANTIQUE—A r[h]ythmic dance, praising the statue of a young Greek god—his graceful movements—'his shining tusks'—'his breast like a guitar'.
4. ROYAUT.—In the square of a pleasant city, a man and a woman demand to become King and Queen. They have seen visions and undergone trials. And King and Queen they are, for one whole afternoon, while the houses are decorated.
5. MARINE.—seascape—ships with steel prows beating the foam and dashing through the shining spray.
6. INTERLUDE—the statement of the motto.
7. BEING BEAUTEOUS—a vision of a being of great beauty, before a background of snow, odur [*sic*] of death, strange music, prismatic colours—. She turns:—'Oh! our bones are covered anew with a body of love.'
8. PARADE. the underworld—Clowns, criminals, deformed creatures—there are youths among them. 'O violent Paradise of mad grimaces!'—Hottentots, bohemians, hyaenas, Molochs, master jugglers who transform places and people. 'I alone hold the key to this savage parade.'

9. DEPARTURE—Enough of visions—departure into love and new sounds.[17]

Sinfonia da Requiem, Op. 20 (1940) (n.d.)[18]

I. Lacrymosa.
II. Dies Irae.
III. Requiem Aeternam.

This work was written in Amityville, Long Island, in the spring of 1940, and is inscribed to the memory of the composer's parents. In spite of being short for a symphony, it was conceived on festival proportions and scored for a large orchestra including triple wood-wind, saxophone, six horns, piano and a considerable array of percussion.

The scheme and the mood of the work are indicated by the Latin titles which are taken from the Requiem Mass; but the connection to the great Catholic ceremony is more emotional than liturgical.

I. LACRYMOSA—Andante ben misurato. A slow marching lament in a persistent 6/8 rhythm with a strong tonal centre on D. There are three main motives (1) a syncopated, sequential theme announced by the cellos and answered by a solo bassoon, (2) a broad theme, based on the interval of a major seventh, (3) alternating chords on Flute and Trombones (outlined by the piano and harps). The first section of the movement is quietly pulsating; the second a long crescendo leading to a climax based on the first cello theme. There is no pause before:

II. DIES IRAE—Allegro con Fuoco. A form of Dance of Death, with occasional moments of quiet marching rhythm. The dominating motif of this movement is announced at the start by the flutes, and includes an important tremolando figure. Other motives are: a triplet repeated-note figure in the trumpets, a slow smooth tune on the saxophone and a livelier syncopated one on the brass. The scheme of the movement is a series of climaxes of which the last is the most powerful, causing the music to disintegrate and to lead directly to:

III. Requiem AETERNAM—Andante piacevole. Very quietly over a background of solo strings and harps; the flutes announce the quiet D major

[17] The first draft (*GB-ALb* 1–02053840) here included:

> Les Illuminations received its first complete performance in London, January 1940 by Sophie Wyss with Boyd Neel conducting—& performed almost immediately afterwards in Basel Switzerland with Paul Sacher conducting. The first American performance was in May 1941 in the I.S.C.M. Festival with Peter Pears as soloist & the composer conducting.

[18] Second draft [typed], n.d. (*GB-ALb* 1–02053826).

tune which is the principle motif of the movement. There is a middle section in which the strings play a flowing melody. This grows to a short climax, but the opening tune is soon resumed, and the work ends quietly in a long sustained clarinet note.

Sinfonia da Requiem, Op. 20 (1940) (1941)[19]

The 'SINFONIA DA REQUIEM' was commissioned by the Japanese Government through the British Council for Cultural Relations with Other Countries, for the celebration of the 2600th anniversary of the Japanese Imperial Dynasty in December 1940. Mr. Britten was then in America and cabled acceptance of the offer on the condition that he was to have a free hand as to the character of the work, and mentioned the plan he had for this Sinfonia together with the titles of the movements. This condition, he understood, was acceptable; accordingly he went to work over the score, and delivered the Sinfonia as agreed in June 1940. The work was to be performed in December 1940. In November, however, Mr. Britten received notice that the Japanese Government did not consider the work as suitable for this particular festival, partly because of its Christian nature. It has not been performed, therefore, in Japan, and the present performances will be the first.

Diversions, Op. 21 (1940) (1941)[20]

For pianoforte (left hand) and orchestra

I wrote this work in Maine in the summer of 1940 at the suggestion of Mr. Paul Wittgenstein. It takes the form of eleven straightforward and concise variations on a simple musical scheme, which is announced by the orchestra without any preamble. I was attracted from the start by the problems involved in writing a work for this particular medium, especially as I was well acquainted with and extremely enthusiastic about Mr. Wittgenstein's skill in overcoming what appear to be insuperable difficulties. In no place in the work did I attempt to imitate a two-handed piano technique, but concentrated on exploiting and emphasising the single line approach. I have tried to treat the problem in every aspect, as a glance at the list of movements will show: special features are trills and scales in the Recitative; wide-spread arpeggios in the Nocturne; agility over the keyboard in the Badinerie and Toccata; and repeated notes in the final Tarantella.

[19] Typescript of programme note for premiere on 29 Mar. 1941, given in New York by New York Philharmonic, John Barbirolli conducting (*GB-ALb* 1–02053841).

[20] Preface to published full score (New York: Boosey & Hawkes, 1941).

Introduction and Rondo alla Burlesca, Op. 23, No. 1 (1940) (1944)[21]

For two pianos

This piece was written in the autumn of 1940 and first performed in New York by Ethel Bartlett and Rae Robertson early in the next year. The Introduction (*grave*) is mainly constructed out of the dotted rhythm given out by the two pianos in close imitation in the first bar. In the Rondo (*allegro*) the main subject, which recurs frequently, is stated right away by the first piano. There is an echo of the Introduction just before a short brilliant coda.

Mazurka Elegiaca, Op. 23, No. 2 (1941) (1944)[22]

For two pianos

Composed in the summer of 1941, this is one of a collection of pieces written by various composers in memory of Paderewski. It is in simple ternary form, with an extended coda founded on one of the accompanying figures to the principal tune.

Scottish Ballad, Op. 26 (1941) (1971)[23]

For two pianos and orchestra

Written for Ethel Bartlett and Rae Robertson, by whom it was first performed with the Cincinnati Symphony Orchestra conducted by Eugène Goossens on 28 November 1941, it starts with the statement of the old hymn tune *Dundee*, followed by a funeral march ('The Flowers of the Forest' and 'Turn ye to me') and an extended Reel. *Dundee* persists to the very end!

[21] Programme note for Wigmore Hall Boosey & Hawkes concert, 29 Mar. 1944 (*GB-ALb* 7–01008549).

[22] Programme note for Wigmore Hall Boosey & Hawkes concert, 29 Mar. 1944 (*GB-ALb* 7–01008549).

[23] Programme note for substitute concert in Aldeburgh Festival, 13 June 1971 (*GB-ALb* 7–02053450).

The Ballad of Little Musgrave and Lady Barnard (1943) (1969)[24]

For male voices and piano

During the 1939–45 war Richard Wood, the singer and an old friend of mine, was a prisoner-of-war for several years in Oflag VIIb, in Eichstätt, Germany. In this camp he started choirs and orchestras among the prisoners; hearing of it, I wrote this piece for him and his friends and somehow, through devious means, his sister Anne Wood managed to get a copy to him (page by page in microfilm). This arrived in time to be performed in a festival which the prisoners had organised for February 1944—and it was given four times.

Peter Grimes, Op. 33 (1945) (1945)[25]

Although I had been planning this opera for sometime, it was Koussevitzky who gave me the actual stimulus in 1942 to go ahead and write it, and he commissioned it in memory of his wife who had recently died. It took Montague [*sic*] Slater and me nearly two years to complete the libretto, and I started writing the music at the beginning of last year. The last notes were written in February this year, and Sadlers Wells Opera started musical rehearsals almost at once. The first performance coincided with the reopening of the Sadlers Wells Theatre on June 7th.

The background of the opera is a small fishing town on the East Coast called the Borough. The period is the beginning of the last century. Life is hard here, and the sea, grey and cold is the dominating factor in the lives of the people—their friend but also their enemy! In the first interlude I have tried to suggest the dawning of a grey cold day, as the people go slowly to their work. [Excerpt 1: first Sea Interlude 'Dawn']

Although here the sea seems calm, there is a feeling of underlying menace, and actually, later in this First Act, one of the periodic storms bursts upon the Borough, and a section of the neighbouring cliffs tumbles into the sea. As you will hear when the opera is broadcast each scene is preceded by a short orchestra piece painting the sea in its various moods.

The Borough has in it all the characters you might expect to find—the pub-keeper, the Rector, the retired sea-captain, the gossiping widow and so forth.

[24] AFPB (1969), 74.

[25] Original typescript (BBCWAC microfilm, *Music Magazine* (32), films 1–2). Broadcast 15 July 1945, BBC Home Service, 11 a.m.: illustrative talk for series *Music Magazine*, presented by Alec Robertson. (Pre-recorded 11 July 1945.) The excerpts were performed by Britten on piano, with Joan Cross as Ellen Orford and Peter Pears as Peter Grimes.

But there are also in the Borough two very unusual people—the fisherman Peter Grimes, and the widowed school-mistress, Mrs. Ellen Orford.

Peter Grimes, a visionary and highly skilled fisherman, is very unpopular with the community, just because he is different. How different can be heard from the song he sings at the pub, while people are sheltering from the storm raging outside. [Excerpt 2: 'Now the Great Bear and Pleiades']

At this moment a particular shadow hangs over Peter Grimes. He is on trial for the loss of one of his apprentices at sea. Murder is suspected. In the First Act he describes that loss to Bulstrode [*sic*], the sympathetic sea captain. [Excerpt 3: 'Picture what that day was like, that evil day!']

Always at the back of Peter Grimes' mind is the vision of an ideal life; he dreams of having vindicated himself in the eyes of the Borough and of himself happily married to Ellen Orford. [Excerpt 4: 'These Borough gossips listen to money']

Ellen Orford is the one person in the Brough [*sic*] who really knows and understands Grimes, and she does her best to protect him against malicious chatter. [Excerpt 5: 'Let her among you without fault cast the first stone']

In the last act when suspicion is steadily mounting to fever-height, Ellen in this next song unwittingly provides the clue which leads to the man-hunt after Grimes and his eventual madness and suicide. She is overheard telling Bulstrode about the discovery of the jersey, on which she had embroidered an anchor for the boy. [Excerpt 6: 'Embroidery in childhood']

Ellen's unwitting betrayal is made all the more poignant when one recalls the tender duet in the Prologue. In that scene after the noisy courtroom is cleared, Ellen and Grimes are left alone. Ellen tries to comfort him, he at first refuses to be comforted, but at the close of the scene they walk out together, hand in hand. [Excerpt 7: 'The truth, the pity and the truth']

Four Sea Interludes from *Peter Grimes*, Op. 33a (1945)

(n.d.)[26]

The second Interlude, which precedes the second Act, is a brilliant summer Sunday morning. The waves are sparkling in the sun, throwing up little jets of water. On shore the church bells are ringing and the people of the Borough, smart in their Sunday clothes, hurry across the stage into the little church. III The Third interlude precedes the 3rd Act. It is a moonlit evening now, the sea

[26] Autograph draft [incomplete], n.d. (*GB-ALb* 1–02053842). Written on the back page of the composition sketch of 'The red fox, the sun' from *This Way to the Tomb*. Possibly written for Britten's introduction to the opera, with some cast and producer Eric Crozier, held at Wigmore Hall on 31 May 1945.

is still, but as always in the North Sea there is a swell. When the curtain goes up a dance band is heard, accompanying a subscription dance in the Moot Hall (the Boro' town hall) but in this Interlude our eyes are now away from the little town and we look out over the quietly moving sea, so soon to be the grave of Peter Grimes, the fisherman in the story of the opera. IV The fourth Interlude, the 2nd of the 1st Act, paints one of those treacherous howling gales so prevalent on the East Coast, which eat away whole stretches of the neighbouring cliffs . . .

Saint Nicolas, Op. 42 (1948) (1949)[27]

Cantata for tenor solo, chorus (SATB), semi-chorus (SA), four boy singers and string orchestra, piano duet, percussion and organ

As stated in the dedication, Saint Nicolas was written to be performed at the centenary of a school, when it was sung by the combined choirs of three boys' schools (the main chorus) and one girls' school (the gallery choir). It is therefore suitable for performance by any numerically big chorus, even if the singers are not very experienced. The choir in the gallery should have a separate conductor.

The string parts are not very sophisticated and can be played by amateur players, preferably led by a professional quintet. The piano duet part is also of only moderate difficulty. The first percussion part is *obligato* and should be played by a professional drummer, who may play as many of the instruments included in the second part as is feasible; the second part is *ad libitum* and may be played by as many gifted and/or enthusiastic amateurs as there are instruments. On the other hand, the solo tenor part, as can easily be seen, is no amateur matter. The conductor must be cool-headed and should turn to the congregation/audience to conduct them in the two hymns.

The Beggar's Opera, Op. 43 (1948) (1948)[28]

A ballad-opera by John Gay (1728)
Realized from the original airs by Benjamin Britten

The tunes to which John Gay wrote his apt and witty lyrics are among our finest national songs. These seventeenth and eighteenth century airs, known usually as 'traditional tunes', seem to me to be the most characteristically *English* of any of our folk-songs. They are often strangely like Purcell and

[27] Preface to published vocal score (London: Boosey & Hawkes, 1949).

[28] Programme note for first production, Arts Theatre, Cambridge, EOG, May 1948 (*GB-ALb* 7–02053439).

Handel: may, perhaps, have influenced them, or have been influenced by them. They have strong, leaping intervals, sometimes in peculiar modes, and are often strange and severe in mood.

A definitive arrangement of them can never be achieved, since each generation sees them from a different aspect, but I feel that most recent arrangements have avoided their toughness and strangeness, and have concentrated only on their lyrical prettiness.

For my arrangements of the tunes I have gone to a contemporary edition of the original arrangements by Dr. Pepusch. Apart from one or two extensions and repetitions I have left the tunes exactly as they stood, except for one or two places where the original seemed confused and inaccurate. Three of them have had to be omitted because of the excessive length of the whole for performance in our time, but a far higher percentage of the sixty-nine tunes will be in this version than in any other recent one.

Spring Symphony, Op. 44 (1949) (1950)[29]

For soprano, contralto and tenor solos, chorus, boys' choir and orchestra

I wrote the Spring Symphony in the Autumn and Winter of 1948/9, and finished the score in the late Spring of 1949. For two years I had been planning such a work, a symphony not only dealing with the Spring itself, but with the progress of Winter to Spring and the re-awakening of the earth and life which that means. Originally I had wanted to use mediæval Latin verse and had made a selection of fine poems; but a re-reading of much English lyric verse and a particularly lovely Spring day in East Suffolk, the Suffolk of Constable and Gainsborough, made me change my mind.

The work is written for a large orchestra, mixed choirs and boys' choir, three soloists (soprano, contralto and tenor) and a cow-horn. It is in the traditional four movement shape of a symphony, but with the movements divided into shorter sections bound together by a similar mood or point of view. Thus after an introduction, which is a prayer, in Winter, for Spring to come, the first movements deal with the arrival of Spring, the cuckoo, the birds, the flowers, the sun and 'May month's beauty'; the second movements paint the darker side of Spring—the fading violets, rain and night; the third is a series of dances, the love of young people; the fourth is a May-day Festival, a kind of bank holiday, which ends with the great 13th Century traditional song 'Sumer is i-cumen in,' sung or rather shouted by the boys.

[29] 'A note on the Spring Symphony', *Music Survey* 2 (Spring 1950).

Spring Symphony, Op. 44 (1949) (1967)[30]

For soprano, contralto and tenor solos, chorus, boys' choir and orchestra

The *Spring Symphony* was written in 1949 for Serge Koussevitzky and the Boston Symphony Orchestra. It was first performed in Amsterdam at the Holland Festival on 9 [*sic*] July 1949. The work consists of settings of English poems from the thirteenth to the twentieth centuries, linked by their allegiance to spring, and grouped to form four 'Parts' corresponding to the traditional movements of a symphony.

The Little Sweep, Op. 45 (1949) (1965)[31]

The opera from *Let's Make an* Opera, an entertainment for young people

This opera is the final section of the entertainment for young people called *Let's Make an Opera!* The first section of this is in the form of a play and illustrates the preparation and rehearsal of an Opera. It will be easily seen that professionals or very gifted amateurs are needed to play the grown-up parts and also the part of Juliet (provided, of course, that she can look convincingly youthful). It is essential that real children should play the children's parts—the boys with unbroken voices who shouldn't be scared of using their chest voices.

The accompaniment is for solo string quartet, piano-duet (four hands on one piano) and percussion (one player can manage). A vocal score containing an arrangement for piano-duet with or without percussion is available (the piano-duet in this vocal score is not the same as the duet part mentioned above, although the percussion part *is* the same). This reduced version can be used for actual performance but the original full version should be used where possible. A rehearsal score with reduction of the accompaniment for solo piano is also available. The string parts are not very easy.

The songs Nos. I, IX, XIV and XVII are to be sung by the whole audience under the direction of the conductor. They must, of course, be rehearsed beforehand. Allowance is made for such rehearsal in Part One of *Let's Make an Opera!* †

If only *The Little Sweep* is to be performed, the conductor will have to take a rehearsal with the audience and orchestra before the opera begins.

† The libretto of *Let's Make an Opera!* can be obtained from the publishers of this score.

[30] AFPB (1967), 24. The first performance was in fact on 14 July 1949.

[31] Preface to published study score (London: Faber Music, 1965).

Lachrymae, Op. 48 (1950) (1952)[32]

Reflections on a song of John Dowland, for viola and piano

Written for William Primrose, this piece was first performed at the Aldeburgh Festival of 1950. It is a series of variations on the first phrase of Dowland's song 'If my complaints could passions move', one of his most characteristically passionate melodies. After a *lento* introduction in which the song is quoted in the bass of the piano-part, the Reflections continue with the following indications: Allegretto molto commodo, Animato, Tranquillo, Allegro con moto, Largamente (big chords for both instruments), Appasionato [*sic*] (in which another song of Dowland's is quoted 'Flow my tears'), Alla valse moderato (Waltz tempo), Allegro marcia (syncopated march rhythms for the viola), Lento (very high on the piano, harmonics on the viola) and L'istesso tempo which after a slow crescendo imperceptibly returns to Dowland's original tune and harmony, completing it for the first time. John Dowland put at the top of one of his pieces 'Semper Dowland, semper dolens', and this piece darkly reflects that introspective melancholy that was so much a part of the Elizabethan temperament.

Three scenes from *Gloriana*, Op. 53 (1953) (1970)[33]

1. The Tournament 2. Lute Song 3. Apotheosis

Gloriana was first produced at the Royal Opera House on June 18th, 1953, as part of the Coronation celebrations. It had a memorable second production in this country in 1966 at Sadler's Wells, when Colin Graham created an impressive production in an ingenious 'permanent' set. This was seen at the Maltings in 1968 with Sylvia Fisher as the Queen, a part she has made her own. For the performance this afternoon I have selected three extracts. The first shows the crowd's reaction to a jousting match; this is witnessed by the Earl of Essex, and to his chagrin Lord Mountjoy (his rival for the Queen's favour) overcomes his opponent. The scene ends with the hymn of loyalty to Her Majesty. The second is the Lute Song sung by Essex to the Queen—a song which becomes a symbol of their strange relationship—sweet, melancholy, and uneasy. The last extract is the same song, played loudly and bitterly on the full orchestra, which follows the Queen's signing of Essex's death-warrant. This leads to the scene descriptive of the Queen's own death. It ends with the loyal hymn sung quietly 'in the distance'. The opera is dedicated, by gracious permission, to Her Majesty the Queen.

[32] AFBP (1952), 36–7. [33] AFPB (1970), 14–15.

Folksong Arrangements, vol. 4, Moore's *Irish Melodies* (1957) (1960)[34]

For high voice and piano

All the texts of these songs are from Thomas Moore's *Irish Melodies*, published between 1808 and 1834—in one case from the slightly later *National Melodies*. In most instances I have also taken the tunes from the same sources (music arranged by Sir John Stevenson); however, in a few cases I have preferred to go back to Bunting's *Ancient Music of Ireland*, which had in the first place inspired Tom Moore to write his lyrics.

Noye's Fludde, Op. 59 (1957) (1958)[35]

The Chester Miracle Play, set for adults' and children's voices, children's chorus, chamber ensemble and children's orchestra

The mediaeval Chester Miracle Plays were performed by ordinary people: local craftsmen and tradesmen of the town and their families, with choristers from the local church or cathedral for the children's parts. Each Guild performed one play from the cycle on a cart (called *pageant*). This cart moved around the town from place to place, and on it the performance had to be entirely contained. The scenic devices, though carefully worked out, had to be extremely simple. *Noye's Fludde*, set to music, is intended for the same style of presentation—though not necessarily on a cart. Some big building should be used, preferably a church—but not a theatre—large enough to accommodate actors and orchestra, with the action raised on rostra, but not on a stage removed from the congregation. No attempt should be made to hide the orchestra from sight. The conductor should be to the side, but placed so that he can easily step forward to conduct the congregation, which has to play a large part in the proceedings. It may be found necessary to have a sub-conductor to relay to the orchestra the conductor's beat during the hymns and the entrance of animals.

The text used in this work was written at the end of the 16th century. The old spelling has been retained, but modern pronunciation should be used throughout, except for the indicated sounding of the final *e*'s: for example, *shippë* should be pronounced 'shippe(r)'; *Noye* should be pronounced in the familiar way as 'Noah'.

[34] Preface to published vocal score (London: Boosey & Hawkes, 1960).

[35] Preface to published vocal score (London: Boosey & Hawkes, 1958). Note by Britten and Colin Graham.

THE CHARACTERS

Mr and Mrs Noye should be accomplished singer-actors.

The Voice of God should not necessarily be spoken by a professional actor, but he should be highly musical and should have a rich speaking voice, with a simple and sincere delivery, without being at all 'stagey'. He should ideally be placed high up and away from the stage.

Sem, Ham and Jaffett and their wives should have well-trained voices and lively personalities. They should not be too young—perhaps between eleven and fifteen—although Jaffett (who is the eldest) may, as at the first performance, have a broken voice (i.e. a tenor). In this case he should sing the part as written (sounding an octave lower), except for the passages marked ⊕ in the vocal score, and his wife should be a little older than the others.

The Gossips should be older girls, with strong voices, especially in the lower register, and chosen for their dramatic capabilities.

As far as the number of *Animals* is concerned, the more the better; there are forty-nine species referred to in the libretto of which thirty-five pairs were used at the first performances: they were in seven groups and varied in age from seven to eighteen and in size accordingly:—

Group 1: Lions, Leopards, Horses, Oxen, Swine, Goats, Sheep
Group 2: Camels, Asses, Buck and Doe
Group 3: Dogs, Otters, Foxes, Polecats, Hares
Group 4: Bears, Wolves, Monkeys, Squirrels, Ferrets
Group 5: Cats, Rats, Mice
Group 6
and *7:* { Birds (Six pairs in each group):
Herons, Owls, Bittern, Peacocks, Redshanks, Ravens, Cock and Hen, Kites, Cuckoos, Curlews, Doves, Duck and Drake }

In any performance it is essential to have seven well-balanced groups, chosen to give as much variety as possible.

A fair number of the boys in Groups 1 and 2 should have broken voices. The Kyries should be sung in the character of the animal being impersonated.

Four Property Men, responsible boys of about 16–17 years, can be used to help build The Ark, move waves, hoist the rainbow, and other odd jobs to help the production.

THE ORCHESTRA

The orchestra is of two kinds, professional and children (amateurs). The placing of the players is highly important. The professional strings and recorder should be as close to the conductor as possible, with contact between them and their amateur counterparts.

Strings ripieno. There are three sorts of amateur *Violins:* the *Firsts* should be capable players, not however going above the 3rd position, and with the simplest double-stops. The *Seconds* do not go out of the 1st position, while the *Thirds* are very elementary, and have long stretches of just open strings. The *Violas* need to be as accomplished as the *1st Violins*, as do the *1st Cellos*, while the *2nd Cellos* have only the simplest music. The *Double Bass* part is very simple. The number of players is of course according to availability, but there should be at least twenty-five in all.

There should be as many *Recorder* players as possible, divided equally into three parts. Less than a dozen would make too small a noise. The parts are not difficult, but slow chromatic scales and quite a few trills are needed. The soloist needs to be accomplished, with a knowledge of *flutter-tongue*.

The Bugles should number about eight, with two players to each part (or just four players can be used). The leader should be a strong player. The part is so divided that less strong players may omit, or play simpler versions of, the more strenuous passages. A good effect can be made by placing the bugles at the far end of the church.

The Percussion should be led by a professional player who plays the timpani, while the other instruments are divided up between the amateur players, who should be at least six in number. The parts show clearly who should play which instrument. Most of the instruments needed are the stock orchestral ones, but a few need a little explanation. The *Wind machine* (a wooden slatted cylinder which revolves against sail-cloth), and the *Whip* (clappers) can be hired, but the *Slung Mugs* and *Sandpaper* can be concocted at home. The former are mugs (or cups) of varying thicknesses and size—so as to make a kind of scale—slung on string by the handles from a wooden stand, and hit with a wooden spoon (by one player). The latter consists of two pieces of sandpaper attached to blocks of wood and rubbed together.

The Hand-bells are in E♭ and need six players, two bells to each player.

Fanfare for St Edmundsbury (1959) (1969)[36]

For three trumpets

This Fanfare was written for the *Pageant of Magna Carta* held in the grounds of Bury St. Edmunds Cathedral. It is in the form of three separate trumpet fanfares (played *attacca*) which combine in conclusion. The solo fanfares may be

[36] Preface to published parts (London: Boosey & Hawkes, 1969).

played rather freely, but when they come together should be in strict time. The trumpeters should be placed as far apart as possible, even when the Fanfare is performed indoors.

Cantata academica, carmen basiliense, Op. 62 (1959) (n.d.)[37]

For soprano, alto, tenor and bass solos, chorus and orchestra

I wrote the Carmen Basiliense (Cantata Academica) in the first months of 1959 to the Latin text of Bernhard Wyss. It is written for four soloists, mixed chorus and orchestra. Although festive in style, it is also—as seemed to me appropriate for the auspicious occasion—formal with plenty of academic, technical devices—canons, fugues, 'mirrors', ostinatos, pedals etc; in fact each of the short sections into which the Cantata is divided is over (or under) a pedal, and these pedals make up a twelve tone series sung by the chorus to a straightforward and chordal accompaniment in No. 8.

I have made use in several of the numbers of a Canto Populari, a Basel tune (suggested to me by Dr. Paul Sacher) 'z'Basel a mym Rhy'. This appears finally on bells in No. 13.

Sonata in C, Op. 65 (1961) (1961)[38]

For cello and piano

First performance

This sonata was planned during a holiday in Greece last autumn and written at Aldeburgh in December and January. It was inspired by the playing of Mstislav Rostropovich, and is dedicated to him.

1. *Dialogo* (*Allegro*). This movement is throughout a discussion of a tiny motive of a rising or falling second. The motive is lengthened to make a lyrical second subject which rises towards and falls from a pianissimo harmonic.

2. *Scherzo-pizzicato* (*Allegretto*). A study in pizzicato, sometimes almost guitar-like in its elaborate right-hand technique.

3. *Elegia* (*Lento*). Against a sombre plain background, the cello sings a long tune. This tune is developed, by means of double, triple and quadruple stopping, to a big climax, and sinks away to a soft conclusion.

[37] Draft (typescript), n.d. (*GB-ALb* 1–02053804).

[38] AFPB (1961), 64. In later versions, the opening sentence was altered, probably not by Britten: 'This sonata was planned during a holiday in Greece in the autumn of 1960 and written in Aldeburgh the following December and January.' AFPB (1979), 30.

4. A brief *Marcia* (*Energico*). The cello plays a rumbustious bass to the jerky tune on the piano. The *Trio* has horn-like calls over a repeated triplet bass. The *March* returns very softly, with the bass (now in the treble) in harmonics.

5. *Moto Perpetuo* (*Poco Presto*). The 6/8 *saltando* theme dominates the entire movement, frequently changing its character, now high and expressive, now low and grumbling, now gay and carefree.

Psalm 150, Op. 67 (1962) (1963)[39]

For two-part children's voices and instruments

The instrumentation of this work is largely left to the choice of the conductor, according to the availability of the instrumentalists.
What are essential are

1) a treble instrument—Recorder, Flute, Oboe, Clarinet, Violin, etc.
2) some sort of drum—Timpani (in C & G), Side Drum, Tenor Drum, Bass Drum, etc.
3) a keyboard instrument.

The more instruments there are, the merrier, but care should be taken not to swamp the voices—the dynamics are anyhow relative.

If there are two *treble instrument* lines, the upper part should be the stronger. If treble recorders are available they should play the *second* line, reading an octave higher. Violas should play (as far as possible) the *bass instrument* line an octave higher.

As for the voices, it is really essential to have two parts. In the Canon (on page 18) entries 2 and 4 can be omitted. Fewer voices might sing the softer parts in the second (F major) section, but *not* a solo voice.

If someone plays a brass instrument (preferably the Trumpet), the passages in small notes for the treble instruments between bar 134 and bar 157 should be left out.

Curlew River, Op. 71 (1964) (1964)[40]

A parable for church performance

It was in Tokyo in January 1956 that I saw a Nō-drama for the first time; and I was lucky enough during my brief stay there to see two different performances of the same play—*Sumida-gawa*. The whole occasion made a tremendous

[39] Preface to published vocal score (London: Boosey & Hawkes, 1963).
[40] AFPB (1964), 19.

impression upon me, the simple touching story, the economy of the style, the intense slowness of the action, the marvellous skill and control of the performers, the beautiful costumes, the mixture of chanting, speech, singing, which with the three instruments made up the strange music—it all offered a totally new 'operatic' experience.

There was no conductor—the instrumentalists sat on the stage, so did the chorus, and the chief characters made their entrance down a long ramp. The lighting was strictly non-theatrical. The cast was all male, the one female character wearing an exquisite mask which made no attempt to hide the male jowl beneath it.

The memory of this play has seldom left my mind in the years since. Was there not something—many things—to be learnt from it? The solemn dedication and skill of the performers were a lesson to any singer or actor of any country and any language. Was it not possible to use just such a story—the simple one of a demented mother seeking her lost child—with an English background, for there was no question in any case of a pastiche from the ancient Japanese? Surely the Medieval Religious Drama in England would have had a comparable setting—an all-male cast of ecclesiastics—a simple austere staging in a church—a very limited instrumental accompaniment—a moral story? And so we came from *Sumida-gawa* to *Curlew River* and a Church in the Fens, but with the same story and similar characters; and whereas in Tokyo the music was the ancient Japanese music jealously preserved by successive generations, here I have started the work with that wonderful plainsong hymn 'Te lucis ante terminum' and from it the whole piece may be said to have grown. There is nothing specifically Japanese left in our Parable, but if we on the stage and you in the audience can achieve half the intensity and concentration of that original drama I shall be happy.

Gemini Variations, Op. 73 (1965) (1966)[41]

Twelve variations and fugue on an epigram of Kodály. Quartet for two (or four) players: flute, violin and piano 4 hands

When in Budapest in the Spring of 1964 at a Music Club meeting for children, I was very taken by the musical gifts of two twelve-year-old twins. Each played the piano, one the flute and the other the violin; they sang, sight-read, and answered difficult musical questions. It turned out that they were the sons

[41] Preface to published score (London: Faber Music, 1966). In the note written for the first performance one year earlier, Britten had included the following sentences: 'The Theme, suitable for our days of tribute to Kodály, is from one of his *Epigrams* (1954). The variations are very short.' There are other minor differences in words and punctuation.

of one of Budapest's most distinguished flute players. At the end of the meeting they approached me and charmingly, if forcefully, asked me to write them a work. Though I claimed that I was too busy, my refusal was brushed aside; however, I insisted on one small bargaining point; I would do it only if they would write me a long letter telling me all about themselves, their work and their play—in *English*. I felt safe. After a week or two, however, the letter arrived, in vivid and idiosyncratic English, and I felt I must honour my promise. Here it is. The boys came to the Aldeburgh Festival to give the first performance of *Gemini Variations* on June 19th, 1965, and subsequently played it in London (recording it for Decca), Brussels, Budapest and all over Hungary.

I realise that some musicians who wish to play the work may not be quite so versatile as these twins, and have prepared a version of it for four players, with extra *ad lib.* passages for the flute and violin so that they should not become bored by long waits. In this edition both versions are combined, with the additional parts in brackets, and in small type in the score.

The following *Note on Performance* was sent to the Jeney twins, suggesting how to change positions and instruments easily.

NOTE ON PERFORMANCE

The boys should sit at the piano on one bench—preferably of smooth wood so that they can slide easily and quickly from one position to another. There should be behind them a music stand on which is the copy of the music for flute and violin. When the last to play leaves this stand or the piano, he should turn to the next page needed (this is indicated in the copies). It is suggested that the flute and violin when not being used should lie on the ledges by the side of the piano music-stand (the flute to the right, the violin to the left) or on small tables placed in convenient positions. For the last chord of the piece the flute and violin should be picked up quickly while the piano pedal is held down.

Voices for Today, Op. 75 (1965) (1965)[42]

Anthem for chorus (men, women and children) with ad libitum accompaniment for organ

This work is written for a large main chorus of men and women, and a smaller chorus of boys (or boys and girls) placed separately (if possible in a gallery) and with its own conductor.

The speeds of the two choruses (see the metronome marks) are usually not the same, but the beats must coincide whenever there is a long barline running

[42] Preface to published score (London: Faber Music, 1965).

from top to bottom of the system. To achieve this, the conductor of one of the choruses must adjust his last beat before a long barline, an adjustment which means that the last note or rest may be either longer or shorter than its written length. This is indicated by a ⌒ ('curlew' sign) over the note or rest.

It will readily be seen which conductor must make this adjustment. For instance, from Fig. 20 to Fig. 22 it is the conductor of the main chorus, and from Fig. 23 to Fig. 24 it is the conductor of the boys' chorus.

The boys' part has no regular measured tempo, but its rhythm is shown by dotted barlines. The vocalising of the boys should be on the vowels indicated: 'ay' rhyming with 'day', and 'rrr' on a voiced rolled 'r'.

The organ part is *ad libitum* and should be used primarily when the resonance of the building is inadequate.

It is desirable that the work, except for Virgil's *Eclogue*, should be sung in the performers' vernacular, and that the complete texts should be reproduced in the programme.

I wish to thank warmly a number of my friends, including several members of Faber's, who helped me, both with suggestions and research, to compile this small anthology of peace. I should also like to thank Ralph Downes for his registrations and editing of the organ part.

The Golden Vanity, Op. 78 (1966) (1967)[43]

A vaudeville for boys and piano after the old English ballad

The Golden Vanity was written last year in answer to a request from the boys of the Wiener Sängerknaben, for them to perform on their tours. They particularly asked that they should not have to play girls' parts.

The Building of the House, Op. 79 (1967) (1967)[44]

Overture with or without chorus

I wrote this true example of Occasional Music during December and January of the past winter. It was certainly inspired by the excitement of the planning and building—and the haste! I wanted to find a suitable text, and to fit it to music singable by an amateur chorus with a professional orchestra. Imogen Holst suggested the text from *The Scottish Psalter*, and the old chorale tune which Bach loved to use.

[43] AFPB (1967), 8. [44] AFPB (1967), 13.

The Building of the House, Op. 79 (1967) (1969)[45]

Overture with or without chorus

This true example of occasional music was written for the Inaugural Concert of the Maltings Concert Hall in June 1967. It was inspired by the excitement of the planning and building—and the haste! It is in several clear sections: an impetuous start, with each section of the orchestra playing in different speeds; a common-chord harmonisation of the chorale for the chorus, with lively woodwind figuration; a quiet string *fugato*; a canonic version of the chorale for brass and wood; a soft recapitulation of the opening which eventually builds up to, and accompanies, the forte second verse of the chorale. The words are adapted by I.H.[46] From *The Whole Book of Psalms*, 1562 and 1677, and set to an old Lutheran hymn-tune.

The Building of the House, Op. 79 (1967) (1971)[47]

Overture with or without chorus

One of the most exciting things for a composer is to have an Occasion to celebrate musically, and history is full of splendid pieces of music written for special Occasions. Every one of Bach's cantatas was written for a special day in the church calendar, and what marvellous pieces every one of those two hundred are! Sometimes the Occasion may not be so inspiring, as Purcell may have felt on having to celebrate 'The King's Return from Newmarket', but being a great composer he managed to produce something very fine.

I was certainly excited by the occasion for which this overture was written—the conversion of a part of the Snape Maltings into a splendid Concert Hall for the Aldeburgh Festival. Imogen Holst suggested that I use the text from the *Whole Book of Psalms* and an old chorale tune which Bach loved. Alas, our prayer in the last two lines was not answered exactly in the expected way, because two years after it was opened the Maltings Concert Hall was destroyed by fire.[48] If you know the history of ERMA, which tells of the tragic loss of Ernest Read's Studio and St Paul's Church House in the 1939–45 war, you will realise what a terrible blow such destruction can be, not only destroying a beautiful building, but the contents too, and the confusion of all immediate plans.

45 AFPB (1969), 19.

46 Imogen Holst.

47 Draft (typescript) (*GB-ALb* 1–02053848). Programme note for Ernest Read Music Association, 30 Dec. 1971.

48 'But they shall thrive whom God doth bless, | Their house shall stand through storm and stress.'

But just as the Ernest Read concerts were resumed, and went forward with additional strength, so a year later the Maltings Concert Hall was rebuilt with improvements and additions too and with the sound as perfect and characteristic as before (I hope many members of tonight's audience will visit the hall before long).

As we had less than a year before the next Festival was due to start, the urgency of the rebuilding was even greater than before; so the overture, which was meant to convey something of the excitement and haste of the planning and building, describes the rebuilding as well.[49]

Children's Crusade, Op. 82 (1969) (1969)[50]

A ballad for children's voices and orchestra

INTERVIEWER: Ben, can you tell me something about the new *Children's Crusade* piece?

BRITTEN: I wrote it last year in October–November, I think, and actually I had thought about setting this particular Brecht poem, this long ballad about the group of children who got displaced at the beginning of the 1939 war, in Poland; I had thought about setting this poem for some time, and when the occasion of the fiftieth anniversary of the Save the Children Fund was proposed and they approached me with the idea of writing a work, I thought this would be an ideal occasion for it and an ideal work for the occasion. He is a poet-playwright that I have had a considerable affection and admiration for for some time. I remember a performance in Zurich just after this last war of the *Mutter Courage*, with Therese Giese, which was an extraordinary experience.[51] I set this in German, this poem, simply because I couldn't find a translation of it which was close enough to the German rhythms, which seemed to be important. So I set it in German, and Hans Keller, with Peter Pears and myself helping a bit, finally put it back into English.

INTERVIEWER: What is the timescale? It's a big piece, is it?

BRITTEN: It lasts about a quarter of an hour–twenty minutes. Actually I've only just recently heard a rehearsal of the work and I think it obviously will

[49] Although, having programmed the Overture for performance in the 1969 Festival, the year in which the Hall burnt down, Britten decided not to tempt fate by programming it for the reopening one year later.

[50] Editor's transcript of recording (NSA LP32386/1LP0195303). Recorded Jan. 1969: interviewer, date of transmission and wavelength unknown.

[51] *Mutter Courage und ihre Kinder* (1941) by Bertold Brecht (1898–1956), the German poet, playwright, and theorist. Therese Giese (1898–1975) was a German actress who, along with Brecht's wife, Helene Weigel, was known for her post-war performances in the title role of Brecht's play.

take a fairly long time. It's written for a rather curious collection of instruments. The setting is for children's voices and an orchestra of children. It's mostly percussion, and there's a great deal of improvisation in the percussion parts, which of course can extend itself.

INTERVIEWER: You mean it might take fifty minutes instead of fifteen?

BRITTEN: Not quite to that degree, but it's that kind of thing. Actually the rehearsal I went to recently was rather exciting, and the children had considerable fun in extending their various bits.

INTERVIEWER: It's mostly then for chorus—children's chorus—is it, or solo parts as well?

BRITTEN: It's got about eight or nine solo parts. The Wandsworth boys are doing it, and they're, I think, using about 120 children.

INTERVIEWER: To have it performed in St Paul's is rather sort of shades of the old Foundling concerts, you know when they did these massive works of Handel and Purcell.

BRITTEN: Yes. I'm hoping that the splendid sound that these boys make may defeat the rather curious accoustics of St Pauls, which is a little bit resonant as you know.

INTERVIEWER: Have you read these articles about yourself in which comments are made about your writing work after work about, really, the subject of innocence.

BRITTEN: I haven't read many of them; I gather they do appear from time to time.

INTERVIEWER: But I mean you are aware that it is a recurring pattern in your creative . . .

BRITTEN: Is one aware of things like that?

INTERVIEWER: I mean I was told, somebody told me that you'd written *The Turn of the Screw* because you really wanted to exorcize it from your thoughts, that it had obssessed you for many years. Is that true?

BRITTEN: No. No, I think that these things seem perhaps clearer to people outside one than they do to oneself. I suppose unconsciously there is something in that rather obsessive subject which can and does excite me, or anyhow occupy me; but I don't say, 'Ah, now I must write another opera about innocence'.

Children's Crusade, Op. 82 (1969) (1969)[52]

A ballad for children's voices and orchestra

For many years I have had the idea of setting Brecht's heart-rending ballad of the wandering band of lost children in the first icy winter of the last war—apparently a true story. The perfect occasion (the 50th anniversary of the Save the Children Fund) following several happy concerts given with the boys of Wandsworth School, was the stimulus to write the work which was completed late last year. I set it in German, but today it is being sung in English.

I would like to acknowledge gratefully the help of James Blades (as on many other occasions) in the planning and making of the percussion instruments played by the Wandsworth boys this afternoon.

Suite for Harp, Op. 83 (1969) (1969)[53]

This short Suite was written in February and March this year especially for our Chosen Artist [Osian Ellis].

1. A classical *Overture*, with dotted rhythms and trumpet chords.
2. *Toccata*, a rondo busy with quavers and semiquavers, with much crossing of parts.
3. *Nocturne*, a clear tune with increasing ornamentation over a low chordal ground.
4. *Fugue*, a brief scherzo, in three voices.
5. *Hymn* (St. Denio), a Welsh tune, a compliment to the dedicatee, with five variants.

A Fanfare for D.W. [David Webster] (1970) (1970)[54]

Fanfare for 4 Trumpets, 4 Trombones and 2 Tubas

This fanfare was written specially for today's occasion. It is based on a series of rising fifths, which celebrate the Royal Opera House (C - - E - - G - - - - -) and its retiring General Administrator (DA - - - - EB - - E -).[55] Over

[52] AFPB (1969), 75.

[53] AFPB (1969), 69.

[54] Draft (typescript), May 1970 (*GB-ALb* 1–02053823).

[55] David Webster (1903–71), skilful English arts administrator, who established Covent Garden as a permanent opera and ballet company immediately after the war, and had close relations with Britten over *Billy Budd* (1951), *Gloriana* (1953), and *The Prince of the Pagodas* (1956).

these are scraps of nine of Sir David's favourite operatic tunes, with one thrown in for historical reasons. No prizes are offered for their identification.[56]

Third Suite for Cello, Op. 87 (1971, rev. 1974)

(1976)[57]

I wrote this suite in the early spring of 1971 and took it as a present to Slava Rostropovich when Peter Pears and I visited Moscow and Leningrad in April of that year. The occasion was a week of British music, and our programme with the London Symphony Orchestra was made memorable by the fact that both Richter and Rostropovich joined us—surely a unique gesture of Anglo-Russian friendship.

As a tribute to a great Russian musician and patriot I based this suite on Russian themes: the first three tunes were taken from Tchaikovsky's volumes of folk-song arrangements; the fourth, the 'Kontakion' (Hymn to the Departed), from the *English Hymnal*. When I played the suite through to Dmitri Shostakovich during our visit to Moscow, he remarked that he had been brought up on a different version of the Kontakion. I consulted my friend Bishop Pimen of Saratov and the Volga, who confirmed that my version was the one he had always known and regularly used. In the score I print both versions, for players to choose whichever they prefer.

The suite is played without a break and consists of variations on the four Russian tunes:

1 Introduzione (lento)—2 Marcia (allegro)—3 Canto (con moto)—4 Barcarolla (lento)—5 Dialogo (allegretto)—6 Fuga (andante espressivo)—7 Recitative (fantastico)—8 Moto perpetuo (presto)—9 Passacaglia (lento solenne) leading to a simple statement of the four themes.

The first performance of the suite took place on 21 December 1974 in the Maltings, Snape.

[56] In an early draft of this note, Britten added the following postscript in pencil: 'About the repeat, I would just as soon it were <u>not</u> made—but if the tunes have not sunk in, & as this will be its only performance, then by all means make it!'

[57] AFPB (1976), 50.

Suite on English Folk Tunes, Op. 90 (1975)[58]
'A time there was' (1974)

A time there was—as one may guess
And as, indeed, earth's testimonies tell—
Before the birth of consciousness
When all went well.

THOMAS HARDY

This work originated with its third movement, *Hankin Booby*, which was commissioned for the opening of the Queen Elizabeth Hall on 1 March 1967; the other four movements were added in the autumn of 1974. The suite is founded on tunes published in the seventeenth century in Playford's *The Dancing Master*, and some folk songs collected orally at the beginning of this century.

1 *Fast and rough* (Dances: 'We'll wed' and 'Stepney Cakes and Ale')
2 *Allegretto* (Songs: 'The Bitter Withy' and 'The Mermaid')
3 *Heavily* (*Hankin Booby*)—wind and drums (Dances: 'Mage on a Cree' and 'Half Hannikin')
4 *Fast and gay*—violins alone (Dances: 'Hunt the Squirrel' and 'The Tuneful Nightingale')
5 *Slow and languid* (Dance: 'Epping Forest' and song: 'Lord Melbourne')

Unlike the fragmentary use I have made of the other tunes in this suite, 'Lord Melbourne', played by the cor anglais, is used complete. It was written down in his usual meticulous detail by Percy Grainger, to whose memory the suite is 'lovingly and reverently' dedicated.

Sacred and Profane, Op. 91 (1975) (1976)[59]

Eight medieval lyrics for unaccompanied voices (SSATB)

1 St. Godric's Hymn 2 I mon waxe wod 3 Lenten is come 4 The long night 5 Yif ic of luve can 6 Carol 7 Ye that pasen by 8 A death

These songs were written early in 1975 for the Wilbye Consort. They are sung in the original medieval English, although some more obscure words are being replaced by their modern equivalents.

[58] AFPB (1975), 33. [59] AFPB (1976), 21.

Phaedra, Op. 93 (1975) (1976)[60]

Dramatic cantata for mezzo-soprano and small orchestra

This work was written during the summer of 1975, for Janet Baker. It is modelled on the Italian cantata form, of which Handel has given us so many noble examples. The recitatives are accompanied by harpsichord and solo cello. The orchestra comprises strings, mostly *divisi*, and percussion.

[60] AFPB (1976), 42.

ON THE MUSIC OF OTHER COMPOSERS

Johann Sebastian Bach (1685–1750) Cantata 'Ich steh mit einem Fuss im Grabe', BWV 156 (1729)

(1949)[1]

SINFONIA. A long, serene tune for solo oboe with light string accompaniment. This beautiful piece is more familiar as the slow movement of the F Minor Harpsichord Concerto.

ARIA with CHORALE (Tenor with sopranos). *Ich steh' mit einem Fuss in Grabe.* The four strands of this intense movement are (i) the choral *Mach's mit mir, Gott,* for sopranos (ii) the tenor solo with its long held, determined notes, (iii) a florid imitation of the voice for violins and viola in unison, (iv) the bass, with its syncopated falling passages.

RECITATIVE (Bass). *Mein Angst und Noth.* A long, anguished secco recitative with surprising and curious harmonies.

ARIA (Alto). *Herr, was du willst.* A florid, brave vocal line with much imitation by the oboe, violin and bass.

RECITATIVE (Bass). *Und willst du, das ich nicht soll kranken?* modulates to the new key of C major for the

CHORALE. *Herr, wie du willst.* A strong noble expression of absolute faith and confidence.

Bach, Cantata 'Komm, du süsse Todesstunde', BWV 161 (1715)

(1949)[2]

ARIA (Alto). Flutes and the key of C major offer a most serene frame for one of Bach's loveliest movements. Against the gentle movement of the voice called the 'süsses Todesstunde' is heard on the organ the old Chorale and tune so familiar from the Passions.

RECITATIVE (Tenor). Each key-word of this secco recitative is pointed. For 'joy', Bach gives us a happy decoration; for 'sighing' there is a leap of a seventh, and the 'cello softly murmurs, in the last bars, the singer's longing to be with Christ.

[1] AFPB (1949), 39. Note by Britten and Pears.

[2] AFPB (1949), 41. Note by Britten and Pears.

ARIA (Tenor). The longing for death which Bach puts so beautifully to music, is here no morbid self-torture but a sure faith in peace to come. The strings alone accompany the voice, and as usual the important words receive the emphasis of musical ornamentation.

RECITATIVE (Alto). In this most expressive recitative, the singer bids farewell to the world, and as she tells the last hour to strike, all the instruments imitate bells.

QUARTET. The flutes ripple peacefully in thirds and sixths, while a sort of cradle song in 3/8 bids Jesus to bear the soul away.

CHORALE. The tune, which was a background in the first aria, is now played full and warm, with a wonderful counterpoint for the flutes.

Balinese Ceremonial Music (transcribed by Colin McPhee) (1944)[3]

Pemoengkah—Gambangan—Taboeh Teloe

Colin McPhee, the American composer and pianist is the leading authority on Balinese music. He lived for eight years in Bali, and took down hundreds of examples of the music of the island. The transcriptions for two pianos are literal, except in so far as the Balinese scale differs slightly from our own tempered scale, and in the second piece (Gambangan) the drum beats are omitted since it is impossible to imitate them on the piano.

I.—*Pemoengkah.* Mr. McPhee tells us that this is from the overture to the Shadow-Play (a popular entertainment in Bali, in which puppets are thrown in silhouette against an illuminated screen). It is played by a quartet of ten-keyed metallophones (*gendér*), two of which double the others an octave higher.

II.—*Gambangan.* Originally written for an orchestra of four *gambang* (an ancient instrument with fourteen wooden keys) and one or two *saron* (an instrument with seven thick metal keys), this piece was transcribed by a modern Balinese musician for a larger orchestra, the *gamelan gong*, with gongs and some thirty players. The melody is played by a group of *gangsa* (metal-keyed instruments) and the figuration on a series of twelve small gongs (*réjong*).

III.—*Taboeh Teloe.* This music is the first to be played at any large ceremony in Bali, such as a cremation or a temple feast, and by the *Gamelan Gong Gedé* (the gamelan with the great gongs), which comprises many metal-keyed instruments, three large gongs, and many small gongs. The melody is played

[3] Programme note for Wigmore Hall Boosey & Hawkes concert, 29 Mar. 1944 (*GB-ALb* 7–01008549).

by a single musician on the *trompong* (a series of ten small gongs mounted horizontally).

Ludwig van Beethoven (1770–1820) (1954)[4]
Piano Trio in B♭ 'The Archduke', Op. 97 (1810–11)

The Archduke Rudolph of Austria was for many years Beethoven's pupil and a close personal friend. The young Archduke's great kindness to the composer was rewarded by many dedications, including the *Missa Solemnis* and this most famous of his Piano Trios. It was written in 1811 and we are told that the Archduke played over the work from the composer's manuscript before it was published. One of Beethoven's last public performances as pianist was in a performance of this work.

The Trio was designed on the broadest lines, and consists of:

1. *Allegro moderato*. Dominated by a proud theme announced immediately by the piano.

2. *Scherzo. Allegro*. Alternating gnome-like and gracious. The *Trio* has splendid outbursts in remote keys.

3. *Andante cantabile, ma però con moto*. A beautiful, solemn theme, five times varied, the last being very quiet and mysterious before the:

4. *Allegro moderato* bursts in with frivolous gaiety. The work ends with a mad *Presto* coda.

Frank Bridge (1879–1941) (1948)[5]
Phantasie Piano Quartet (1910)

Finished in June 1910, this work is written in Bridge's early style—sonorous yet lucid, with clear, clean lines, grateful to listen to and to play. It is the music of a practical musician, brought up in German orthodoxy, but who loved French romanticism and conception of sound—Brahms happily tempered with Fauré.

Like the many other Phantasies written in England in the first quarter of this century, inspired by the enthusiasm and generosity of W.W. Cobbett, the work is in several sections, played continuously. The first, a Barcarolle, contains many ideas which run throughout the piece. The second is a rhythmic scherzo with a *cantabile* trio. The third section consists of a recitative leading to a recapitulation of the first section with a finely engineered climax. There is a short coda which suggests the deep red afterglow of a sunset.

[4] AFPB (1954), 37–8. [5] AFPB (1948), 26.

Bridge, Piano Quintet (1904–12) (1951)[6]

This quintet was written in four-movement form when Bridge was twenty-five. In 1912, he thoroughly revised it and condensed the second and third movement into one movement. All the same, the style and content remain those of a young man, highly romantic and exuberant. In spite of the later revision, it may lack that strong control and selection which characterizes the later Bridge works, but it is full of warm, and highly personal melodies, and is most richly scored for the five instruments.

(i) *Adagio—Allegro Moderato*. The first subject, an uneasy melody, is announced, as so often in Bridge's works, by the viola. The second subject, more confident, starts quietly on the piano. It is taken up by the strings one after another, with increasing passion and in moving modulations until a fine climax is reached. The development starts mysteriously. The recapitulation is quite regular, and at the end there is a return to the slow tempo of the Introduction.

(ii) *Adagio—Allegro con brio—Adagio.* The slow sections of this movement are dominated by a fine soaring tune of which beautiful and resonant use is made. The quick section, the Scherzo of the work, has highly ingenious rhythms and a gnome-like grotesque character.

(iii) *Allegro Energico.* The main theme is harsh and angular, announced by all four strings in unison with a brilliant piano accompaniment, and there is a tender subsidiary theme. The final climax of the movement is built on subjects from the first movement worked into the form with great ingenuity.

Bridge, *The Sea* (1910–11) (1971)[7]

Apart from an early unpublished symphonic poem, this Suite (written in 1910–11) was Bridge's first major work for orchestra. But by 1910 he had already had much conducting experience, and his writing for orchestra was confident, clear and personal. *The Sea* was conducted by the composer at the Norwich Festival in 1924, when it was so successful that he was invited to write a work specially for the next (1927) Festival. This was *Enter Spring*; but in the intervening years his style had deepened and rarefied, and the new work was altogether too much for the critics and most of the public. Bridge's love of the sea and the rocky seashore led him to build a house a mile or so from Beachy Head, some fifteen years later than this Suite, where he lived until his death. It was his habit to take his friends walking over the cliffs with the superb view of the Channel, and also (whenever it was fine) he would enjoy going prawning before breakfast.

6 AFPB (1951), 30.

7 AFPB (1971), 71.

Bridge, String Sextet (1906–12) (1949)[8]

The dates 1906–1912 are printed at the end of the score of this work. This is interesting for two reasons. First, it is indicative of Bridge's self-criticism. He was always determined to approach perfection as nearly as possible, even though writing a work of less than thirty minutes in length might take him six years. Secondly, the dates show that the *Sextet* was begun in his carefree romantic twenties, when he revelled in luscious sonorities and passionate sweeping themes. This was tempered by the austerity that began to develop in his early thirties and only came to complete fruition after the first World War in the superb and strange later chamber music and orchestral music, such as his last two quartets, his piano trio and in 'There is a Willow', which was performed at last year's Aldeburgh Festival.

The *Sextet* is in three movements.

I. *Allegro Moderato.* A spacious movement, with a memorable opening tune, played *forte* with great warmth and expansion, and a tender and reflective second subject, *Meno mosso e tranquillo*. The great resonance of the string writing throughout this movement is produced by most careful spacing of the parts and by the general gratefulness of the writing for the instruments.

II. *Andante con moto—Allegro—Tempo I.* The movement opens with a simple, slowly moving harmonic passage, which later becomes the accompaniment to a tender first violin melody. The second section is a *scherzo*, alternately mysterious and forceful. The third section, in the tempo and mood of the first, varies most subtly the accompaniment and melody mentioned above.

III. *Allegro ben moderato* leading to *a tempo moderato*. The short introduction is largely for the four upper instruments and leads to an impetuous *animato*. As in the first movement there is a slow and reflective second subject. The development section is thinner and more contrapuntal in texture, and much use is made of material from the two preceding movements. In fact, the second half of this movement is seen, as it were, through the eyes of the earlier movements.

Bridge, String Quartet No. 3 (1926) (1955)[9]

Frank Bridge is known almost entirely by his early works, those written before the first world war; such as the Sextet for Strings, the Piano Quartet-Phantasy, the first two quartets, the Suite 'The Sea', and the many and lovely songs. To those who know only this period of his work the later pieces must seem like those of another composer. The earlier works are tonal, and harmonically direct; the melodies clear and strong; the rhythms if not square, then rather

[8] AFPB (1949), 43. [9] AFPB (1955), 30–1.

regular. The later works have no clear keys, are acid in harmony, the melodies have a curious conversation-like character, and the rhythms are usually irregular, and definite rhythmic patterns are rare. But to one more familiar with all his works the connection between the two periods is clear—the seed of the later works is in the earlier; not just as the later more contrapuntal Mozart (and Verdi) grew gradually out of the young composer's clear and pure attitude to harmony; just as the chromatic yearning of Tannhäuser points to Parsifal; just as an impatience of tonality is there in the earliest work of Schönberg. These changes are always evolutionary—Mozart's technique was ready for the shock of J. S. Bach when he discovered him, and the absorption of the new contrapuntal attitude came naturally. So with Frank Bridge the later works are an evolution from the earlier—stemming from a desire to say more personal and subtler things. They can be difficult at first to follow, apart of course from the invariable fascination of the sound; the conversational melodies can be difficult to recognise, but the moods are clear, and the drama and tensions easy to feel.

The Third String Quartet was written in 1927 and dedicated (like the Fourth, and the splendid late Piano Trio) to that great American patron of chamber music, Mrs Sprague Coolidge. The enthusiasm and confidence of Mrs Coolidge was a great inspiration to Bridge during his last years when so many musical friends were disappointed and bewildered by his later developments.

I. *Andante Moderato—Allegro Moderato*. The brief searching introduction is answered by a brusque Allegro. Gradually the germ theme of the whole work (a rising minor triad falling a semitone), which also gives the tonality of the piece (F sharp), becomes apparent. The tension relaxes into a calmer passage of common chords with a discordant bass. This is followed by a gentler tune on the viola (the second subject). The development starts hesitantly, fragments of themes here and there, until a big crescendo (over a cello *ostinato*) leads to a *fortissimo* statement of the Exposition. The cello plays the second subject now, to a different accompaniment from before. The Coda is violent, and dominated by the germ theme.

II. *Andante con moto*. Muted throughout. The movement starts with a sensitive duet for the two violins over a rocking accompaniment in the viola and cello. The harmony throughout is of a very personal Frank Bridge flavour—bittersweet. There is a big, strained climax (the germ theme in the viola and cello). A hesitant restart of the violin duet, interrupted by a beautiful high cello solo with curious accompaniment (including a *ponticello* tremolo). The duet is resumed and the movement fades away.

III. *Allegro energico*. The germ theme introduces a tempestuous first subject—more perhaps a first mood than a subject, but made of quite definite melodic shapes. The second subject is a passionate high cello melody. The tension relaxes and there is a soothing chordal passage over a rocking viola figure. The development starts with an uneasy recollection of a melody from the first movement on the second violin. This is repeated with mounting excitement by the other instruments, and leads to an agitated recapitulation. A tremendous climax is reached, collapses, and the instruments mute. There is a recollection of the slow movement, and the movement dies away with the germ theme low in the cello.

Bridge, Trio (Rhapsody) (1928) (1965)[10]

The MS. of this trio which has recently come to light is dated March 1928 (a year before the magnificent Piano Trio which we performed two years ago), and in pencil it has scribbled on it 'Version 2—no bon'. I can well remember discussions about this work, when as a boy I was working with Bridge, and a try through of it, but I cannot remember that he was dissatisfied with it, although no public performance followed: that may of course have been because the interest in his later music was virtually nil. In my opinion the work is decidedly worth reviving; it has a strong, fantastic character, very personal themes, and wonderfully resourceful writing for the instruments. It is in a kind of extended sonata form. The speed fluctuates frequently and cunningly between *Allegro* and *Andante*.

Claude Debussy (1862–1918) (1961)[11]
Sonata, for cello and piano (1915)

In 1914 Debussy was already seriously ill, but composed steadily until the outbreak of war with Germany. He was so shocked by this catastrophe that, apart from a *Berceuse Héroique* (a tribute to the Belgian people), he felt there was no point in writing music any longer. He occupied himself with making an edition of Chopin to replace the German ones. But in the middle of 1915 his natural creative impulse asserted itself again, and he now felt his duty was to create beauty while so much was being destroyed around him. By the end of September that year he had already written the *En Blanc et Noir* for two pianos, the fantastic *12 Études* for piano, and this cello sonata. This was to have been the first of *Six Sonates pour divers Instruments composées par C. Debussy, Musicien Français*. Alas, only three of these were completed when he succumbed to cancer in 1918.

The cello sonata shows little of the direct influence of war (unlike the terrifying second movement of the two-piano suite), although there is

[10] AFPB (1965), 30. [11] AFPB (1961), 64.

severity and tragedy in the beginning of the first movement (*Slow*). The writing for the instruments is original and resourceful throughout, and the second and third movements (*Serenade* and *Finale*) have extensive use of pizzicato, *saltando* bowing, *ponticello*, and harmonics. But these are never used for display: they lead us into Debussy's personal world of gaiety, sensitivity, mystery and irony.

Edward Elgar (1857–1934) *Introduction and Allegro*, Op. 47 (1905) (1969)[12]

First performed in the Queen's Hall, London, on 8th March 1905, this work was dedicated to Professor S.S. Sanford, of Yale, at which University Elgar was made and Honorary Doctor of Music in June of that year. The Introduction is fragmentary, with much foreshadowing of the thematic material of the Allegro—the 'nobilmente' second theme, the ambling first theme with its rising fifths and sixths, but principally the haunting melody of the work—supposedly a folk-melody, which Elgar heard sung in the Welsh mountains, characterised by a repeated falling third. There had been many great works for strings before this: one thinks of Purcell's Chacony, the third Brandenburg, Handel, Mozart, Tchaikovsky and Grieg, but these subtle sonorities, contrasting and combining the quartet and the orchestra, and, above all, the brilliant Kreutzer-like scales and arpeggios, were something quite new.

Elgar, *For the Fallen* (No. 3 of *The Spirit of England*, Op. 80) (1915) (1969)[13]

It is not surprising that the war of 1914–18 produced from the red-hot patriot Elgar many immediately inspiring works: *Carillon*, *Polonia*, *Le Drapeau Belge*, and the *Spirit of England* (*The Fourth of August*, *To Women* and *For the Fallen*). In the rather different atmosphere of today some of these works have lost their immediacy, but *For the Fallen* has always seemed to me to have in its opening bars a personal tenderness and grief, in the grotesque march an agony of distortion, and in the final sequences a ring of genuine splendour. It was first performed in Leeds on 3rd May 1916, and in London the following week at a series of concerts in aid of the Red Cross, during which week *The Dream of Gerontius* was performed daily.

[12] AFPB (1969), 38.

[13] AFPB (1969), 38.

Orlando Gibbons (1583–1625) (1948)[14]
Fantasia in four parts in F

Originally written for a consort of viols, this piece has been transposed up a fourth for performance by a string quartet, and edited by Edmund H. Fellowes. It is characterized by great freshness and gaiety, and the wonderful memorability of its themes. As was the tradition of Fantasies of the early seventeenth century, it is composed of many short sections, starting with a buoyant fugato, and including a short piece in galliard rhythm, and, towards the close, a quotation from a contemporary Morris dance appears with touching effect.

Joseph Haydn (1732–1809), (1949)[15]
String Quartet in C 'The Bird'
Op. 33, No. 3 (1781)

Although Haydn had been in his service for many years previously, in 1766 he became head of the Esterhazy Capelle, under the generous and discriminating patronage of Nicolaus, Prince Esterhazy, 'The Magnificent'. For twenty-four years Haydn held this post, and musically it was the happiest part of his life. Perhaps it was even the happiest situation in which any musician could find himself. He had an enthusiastic and adventurous patron, a first-class ensemble of players to work for, and innumerable occasions to excite his inspiration and imagination. He was also in close touch with Vienna, the musical centre of his time, and his beloved friend Mozart.

At Esterhazy he wrote about forty quartets and can be said to have perfected this superb and subtle medium during those years. The six quartets of Op. 33 were among the earliest written at Esterhazy. Perhaps here the writing has not the divine conversational quality that marks the later quartets, but the music already shows the easy relaxation and general good-humour which can never be mistaken for superficiality or thinness. There is a fire burning beneath this benign surface.

The Quartet in C Major is in four movements. 1. *Allegro moderato*. Built on the slightest material, almost on a crescendo and a grace-note, this movement might be called 'The apotheosis of the grace-note'. 2. *Scherzando*. The main part is low, sotto-voce and smooth—almost sinister. Throughout the compass of the instruments is never more than a seventh. The *trio*, a bright, gay duet for two violins, is a complete contrast. 3. *Adagio*. Principally a solo for the first violin—a serene, operatic tune, with more and more decoration and melismae.

[14] AFPB (1948), 25.

[15] AFPB (1949), 42.

4. *Rondo, Presto.* One of Haydn's gayest 2/4 tunes, leading breathlessly to the superbly ridiculous end.

Gustav Holst (1874–1934) (1971)[16]
The Wandering Scholar, Op. 50 (1929–30)

The Wandering Scholar, Holst's last opera, was written in 1929–30: its original title was 'The Tale of the Wandering Scholar'. It was first performed in the David Lewis Theatre, Liverpool, in 1934, conducted by Dr. J. E. Wallace and produced by Frederick Wilkinson. This was a few months before Holst's death and he was too ill to go to the performance. He had no chance to revise the score, which remained unpublished until 1971. He left some pencil queries in the margins of his vocal score, such as 'Tempo?', 'More?', 'More harmony?', etc. And in one of his notebooks he left queries about several words in the libretto which he had doubts about. The editors have answered these queries by making some alterations in speeds and dynamics. They have suggested metronome marks throughout the work, as a help in keeping the continuity of the music at each change of action. In order to make Holst's intentions clearer they have added *tenuto* lines to his *pesante* notes and *staccato* dashes in his *non legato* passages, and they have occasionally indicated the subtlety of a mood, as at the 'cold and casual' woodwind phrase after [22]. They have also made several alterations in the libretto which they feel that Holst might have made himself if he had had the chance to revise the work with his friend Clifford Bax.

When the English Opera Group performed *The Wandering Scholar* at the Cheltenham Festival in 1951, Benjamin Britten adapted Holst's own suggestions for cueing-in for single wind, and wrote new parts for harp and percussion so that the work could be performed with the normal English Opera Group orchestra: Flute (alternating Piccolo), Oboe (alternating English Horn), Clarinet, Bassoon, Horn, Percussion, Harp, String Quartet and Double Bass. This version is available on hire. (The printed Vocal Score can be used in rehearsal for either version: the instrumentation indicated in the piano part agrees with this Study Score.)

John Ireland (1879–1962) (1959)[17]
The Land of Lost Content (1920–1)

John Ireland will be eighty years of age this August, and so we are giving this Cycle tonight as a tribute to a composer of strong personal gifts and real

[16] Preface to published score (London: Faber Music, 1971). Note probably by Britten and Imogen Holst.

[17] AFPB (1959), 49.

single-mindedness of purpose. Ireland is best known for his songs and chamber music, and rightly so, because they form the bulk of his output and contain his most individual thoughts. His first great impact on the public was with his Second Violin Sonata (1917) written under the terrible shadow of the First World War.

This Cycle, perhaps his most personal, certainly his most famous, was published in 1921. There have been many English composers to set Housman's poems, and none, to my mind, more sympathetically successful than Ireland; there is much in common between Ireland and Housman, who 'in his strange, magical, musical, and at times sentimental way . . . seems to say good-bye to the vanishing peacefulness of the country, and to the freshness and innocence of its young men'. These words come from a recent broadcast by William Plomer on the centenary of the birth of the poet. It is good that we can also pay tribute to Housman by including these settings of some of his most succinct and characteristic poems.

The six songs are: 1 *Lent Lily*, typical of Ireland's rhythmic suppleness; 2 *Ladslove*, a crystalline setting of the Narcissus legend; 3 *Goal and Wicket*, tough and bitter; 4 *The Vain Desire*, very personal tonal ambiguity; 5 *The Encounter*, strong and rhythmic with a fine tritonic bass; 6 *Epilogue*, in which is embedded a quotation from his setting of 'My true love hath my heart'—a phrase with great significance for the composer.

Gustav Mahler (1860–1911) (1961)[18]
Symphony No. 4 (1892, 1899–1900, rev. 1901–10)

An impressive number of musicians, including Otto Klemperer, Arnold Schoenberg and Erwin Stein, has testified that Mahler was the greatest of operatic conductors. He was for ten years the director of the Vienna Opera, and intensive work there, as well as artistic battles, prevented him from composing, except in his summer holiday months. Thus the first three movements of this symphony were written in the summers of 1899 and 1900. The fourth movement had been written as part of the third symphony (1895–6).

[18] AFPB (1961), 60. Britten's 1969 revision of this article concluded thus:

> In most of his works Mahler continued after performance and even after publication to make subtle changes in the orchestration. The Fourth Symphony is no exception, and the final alterations were made in the proofs of the work around the time he last conducted it—in New York on 17th January 1911. In the latest Eulenburg score (1966) these changes are, oddly enough, ignored; but we are using them, agreeing as we do with the late Erwin Stein, that they are 'improvements of great significance'. Anyhow, they are Mahler's final thoughts on the matter.

This movement, a setting of a poem from *Des Knaben Wunderhorn*, gives in effect the theme of the whole work. The poem paints a charming children's picture of life in heaven, without a trace of sentimentality, and the whole symphony can be said to be a child's world—of intense but clear emotions, of sudden changes of mood from gaiety to anxiety—a world of sensitivity without sophistication.

1. *Moderato.* The first light-hearted group of themes soon gives way to a singing, tender second subject with a moment of passion. The exposition finishes with a deceptively innocent, jerky little tune on the oboe, and a calming phrase from the cellos. The long development, with its many different moods, its outbursts of temper and gaiety, all skilfully bound together, leads to a triumphant climax, with a bold trumpet solo which could be a nursery rhyme. The recapitulation creeps in surreptitiously.

2. *With easy movement.* An extended Rondo. There are three main ideas, which alternate with subtle variations—a mysterious waltz on the solo fiddle (tuned a tone higher than usual), a gracious flowing tune, cheekily punctuated, and a slower *Ländler* tune, with many trills. Towards the end the last tune is extended in quiet ecstasy, before the mysterious fiddle takes over once again.

3. *Quietly.* Again in rondo-like form, the movement of 'heavenly length' is dominated by a relaxed section in G major, with a clear mood but with few features except for a Schubert-like pizzicato bass. The second section starts with an oboe tune (with the same bass as before) and leads to a passionate pleading phrase which recurs all through Mahler's music. One reappearance of the main subject is fascinating: four statements in abruptly increased speeds. Just before the end, as the music seems to be fading out, there is an ecstatic outburst, culminating in the nursery rhyme tune from the first movement, fortissimo in the horns. Then follows:

4. *Very peacefully*, the setting of the *Knaben Wunderhorn* verses. We now see from where the 'nursery rhyme' tune comes, and from where the little repeated flute grace-notes (which started the symphony) come. So much, in fact, of the previous movements stems from this artless song that it seems to be a theme preceded by its variation. For the last verse we move from the casual world of G major into a heavenly E major, with one of the most serenely beautiful tunes Mahler ever wrote.

In this performance some of the latest (unpublished) changes Mahler made are being used. These are described in fascinating detail in Erwin Stein's book *Orpheus in New Guises*.

Felix Mendelssohn (1809–47) (1969)[19]
String Quintet No. 1, Op. 18 (1826, rev. 1932)

1. *Allegro con moto* 2. *Scherzo: Allegro di molto*
The original version of this Quintet was written when Mendelssohn was sixteen—a year later than the better-known Octet. It was in four movements, the third of which, a minuet which seems to be lost, was replaced in 1832 by an Intermezzo. We are playing today the first two movements of the original version. The second movement is one of the famous Mendelssohn scherzos (the ones to *A Midsummer Night's Dream* and the Octet are other examples)—brilliant yet ghostlike, advancing and receding, 'swifter than the Moone's sphere'.

Mendelssohn, Symphony No. 3 (1970)[20]
'Scottish', Op. 56 (1842)

1. *Adagio* 2. *Scherzo: Vivace non troppo*
Mendelssohn paid a fruitful visit to Scotland in 1829, when he was little more than a boy. On this trip the idea (and some of the musical phrases) of both the Hebrides Overture and this symphony, two of his finest works, came to him. The latter work was not completed until 1842, when Mendelssohn was already a firm favourite in England; and it was in London in the same year that it had its triumphant second performance. Shortly before this Mendelssohn had visited Queen Victoria and the Prince Consort at Buckingham Palace, when Her Majesty sang some of his songs (sight-reading one of them) and His Royal Highness enjoyed himself pulling out the stops while Mendelssohn played the organ. His request to be allowed to dedicate this symphony to the Queen was readily granted. The *Adagio* starts with a characteristic melancholy tune for the violins; this alternates with a threatening little march for wind instruments. The Scherzo is delightfully scored, and starts with the clarinet playing the curling first tune against the repeated semiquavers in the strings. These two ideas provide the bulk of the material for this short but masterly movement.

E. J. Moeran (1894–1950) (1973)[21]
Nocturne (1934)

During the first few years of the thirties, E. J. Moeran recuperated from a nervous illness at the house of his parents, a few miles outside Norwich. My parents were then still living in Lowestoft, and most of my holidays were spent

[19] AFPB (1969), 67. [20] AFPB (1970), 14. [21] AFPB (1973), 56.

there. Jack Moeran and I became warm friends despite the disparity of our ages, and it was a privilege to get to know this charming and affectionate Irishman. He was a near-invalid, broken by the 1914–18 war, but he struggled manfully with his problems and produced music of personality and beauty. His approach to music was passionately subjective, and his occasional amateur flounderings came in for some rather bossy teenage criticisms from me—which he accepted gratefully and humbly. His *Songs of Springtime* for unaccompanied choir came from this time, and a rather wild but not unimpressive Symphony in G minor, and, in the early months of 1934, this *Nocturne*, dedicated to the memory of his beloved Delius. Of course the *Nocturne* owes much to the shifting harmonies of the senior master, but the twilight nostalgic beauty of this music is Moeran's own. The poem is an 'Address to the Sunset' from *Don Juan Tenorio, the Great*, a play by Robert Nichols—friend of poets, painters, and composers of that time, and whose widow lived for many years in Aldeburgh and who was a good friend to music and the Festival. The *Nocturne* was written for the Norwich Philharmonic Society and performed by them early in 1934, with Roy Henderson as baritone soloist. It was repeated soon after, if my memory is right, at the Norwich Festival with Keith Falkner.

Wolfgang Amadeus Mozart (1756–91) Symphony in D, K. 84 (1770); Sinfonia Concertante, K. 364 (1779); Piano Concerto, K. 459 (1784); Adagio and Rondo, K. 617 (1791).

(1951)[22]

The compositions to be performed tonight range over more than twenty years—the Symphony in D, written when Mozart was fourteen, the Sinfonia Concertante when he was twenty-three, the Piano Concerto five years later, and finally the Adagio and Rondo six months before his death at the age of thirty-five. But from his earliest years, Mozart's music is complete and satisfactory. In the little boyish Symphony the forms are conventional, it is scarcely more than an Overture, but the tenderness of the slow movement, the gaiety of the others is surely recognizable Mozart. Mozart was certainly here under the influence of J. C. Bach, the London Bach who was such a dear friend of the young boy. All his life, Mozart had the wit to be influenced by great composers, especially of course Haydn and J. S. Bach—but then he assimilated these influences and made them part of his own character. The Sinfonia Concertante is certainly the greatest of his Concertos for stringed

[22] AFPB (1951), 25–6.

instruments. The viola always drew something special, something rich and strange, from Mozart. The first and last movements are in his *gallant* manner, but every gesture has meaning and the form is balanced with incomparable nicety. The slow movement is tragedy in the grandest manner, dark and sombre with cries of extraordinary poignancy from the viola. Mozart, himself, has supplied cadenzas for the first two movements of great beauty and elaboration.

The Adagio and Rondo in C was written in 1791 for Marian Kirchgaessner—a virtuoso of the newly-invented glass-harmonica (the nearest contemporary instrument is the Celesta, or the Dulcitone). Like the music Mozart wrote for the clockwork organ, and above all the 'Organ piece for a Clock' (the famous F Minor Fantasia), Mozart was inspired to extraordinary heights by the unlikely job of having to write music for a mechanical and fashionable 'novelty' instrument. The Adagio in C Minor is of a 'Magic Flute' depth, and the serene and graceful Allegretto Rondo reminds us at times of the same masterpiece.

Mozart wrote the piano concerto K. 459 in December, 1784, probably for himself to play. It is a 'virtuoso' one, filled with most brilliant writing for the solo instrument (particularly in the Presto, an especially popular movement)—even the usual slow movement being replaced by an Allegretto of gracious character—but every scrap of it has a warmth and seriousness and a melodic memorability unsurpassed by Mozart himself. The Cadenzas played this evening are Mozart's own.

Mozart, Sinfonia Concertante, K. 297b (1778) (1960)[23]

1 *Allegro* 2 *Adagio* 3 *Andantino con variazioni*

This work was written in Paris in 1778 for four celebrated virtuosi: Wendling (flute), Ramm (oboe), Punto (horn) and Ritter (bassoon). This form of the work is lost, and where the present version comes from no one knows, except that there is no sign of any 'arrangement' of the solo parts, and the clarinet part is unmistakably 'Mozartian'—with the knowledge and understanding of the instrument worthy of the composer of the Clarinet Concerto and Quintet.

The work is conceived on a grand scale; the first movement, in particular, with its three statements of the formal opening subject (for orchestra and then for each pair of soloists), its big *tutti* at the beginning of the development section, and its fine long original cadenza. The second movement is, like the

[23] AFPB (1960), 80.

first and last movements, in E flat; this gives a particularly monumental feeling and a strong sense of continuity to the whole work. The ten variations of the last movement are of great brilliance for the solo instruments, with an expressive little coda for orchestra which connects each variation. The movement ends with a gay little 6/8 *Allegro*.

Mozart, String Quintet in C, K. 515 (1787) (1973)[24]

Mozart's Quintet in C is dated 'Vienna, April 19, 1787'. Less than four weeks later he had already finished the passionately tragic G minor Quintet. Throughout these two months of April and May he was anxiously waiting for news from Salzburg of his father, who was in his last illness. At this time the thought of death was never far from Mozart's mind. A letter to his father says: 'I never lie down at night without reflecting that—young as I am—I may not live to see another day. Yet no one of my acquaintances could say that in company I am morose or disgruntled.' It is this mood that is reflected in the C major Quintet. No music could be further removed from morose or disgruntled thoughts or feelings. But the happiness that shines through it is not the relaxed indifference of evasion: it is the result of having considered death to be 'the best and truest friend of mankind'.

1. *Allegro* The movement grows from the quickly pulsating triad of the second violin and violas, the determination of the cello's mounting arpeggio, and the expressive query of the first violin.

2. *Menuetto* (*Allegretto*) Formal and courteous, but with warmth in its legato gestures. The rising seventh at the beginning of the trio leads to poignant modulations.

3. *Andante* One of Mozart's unforgettable 3/4 tunes in F major. The first violin and first viola offer each other jewelled phrases throughout their long dialogue, while the remaining strings support them with their comments of agreement.

4. *Allegro* The quintet returns to C major for a cheerful 2/4 tune that is characteristic of a rondo. There are occasional glances towards more remote keys, with sudden dynamic outbursts, but nothing destroys the underlying assurance of the music.

[24] AFPB (1973), 26.

Mozart, Adagio and Fugue in C minor, K. 546 (1788) (1972)[25]

The short Adagio 'for the Fugue which I wrote long ago for two pianos' (as Mozart said) was composed in Vienna on 26 June 1788; at the same time, presumably, he wrote the string version of the four-and-a-half-year-old Fugue. The latter is a fine work full of the dramatic intensity which he gave to the form, but the Adagio has in its fifty-two solemn bars a series of the most extraordinary modulations even Mozart ever contrived.

Mozart, Requiem, K. 626 (1791) (1971)[26]

Everyone knows the story of the mysterious 'grey stranger' who arrived at Mozart's house six months before he died, and whom he felt to be a presage of his own death. This mystery has long been solved (it was a servant of Count Walsegg-Stuppach, who wanted this work to commemorate his recently deceased wife); but the other mystery, of how much Mozart actually wrote of this great fragment, has not been solved, and probably never will be. He had already much to do—*The Magic Flute*, the opera seria 'Titus', two Masonic cantatas, a Clarinet Concerto. It seemed inconceivable that he should add to this schedule, but he did, working on the Requiem on and off through those last hectic six months.

In Mozart's own writing we have the *Requiem aeternam* and *Kyrie eleison* (complete); the *Dies irae*, *Rex tremendae*, *Confutatis*, *Domine Jesu*, *Hostias* (complete vocal parts and bass, and sketches for the other instruments); and the first eight bars of the *Lacrimosa* only. At his death his wife was determined to get the work completed: the rest of the commission fee was needed, since money was short. First she tried Joseph Eybler, who did splendidly until he came to the eight bars of the *Lacrimosa*, when his courage failed him and he gave up. Constanza tried other composers, who understandably wouldn't attempt such an intimidating task, until Süssmayr (a twenty-five-year-old pupil of Mozart) agreed to undertake it. He started from scratch, perhaps not doing such a polished job as Eybler, but he had the courage to go on with the *Lacrimosa* and found his own answer to those tremendous eight bars—or *was* it his own answer? Perhaps one day we shall know. It seems unlikely that he was solely responsible for the flaming *Sanctus*, the gracious tune of the *Benedictus*, or the brooding *Agnus Dei*. If so he would surely have developed into a wonderful composer himself. There are stories of Mozart on his death-bed indicating some drum rhythms for the *Sanctus* to Süssmayr, of the *Benedictus*

[25] AFPB (1972), 32. [26] AFPB (1971), 61–2.

melody being found on a scrap of paper, and of him showing the way to fit the 'Lux aeterna' and 'Cum Sanctis' words to the music of the *Introitus* and *Kyrie*. Actually Plath discovered in the Berlin State Library a sheet of sketches (a cancelled continuation of the *Rex tremendae*, and a splendid start to an 'Amen' fugue). Professor Nowak (who has done much excellent detective work) considers this proof that there were other sketches and notes, and I think he is probably right. The story is that Constanza destroyed these other sketches, but I can never understand what compelled her to do so—the existence of more sketches would not seem to prove anything.

Since the recent publication of the whole of the Eybler version, we have been able to compare it with the familiar version of Süssmayr, which has been used for nearly two hundred years. One notices that occasionally Eybler's compares favourably with it: in the richness of some of the counterpoint, the rhythmic vividness of the trumpets and drums, and some more effective woodwind writing. For this performance I have made use of several of Eybler's solutions, and in one case I have attempted one of my own.

Giovanni Battista Pergolesi (1710–36) (1949)[27]
Concertino No. 6 in B♭ for strings and continuo

Andante—Presto . . . a capella—Adagio affettuoso—Allegro moderato

Pergolesi wrote his first stage works for a Court theatre and was later appointed organist at the Neapolitan Royal Chapel, but when his opera *L'Olimpiade* failed at Rome, he decided to devote himself only to sacred music. He died of consumption at the age of twenty-six, having written six operas, five *intermezzi* (including the famous *Serva Padrona*), two oratorios, twelve cantatas, twenty-six sonatas for violins and bass, and much church music.

He entitles this graceful and lyrical work *Concertino No. 6 per 4 Violini, Viola, Violoncello e Basso continuo*, and there are actually seven independent voices. But the two first violins continually lead, and the work is in effect a two-violin concerto.

The *Adagio* is a passionate Siciliana, in the dotted rhythm so often used by Pergolesi. The widely spread arpeggios are typical of the beautifully contrived violin writing throughout.

The last movement has special interest as being the origin of the Tarantella from Stravinsky's ballet *Pulcinella* based on Pergolesi's themes, but while in Pergolesi the quaver movement is confined to the two solo violins, with a solemn sustained background for the lower strings, in Stravinsky the movement is general.

[27] AFPB (1949), 19.

Henry Purcell (1659–95) Chacony in G minor, Z730 (*c.*1678) (1955)[28]

This chacony seems to have been written in the early 1680s, but it is not known for what occasion. Although written for viols, the transcription on to our modern stringed instruments can be made without changing a note. The manuscript is in the British Museum.

The theme, first of all in the basses, moves in stately fashion from a high to a low G. It is repeated many times in the bass with varying textures above. It then starts moving around the orchestra. There is a quaver version with heavy chords above it, which provides the material for several repetitions. There are some free and modulating versions of it, and a connecting passage leads to a forceful and rhythmic statement in G minor. The end is remarkable; a pathetic variation, with dropping semiquavers, and repeated 'soft'—Purcell's own instruction.

Purcell, *Dido and Aeneas*, Z626 (*c.*1689) (1961)[29]

This is a working edition, intended chiefly for performance. It is also intended for reference, because at present it is the only full score that can be bought. The Purcell Society edition, published in 1889, has been out of print for many years and in later versions the full score has been available only on hire. A masterpiece such as *Dido and Aeneas* should have a scholarly edition of the score, reproducing Purcell's intentions as nearly as possible, but as the autograph score has not yet been discovered there can be no authentic edition.

[28] AFPB (1955), 47.

Britten's note for his published edition of this piece (B&H, 1965) included this preface:

> It is not known when Purcell composed this isolated, independent Chacony, nor for what occasion if any he wrote it. It was most probably written as incidental music for a play—most likely a tragedy, judging by the serious and severe nature of the music.
>
> The autograph score is in the British Museum (Add. mss. 30930), which was used as the basis for this edition.
>
> This edition is a practical one, the result of the experience gained in performing the work many times. The interpretation is of course a personal one, including dynamics, phrasing, gracing, and the 'double-dotting' of many of the rhythms. In rehearsal it has been found helpful to regard the characteristic rhythm of ♪. ♬ as a form of ♩ ♬ [5] with the ♩ played *staccato* and the ♬ emphasised.
>
> The Chacony can be played by string quartet or string orchestra, with or without a harpsichord. A separate harpsichord part is available on hire from the publishers.

[29] Preface to published miniature score (London: Boosey & Hawkes, 1961).

The Existing Manuscripts

There are two manuscripts of the work, in the handwriting of two different copyists. The one in the Library of St. Michael's College, Tenbury, is described in the Purcell Society edition as 'a fine MS. score written by John Travers, about 1720', but the writing is unlike that of Travers, and the watermark of the paper shows that it cannot be dated before the second half of the eighteenth century,[30] also there are many copyist's errors.

The other manuscript was for many years in the possession of W. H. Cummings, the editor of the Purcell Society score. After his death it was sold in 1917 to the late Marquis Tokugawa and placed in the Nanki Music Library at Tokyo. The present owner, Mr. Kyuhei Oki, lent the manuscript to the Purcell–Handel exhibition in London during the summer of 1959. He also very generously allowed us to work from a microfilm while preparing this present edition of the work.

Miss Pamela Willetts of the Department of Manuscripts in the British Museum has found that the handwriting of the Oki MS. (approximately 1800) is the same as that in several volumes of works by Handel and Arne which were the property of Dr. Samuel Arnold (1740–1802). There are fewer copyists' errors in this MS. than in the Tenbury MS., but neither copy shows any sign of having been used in performance.

Previous Published Editions

The earliest published edition was an incomplete version edited by G. A. Macfarren for the Musical Antiquarian Society in 1841. At that time no libretto had been discovered. In 1870 E. F. Rimbault published a vocal score. A copy of the libretto had then been found, and Rimbault learnt that a good deal of the music was missing, but in spite of 'diligent searches' he failed to discover other manuscripts.

When W. H. Cummings made his Purcell Society edition of 1889 he was able to consult not only his own manuscript (now the Oki MS.) which he had purchased in 1877, but also the Tenbury MS., (then in the private library of the Rev. Sir Frederick Ouseley), and a set of manuscript parts which Edward J. Dent later identified as agreeing with the Musical Antiquarian Society edition of 1841. Unfortunately Cummings left no record in his Purcell Society edition of where his own manuscript score had differed from the Tenbury MS. or from the set of parts. Now that a comparison of the manuscripts is possible, it can clearly be seen that he often preferred the Musical Antiquarian version to either of the others.

[30] Original footnote: See 'New Light on *Dido and Aeneas*' by Eric Walter White, in *Henry Purcell: Essays on his Music*, edited Imogen Holst, O.U.P. 1959.

When Dent prepared his edition of the work for the Oxford University Press in 1925 he based it on the Tenbury MS. as he did not know where the other MS. was.

We have compared the two manuscripts in detail. There is a list of the variants on page I–XXIV. Any collation of the two manuscripts can only be guesswork. We have aimed at getting as near as possible to what we think the composer intended, reaching each decision partly as the result of contemporary evidence but mostly as the result of a working familiarity with other music by Purcell.

Speeds and Dynamics

The occasional indications of 'quick' and 'slow', 'loud' and 'soft' and other headings in the Tenbury and Oki MSS. are here reproduced in larger type to distinguish them from our own editorial suggestions.

Key signatures and Accidentals

Key signatures have been modernized. (Tenbury's two flats for C minor and three flats for F minor are listed on pages II and V). As this is a working edition the accidentals that are taken for granted in the manuscripts are here shown on the stave instead of above it. (This decision was reached with reluctance, but having no authentic manuscript to work from it would have been intolerably fussy to give alternative accidentals in the same bar. The only scholarly approach to the problem would be a facsimile edition of both manuscripts: perhaps some publisher may one day make this possible.) In supplying these missing accidentals we have followed the late seventeenth century evidence that an accidental applies only to the particular note before which it is placed; that in an ascending minor scale the sixth as well as the seventh note is raised a semitone, although only the seventh may be sharpened on paper; and that in a descending minor scale the seventh and sixth will both be flattened unless there is an indication to the contrary.

The major third in the final chord of a minor tune was usually taken for granted where only a bare fifth was supplied, but late seventeenth century evidence says 'French composers do the opposite', and as Purcell was influenced by Lully as well as by the Italians it would be a mistake to keep too rigidly to this convention.

There is very little figuring in either manuscript that gives direct guidance in the choice of accidentals.

Time signatures, dotted notes and inequality

Time signatures have been modernized. Tenbury's **3**, ¢ etc. are listed on pages II to XXIII. The difference between **C** and ¢ is not clearly defined in the seventeenth century: a writer of 1650 says that both signs were often used for the same thing. The time signature **2** was considered to be quicker than ¢, but this rule cannot have been invariable, for it would be impossible to take the beginning of Act I Scene 2 (page 33) at a quick two in a bar.

The indication that a dotted note should be doubly dotted is shown in the full score above the stave.[31] Suggestions for the inequality of evenly-written quavers are also above the stave. Inequality should ideally sound like an improvisation, and it is quite likely to vary from one performance to the next. For instance, we had originally thought of writing Aeneas's protesting 'Tonight?' on page 67 with a semiquaver for the first syllable, but during rehearsals for a recent recording by the B.B.C. Transcription Service we found that the word needed the full dramatic weight of a quaver.

Gracing

Purcell, like Bach, wrote out far more of his graces than was usual with his contemporaries. The few editorial suggestions in this opera are mostly concerned with smoothing over the gap of a falling third at a cadence. This gracing is written in small notes on the stave: before the note where time is to be taken from that note, and after the first of two repeated quavers where the grace-note is an alternative to the first quaver. Trills that are not in either MS. are shown in small type.

Interpretation of Graces and Dotted notes

All trills begin on the upper note. The trill should come to rest on the final beat. Dotted notes without a trill are, except in obviously legato passages, sung or played with a silence on the dot, as in 'drive 'em back' on page 46. This 'silence of articulation' is important from the first bar of the opera.

Double bars

One of the chief differences between the Tenbury and Oki MSS. is their use of double bars. The Oki MS. uses double bars in the late eighteenth-century way, as we use them today. In the Tenbury MS. a slow **C** aria leads straight into a quick **3** chorus, without a double bar between them, an indication of an *attaca* that was still in use for some of the Bach cantatas. We have kept to the Tenbury method because it gives such a clear indication of the continuity of Purcell's music. But we have not kept to the Tenbury habit of changing the last bar of a **C** aria to **3**, in anticipation of the following change of time signature. This is a device corresponding to the modern warning ‖$^{3}_{4}$ at the end of a line: its appearance is so unusual that it would be out of place in a working edition.

[31] Original footnote: In the vocal score all such indications are shown on the stave.

The Libretto[32]

Nahum Tate's libretto was published in 1689 or 1690, with a heading describing it as 'AN OPERA Perform'd at Mr JOSIAS PRIEST's Boarding-School at CHELSEY By Young Gentlewomen'. No music has survived for the pastoral Prologue which gives opportunities for Mr. Priest's dancing pupils to perform six extra dances.

Six lines of libretto at the end of Act II are also without any music. These lines are important, as it seems obvious that Aeneas's recitative in A minor and his exit without any curtain music or chorus cannot be the real end of the act, which needs to return to the D minor of the beginning of the act, or to its relative or tonic major, as each of the other scenes does. When we first saw the Oki MS. we hoped the missing music might be there, but alas, it ends in the same way as the Tenbury MS. We have therefore included music for these six lines from other works by Purcell, as used in the edition prepared for the English Opera Group's production in 1951.

The extra music in Act II

The Trio for the Sorceress and the two witches, page 71, is transposed from a trio in *The Indian Queen* (1690). The Chorus is transposed from the *Welcome Song* of 1687, and the Dance is taken from the overture to *Sir Anthony Love* (1690).

Purcell, *Dido and Aeneas*, Z626 (*c.*1689) (1962)[33]

The greatest piece of English operatic literature was written for a girls' school. In 1689 Mr. Josias Priest, a gentleman of the theatre, who ran a dancing academy for young gentlewomen in Chelsea, had the good fortune to have *Dido and Aeneas* written for him by the twenty-nine-year-old Purcell. The libretto was written by Nahum Tate, a poet of no great distinction in his own right, who nevertheless happened to produce for this occasion an almost perfect small-scale opera libretto.

Dido, Queen of Carthage, is beset by anxiety, and, when charged by her attendant Belinda, admits that her heart is captured by her Trojan guest, the Prince Aeneas. He himself enters, and persuades her to have pity on him. Love triumphs, and the scene ends with a dance. In the next scene we are taken to

[32] Original footnote: For more detailed information about the libretto, see the footnote to page (iii) [i.e. Eric Walter White's essay].

[33] AFPB (1962), 32–3. Note written by Britten, Pears, and Imogen Holst. The first three paragraphs are taken from an article Pears wrote for the 1951 Festival book, before the Tokyo microfilm was known about.

the cave of the witches who are plotting ruin for Dido: they will make Aeneas think that Jove commands him to leave Carthage at once and continue his journey to be the founder of the Roman Empire. In the third scene, the happy Dido and Aeneas are enjoying a *fête-champêtre*, when a storm interrupts them and an evil spirit, disguised as Mercury, appears to tell Aeneas that he must sail away at once. The witches rejoice in their triumph. The scene changes. The sailors are making ready to be off; they have a characteristic song and dance. The witches appear and plot further mischief; 'destruction's our delight', they sing. Meanwhile, the tragic queen realises her fate. Aeneas comes to break to her the news of his departure, and after a sad and bitter duet Dido dismisses him. Her heart is broken and death is near. She bids her faithful Belinda farewell, and the opera ends with a chorus of mourning.

Dido was not printed in Purcell's lifetime; one or two songs appeared in collections after his death, but no score was published until 1840, and by then the original manuscript had long since disappeared. The earliest surviving manuscript is the eighteenth-century copy in St. Michael's College, Tenbury. (This was the basis of the English Opera Group's production in 1951.) The Tenbury copy was clearly never used for performance, and it contains many uncorrected mistakes. The only other surviving manuscript has been in Tokyo since 1917. Various legends have sprung up concerning this Tokyo copy. At one time it was considered as 'lost'. Later on, there was a rumour—fortunately unfounded—that it had been sold to an American collector in Baltimore, who had locked it up in a cellar, refusing to let anyone have a look at it. After many searches had been made, the manuscript was traced by the Tokyo representatives of the British Council, and the present owner, Mr Kyuhei Oki, generously allowed a photographed copy to be used in preparing the edition of the opera which will be heard this evening.

It was an exciting moment when the microfilm from Tokyo reached Aldeburgh. Our first glance was for the end of Act II, in the feverish hopes of finding the missing music to the last six lines of the libretto. Alas, it was not there. But throughout the photographed pages of this 1800 manuscript there were fascinating details where the music differed from the more familiar version.

The new edition of the music for this year's festival is based on a collation of the two manuscripts, in which we have aimed at getting as near as possible to the composer's intentions, reaching each decision partly as the result of contemporary evidence but mostly as the result of a working familiarity with other music by Purcell.

The extra music for the end of Act II is the same as in the 1951 production: the Trio for the Sorceress and Witches is from *The Indian Queen* (1695); the Chorus is from the *Welcome Song* of 1687, and the dance is from *Sir Anthony Love* (1690).

Purcell, *The Fairy Queen*, Z629 (1792) (1970)[34]

1. *The changed order of the music in this shortened version*

A staged production of *The Fairy Queen* in its entirety is too unwieldy for most twentieth-century audiences, who are not used to sitting through all five acts of a spoken play with 'Singing, Dancing and Machines interwoven with 'em, after the manner of an Opera'. Even a concert performance has to be cut, and in planning this new version we have regretfully left out some of our favourite songs and dances. Cutting out items here and there cannot provide a satisfying shape. It was Peter Pears' suggestion that we should change the order of the scenes and transform the work into four parts—*Oberon's Birthday*, *Night and Silence*, *The Sweet Passion* and *Epithalamium*. Each part is dramatically convincing on its own, and we have kept the clear musical framework of the key sequences so characteristic of Purcell.

2. *The sources*

There is no autograph manuscript of the work. The score that was used at the first performance at the Queen's (formerly the Dorset Gardens) Theatre in 1692 was written by several copyists, and pages were left blank for music that was not ready. Only two songs and four dances are in Purcell's own handwriting. After his death in 1695 some of the music from *The Fairy Queen* was published in *Orpheus Britannicus* and *Ayres for the Theatre*, but the manuscript full score was lost and nothing was heard of it until nearly two hundred years later, when it was discovered to be in the library of the Royal Academy of Music. Owing to the kindness of the Librarian we have been able to study this score in detail and to use it as our main source for this new edition. We are also very grateful to the Clerk of the Gresham Committee for allowing us to see the Gresham College M.S.VI.5.6 (now in the Guildhall) which contains several songs from *The Fairy Queen* in Purcell's own writing.

3. *Duration*

The approximate duration is 96 minutes.
(Part I 28′ Part II 28′ Part III 22′ Part IV 18′)

4. *The number of soloists needed*

This edition has been planned for two sopranos, one mezzo-soprano, two counter-tenors, two tenors and two basses. This is the ideal number, but it can, if necessary, be performed with fewer voices:—two sopranos, mezzo-soprano,

[34] Preface to published vocal score (London: Faber Music, 1970). This note was written by Britten and Imogen Holst.

counter-tenor, tenor and bass. In this case the counter-tenor, tenor and bass soloists will sing all the music allotted to counter-tenor, tenor and bass. In No. 3 the second counter-tenor line should be taken by the tenor, and in No. 13 a high tenor can replace the counter-tenor at will. The repeat of the trio in No. 38 should be sung by mezzo-soprano, counter-tenor, and tenor singing the bass part with alternative small notes.

5. *Transpositions*

Purcell wrote the *Dialogue between Coridon and Mopsa* (No. 27) in G for counter-tenor and bass as a comic scene in the original staged production. In this concert edition we have transposed it to B flat for mezzo-soprano and tenor, and we have followed the variants in the Gresham M.S., where Purcell has transposed it to F with both voices in the G clef. We have also transposed the *Dance for the Haymakers* (No. 28) from G to F. Everything else is in its original key.

6. *Instrumentation*

The instrumentation for each number is given in the Contents (page vi), with editorial additions shown in brackets. The original score is written for 2 flutes (recorders in the seventeenth century), 2 oboes, 2 trumpets, kettledrums and strings. The bass line represents the *basso continuo*, which would have included harpsichord throughout. In this vocal score the realization of the harpsichord part is shown in normal-sized notes. At performances where the harpsichord player prefers to make his own realization of the part, the soloists must be prepared to hear a different rhythm, spacing and texture of the upper-stave notes in any of the passages marked 'harpsichord'. The *continuo* in Purcell's time would have included cello and double bass whenever they were needed, and the bassoon would always have joined in where there were oboes playing. The drums were always required where there were trumpets. (The drum parts in Nos. 1, 4 and 11 are original: in Nos. 32, 38 and 40 they are editorial.) In several of the choruses and dances we have added optional woodwind, remembering the late seventeenth-century tradition of doubling the string parts on oboes and bassoon whenever the music seemed to call for it. In No. 14 the high, chirruping tune of 'the songsters of the sky' is marked 'Violins' in the manuscript score, but the word has been added in a much later writing than the music, so we have given the part to oboes and the modern equivalent of Purcell's sopranino recorders. In *The Plaint* (No. 26) we have given the tune to the oboe instead of the violin because it was written for oboe in an early eighteenth-century manuscript that was once in the library of the Royal College of Music: unfortunately this M.S. is now lost. In *Hark! th' echoing air* (No. 33), in the original manuscript the trumpet stops playing after bar 6 and does not come in again until the last three bars: the trumpet part that we have shown between bar 7 and bar 35 is an editorial addition.

7. *Time signatures*

We have kept the original time-values of the notes throughout the work, but we have modernised the time signatures.

8. *Tempo indications*

The very few tempo indications given in the manuscript score are shown here in their original Italian. The remaining indications in English, as well as the metronome marks, are editorial suggestions.

9. *Double bars*

Double bars are only written in the original manuscript when a number has come to an end and there is to be a definite break before the next number begins. We have shown these with thick double bars, and we have used thin double bars where the music is to lead straight on with an *attacca.*

10. *Repeats*

Purcell wrote the music of *The Fairy Queen* for performance in a theatre, with frequent dances and with stage directions asking for 'vast Quantities of Water falling in mighty Cascades', and for 'numbers of strange Birds flying in the Air'; all his repeats were needed. We have shown them all, but conductors will decide how many are required in a concert performance. The repeats in *If Love's a sweet passion* (No. 25) might seem unnecessary without any dancers, and the players in No. 16, *Echo*, may find the repeat too exhausting.

11. *Dynamics*

The only dynamics that are marked in the manuscripts are the 'loud', 'soft' and 'softer' of the echo effect in Nos. 15 and 16, the alternating 'loud' and 'soft' in the first half of *Turn then thine eyes* (No. 36), the 'Violins with sourdines' in *See, even Night herself is here* (No. 19) and the 'soft' for the last six bars of *The Plaint* (No. 26). These are shown in their modern equivalents. All other indications are editorial.

12. *Accidentals*

Notes that have been editorially sharpened or flattened are listed in the Full Score.

13. *Phrase marks*

The slurs shown in the manuscripts are inconsistent and incomplete from the point of view of modern performers. We have followed what we believe to have been Purcell's intentions, and in the voice parts we have avoided using a slur where there are several notes to one syllable unless the music needs to be smooth. The staccato dots, which are all editorial, are to point the phrasing.

14. *Ornaments*

As was customary in the late seventeenth-century, Purcell indicated some of the trills and ornaments he wanted, and trusted his performers to supply the others where needed. We have added our suggestions.

15. *Inequality and rubato*

We have also suggested the occasional transformation of even quavers into dotted quavers. This 'inequality' is so subtle that it is difficult to convey it on the printed page. The rhythm at bar 80 in the *Chaconne* (No. 39) is almost like triplets, but it would give a false impression to rewrite it in 9/8. The notation can only be approximate, and the freedom has to be felt. This also applies to *rubato*. We have made several suggestions, such as taking time over the echoes in Nos. 15 and 16, and speeding up the end of *Coridon and Mopsa* (No. 27) and broadening out for the words 'Before thy shrine the Seasons fall' in No. 6. But there are many other occasions for rubato where the performer has to rely on the sound and the feel of the music. It is worth remembering that Purcell's contemporary, Thomas Mace, said: 'When we come to be Masters, so that we can command all manner of Time at our own Pleasures, we then take Liberty (and very often, for good Adornment-sake) to break time; sometimes Faster, and sometimes Slower, as we perceive it the Nature of the thing requires'.

Purcell, *Harmonia Sacra* (realized Britten and Pears, 1944–5) (1947)[35]

This edition of Purcell's music which will eventually, it is hoped, include most of the songs from the Orpheus Britannicus and the Harmonia Sacra, as well as much of the chamber music, choral and orchestral music, is not intended to be a definitive edition or a work of reference. It is a performing edition for contemporary conditions.

Many of the pieces to be published have not been printed for 100 years, others are only available today in the admirable but expensive folios of the Purcell Society. Many more are published in all sorts of arrangements which do not seem to us to contain much of the Purcellian spirit. This edition is not the work of musicologists and therefore the solution of problems such as

[35] Preface to published score (London: Boosey & Hawkes, 1947). This note was written by Britten and Pears. It appeared in a number of Britten's Purcell collections.

ornamentation has not been attempted. Most singers today are either unwilling or unable to perform the 'Graces'—which Purcell may have expected and we have therefore only printed the notes which Purcell himself printed. Those singers who wish to 'grace' the songs will do so at their own pleasure.

It is clear that the figured basses in Purcell's day were realised in a manner personal to the player. In this edition the basses have also, inevitably, been realised in a personal way. But it has been the constant endeavour of the arranger to apply to these realisations something of that mixture of clarity, brilliance, tenderness and strangeness which shines out in all Purcell's music.

Franz Schubert (1797–1828) (1955)[36]
Piano Quintet in A 'Die Forelle', D. 667 (1819)

Sylvester Paumgartner, a rich amateur of music, commissioned this Quintet in 1819 for performance in his house in Steyr. Schubert completed the work on 2 July and it was apparently performed there that year, with Paumgartner giving, we are told, only a 'modest' account of the cello part. We are also told that Schubert was late in writing the work for the first performance and that he wrote it out in the separate string parts and played the piano part from memory! The work was not published until 1829 (by Josef Czerny).

The Quintet is as notable for its richness of invention as for the amazing richness of its scoring. Each instrument (including the double-bass) has a solo part of great virtuosity. Because of the preponderance of lower strings the piano part often lies high, giving a great brilliance to the texture.

I. *Allegro vivace.* A clear, resonant arpeggio is followed by a warm, simple tune. This is developed with Schubertian generosity to make the principal subject. A gay little melody, of repeated crotchets and jerky figures, is the second subject. The development section is remarkable, even for Schubert, for its wealth of modulation. The recapitulation is the exposition transposed a fourth higher (or a fifth lower)—a method which Schubert often adopted, and which makes the movement end in the right key with no alterations.

II. *Andante.* The long and ornate first subject (piano, repeated by violin) is in F major. The warm smooth second subject (viola and cello) is in F sharp minor. The codetta, gay and rhythmic, is in D major, settling down to G. The recapitulation echoes all this in A flat, A minor and F. All these modulations are handled with such magical skill that the movement sounds almost casual.

III. *Scherzo and Trio.* A *presto* scherzo, all in crotchets except an occasional scurry of quavers up to the first beat of the bar. A very gracious and lilting Trio.

[36] AFPB (1955), 17–18.

IV. *Theme and Variations*. The theme is the first half of the song *Die Forelle*, but played *Andantino*. It is only in the Coda that the tune is played in its original quicker tempo. *Var. I*. Tune on the piano with smooth string background in triplets. *Var. II*. Tune on the viola, echoed by the piano. *Var. III*. Tune on cello and double-bass accompanied by very brilliant (and horribly difficult) running passages on the piano. *Var. IV. Minore*. The outlines of the tune are clear in the dramatic gestures. *Var. V*. The cello plays a graceful variant of the tune. *Coda*. The tune is now heard against the original triplet accompaniment of the song.

V. *Finale: Allegro guisto*. The movement is dominated by a spiky little march tune, often heralded by an imitation horn call. There are graceful moments, a gentler second subject, and a chorale-like codetta, but they are all brushed aside by the relentless march rhythm.

Schubert, Symphony No. 8 in B minor ('Unfinished'), D. 759 (1822) (1970)[37]

1. *Allegro moderato* 2. *Andante con moto*
These two movements—two of the subtlest, warmest and most original that Schubert ever wrote—were written in October 1822, and the original manuscript is prefaced by a bold, confident title-page. At what point did Schubert decide not to go on with this masterpiece, and why? We know that he started a third movement: there are full sketches of it, and one page fully scored. We also know that as early as 1823 he sent the score of the first two movements (most likely his only copies apart from possible sketches) to his friend Anselm Hüttenbrenner in Graz, so it looks as if he had pretty soon given up hope of matching the extraordinary quality of the Allegro and Andante; the sketched third movement, although fine and energetic, is, to be honest, rather routine. Did he perhaps realise, since he had an extraordinary sense of the overall form of his works, that another movement in triple time would be straining even *his* resources; that this symphony so far was so rich in content and expression that even a Schubert routine would seem a let-down? Anyhow, we can be eternally grateful that when in 1865 Hüttenbrenner's friend, the conductor Johann Herbeck, asked him if he had any Schubert music as yet unplayed, these precious two movements had not been mislaid; and so we possess some of the loveliest music that exists—endless playing can never stale its freshness.

[37] AFPB (1970), 66–7.

Schubert, *Introduction and Variations*, D. 802 (1824) (1958)[38]

The theme of these variations is the tragic song *Trock'ne Blumen* which follows the stormy climax of *Die böse Farbe* in the second half of the song cycle, *Die schöne Müllerin*. They were written probably in January 1824 (two months after the cycle was completed), and most likely for the flautist Ferdinand Bogner.

The storm which withers these flowers is a spiritual one. The *Introduction* (establishing the key and the basic rhythm of the variations) is cold and lost—only inwardly tempestuous; there are even echoes of the other storm in *Die junge Nonne*. The *Theme*, slightly more symmetrical than the original song, is in the piano, and repeated section by section on the flute.

Variation 1: The florid flute passages start rather deliberately and severely. *Variation* 2: Stormy left hand octaves in the piano. *Variation* 3: The sun shines through in a ravishing *major* duet for the flute and piano right hand, but *Variation* 4 breaks out again with stormy arpeggios in the piano. *Variation* 5 is the climax of frenzied agility. *Variation* 6 has a lighter mood—with gay little imitations over a staccato bass—and leads directly into *Variation* 7, a brilliant and triumphant march. But two Schubertian, deeply-felt modulations remind us that the storm is not long past, and that flowers will once again be withered.

Schubert, String Quartet in D minor 'Der Tod und das Mädchen', D. 810 (1824) (1973)[39]

In September 1824 the Viennese publishing house, Sauer and Leidesdorf, announced the appearance of three quartets by Schubert. Actually only one (in A minor) appeared. The publication of the other two (tonight's D minor, and probably the G major) was dropped owing to lack of public interest. Schubert offered them to Schott's of Mainz in 1828, but they were not interested. The world had to wait for the appearance of this masterpiece until it was performed in Berlin in 1833.

1 *Allegro* A fierce gesture, including a quaver triplet, starts the work. There is a lulling second subject (accompanied by a quaver triplet). The first half ends

[38] AFPB (1958), 84–5.

[39] AFPB (1973), 27. Written for AFPB (1954), 28. Some minor alterations were made in the later version.

with a pathetic phrase (first violin and viola in octaves) with a flattened seventh in a characteristic rhythm; much of the development is also based on this phrase.

2 *Andante con moto* Five variations on a section of the song 'Death and the Maiden'. The variations are mostly of mood and texture, the harmony remaining constant throughout. The last variation works up to a terrific climax, and slowly relaxes into an infinitely touching and simple codetta.

3 *Scherzo and Trio* (*Allegro molto*) A dramatic scherzo, with harsh harmonies and biting rhythms, is followed by a tender major trio, with distant echoes of the scherzo rhythm.

4 *Presto* A tremendous, breathless dance of death. Sudden fortissimo outbursts and seductive tunes remind one of the Erl King. There is no escaping this relentless flood of music, which has the drive and power of a full orchestra, and yet because of the infinite skill and hypnotic power of the composer, the string quartet medium is never strained.

Schubert, Sonata in A minor 'The Arpeggione', D. 821 (1824) (1961)[40]

1. *Allegro moderato* 2. *Adagio*, leading to 3. *Allegretto*

This sonata was written in November 1824 (and first performed in December that year) for an arpeggione, a guitar-like cello which had been invented by G. Stauffer in Vienna in 1823. It had six strings, and was shaped and tuned like a guitar but played with a bow. It never caught on, and when the music was published in 1871 an adaptation for cello was included. This meant changing some of the levels of the highest passage work, but it remains ferociously difficult technically, although nothing could be simpler or more transparent and charming than the music itself.

Schubert, String Quintet in C, D. 956 (1828) (1955)[41]

Schubert wrote this great Quintet in 1828, during the last few months of his life. He never heard it played, even by his amateur friends. The first concert performance was in 1850, and it was not published until 1853.

[40] AFPB (1961), 63.

[41] AFPB (1955), 18–19. A later version of this note contained some small changes in the first half, and some more significant ones in the second. This is how Britten later described the last three movements:

This was the work that Grove had in mind when he wrote: 'It is difficult to speak of it too highly. . . . Think of the abundance of the thoughts, the sudden surprises, the wonderful transitions, the extraordinary pathos of the turns of melody and modulation, the absolute manner in which they bring you into contact with the affectionate, tender, suffering personality of the composer'.

Listening to it, as the beauties unfold one after another and the mood changes from light to darkness and back again to light, the overwhelming impression is of the wholeness of the music. Schubert's effortless spontaneity is not only the result of his rapid and 'instinctive' writing; it is also the result of his miraculously mature understanding of form.

In the very opening bars of the *Allegro ma non troppo*, the mood and structure of the whole work can be heard in the serenity of the C major chord and its passionate crescendo towards the tragic diminished seventh and its gradual lessening of the tension. The first violin lifts the held C into a phrase which leads to a high pianissimo question; its semiquaver upbeat grows nearer and more insistent until it sweeps the music into a fortissimo declamation of the opening chords, now broken up into detached arpeggios. After the climax of a chromatic crescendo, the sforzando of the cellos' held G melts into the wonderful legato of their E flat tune in thirds and sixths. It is one of those tunes that one longs to hear again. Fortunately Schubert was never afraid of repeating himself; he immediately gives it to the violins, while the second cello touches the root of each harmony with its pianissimo pizzicato—a gesture of disarming simplicity which only a very great composer could have achieved.

The calm ending of the first movement, over its long held C, is followed by

In the tranquil 12/8 of the E major *Adagio*, the slow, sustained notes of the second violin, viola and first cello are so perfectly balanced that they seem to hang motionless in the air; while the first violin breathes a poignantly expressive tune, hesitantly returning over and over again to its short phrase, and the second cello's slow *pizzicato* brings an audible pulse to the texture of the music. After a dramatic outburst in F minor the music returns to the *sostenuto* in E.

The lively theme of the *Scherzo*, in C, is founded on the notes of a horn-call and carries a memory of the *Schöne Müllerin*. Abruptly the music leaves the security of C and plunges into A flat. At the triumphant return to C major there is an astonishing brilliance in the double stops of the five instruments, with their resounding open strings. The short D flat *Trio* gives an impression of reaching immense distances, owing to its unfettered modulations and enharmonic changes.

The finale has the rhythm of a dance which is kept tirelessly moving by the vitality of its syncopated *sforzandos*. The second subject is another of Schubert's unforgettably gracious tunes, and brings with it a recollection of the mood of the opening of the first movement. Then the dance becomes wilder, until all the threads of the work are drawn together in the final sweep from D flat to C.

the tranquil twelve-eight of the E major *Adagio*, where the slow, sustained notes of the second violin, viola and first cello are so perfectly balanced that they seem to hang motionless in the air while they are flowing onwards. The first violin breathes a poignantly expressive tune, hesitantly returning over and over again to its short phrase, as if recollecting a song, while the second cello's slow pizzicato brings an audible pulse to the texture of the music.

At the quietest moment of the hushed cadence the E is suddenly snatched up and transformed into the leading note of a passionate fortissimo in F minor, where the relentlessly repeated rising triplets of the second cello are heavily laden with a weight of sorrow.

After such a dramatic outburst, the music needs time to recover its lost quiet. At the return to the *sostenuto* in E, the second cello's mood is still perturbed; then, at last, its rising demisemiquavers give way to the tranquil pizzicato. At the very end of the movement, when the journey is over, there is a backward glance at the darkness of F minor, but it is only for an instant, and the final chord of E major is utterly untroubled.

In the *Scherzo* the music returns to C for its lively theme which is founded on the notes of a horn-call and which brings with it a memory of the *Schöne Müllerin*. Abruptly the music leaves the security of C and plunges into A flat; it is tossed to and fro by its sudden modulations and pulled this way and that by the accents of its syncopation, before returning to a triumphant C major, where there is an astonishing brilliance in the double stops of the five instruments with their resounding open strings.

The *Andante sostenuto* enters dramatically into its key of D flat, with sad descending octaves which lead to the resignation of the long-drawn-out cadences. This short interlude gives an impression of reaching immense distances owing to its unfettered modulations and enharmonic changes.

The *Allegretto* has the rhythm of a dance which is kept tirelessly moving by the vitality of its syncopated sforzandos. There is a suggestion of sadness in the C minor opening, but the cloud soon lifts and the tune enters its own key of C major.

The second subject is another of those unforgettably gracious tunes of which Schubert possessed such an inexhaustible store. The sparkling triplets which embroider it are later transformed into sweeping arpeggios, bring with them a recollection of the mood of the opening of the first movement. Then the pace quickens to *Più presto* and the dance becomes wilder until it ends in a gesture that draws all the threads of the work together in its final sweep from D flat to C.

Robert Schumann (1810–56) Piano Quartet in E♭, Op. 47 (1842) (1973)[42]

This was the last of the great chamber works written by Schumann in 1842. This 'annus mirabilis' produced 3 full sized string quartets (of wonderful invention & originality) & 2 big works for strings & piano—but somehow the Piano quartet has remained the Cinderella of them all. It is difficult to see why. It is brimming over with ideas. The slow movement has one of the loveliest tunes that Schumann every wrote, as well as one of the most magical effects in its 'coda'. The form is highly satisfactory, although some might claim (from excess of 20th century fidgets) that it is a little over-extended; but surely the warmth of the climaxes must excite & satisfy most listeners. Perhaps the instrumental texture, with an amount of 'doubleing' & repeated notes, has its problems, but not more so than the popular piano 5tet; and it is easily overcome if one takes note of the comparative weight of the early 19C pianoforte against the strings, and if one remembers the magical pedalling effects of Schumann's superb piano music—there are occasions when the pianist can feel that he is pedalling the stringed instruments.

I Sostenuto Assai—Allegro ma non troppo. A solemn little introduction foreshadows one of the many melodic fragments of the Allegro. The adorably warm dialogues of this movement lead us through every key, & a wide range of moods.

II Scherzo—Molto vivace. A fantastic scurrying scherzo with two trios: one, gently melancholic, & the other with mysterious shifting chords (with the barlines forgotten) alternating with explosive pizzicatos.

III Andante Cantabile. Each stringed instrument in turn has the gorgeous tune with its sequential sevenths (a feature so enjoyed by Elgar half a century later). There is a hushed chorale-like interlude before the viola puts even more meaning into the great tune. In the coda the cellist tunes his C string a tone lower, which produces a mysterious pedal to the scales of the other instruments.

IV Finale—Vivace. Schumann out does the last movement of the 5tet in bustling fugatos. He borrows a famous theme from the Jupiter Symphony but does quite different things with it. In the midst of all the bustle haunting themes appear.

Schumann, Andante and Variations, Op. 46 (1843) (1956)[43]

This work was originally written (in 1843) for the curious combination of horn solo, two cellos, and two pianos. Before it was performed, however,

[42] Autograph draft, [9 Mar. 1973] (*GB-ALb* 1-02052218).

[43] AFPB (1956), 62.

Schumann withdrew it, rearranged it for two pianos alone, and then the year after, it was performed in the new version by Clara Schumann and Mendelssohn. The original version was not performed until 1868 (by Clara Schumann and Brahms).

The work consists of a charming theme, sequential, mostly in flowing quavers; and nine simple and direct variations, mostly variations in figuration with the harmony unchanged. The fifth and eighth show clear signs of the horn from the original scoring. The sixth is most original, a kind of meditation on the first theme, with quite different harmonies. The coda starts with a subdued statement of the theme, which dissolves into floating semiquavers.

Schumann, *Fünf Stücke im Volkston*, Op. 102 (1849) (1961)[44]

Between 1849 and 1853 Schumann became interested in some of the less usual solo instruments. It may have been that there were fine players in the Düsseldorf Orchestra of which he was at that time conductor, and for whom he may have written some of these works—for various combinations of horn, oboe, clarinet, viola, cello, etc.

The cello pieces are more relaxed and less intense and strange harmonically than many of the others (especially the ones for viola)—hence, perhaps, 'im Volkston'.

1. *With humour* ('vanitas vanitatum') in A minor with a violent middle section in F.
2. *Slow.* A serene F major tune in subtle and irregular phrases.
3. *Not fast* in A minor, and a warm D major tune, with high double-stops, for the cello.
4. *Not too fast* in D major; the angular arpeggio of the first theme is used as the accompaniment of the gracious second subject.
5. *Strong and marked* in A minor—characteristic Schumann in its alternating rhythms of twos and threes.

Schumann, Concerto for Cello and Orchestra, Op. 129 (1850) (1961)[45]

It is not known for whom Schumann composed this concerto in 1850, and it was certainly not performed in his lifetime. Here, as so often, Schumann shows

[44] AFPB (1961), 64. [45] AFPB (1961), 59.

a warm and original understanding of the character of the instrument, but without much sympathy for its technique; this makes the concerto somewhat ungrateful to play. In fact it is only with the emergence recently of great technical virtuosos, who are also fine musicians, that this work has come into its own—as being one of the most beautiful and profound of concertos.

1. *Not too fast.* A movement of dark, lyrical beauty. The passage work is always subtly integrated, although the impression is one of complete spontaneity—notice, for instance, how the little quaver triplets in the development grow naturally out of the cadential figures of the solo instrument. The movement leads to:

2. *Slow.* Thrummed pizzicato chords accompany a sighing melody, the wind instruments imitating and commenting. A recitative-like passage, with references to the first movement, leads to:

3. *Very lively.* A characteristic motive—strong chords, answered by a twisting arpeggio—dominates the movement. There are warm lyrical passages, but the general mood, with scurrying semi-quaver figures in the solo instrument, and leaps to high positions, is tense and agitated. Before the end there is a remarkable and strange accompanied cadenza.

Schumann, *Szenen aus Goethes Faust*, WoO3 (1844–53) (1972)[46]

Goethe's *Faust*, Part I, was published in 1808; Part II, after his death in 1832. Beethoven had talked of writing a work on Part I, but never did, and when in 1848 Schumann set the last scene of Part II (Faust's Redemption), he was the first composer to do so. Since then Liszt, Mahler and others have used those famous lines, and Berlioz, Gounod and Busoni are only three of the many who have taken something for themselves out of Goethe's extraordinary treasure of ideas and characters. In the first edition of *Grove's Dictionary* (1889) Philip Spitta, the biographer of Bach, could write: 'To Schumann is due the chief meed of praise for having popularised the second part of *Faust*.' At the first (private) performance in 1848 of today's last movement, it was felt that 'the meaning of Goethe's words was made clear for the first time, so deeply imbued was the composer with the poet's inmost spirit'. Schumann never intended the work as we have it for the stage, and of its sections, the Overture was the last composed, in 1853, the first three scenes and 'Ariel' in 1849, *Mitternacht* in 1850, and Faust's Death in 1853. It has often been said that along with Schumann's

[46] AFPB (1972), 52. Note written by Britten and Pears.

decline in health went a decline in creative powers, but that this work shows the decline in progress is questionable. Such an emphasis can be much exaggerated: it is not so simple. Perhaps it is fairer to point out that Schumann was trying to turn what was begun as a possible opera into what became an impossible oratorio. Finally he pronounced against a total performance of the music, unless 'as a curiosity', and so rare have performances become in spite of early enthusiasm (for instance, Novello published an English version very soon after the German one) that each performance may still qualify as just that. But that Schumann's interest lagged in his whole *Faust* project would be a misapprehension, since the Overture was the last music to be written, and it gives a very strong and characterful start to the whole. At the end of the fresh and lyrical love duet for Faust and Gretchen, there appears with Mephistopheles the phrase (on the bassoon) which returns as often as the evil spirits appear (for instance, in the Cathedral scene of Gretchen's remorse, which follows). The Gretchen episode over, Faust is spurred to higher aspiration by the fair sights and sounds in Nature; in the next scene, however, the spectre of all-powerful Care, though defied by him, robs him of his sight. Yet Faust is still confident in his powers. In the last scene of Part II, Faust, surrounded by the creatures of dissolution, triumphantly utters his phrases of confidence until the very moment of quick dying—referred to by Mephistopheles as 'the last, wretched empty moment'—a moment which is transformed in Schumann's Part III to a slow progress up from Earth, past the abodes of the Holy Fathers and Saints and Angels, where Love, known at first as the unselfish love of Woman, draws Faust's soul upward to the contemplation of higher Love, until it is at last recognised to be a spark of the eternally tender (or feminine) element of the Divine Nature. As Robert Schumann had written to Clara, 'it is you who will bring me peace and healing'. This whole last section is rightly accepted as one of Schumann's grandest creations.

Schumann, essentially a piano composer, hoped to create on the orchestra the resonance which he so beautifully achieved with the piano's pedal and half-pedal. In his attempts to effect this, however, he came to rely excessively on tremolando in the middle strings, somehow trusting that the players would be as sensitive and sympathetic as his own two hands and feet were. We have made some small excisions of these tremolandi as well as a very little thinning out of the wind for this performance. We have cut part of the first scene of Part II, as well as a section of Part III, to keep the work to a manageable size. In the Cathedral scene's opening bars, we have preferred the piano version (sketches?) and have added a note or two here and there.

Dmitri Shostakovich (1906–75) (1973)[47]
String Quartet No. 13, Op. 138 (1970)

Dmitri Shostakovich's Thirteenth Quartet was composed in 1970. It is in one movement, consisting of five clear sections linked together. The first section begins with an expressive theme on the viola. The mournful motives on which it is founded are based on 'the intonation of a sigh'. The whole of the first section of the quartet (*Adagio*) is reflective and sad in character: the even sonority and clear four-part writing occasionally suggest a chorale.

The second section (*Doppio movimento*—twice as fast as the preceding *Adagio*) begins with a pointed scherzo theme on the first violin, the speedy development of which leads to an expressive climax, saturated with dissonant sounds.

The intensity and passion of the music changes abruptly at the beginning of the third section, which consists of variations over an ostinato bass in the midst of which, from time to time, one hears ghostly tappings made by the bow on the body of the instruments. Firm rhythm dominates the whole of the central section.

The sections now appear in reverse order. A brief repeat of the second section gives way to an expanded version of the first, and a return to the tempo of the *Adagio*. The development of the first viola theme is accompanied by the tappings to which we have already been introduced. The work's ending is enigmatic. A solo recitative on the viola concludes with a sudden leap up to a very high note, and the first and second violins join in unison. There is a quick crescendo and the work stops abruptly.

One of the most striking features of this quartet is the strict classical control of the metre which, except for a few bars in the middle, does not vary from the metronomic beat of 80. There are no accelerandos or ritardandos and not one single pause to break its smooth surface, which nevertheless covers an intense passion.

Giuseppe Verdi (1813–1901) (1951)[48]
String Quartet in E minor (1873)

This Quartet was written during a delay in the rehearsals for the first performance of *Aïda* in Naples in 1873, 'for mere amusement'! Apart from some unpublished Juvenilia, it is the only purely instrumental work Verdi ever wrote, but it is full of the same honesty, simplicity and melodic strength which characterize all the operas we know and love so well. Although the composer was

[47] AFPB (1973), 27. [48] AFPB (1951), 29–30.

not proud of it, and even discouraged performances, the work survives for more than historical reasons.

(i) *Allegro.* In strict sonata form with a memorable first subject announced by the second violin, and a serene chorale-like second subject. The whole movement is rich in invention.

(ii) *Andante.* Deeply serious beneath the elegant and operatic surface.

(iii) *Prestissimo.* A brilliant witch-like Scherzo, and a suave trio with a long and dignified tune for 'cello.

(iv) *Scherzo Fuga—Allegro assai mosso.* A Fugue, brilliantly exploiting the spiky, angular theme. There are many violent contrasts of ***pp*** and ***ff***, harshness and tenderness.

INDEX OF BRITTEN'S WORKS

GENERAL INDEX